Conceptual Spaces

Conceptual Spaces

The Geometry of Thought

Peter Gärdenfors

A Bradford Book

The MIT Press
Cambridge, Massachusetts
London, England

This book was set in Palatino by Best-set Typesetter Ltd., Hong Kong.
Printed and bound in the United States of America.

Library of Congress Cataloging-in-Publication Data

Gärdenfors, Peter.
    Conceptual spaces : the geometry of thought / Peter Gärdenfors.
        p.   cm.
    "A Bradford book."
    Includes bibliographical references and index.
    ISBN 0-262-07199-1 (alk. paper)
    1. Artificial intelligence.   2. Cognitive science.   I. Title.
Q335 .G358 2000
006.3—dc21   99-046109

10   9   8   7   6   5   4   3   2

Contents

Preface

A central problem for cognitive science is how representations should be modeled. This book proposes a geometrical mode of representation based on what I call conceptual spaces. It presents a metatheory on the same level as the symbolic and connectionist modes of representation that, so far, have been dominant within cognitive science. I cast my net widely, trying to show that geometrical representations are viable for many areas within cognitive science. In particular, I suggest new ways of modeling concept formation, semantics, nonmonotonic inferences, and inductive reasoning.

While writing the text, I felt like a centaur, standing on four legs and waving two hands. The four legs are supported by four disciplines: philosophy, computer science, psychology, and linguistics (and there is a tail of neuroscience). Since these disciplines pull in different directions—in particular when it comes to methodological questions—there is a considerable risk that my centaur has ended up in a four-legged split.

A consequence of this split is that I will satisfy no one. Philosophers will complain that my arguments are weak; psychologists will point to a wealth of evidence about concept formation that I have not accounted for; linguistics will indict me for glossing over the intricacies of language in my analysis of semantics; and computer scientists will ridicule me for not developing algorithms for the various processes that I describe.

I plead guilty to all four charges. My aim is to unify ideas from different disciplines into a general theory of representation. This is a work within cognitive science and not one in philosophy, psychology, linguistics, or computer science. My ambition here is to present a coherent research program that others will find attractive and use as a basis for more detailed investigations.

On the one hand, the book aims at presenting a constructive model, based on conceptual spaces, of how information is to be represented. This hand is waving to attract engineers and robot constructors who are developing artificial systems capable of solving cognitive tasks and who want suggestions for how to represent the information handled by the systems.

On the other hand, the book also has an explanatory aim. This hand is trying to lure empirical scientists (mainly from linguistics and psychology). In particular, I aim to explain some aspects of concept formation, inductive reasoning, and the semantics of natural languages. In these areas, however, I cannot display the amount of honest toil that would be necessary to give the ideas a sturdy empirical grounding. But I hope that my bait provides some form of attractive power for experimentalists.

The research for this book has been supported by the Swedish Council for Research in the Humanities and Social Sciences, by the Erik Philip-Sörensen Foundation, and by the Swedish Foundation for Strategic Research.

The writing of the book has a rather long history. Parts of the material have been presented in a number of articles from 1988 and on. Many friends and colleagues have read and commented on the manuscript of the book at various stages. Kenneth Holmqvist joined me during the first years. We had an enlightening research period creating the shell pictures and testing the model presented in chapter 4. Early versions of the book manuscript were presented at the ESSLLI summer School in Prague 1996, the Autumn School in Cognitive Science in Saarbrücken in 1996, and the Cognitive Science seminar at Lund University in 1997. The discussions there helped me develop much of the material. Several people have provided me with extensive comments on later versions of the manuscipt. I want to thank Ingar Brinck for her astute mind, Jens Erik Fenstad for seeing the grand picture, Renata Wassermann for trying to make logic out of it, and Mary-Anne Williams for her pertinent as well as her impertinent comments. MIT Press brought me very useful criticism from Annette Herskovits and two anonymous readers. Elisabeth Engberg Pedersen, Peter Harder, and Jordan Zlatev have given me constructive comments on chapter 5, Timo Honkela on chapter 6, and Christian Balkenius on chapter 7. I also want to thank Lukas Böök, Antonio Chella, Agneta Gulz, Ulrike Haas-Spohn, Christopher Habel, Frederique Harmsze, Paul Hemeren, Måns Holgersson, Jana Holsánová, Mikael Johannesson, Lars Kopp, David de Léon, Jan Morén, Annemarie Peltzer-Karpf, Jean Petitot, Fiora Pirri, Hans Rott, Johanna Seibt, John Sowa, Annika Wallin, and Simon Winter. Jens Månsson did a great job in creating some of the art. Finally, thanks are due to my family who rather tolerantly endured my sitting in front of the computer during a couple of rainy summers.

Chapter 1

Dimensions

1.1 The Problem of Modeling Representations

1.1.1 Three Levels of Representation

Cognitive science has two overarching goals. One is *explanatory*: by studying the cognitive activities of humans and other animals, the scientist formulates *theories* of different aspects of cognition. The theories are tested by experiments or by computer simulations. The other goal is *constructive*: by building *artifacts* like robots, animats, chess-playing programs, and so forth, cognitive scientists aspire to construct systems that can accomplish various cognitive tasks. A key problem for both kinds of goals is how the *representations* used by the cognitive system are to be modeled in an appropriate way.

Within cognitive science, there are currently two dominating approaches to the problem of modeling representations. The *symbolic* approach starts from the assumption that cognitive systems can be described as Turing machines. From this view, cognition is seen as essentially being *computation*, involving symbol manipulation. The second approach is *associationism*, where associations among different kinds of information elements carry the main burden of representation.[1] *Connectionism* is a special case of associationism that models associations using artificial neuron networks. Both the symbolic and the associationistic approaches have their advantages and disadvantages. They are often presented as competing paradigms, but since they attack cognitive problems on different levels, I argue later that they should rather be seen as complementary methodologies.

There are aspects of cognitive phenomena, however, for which neither symbolic representation nor associationism appear to offer appropriate modeling tools. In particular it appears that mechanisms of *concept acquisition*, which are paramount for the understanding of many cognitive phenomena, cannot be given a satisfactory treatment in any of these representational forms. Concept learning is closely tied to the notion of *similarity*, which has turned out to be problematic for the symbolic and associationistic approaches.

Here, I advocate a third form of representing information that is based on using *geometrical* structures rather than symbols or connections among neurons. On the basis of these structures, similarity relations can be modeled in a natural way. I call my way of representing information the *conceptual* form because I believe that the essential aspects of concept formation are best described using this kind of representation.

The geometrical form of representation has already been used in several areas of the cognitive sciences. In particular, dimensional representations are frequently employed within cognitive psychology. As will be seen later in the book, many models of concept formation and learning are based on spatial structures. Suppes et al. (1989) present the general mathematics that are applied in such models. But geometrical and topological notions also have been exploited in linguistics. There is a French tradition exemplified by Thom (1970), who very early applied catastrophe theory to linguistics, and Petitot (1985, 1989, 1995). And there is a more recent development within cognitive linguistics where researchers like Langacker (1987), Lakoff (1987), and Talmy (1988) initiated a study of the spatial and dynamic structure of "image schemas," which clearly are of a conceptual form.[2] As will be seen in the following chapter, several spatial models have also been proposed within the neurosciences.

The conceptual form of representions, however, has to a large extent been neglected in the foundational discussions of representations. It has been a common prejudice in cognitive science that the brain is either a Turing machine working with symbols or a connectionist system using neural networks. One of my objectives here is to show that a conceptual mode based on geometrical and topological representations deserves at least as much attention in cognitive science as the symbolic and the associationistic approaches.

Again, the conceptual representations should not be seen as competing with symbolic or connectionist (associationist) representations. There is no unique correct way of describing cognition. Rather, the three kinds mentioned here can be seen as three *levels* of representations of cognition with different scales of resolution.[3] Which level provides the best explanation or ground for technical constructions depends on the cognitive problem area that is being modeled.

1.1.2 Synopsis

This is a book about the geometry of thought. A theory of *conceptual spaces* will be developed as a particular framework for representing information on the conceptual level. A conceptual space is built upon geometrical structures based on a number of *quality dimensions*. The main applications of the theory will be on the constructive side of cognitive science. I believe, however, that the theory can also explain several aspects of what is known about representations in various biological systems. Hence, I also attempt to connect the theory of conceptual spaces to empirical findings in psychology and neuroscience.

Chapter 1 presents the basic theory of conceptual spaces and, in a rather informal manner, some of the underlying mathematical notions. In chapter 2, representations in conceptual spaces are contrasted to those in symbolic and connectionistic models. It argues that symbolic and connectionistic representations are not sufficient for the aims of cognitive science; many representational problems are best handled by using geometrical structures on the conceptual level.

In the remainder of the book, the theory of conceptual spaces is used as a basis for a constructive analysis of several fundamental notions in philosophy and cognitive science. In chapter 3 is argued that the traditional analysis of *properties* in terms of possible worlds semantics is misguided and that a much more natural account can be given with the aid of conceptual spaces. In chapter 4, this analysis is extended to *concepts* in general. Some experimental results about concept formation will be presented in this chapter. In both chapters 3 and 4, the notion of similarity will be central.

In chapter 5, a general theory for cognitive *semantics* based on conceptual spaces is outlined. In contrast to traditional philosophical theories, this kind of semantics is connected to perception, imagination, memory, communication, and other cognitive mechanisms.

The problem of *induction* is an enigma for the philosophy of science, and it has turned out to be a problem also for systems within artificial intelligence. This is the topic of chapter 6 where it is argued that the classical riddles of induction can be circumvented, if inductive reasoning is studied on the conceptual level of representation instead of on the symbolic level.

The three levels of representation will motivate different types of computations. Chapter 7 is devoted to some computational aspects with the conceptual mode of representation as the focus. Finally, in chapter 8 the research program associated with representations in conceptual spaces is summarized and a general methodological program is proposed.

As can be seen from this overview, I throw my net widely around several problem areas within the cognitive science. The book has two main aims. One is to argue that the conceptual level is the best mode of representation for many problem areas within cognitive science. The other aim is more specific; I want to establish that conceptual spaces can serve as a framework for a number of empirical theories, in particular concerning concept formation, induction, and semantics. I also claim that conceptual spaces are useful representational tools for the constructive side of cognitive science. As an independent issue, I argue that conceptual representations serve as a bridge between symbolic and connectionist ones. In support of this position, Jackendoff (1983, 17) writes: "There is a single level of mental representation, *conceptual structure*, at which linguistic, sensory, and motor information are compatible." The upshot is that the conceptual level of representation ought to be given much more emphasis in future research on cognition.

It should be obvious by now that it is well nigh impossible to give a thorough treatment of all the areas mentioned above within the covers of a single book. Much of my presentation will, unavoidably, be programmatic and some arguments will, no doubt, be seen as rhetorical. I hope, however, that the examples of applications of conceptual spaces presented in this book inspire new investigations into the conceptual forms of representation and further discussions of representations within the cognitive sciences.

1.2 Conceptual Spaces as a Framework for Representations

We frequently compare the experiences we are currently having to memories of earlier episodes. Sometimes, we experience something entirely new, but most of the time what we see or hear is, more or less, the same as what we have already encountered. This cognitive capacity shows that we can judge, consciously or not, various relations among our experiences. In particular, we can tell how *similar* a new phenomenon is to an old one.

With the capacity for such judgments of similarity as a background, philosophers have proposed different kinds of theories about how humans concepts are structured. For example, Armstrong (1978, 116) presents the following desiderata for *an analysis* of what unites concepts:[4]

> If we consider the class of shapes and the class of colours, then both classes exhibit the following interesting but puzzling characteristics which it should be able to understand:
> (a) the members of the two classes all have something in common (they are all shapes, they are all colours)
> (b) but while they have something in common, they differ in that very respect (they all differ as shapes, they all differ as colours)
> (c) they exhibit a resemblance order based upon their intrinsic nature (*triangularity* is like *circularity*, *redness* is more like *orangeness* than *redness* is like *blueness*), where closeness of resemblance has a limit in identity

(d) they form a set of incompatibles (the same particular cannot be simultaneously triangular and circular, or red and blue all over).

The epistemological role of the theory of conceptual spaces to be presented here is to serve as a tool in modeling various *relations* among our experiences, that is, what we perceive, remember, or imagine. In particular, the theory will satisfy Armstrong's desiderata as shown in chapter 3. In contrast, it appears that in symbolic representations the notion of similarity has been severely downplayed. Judgments of similarity, however, are central for a large number of cognitive processes. As will be seen later in this chapter, such judgments reveal the *dimensions* of our perceptions and their structures (compare Austen Clark 1993).

When attacking the problem of representing concepts, an important aspect is that the concepts are not independent of each other but can be structured into *domains*; spatial concepts belong to one domain, concepts for colors to a different domain, kinship relations to a third, concepts for sounds to a fourth, and so on. For many modeling applications within cognitive science it will turn out to be necessary to separate the information to be represented into different domains.

The key notion in the conceptual framework to be presented is that of a *quality dimension*. The fundamental role of the quality dimensions is to build up the domains needed for representing concepts. Quality dimensions will be introduced in the following section via some basal examples.

The structure of many quality dimensions of a conceptual space will make it possible to talk about *distances* along the dimensions. There is a tight connection between distances in a conceptual space and similarity judgments: the smaller the distances is between the representations of two objects, the more similar they are. In this way, the similarity of two objects can be defined via the distance between their representing points in the space. Consequently, conceptual spaces provide us with a natural way of representing similarities.

Depending on whether the explanatory or the constructive goal of cognitive science is in focus, two different interpretations of the quality dimensions will be relevant. One is *phenomenal*, aimed at describing the psychological structure of the perceptions and memories of humans and animals. Under this interpretation the theory of conceptual space will be seen as a theory with testable consequences in human and animal behavior.

The other interpretation is *scientific* where the structure of the dimensions used is often taken from some scientific theory. Under this interpretation the dimensions are not assumed to have any psychological validity but are seen as instruments for predictions. This interpretation is oriented more toward the constructive goals of cognitive science. The two interpretations of the quality dimensions are discussed in section 1.4.

1.3 Quality Dimensions

As first examples of quality dimensions, one can mention *temperature*, *weight*, *brightness*, *pitch* and the three ordinary spatial dimensions *height*, *width*, and *depth*. I have chosen these examples because they are closely connected to what is produced by our sensory receptors (Schiffman 1982). The spatial dimensions height, width, and depth as well as brightness are perceived by the visual sensory system,[5] pitch by the auditory system, temperature by thermal sensors and weight, finally, by the kinaesthetic sensors. As explained later in this chapter, however, there is also a wealth of quality dimensions that are of an abstract non-sensory character.

The primary function of the quality dimensions is to represent various "qualities" of objects.[6] The dimensions correspond to the different ways stimuli are judged to be similar or different.[7] In most cases, judgments of similarity and difference generate an *ordering relation* of stimuli. For example, one can judge tones by their pitch, which will generate an ordering from "low" to "high" of the perceptions.

The dimensions form the framework used to assign *properties* to objects and to specify *relations* among them. The coordinates of a point within a conceptual space represent particular instances of each dimension, for example, a particular temperature, a particular weight, and so forth. Chapter 3 will be devoted to how properties can be described with the aid of quality dimensions in conceptual spaces. The main idea is that a property corresponds to a *region* of a domain of a space.

The notion of a dimension should be understood literally. It is assumed that each of the quality dimensions is endowed with certain *geometrical* structures (in some cases they are *topological* or *ordering* structures). I take the dimension of "time" as a first example to illustrate such a structure (see figure 1.1). In science, time is modeled as a one-dimensional structure that is isomorphic to the line of real

Figure 1.1
The time dimension.

numbers. If "now" is seen as the zero point on the line, the future corresponds to the infinite positive real line and the past to the infinite negative line.

This representation of time is not phenomenally given but is to some extent culturally dependent. People in other cultures have a different time dimension as a part of their cognitive structures. For example, in some cultural contexts, time is viewed as a *circular* structure. There is, in general, no unique way of choosing a dimension to represent a particular quality but a wide array of possibilities.

Another example is the dimension of "weight" which is one-dimensional with a zero point and thus isomorphic to the half-line of nonnegative numbers (see figure 1.2). A basic constraint on this dimension that is commonly made in science is that there are no negative weights.[8]

It should be noted that some quality "dimensions" have only a *discrete* structure, that is, they merely divide objects into disjoint classes. Two examples are classifications of biological species and kinship relations in a human society. One example of a phylogenetic tree of the kind found in biology is shown in figure 1.3. Here the nodes represent different species in the evolution of, for example, a family of organisms, where nodes higher up in the tree represent evolutionarily older (extinct) species.

The distance between two nodes can be measured by the length of the path that connects them. This means that even for discrete

0

Figure 1.2
The weight dimension.

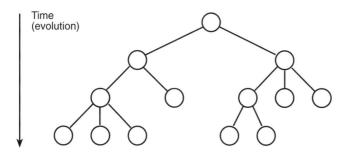

Figure 1.3
A phylogenetic tree.

dimensions one can distinguish a rudimentary geometrical structure. For example, in the phylogenetic classification of animals, it is meaningful to say that birds and reptiles are *more closely related* than reptiles and crocodiles. Some of the properties of discrete dimensions, in particular in graphs, are further discussed in section 1.6 where a general mathematical framework for describing the structures of different quality dimensions will be provided.

1.4 Phenomenal and Scientific Interpretations of Dimensions

To separate different uses of quality dimensions it is important to introduce a distinction between a *phenomenal* (or *psychological*) and a *scientific* (or *theoretical*) interpretation (compare Jackendoff 1983, 31–34). The phenomenal interpretation concerns the cognitive structures (perceptions, memories, etc.) of humans or other organisms. The scientific interpretation, on the other hand, treats dimensions as a part of a scientific theory.[9]

As an example of the distinction, our phenomenal visual space is not a perfect 3-D Euclidean space, since it is not invariant under all linear transformations. Partly because of the effects of gravity on our perception, the vertical dimension (height) is, in general, overestimated in relation to the two horizontal dimensions. That is why the moon looks bigger when it is closer to the horizon, while it in fact has the same "objective" size all the time. The scientific representation of visual space as a 3-D Euclidean space, however, is an idealization that is mathematically amenable. Under this description, all spatial directions have the same status while "verticality" is treated differently under the phenomenal interpretation. As a consequence, all linear coordinate changes of the scientific space preserve the structure of the space.

Another example of the distinction is color which is supported here by Gallistel (1990, 518–519) who writes:

> The facts about color vision suggest how deeply the nervous system may be committed to representing stimuli as points in descriptive spaces of modest dimensionality. It does this even for spectral compositions, which does not lend itself to such a representation. The resulting lack of correspondence between the psychological representation of spectral composition and spectral composition itself is a source of confusion and misunderstanding in scientific discussions of color. Scientists persist in refering to the physical characteristics of the stimulus and to the tuning characteristics of the transducers (the cones) as if psychological color terms like *red*, *green*, and *blue* had some straightforward translation into physical reality, when in fact they do not.

Gallistel's warning against confusion and misunderstanding of the two types of representation should be taken seriously.[10] It is very easy to confound what science says about the characteristics of reality and our perceptions of it.

The distinction between the phenomenal and the scientific interpretation is relevant in relation to the two goals of cognitive science presented above. When the dimensions are seen as cognitive entities—that is, when the goal is to explain naturally occuring cognitive processes—their geometrical structure should not be derived from scientific theories that attempt to give a "realistic" description of the world, but from *psychophysical* measurements that determine how our phenomenal spaces are structured. Furthermore, when it comes to providing a semantics for a natural language, it is the phenomenal interpretations of the quality dimensions that are in focus, as argued in chapter 5.

On the other hand, when we are *constructing* an artificial system, the function of sensors, effectors, and various control devices are in general described in scientifically modeled dimensions. For example, the input variables of a robot may be a small number of physically measured magnitudes, like the brightness of a patch from a video image, the delay of a radar echo, or the pressure from a mechanical grip. Driven by the programmed goals of the robot, these variables can then be transformed into a number of physical output magnitudes, for example, as the voltages of the motors controlling the left and the right wheels.

1.5 Three Sensory Examples: Color, Sound, and Taste

A phenomenally interesting example of a set of quality dimensions concerns *color perception*. According to the most common perceptual models, our cognitive representation of colors can be described by three dimensions: hue, chromaticness, and brightness. These dimensions are given slightly different mathematical mappings in different models. Here, I focus on the Swedish natural color system (NCS) (Hård and Sivik 1981) which is extensively discussed by Hardin (1988, chapter 3). NCS is a descriptive model—it represents the phenomenal structure of colors, not their scientific properties.

The first dimension of NCS is *hue*, which is represented by the familiar *color circle*. The value of this dimension is given by a *polar* coordinate describing the angle of the color around the circle (see figure 1.4). The geometrical structure of this dimension is thus different from the quality dimensions representing time or weight which are isomorphic to the real line. One way of illustrating the differences in geometry is to note that we can talk about phenomenologically *complementary*

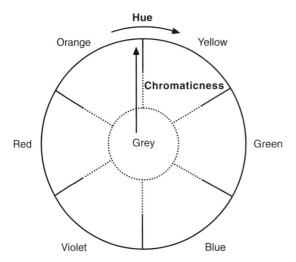

Figure 1.4
The color circle.

colors—colors that lie *opposite* each other on the color circle. In contrast it is *not meaningful* to talk about two points of time or two weights being "opposite" each other.

The second phenomenal dimension of color is *chromaticness* (saturation), which ranges from grey (zero color intensity) to increasingly greater intensities. This dimension is isomorphic to an interval of the real line.[11] The third dimension is *brightness* which varies from white to black and is thus a linear dimension with two end points. The two latter dimensions are not totally independent, since the possible variation of the chromaticness dimension decreases as the values of the brightness dimension approaches the extreme points of black and white, respectively. In other words, for an almost white or almost black color, there can be very little variation in its chromaticness. This is modeled by letting that chromaticness and brightness dimension together generate a triangular representation (see figure 1.5). Together these three dimensions, one with circular structure and two with linear, make up the color space. This space is often illustrated by the so called *color spindle* (see figure 1.6).

The color circle of figure 1.4 can be obtained by making a *horizontal* cut in the spindle. Different triangles like the one in figure 1.5 can be generated by making a *vertical* cut along the central axis of the color spindle.

As mentioned above, the NCS representation is not the only mathematical model of color space (see Hardin 1988 and Rott 1997 for some

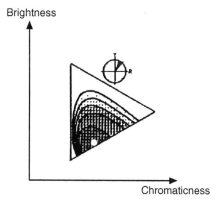

Figure 1.5
The chromaticness-brightness triangle of the NCS (from Sivik and Taft 1994, 150). The small circle marks which sector of the color spindle has been cut out.

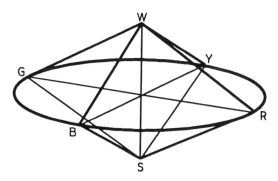

Figure 1.6
The NCS color spindle (from Sivik and Taft 1994, 148).

alternatives). All the alternative models use dimensions, however, and all of them are three-dimensional. Some alternatives replace the circular hue by a structure with corners. A controversy exists over which geometry of the color space best represents human perception. There is no unique answer, since the evaluation partly depends on the aims of the model. By focusing on the NCS color spindle in my applications, I do not claim that this is the optimal representation, but only that it is suitable for illustrating some aspects of color perception and of conceptual spaces in general.

The color spindle represents the phenomenal color space. Austen Clark (1993, 181) argues that physical properties of light are not relevant when describing color space. His distinction between intrinsic and extrinsic features in the following quotation corresponds to the distinction between phenomenal features and those described by scientific theories:

> [A]n analysis of sensory qualities should mention only intrinsic features of the quality space: extrinsic features can be no part of the analysis.
>
> This suggestion implies that the meaning of a colour predicate can be given only in terms of its relations to other colour predicates. The place of the colour in the psychological colour solid is defined by those relations, and it is only its place in the solid that is relevant to its identity. . . .

More general support for the second part of the quotation have been given by Shepard and Chipman (1970, 2) who point out that what is important about a representation is not how it relates to *what* is represented, but how it relates to *other* representations:[12]

> [T]he isomorphism should be sought—not in the first-order relation between (a) an individual object, and (b) its corresponding internal representation—but in the second-order relation between (a) the relations among alternative external objects, and (b) the relations among their corresponding internal representations. Thus, although the internal representation need not itself be square, it should (whatever it is) at least have a closer functional relation to the internal representation for a rectangle than to that, say, for a green flash or the taste of persimmon.

The "functional relation" they refer to concerns the tendency of different responses to be activated together. Such tendencies typically show up in similarity judgments. Thus, because of the structure of the color space, we judge that red is more similar to purple than to yellow, for example, even though we cannot say what it is in the subjective experience of the colors that causes this judgment.[13]

Nevertheless, there are interesting connections between phenomenal and physical dimensions, even if they are not perfectly matched. The hue of a color is related to the wavelengths of light, which thus is the main dimension used in the scientific description of color. Visible light occurs in the range of 420–700 nm. The geometrical structure of the (scientific) wavelength dimension is thus linear, in contrast to the circular structure of the (phenomenal) hue dimension.

The neurophysiological mechanisms underlying the mental representation of color space are comparatively well understood. In particular, it has been established that human color vision is mediated by the cones in the retina which contain three kinds of pigments. These pigments are maximally sensitive at 445 nm (blue-violet), 535 nm (green)

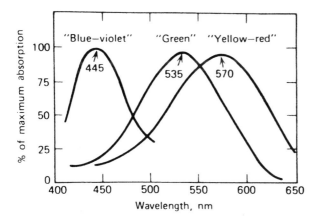

Figure 1.7
Absorption spectra for three types of cone pigments (from Buss 1973, 203).

and 570 nm (yellow-red) (see figure 1.7). The perceived color emerges as a mixture of input from different kinds of cones. For instance, "pure" red is generated by a mixture of signals from the blue-violet and the yellow-red sensitive cones.

The connections between what excites the cones and rods in the retina, however, and what color is *perceived* is far from trivial. According to Land's (1977) results, the perceived color is not directly a function of radiant energy received by the cones and rods, but rather it is determined by "lightness" values computed at three wavelengths.[14]

Human color vision is thus trichromatic. In the animal kingdom we find a large variation of color systems (see for example Thompson 1995); many mammals are dichromats, while others (like goldfish and turtles) appear to be tetrachromats; and some may even be pentachromats (pigeons and ducks). The precise geometric structures of the color spaces of the different species remain to be established (research which will involve very laborious empirical work). Here, it suffices to say that the human color space is but one of many evolutionary solutions to color perception.

We can also find related spatial structures for other sensory qualities. For example, consider the quality dimension of *pitch*, which is basically a continuous one-dimensional structure going from low tones to high. This representation is directly connected to the neurophysiology of pitch perception (see section 2.5).

Apart from the basic frequency dimension of tones, we can find some interesting further structure in the cognitive representation of tones. Natural tones are not simple sinusoidal tones of one frequency only but constituted of a number of higher harmonics. The timbre of a tone, which is a phenomenal dimension, is determined by the relative strength of the higher harmonics of the fundamental frequency of the tone. An interesting perceptual phenomenon is "the case of the missing fundamental." This means that if the fundamental frequency is removed by artificial methods from a complex physical tone, the phenomenal pitch of the tone is still perceived as that corresponding to the removed fundamental.[15] Apparently, the fundamental frequency is not indispensable for pitch perception, but the perceived pitch is determined by a combination of the lower harmonics (compare the "vowel space" presented in section 3.8).

Thus, the harmonics of a tone are essential for how it is perceived: tones that share a number of harmonics will be perceived to be similar. The tone that shares the most harmonics with a given tone is its octave, the second most similar is the fifth, the third most similar is the fourth, and so on. This additional "geometrical" structure on the pitch dimension, which can be derived from the wave structure of tones, provides the foundational explanation for the perception of musical *intervals*.[16] This is an example of higher level structures of conceptual spaces to be discussed in section 3.10.

As a third example of sensory space representations, the human perception of *taste* appears to be generated from four distinct types of receptors: salt, sour, sweet, and bitter. Thus the quality space representing taste could be described as a four-dimensional space. One such model was put forward by Henning (1916), who suggested that phenomenal gustatory space could be described as a tetrahedron (see figure 1.8). Henning speculated that any taste could be described as a mixture of only three primaries. This means that any taste can be rep-

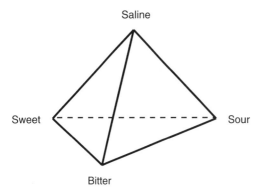

Figure 1.8
Henning's taste tetrahedron.

resented as a point on one of the *planes* of the tetrahedron, so that no taste is mapped onto the interior of the tetrahedron.

There are other models, however, that propose more than four fundamental tastes.[17] Which is the best model of the phenomenal gustatory space remains to be established. This will involve sophisticated psychophysical measurement techniques. Suffice it to say that the gustatory space quite clearly has some nontrivial geometrical structure. For instance, we can meaningfully claim that the taste of a walnut is closer to the taste of a hazelnut than to the taste of popcorn in the same way as we can say that the color orange is closer to yellow than to blue.

1.6 Some Mathematical Notions

The dimensions of conceptual spaces, as illustrated in these examples, are supposed to satisfy certain structural constraints. In this section, some of the mathematical concepts that will be used in the following chapters are presented in greater detail. Since most of the examples of quality dimensions will have geometrical structures, I focus here on some fundamental notions of geometry.[18]

An axiomatic system for geometry can, in principle, be constructed from two primitive relations, namely *betweenness* and *equidistance* defined over a space of *points*. In most treatments, however, *lines* and *planes* are also taken to be primitive concepts (see, for example, Borsuk and Szmielew 1960), but these notions will only play a marginal role here.

1.6.1 Betweenness

One of the fundamental geometrical relations is betweenness, a concept frequently applied in this book. Let S denote the set of all points in a space. The betweenness relation is a ternary relation $B(a, b, c)$ over points in S, which is read as "point b lies between points a and c." The relation is supposed to satisfy some fundamental axioms. The simplest ones are the following:[19]

> *B0*: If $B(a, b, c)$, then a, b and c are distinct points.
> *B1*: If $B(a, b, c)$, then $B(c, b, a)$.

In words: "If b is between a and c, then b is between c and a."

> *B2*: If $B(a, b, c)$, then not $B(b, a, c)$.

"If b is between a and c, then a is not between c and b."

> *B3*: If $B(a, b, c)$ and $B(b, c, d)$, then $B(a, b, d)$.

"If b is between a and c and c is between b and d, then b is between a and d."

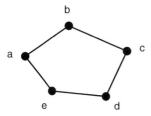

Figure 1.9
Graph violating axiom B3 when $B(a, b, c)$ is defined as "b is on the *shortest* path from a to c."

B4: If $B(a, b, d)$ and $B(b, c, d)$, then $B(a, b, c)$.

"If b is between a and d and c is between b and d, then b is between a and c."

These axioms are satisfied for a large number of ordered structures.[20] It is easy to see that they are true of ordinary Euclidean geometry; however, they may also be valid in some "weaker" structures like graphs. If we define $B(a, b, c)$ as "there is some path from a to c that passes through b," then axioms B1, B3, and B4 are all valid. B2 is also valid if the graph is a tree (that is, if it does not contain any loops).

In contrast, if $B(a, b, c)$ is defined as "b is on the *shortest* path from a to c," then axiom B3 need not be valid in all graphs as figure 1.9 shows. In this figure, b is on the shortest path from a to c, and c is on the shortest path from b to d, but b is not on the shortest path from a to d (nor is c).

This example shows that for a given ordered structure there may be *more than one way* of defining a betweenness relation. I will come back to this point in the following chapters, as it is important for an analysis of concept formation.

From B1–B4 it immediately follows:

LEMMA 1.1   (i) If $B(a, b, c)$ and $B(b, c, d)$, then $B(a, c, d)$; (ii) If $B(a, b, d)$ and $B(b, c, d)$, then $B(a, c, d)$.

In principle, the notion of a *line* can be defined with the aid of the betweenness relation (Borsuk and Szmielew 1960, 57), by saying that the line through points a and c, in symbols L_{ac}, consists of the set of points b such that $B(a, b, c)$ or $B(b, a, c)$ or $B(a, c, b)$ (together with the points a and c themselves). Unless further assumptions are made, however, concerning the structure of the set S of points, the lines defined in this way may not look like the lines we know from ordinary geometry. For example, the line between a and d in figure 1.9 will consist of all the points a, b, c, d and e.[21] Still, one can prove the following property of all lines:

LEMMA 1.2   If a, b, c and d are four points on a line and $B(a, b, d)$ and $B(a, c, d)$, then either $B(a, b, c)$ or $B(a, c, b)$ or $b = c$.

Furthermore, a *plane* can be defined with the aid of lines and the betweenness relation.[22] Once we have the notions of lines and planes, most of traditional geometry can be constructed.

The basic axioms for betweenness can be supplemented with an axiom for *density*:

> B5: For any two points a and c in S, there is some point b such that $B(a, b, c)$.

Of course, there are quality dimensions; for example, all discrete dimensions, for which axiom B5 is not valid.

As is well known from the theory of rational numbers, density does not imply *continuity*.[23]

1.6.2 Equidistance

The second primitive notion of geometry is that of *equidistance*. It is a four-place relation $E(a, b, c, d)$ which is read as "point a is just as far from point b as point c is from point d." The basic axioms for the relation E are the following (Borsuk and Szmielew 1960, 60):

> E1: If $E(a, a, p, q)$, then $p = q$.
> E2: $E(a, b, b, a)$.
> E3: If $E(a, b, c, d)$ and $E(a, b, e, f)$, then $E(c, d, e, f)$.

LEMMA 1.3   (i) If $E(a, b, c, d)$ and $E(c, d, e, f)$, then $E(a, b, e, f)$. (ii) If $E(a, b, c, d)$, then $E(a, b, d, c)$.[24]

The following axiom connects the betweenness relation B with the equidistance relation E:

> E4: If $B(a, b, c)$, $B(d, e, f)$, $E(a, b, d, e)$ and $E(b, c, e, f)$, then $E(a, c, d, f)$.

E4 says essentially that if b is between a and c, then the distance between a and c is the sum of the distance between a and b and the distances between b and c. Because sums of distances cannot be defined explicitly using only the relations B and E, however, the condition is expressed in a purely relational way.

1.6.3 Metric Spaces

The equidistance relation is a qualitative notion of distance. A stronger notion is that of a *metric* space. A real-valued function $d(a,b)$ is said to be a *distance function* for the space S if it satisfies the following conditions for all points a, b, and c in S:

D1: $d(a, b) \geq 0$ and $d(a, b) = 0$ only if $a = b$. (minimality)
D2: $d(a, b) = d(b, a)$. (symmetry)
D3: $d(a, b) + d(b, c) \geq d(a, c)$. (triangle inequality)

A space that has a distance function is called a metric space. For example, in the two-dimensional space R^2, the *Euclidean* distance $d_E(x, y) = \sqrt{((x_1 - y_1)^2 + (x_2 - y_2)^2)}$ satisfies D1–D3. Also a finite graph where the distance between points a and b is defined as the number of steps on the shortest path between a and b is a metric space.

In a metric space, one can *define* a betweenness relation B and an equidistance relation E in the following way:

Def B: $B(a, b, c)$ if and only if $d(a, b) + d(b, c) = d(a, c)$.
Def E: $E(a, b, c, d)$ if and only if $d(a, b) = d(c, d)$.

It is easy to show that if d satisfies D1–D3, then B and E defined in this way satisfies B1, B2, B4, and E1–E4. B3 is not valid in general as is shown by the graph in figure 1.9, where the distance between points a and b is defined as the number of steps on the shortest path between a and b. B3, however, is valid in tree graphs.

1.6.4 Euclidean and City-Block Metrics

For the Euclidean distance function, the betweenness relation defined by Def B, results in the standard meaning so that all points between a and b are the ones on the *straight line* between a and b. As illustrated in figure 1.10, equidistance can be represented by *circles* in the sense that the set of points at distance d from a point c form a circle with c as center and d as the radius.

There is more then one way, however, of defining a metric on R^2. Another common metric is the so called *city-block* metric, defined as follows, where $|x_1 - y_1|$ denotes the absolute distance between x_1 and y_1:

$$d_C(x, y) = |x_1 - y_1| + |x_2 - y_2|. \tag{1.1}$$

For the city-block measure, the set of points at distance d from a point c form a *diamond* with c as center (see figure 1.11).

It should be noted that the city-block metric depends on the *direction* of the x and y axes in R^2, in contrast to the Euclidean metric, which is invariant under all rotations of the axes. The set of points between points a and b, as given by Def B, is not a straight line for the city-block metric, but the rectangle generated by a and b and the directions of the axes (see figure 1.12).

It follows that, for a given space, there is not a unique meaning of "between"; different metrics generate different betweenness relations. Further examples of this are given in chapter 3.

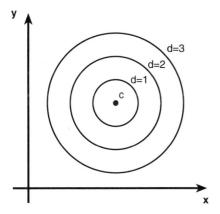

Figure 1.10
Equidistances under the Euclidean metric.

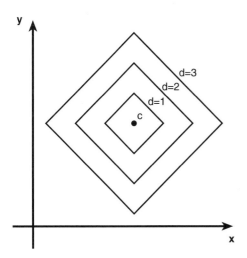

Figure 1.11
Equidistances under the city-block metric.

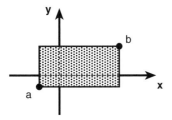

Figure 1.12
The set of points *between* a and b defined by the city-block metric.

The Euclidean and city-block metrics can be generalized in a straightforward way to the n-dimensional Cartesian space R^n by the following equations:

$$d_E(x, y) = \sqrt{\Sigma_i(x_i - y_i)^2}.$$ (1.2)

$$d_C(x, y) = \Sigma_i|x_i - y_i|.$$ (1.3)

They are special cases of the class of *Minkowski metrics* defined by

$$d_k(x, y) = \sqrt[k]{\Sigma_i|x_i - y_i|^k},$$ (1.4)

where we thus have as special cases $d_E(x, y) = d_2(x, y)$ and $d_C(x, y) = d_1(x, y)$.[25]

Equations (1.2)–(1.4) presume that the *scales* of the different dimensions are identical so that the distance measured along one of the axes is the same as that measured along another. In psychological contexts, however, this assumption is often violated. A more general form of distance is obtained by putting a weight w_i on the distance measured along dimension i (see, for example, Nosofsky 1986):

$$d_E(x, y) = \sqrt{\Sigma_i w_i \cdot (x_i - y_i)^2}.$$ (1.5)

$$d_C(x, y) = \Sigma_i w_i \cdot |x_i - y_i|.$$ (1.6)

In these equations, w_i is the "attention-weight" given to dimension i (the role of attention-weights in determining the "salience" of dimensions discussed in section 4.2). Large values of w_i "stretch" the conceptual space along dimension i, while small values of w_i will "shrink" the space along that dimension. In the following, I refer to the more general definitions given by equations (1.5) and (1.6) when Euclidean or city-block distances are mentioned.

1.6.5 Similarity as a Function of Distance

In studies of categorization and concept formation, it is often assumed that the *similarity* of two stimuli can be determined from the distances between the representations of the stimuli in the underlying psychological space. But then what is this functional relation between similarity and distance? A common assumption in the psychological literature (Shepard 1987, Nosofsky 1988a, 1988b, 1992, Hahn and Chater 1997) is that similarity is an *exponentially decaying function* of distance. If s_{ij} expresses the similarity between two objects i and j and d_{ij} their distance, then the following formula, where c is a general "sensitivity" parameter, expresses the relation between the two measures:

$$s_{ij} = e^{-c \cdot d_{ij}}.$$ (1.7)

Shepard (1987) calls this the *universal law of generalization* and he argues that it captures the similarity-based generalization performances of subjects in a variety of settings. An underlying motivation for the equation is that matching and mismatching properties are combined multiplicatively rather than additively (Nosofsky 1992, Medin, Goldstone, and Gentner 1993, 258). Given some additional mathematical assumptions, this corresponds to an exponential decay of similarity.

Nosofsky (1986) argues that the exponential function in (1.7) should be replaced by a Gaussian function of the following form:

$$s_{ij} = e^{-c \cdot d_{ij}^2}. \tag{1.8}$$

I will not enter the debate on which of these two functional forms is the more generally valid. Here it suffices to notice that for both equations the similarity between two objects drops quickly when the distance between the objects is relatively small, while it drops much more slowly when the distance is relatively large.

The mathematical notions that have been introduced in this section will prove their usefulness when the theories of properties and concepts are presented in chapters 3 and 4.

1.7 How Dimensions Are Identified

In a conceptual space that is used as a framework for a scientific theory or for construction of an artificial cognitive system, the geometrical or topological structures of the dimensions are *chosen* by the scientist proposing the theory or the constructor building the system. The structures of the dimensions are tightly connected to the *measurement methods* employed to determine the values on the dimensions in experimental situations (compare Sneed 1971 and Suppes et al. 1989). Thus, the choice of dimensions in a given constructive situation will partly depend on what sensors are assumed to be used and their function.

In contrast, the dimensions of a *phenomenal* conceptual space are not obtainable immediately from the perceptions or actions of the subjects, but have to be *infered* from their behavior. There are a number of statistical techniques for identifying the dimensions of a phenomenal space. Here, I only introduce one of the most well-known methods, namely *multidimensional scaling* (MDS).[26] In section 4.10, a different technique will be presented in connection with an analysis of "shell space," and in section 6.5 a method based on artificial neuron networks is described.

If the coordinates of two points are known for all dimensions of a metric conceptual space, it is easy to calculate the *distance* between the points using the metric that goes along with the space. MDS concerns the reverse problem; starting from subjects' judgments about the similarities of two stimuli, MDS is used to determine the number of dimensions in the underlying phenomenal space and the scaling of the space. The goal is to obtain as high a correlation as possible between the similarity judgments of the subjects and the corresponding distances in the estimated dimensional space.

A MDS analysis starts out from a set of data concerning judgments of similarities of a class of stimuli. The similarity judgments can be numerical, but they are often given in an ordinal form obtained from a scale ranging from "very similar" to "very dissimilar." The judgments given by the individual subjects are normally averaged before they are fed into a MDS algorithm (such as Kruskal's 1964 KYST).

The investigator chooses the number n of dimensions in the space to be estimated and the metric (normally Euclidean or city-block) to be used in defining distances in the space. Starting from an initial assignment of coordinates to the stimuli in an n-dimensional space, the MDS algorithm then systematically adjusts the coordinates to achieve a progressively better fit to the data from the similarity judgments. The degree of misfit between the data and the estimated space is normally measured by a "stress function."[27] The algorithm stops when the stress of the estimated space no longer decreases.

As an example, Shepard (1962a,b) applied "proximity analysis," which is a variant of MDS to a selection of fourteen hues. Subjects were asked to rate the similarity of each pair of hues on an ordinal scale from 1 to 5. The result of the analysis was the structure shown in figure 1.13. In this figure, the MDS program placed the stimuli points in a two-dimensional space. The curved line connecting them was drawn by Shepard. As can be seen, it forms a circle based on two opponent axes, red-green and blue-yellow, in almost perfect fit with the hypothesized color circle.

The higher the dimension n of the estimated space, the smaller is the resulting minimal stress. Thus, arbitrarily good fit can be achieved by increasing n. This means that it is a methodological problem to decide what value of n to use in a model. Unless there are strong a priori reasons for assuming that the underlying phenomenal space has a certain number of dimensions, one often looks for a (rather small) number n where the computed stress of $n + 1$ dimensions is not significantly smaller than the stress of n dimensions.[28]

One problem with MDS is that it can be difficult to give a psychological *interpretation* of the dimensions generated by the algorithm (given a choice of n). Austen Clark (1993, 124) formulates the problem as follows:

> The number of dimensions of the MDS space corresponds to the number of independent ways in which stimuli in that modality

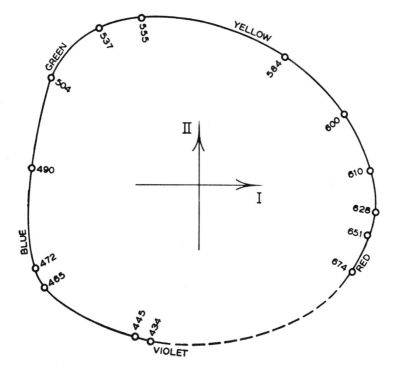

Figure 1.13
A MDS analysis of hues. Stimuli are marked by wavelength in nanometers (from Shepard 1962b, 236).

can be sensed to resemble or differ, but the dimensions *per se* have no meaning. Indeed, it will be seen that a key step in explaining a quality space is to find interpretable axes. Sometimes one can provide them with a neurophysiological interpretation. Only then can one claim to have determined *what* the differentiative attributes of encodings are, as opposed to knowing simply how many of them there are.

Apart from the neurophysiological interpretations that Clark mentions, investigators often have hypotheses about quality dimensions that could generate the subjects' similarity judgments. So-called "property vector fitting" can then be used to verify the presence of such hypothesized dimensions.[29] This means that, by regression analysis, a stimulus attribute can be correlated with a vector in the space generated by an MDS method. If a high correlation can be found, this indicates that a dimension corresponding to the stimulus attribute is represented in the space. This technique does not guarantee, however, that all the dimensions in a space generated by MDS can be given a meaningful psychological interpretation.

1.8 Integral and Separable Dimensions

A conceptual space is defined here as a set of quality dimensions with a geometrical structure. Now it is time to consider the relations among the dimensions in a conceptual space.

Certain quality dimensions are *integral* in the sense that one cannot assign an object a value on one dimension without giving it a value on the other (Garner 1974, Maddox 1992, Melara 1992). For example, an object cannot be given a hue without also giving it a brightness value. Or a pitch of a sound always goes along with a certain loudness. Dimensions that are not integral are said to be *separable*, as for example the size and hue dimensions.[30] The distinction between integral and separable dimensions will play an important role in the analysis of properties and concepts in chapters 3 and 4. Melara (1992, 274) presents the distinction as follows:

> What is the difference psychologically, then, between interacting [integral] and separable dimensions? In my view, these dimensions differ in their similarity relations. Specifically, interacting and separable dimensions differ in their degree of *cross-dimensional similarity*, a construct defined as the phenomenal similarity of one dimension of experience with another. I propose that interacting dimensions are higher in cross-dimensional similarity than separable dimensions.

Several empirical tests have been proposed to decide whether two perceptual dimensions are separable or integral (see Maddox 1992 for an excellent survey and analysis of these tests). One test is called "speeded classification." The stimuli in this test consists of four combinations of two levels of two dimensions x and y (say size and hue). If the x-levels are x_1 and x_2 (for example, large and small) and the y-values y_1 and y_2 (for example, green and yellow), we can denote the four stimuli (x_1, y_1), (x_1, y_2), (x_2, y_1), and (x_2, y_2) respectively. In the *control* condition, subjects are asked to categorize, as quickly as possible, the level of one dimension, say x, while the other is held constant, by being presented with either (x_1, y_1) or (x_2, y_1) as stimulus (alternatively, (x_1, y_2) or (x_2, y_2)). In the *filtering* condition, the subjects are asked to categorize the level of the same dimension while the other is varied independently. In this condition, the stimulus set thus consists of all four stimuli. Now, if the mean reaction time in the filtering condition is longer than in the control condition, the irrelevant dimension, in this case y, is said to *interfere* with the test dimension x. According to the speeded classification test, x and y are then classified as integral. The underlying assumption is that two separable dimensions can be attended *selectively*, while this is difficult for two integral dimensions; in separable dimensions, the subjects can "filter out" information from the irrelevant dimension.

Another test is the "redundancy task" (Garner 1974). The stimuli and the control condition are the same as in the previous test. In the *redundancy* condition, only two of the four stimuli are utilized, either (x_1, y_1) and (x_2, y_2) or (x_1, y_2) and (x_2, y_1). The values of the two dimension are thus correlated so that the value of one allows the subject to predict the value of the other. The subject is presented with one of the two stimuli and is also here asked to categorize, as quickly as possible, the value of one dimension, say x. If the mean reaction time is shorter than in the control condition, the subjects are said to exhibit a *redundancy gain*. According to the redundancy task, the dimensions are then classified as integral.

A third test, the so-called "direct dissimilarity scaling," concerns the *metric* of the conceptual space that best explains how subjects judge the similarity of different stimuli that vary along the two dimensions (Attneave 1950, Shepard 1964). In this test, the stimuli consist of all combinations of several levels of the two dimensions x and y. The subjects are then presented with all possible pairs of stimuli, one at a time, and are asked to judge the *dissimilarity* of the stimuli on a scale from 1 to 10. This test is an operational way of deciding the distance function in a metric perceptual space.

Using MDS or some other method, the data are fitted into a two-dimensional space. If the Euclidean metric fits the data best, the dimensions are classified as integral; while if the city-block metric gives the best result, they are classified as separable. If two dimensions are separable, the dissimilarity of two stimuli is obtained by adding the dissimilarity along each of the two dimensions, as is done in the city-block metric. In contrast, when the dimensions are integral, the dissimilarity is determined by both dimensions taken together, which motivates a Euclidean metric (compare the above quotation from Melara on cross-dimensional similarity).

Conversely, suppose we are in the constructive mode and attempt to design a conceptual space for solving some cognitive task. If we decide that two dimensions are integral, we should use the Euclidean metric to determine distances and degrees of similarity; while if we decide that the dimensions are separable, the city-block metric should be used instead. Even in scientific theories the relations among dimensions can vary. For example, time and space are treated as separable in

Newtonian mechanics, while the four-dimensional space-time forms an integral set of dimensions in relativity theory (with its own special Minkowski metric).

The notion of a *domain* is central in this book, and it is used in connection with concept formation in chapter 4, with cognitive semantics in chapter 5, and with induction in chapter 6. Using the concepts of this section, I can now define a domain as *a set of integral dimensions that are separable from all other dimensions.* The three-color dimensions are a prime example of a domain in this sense since hue, chromaticness, and brightness are integral dimensions that presumably are separable from other quality dimensions.[31] Another example could be the *tone* domain with the basic dimensions of *pitch* and *loudness.*[32] The most fundamental reason for decomposing a cognitive structure into domains is the assumption that an object can be assigned certain properties *independently* of other properties. An object can be assigned the weight of "one kilo" independently of its temperature or color.

A *conceptual space* can then be defined as a collection of one or more domains. It should be emphasized that not all domains in conceptual spaces are assumed to be metric. Sometimes a domain is just an ordering or a graph with no distance defined. And even if distances are defined for the different domains of a conceptual space, the domains may be "incommensurable" in the sense that there is no common scale to express distances on the entire space.

The domains of a conceptual space should not be seen as totally independent entities, but they are *correlated* in various ways since the properties of the objects modeled in the space covary. For example, ripeness and color domains covary in the space of fruits. These correlations are discussed in connection with the model of concepts in section 4.3 and in connection with induction in section 6.6.[33]

Conceptual spaces will be the focus of my study of representations on the conceptual level. A *point* in a space represents a possible object (see section 4.8). The properties of the objects are determined by its location in the space. As will be argued in chapter 3, properties are represented by *regions* of a domain. As was seen in section 1.5, however, what is important is not the exact form of the representation but rather the *relations* between different areas of a conceptual space.

1.9 On the Origins of Quality Dimensions

In the previous sections I have given several examples of quality dimensions from different kinds of domains. There appears to be different types of dimensions, so a warranted question is: Where do the dimensions come from? I do not believe there is a unique answer to this question. In this section, I will try to trace the origins of different kinds of quality dimensions.

First, some of the quality dimensions appear to be *innate* or developed very early in life. They are to some extent hard-wired in our nervous system, as for example the sensory dimensions presented in section 1.5. This probably also applies to our representations of ordinary space. Since domains of this kind are obviously extremely important for basic activities like getting around in the environment, finding food, and avoiding danger, there is evolutionary justification for the innateness assumption. Humans and other animals that did not have a sufficiently adequate representation of the spatial structure of the external world were disadvantaged by natural selection.

The brains of humans and animals contain topographic areas that map different kinds of sense modalities onto spatial areas (see section 2.5 for more connections to neuroscience). The structuring principles of these mappings are basically innate, even if the fine tuning is established during the development of the human or animal.[34] The same principles appear to govern most of the animal kingdom. Gallistel (1990, 105) argues:

> [T]he intuitive belief that the cognitive maps of "lower" animals are weaker than our own is not well founded. They may be impoverished relative to our own (have less on them) but they are not weaker in their formal characteristics. There is experimental evidence that even insect maps are metric maps.

Quine (1969, 123) notes that something like innate quality dimensions are needed to make *learning* possible:

> Without some such prior spacing of qualities, we could never acquire a habit; all stimuli would be equally alike and equally different. These spacings of qualities, on the part of men and other animals, can be explored and mapped in the laboratory by experiments in conditioning and extinction. Needed as they are for all learning, these distinctive spacings cannot themselves all be learned; some must be innate.

The point is that without an initial structure, the world would be just a "blooming, buzzing confusion" (James 1890). We need some dimensions to get learning going.

Once the process has started, however, new dimensions can be added by the learning process.[35] One kind of example comes from studies of children's cognitive development. Smith (1989, 146–47) argues that working out a system of perceptual dimension, a system of *kinds* of similarities, may be one of the major intellectual achievements of early childhood. . . . The basic developmental notion is one of differentiation, from global syncretic classes of perceptual resemblance and magnitude to dimensionally specific kinds of sameness and magnitude.

Two-year-olds can represent whole objects, but they cannot reason about the dimensions of these objects. Goldstone and Barsalou (1998, 252) note:[36]

Evidence suggests that dimensions that are easily separated by adults, such as the brightness and size of a square, are treated as fused together for children. . . . For example, children have difficulty identifying whether two objects differ on their brightness or size even though they can easily see that they differ in some way. Both differentiation and dimensionalization occur throughout one's lifetime.

Consequently, learning new concepts is often connected with *expanding* one's conceptual space with new quality dimensions. For example, consider the (phenomenal) dimension of *volume*. The experiments on "conservation" performed by Piaget and his followers indicate that small children have no separate representation of volume; they confuse the volume of a liquid with the *height* of the liquid in its container. It is only at about the age of five years that they learn to represent the two dimensions separately. Similarly, three- and four-year-olds confuse *high* with *tall*, *big* with *bright*, and so forth (Carey 1978).[37]

Along the same lines, Shepp (1983) argues that the developmental shift is from integral dimensions to separable:

[Y]ounger children have been described as perceiving objects as unitary wholes and failing to attend selectively. This characterization is strikingly similar to the perception and attention of an adult when performing with integral dimensions. In contrast, older children are characterized as perceiving objects according to values on specific dimensions and as succeeding in selective attention. Such a description accurately describes an adult's perception and attention when confronted with separable dimensions. On the basis of these parallels, we have suggested the hypothesis that dimensional combinations that are perceived as separable by the older child and adult are perceived as integral by the young child.

Still other dimensions may be *culturally* dependent.[38] Take time, for example; in some cultures time is conceived to be *circular*—the world keeps returning to the same point in time and the same events occur over and over again; and in other cultures it is hardly meaningful at all to speak of time as a dimension. A sophisticated time dimension, with a full metric structure, is needed for advanced forms of planning and coordination with other individuals, but it is not necessary for the most basic activities of an organism. As a matter of fact, the standard Western conception of time is a comparatively recent phenomenon (Toulmin and Goodfield 1965).

The examples given here indicate that many of the quality dimensions of human conceptual spaces are not directly generated from sensory inputs.[39] This is even clearer when we use concepts based on the *functions* of artifacts or the *social roles* of people in a society. Even if we do not know much about the geometrical structures of these dimensions, it is quite obvious that there is some such nontrivial structure. This has been argued by Marr and Vaina (1982) and Vaina (1983), who give an analysis of functional representation where functions of an object are determined by the actions it allows. I return to the analysis of actions and functional properties in section 3.10.3.

Culture, in the form of interactions among people, may in itself generate constraints on conceptual spaces. For example, Freyd (1983, 193–194) puts forward the intriguing proposal that conceptual spaces may evolve as a representational form in a community just because people have to *share* knowledge:

> There have been a number of different approaches towards analyzing the structures in semantic domains, but what these approaches have in common is the goal of discovering constraints on knowledge representation. I argue that the structures the different semantic analyses uncover may stem from shareability constraints on knowledge representation. . . . So, if a set of terms can be shown to behave as if they are represented in a three-dimensional space, one inference that is often made is that there is both some psychological reality to the spatial reality (or some formally equivalent formulation) and some innate necessity to it. But it might be that the structural properties of the knowledge domain came about because such structural properties provide for the most efficient sharing of concepts. That is, we cannot be sure that the regularities tell us anything about how the brain can represent things, or even "prefer" to, if it didn't have to share concepts with other brains.

Here Freyd hints at an *economic* explanation of why we have conceptual spaces; they facilitate the sharing of knowledge.[40] Section 5.8 shows that since efficient sharing of knowledge is one of the fundamental requirements of *communication*, Freyd's argument will provide an independent justification for the representational role of conceptual spaces.

Finally, some quality dimensions are introduced by *science*. Witness, for example, Newton's distinction between *weight* and *mass*, which is of pivotal importance for the development of his celestial mechanics but which has hardly any correspondence in human perception. To the extent we have mental representations of the masses of objects in distinction to their weights, these are not given by the senses but have to be learned by adopting the conceptual space of Newtonian mechanics in our representations. The role of new dimensions in science will be further discussed in section 6.4.

1.10 Conclusion

The main purpose of this chapter has been to present the notions of dimensions and domains that constitute the fundamentals of the theory of conceptual spaces. Throughout the book, I apply constructions using conceptual spaces to material from several research areas like semantics, cognitive psychology, philosophy of science, neuroscience, neural networks, and machine learning. I hope that these constructions will establish the viability of the conceptual level of representation.

So what *kind* of theory is the theory of conceptual spaces? Is it an empirical, normative, computational, psychological, neuroscientific, or linguistic theory? The answer is that the theory of conceptual spaces is used in two ways in this book. On a general level, it is a *framework for cognitive representations*. It should be seen as a complement to the symbolic and the connectionist approaches that forms a bridge between these two forms of representation. On a more specific level, the framework of conceptual spaces can then be turned into *empirically testable theories* or *constructive models* by filling in specific dimensions with certain geometrical structures, specific measurement methods, specific connections to other empirical phenomena, and so forth.

Cognitive science has two predominant goals: to *explain* cognitive phenomena and to *construct* artificial systems that can solve various cognitive tasks. My primary aim here is to use conceptual spaces in constructive tasks. In the following chapters, I outline how they can be used in computational models of *concept formation* and *induction* and I also show that they are useful for representing the *meanings* of different kinds of linguistic expressions in a computational approach to semantics. The confidence in the aptness of the theory of conceptual spaces should increase, however, if the theory can also be used to explain various empirical phenomena. Consequently, I also connect the theory to empirical material from psychology, neuroscience, and linguistics, even though I do not attempt to give a complete evaluation of the empirical potency of the theory.

Conceptual spaces are static in the sense that they only describe the *structure* of representations. A full model of cognitive mechanisms not only includes the representational form, but also a description of the *processes* operating on the representations. A particular conceptual space is, in general, compatible with several types of processes, and it must therefore be complemented with a description of the *dynamics* of the representations to generate testable predictions (see, for example, Port and van Gelder 1995, Scott Kelso 1995, van Gelder 1998). This topic is treated in chapter 7.

Finally, a philosophical question: What is the ontological status of conceptual spaces? I view conceptual spaces as *theoretical entities* that can be used to explain and predict various empirical phenomena concerning concept formation (the role of theoretical entities is discussed further in section 6.4). In particular, the distances associated with metric space should be seen as theoretical terms. And if similarity is defined by distances via equation (1.7) or (1.8), similarity will be a theoretical term, too (compare Medin, Goldstone, and Gentner 1993, 255). Since my basic methodological position is *instrumentalistic*, I avoid questions about how real the dimensions of conceptual spaces are but view them as instruments for predictive and constructive purposes (compare, for example, the question of what the equator is).

Some of the neurophysiological correlates of the phenomenal dimensions are presented in section 2.5. By being correlated to empirical phenomena in different ways, the assumptions about the dimensions will have testable empirical consequences. These consequences can then be seen as defining the *content* of the theory (compare Sneed 1971 and Stegmüller 1976). Furthermore, when constructing artificial systems, the dimensions of the conceptual spaces will function as the framework for the architecture of the systems that, for example, will determine the role of the sensors in the system.

In brief, my instrumentalist standing means that I eschew philosophical discussions of how "real" conceptual spaces are. The important thing is that we can *do* things with them. To manifest this is the objective of the rest of the book.

Chapter 2
Symbolic, Conceptual, and
Subconceptual Representations

2.1 An Analogy for the Three Kinds of Representations

The previous chapter introduced three levels of representation within cognitive science—the symbolic, the conceptual, and the associationist levels. Since associationist representations occur at the most fine-grained level, I call them *subconceptual* representations.[41] The main goal of this chapter is to argue that all three levels are needed to cover the problems of representation the cognitive scientist faces when explaining cognitive phenomena and building artificial agents.

To provide an introductory illustration of the roles of the three levels in representing information, an analogy may be helpful.[42] Let me assume that the world represented here is a jungle. People move around in the undergrowth pursuing different kinds of goals. Suppose that my aim is explanatory—I want to describe their travelings through the jungle.

On a myopic scale, the movements of the jungle inhabitants are constrained in two ways. First, by the *environment*—rocks, trees, bushes, vines, rivers, and so forth, block their way and prevent them from moving in straight lines and from seeing very far ahead. Second, their *bodies* only allow certain movements; they cannot take three-meter steps, they cannot squeeze through passages that are only 10 centimeters wide, they cannot climb very steep cliffs, and so forth.

These constraints determine a class of possible trajectories through the jungle. Among the various possibilities, people tend to choose the most efficient paths. What is efficient, however, can only be determined locally, since there is no way of surveying the whole area.

At this stage, the trajectories chosen by the inhabitants can be described only on a very low and detailed level. Language is not even sufficient for this task, but traveling instructions are best given by *praxis*, that is, *showing* somebody the way. The closest verbal representation would be cumbersome instructions like "two steps towards the trunk of the tree, then take a left turn and bend under the branch, turn 45° to the right and step over the rock. . . ." Since the trajectories are determined by the dynamic interactions between the people and their environment, this level of representation corresponds to the subconceptual level. This is in analogy with connectionist systems, where the activities of the neurons depend on the dynamic structure of the artificial neuron network. A full description of people's movement in the jungle can only be made on a *local* level in analogy with the descriptions of the activities of the neurons in an artificial neuron network.

In the long run, the people's movements will cause certain changes in the environment; somebody lifts aside a rock that blocks the way, somebody breaks a branch that hangs down, and general wear and tear makes certain routes easier to follow. In this way, *paths* through the jungle are established that make traveling more efficient. The paths make it possible to find *directions* and thus plan further ahead. This process corresponds to *learning* in artificial neuron networks. Indeed, the paths can be seen as analogous to the "valleys" of the energy function of the network (see Rumelhart and McClelland 1986).

Let us assume that the information available to the jungle people is of the kind that makes it possible to draw a *map* of the system of paths. Even though a map cannot be transfered completely to a verbal form, a different kind of route description would now become possible. One can say, "go 30 meters to the west, turn right, and follow the path down the hill and at the crossroads take the left branch. . . ." These descriptions would be less cumbersome than those on the level of trajectories. It is no longer necessary to consider the areas *outside* the paths, since it can be assumed that the physical constraints make it so much easier to follow the paths. The new kind of description of the travelings presumes that *spatial dimensions* (generating directions like north, west, etc.) are available in the representation. Furthermore, one must be able to determine *distances* in the area. We are now representing traveling information in a spatial form on what corresponds to what I call the *conceptual* level. The *geometrical* structure of the problem space is constitutive for this type of representation.

When the travelings of the jungle people result in a complex system of paths, the paths naturally cross each other at various points. If the crossings and other places are given *names* and road marks are put up, an even more efficient type of route descriptions will emerge: "go from A to B, turn left and go to C. . . ." The details of what happens between the crossing points are no longer necessary to mention, since it is presupposed that there is a (unique) path between A and B that can be traversed without problems. We have now reached what corresponds to the *symbolic* level of representation, where the road marks are the most prominent symbols. If this kind of representation is to function as a tool for communication, it is also required that there is *common knowledge* of what places the names refer to.

The most important lesson to be drawn from this analogy is that there is *no unique way* of representing what is going on in the world. On all three levels, it is the same phenomena that are represented, namely, people's movements through the jungle. The difference is mainly a matter of the *level of detail* used in the representations of their movements. One should also note that the lowest level of description is, in principle, always applicable, while the conceptual and symbolic levels presume that further conditions are satisfied. As soon as these conditions are fulfilled, however, descriptions on the lowest level become unnecessarily complex.

The analogy presented here is not perfect, but it is a useful guide for the following sections where the three different forms of representation are presented in greater detail and their merits and problems are discussed. In section 2.2, the symbolic approach is discussed since this is the classic form of representation within artificial intelligence (AI) and cognitive science. Section 2.3 deals with connectionist representations and other subconceptual forms. In section 2.4 the comparatively lesser known conceptual form based on points or vectors in conceptual spaces is discussed. This level of representation, in terms of its scale, comes in between the symbolic and the subconceptual levels. Further computational aspects of the three different levels are discussed in chapters 6 through 8.

2.2 Symbolic Representations

2.2.1 Computationalism

The outline of the symbolic paradigm of representing information presented here will not be explicitly found in the works of any particular author. It forms an implicit methodology for most research in AI. The classical sources are the works of Newell and Simon (1976). A defence of the general reasoning can be found, for example, in the writings of Fodor (1981, introduction, and chapters 7 and 9) and Pylyshyn (1984), and in the joint article of Fodor and Pylyshyn (1988). Since the position is well-known, a sketch of the most relevant features will suffice here.[43]

The central tenet of the symbolic paradigm is that representing and processing information essentially consists of *symbol manipulation* according to explicit *rules*.[44] The symbols can be concatenated to form expressions in a *language of thought* (Fodor 1975), which is sometimes called Mentalese. The content of a sentence in Mentalese is a belief or a thought of an agent. The different beliefs in the cognitive states of a person are connected via their *logical* or *inferential relations*. Pylyshyn writes (1984, 194): "If a person believes (wants, fears) P, then that person's behavior depends on the form the expression of P takes rather than the state of affairs P refers to. . . ." Thus, the manipulations of symbols are performed without considering the semantic content of the symbols. In applications within AI, first-order logic has been the dominating inferential system (or some related programming version of it, such as Prolog). In other areas, however, more general forms of inference, like those provided by inductive logic or decision theory, have been utilized.

Within the symbolic tradition there are two dominating application areas for cognitive processes. One is modeling logical *inferences* and the other is syntactic *parsing*. When the symbols are used for modeling logical inferences, the expressions represent *propositions* and they stand in various *logical relations* to each other. Information processing involves above all *computations* of logical consequences.[45] In brief, a cognitive agent is seen as a kind of logic machine that operates on sentences from some formal language. The following quotation from Fodor (1981, 230) is a typical formulation of the symbolic paradigm:

> Insofar as we think of mental processes as computational (hence as formal operations defined on representations), it will be natural to take the mind to be, inter alia, a kind of computer. That is, we will think of the mind as carrying out whatever symbol manipulations are constitutive of the hypothesized computational processes. To a first approximation, we may thus construe mental operations as pretty directly analogous to those of a Turing machine.

Similarly, the Chomskian tradition in linguistics focuses on the *syntax* of language. Language is seen as strings of symbols that can be processed by different kinds of *automata*, of which the Turing machine is the most advanced. The main operations are *parsing* of a string of symbols according to a (recursive) set of grammatical rules, and, conversely, *generation* of strings according to the grammatical rules.

The *material basis* for the symbolic processes—be it logical, linguistic, or of a more general psychological nature—is irrelevant to the description of their results. The same mental state with all its sentential attitudes can be realized in a brain as well as in a computer. Thus, the symbolic paradigm clearly presupposes a *functionalist* philosophy of mind. In brief, the mind is conceived of as a computing device, that generates symbolic sentences as inputs from sensory channels, performs logical operations on these sentences, and then transforms them into verbal or nonverbal behaviors as output. Symbol manipulation is supposed to be detached from the environment in the sense that once the "program" has been given its input (in symbolic form), the processing can be performed independently of what happens around the agent.[46]

A further claim of the symbolic paradigm is that mental representations *cannot be reduced* to neurobiological or other physicalistic categories (see P. S. Churchland 1986, section 9.5). The reason is that the functional role of the symbolic representations and the inference rules can be given many different realizations, neurophysiological, electronic, or others. The causal relations governing such a material realization of a mental state will be different for different realizations, even if they represent the same logical relations. Pylyshyn writes (1984, 27): "My brain states are not, as we have noted, causally connected in appropriate ways to walking and to mountains. The relationship must be one of content: a semantic, not a causal relation."

2.2.2 The Limitations of Symbolic Representations

After outlining this position, I now turn to the limitations of the representational power of the symbolic approach. One of the major problems encountered in the classical form of AI is the *frame problem* (McCarthy and Hayes 1969, Dennett 1987, Janlert 1987). Within the early AI community, it was hoped that if we could represent the knowledge necessary to describe the world and the possible actions in a suitable symbolic formalism, then by coupling this world description with a powerful inference machine one could construct an artificial agent capable of planning and problem solving. It soon turned out, however, that describing actions and their consequences in a symbolic form leads to a combinatorial explosion of the logical inferences that are needed. The frame problem can be defined as the problem of specifying on the symbolic level what changes and what stays constant in the particular domain when a particular action is performed.

Some changes are *relevant* for the planning, while others are totally irrelevant. Propositional representations are not well suited for representing causal connections or dynamic interactions. One of the main reasons for this is that they do not provide any natural way to separate different *domains* of information. Various escape routes were tried, but the frame problem persisted in one form or another. The entire program of building planning agents based on purely symbolic representations more or less came to a stall. In brief, a substantial part of the knowledge about the relevant domains cannot be expressed in the format required by symbolic representations (compare Tirri 1991, 56).

The frame problem is linked to the fact that the central bearers of the symbolic representations based on first-order languages are the *predicates* of the language. These predicates are supposed to be *given* to the system.[47] Stewart (1996, 317) says, "In the computational paradigm, symbolic representations are theoretical primitives so that it is not really possible to study their evolutionary emergence, because there are no conceptual categories available for specifying the situation *before* symbols came into being." A successful system, however, must be able to *learn* radically new properties from its interactions with the world and not only form new combinations of the given predicates. This has turned out to be an enigma for symbolic representations. This gives rise to an essential question for a theory of cognitive representation: *where do new predicates come from*?

Furthermore, not only is there a problem of describing the genesis of predicates, but their *development* in a cognitive system is not easily modeled on the symbolic level. Even after an agent has learned a concept, the meaning of the concept very often changes as a result of new experiences. In the symbolic mode of representation, there has been no satisfactory way of modeling the dynamics of concepts. The fact that artificial neuron networks can adapt their categorizations to new experiences has been claimed as an advantage of the networks over symbolic systems, but I argue that the conceptual level is the most appropriate to model this kind of process.

Yet another problem for the symbolic approach is highlighted by Harnad (1990). He asks the following questions: "How can the semantic interpretation of a formal symbol system be made *intrinsic* to the system, rather than just parasitic on the meanings in our heads? How can the meanings of the meaningless symbol tokens, manipulated solely on the basis of their (arbitrary) shapes, be grounded in anything but other meaningless symbols?"

Harnad calls this problem the *symbol grounding problem*. He concludes: "[T]he problem of connecting up with the world in the right way is virtually coextensive with the problem of cognition itself." Thus the symbol grounding problem can be argued to be an *artifact* of the symbolic position. In the same vein, Stewart (1996, 323) says:[48]

> [S]ince linguistic symbols emerge from the precursors of the semiotic signals of animal communication, they *always already* have meaning, even before they acquire the status of symbols. On this view, formal symbols devoid of meaning are *derivative*, being obtained by positively *divesting* previously meaningful symbols of their significance. Quite concretely, this process occurred historically in the course of the history of axiomatic mathematics from Euclid to Hilbert. From this point of view, the "symbol-grounding problem" of computation cognitive science looks

rather bizarre and somewhat perverse: why go to all the bother of divesting "natural symbols" of their meaning, and then desperately trying to put it back, when it would seem so simple to leave them as they are!

These problems have been swept under the carpet within the symbolic tradition.[49] And among those who have addressed the problem, no satisfactory solution has been provided. In his despair of circumventing the problems of the genesis of the predicates, Fodor (1975) goes so far as to claim that all predicates that an agent may use during its entire cognitive history are *innate* to the system.

The problems concerning the formation and dynamics of predicates become most pressing when one scrutinizes the attempts within the symbolic tradition to explain *inductive inferences*. The most ambitious project of analyzing induction during this century has been that of the logical positivists. Inductive inferences were important for them, since such inferences were necessary for their verificationist aims. The basic objects of study for them were sentences in some more or less regimented language. It became apparent, however, that the methodology of the positivists led to serious problems in relation to induction. The most famous ones are Hempel's (1965) "paradox of confirmation" and Goodman's (1955) "riddle of induction." These problems will be addressed in chapters 3 and 6.

What is needed is a *nonlogical* way of distinguishing the predicates that may be used in inductive inferences from those that may not. There are several suggestions for such a distinction in the literature. One idea is that some predicates denote "natural kinds" or "natural properties" while others do not, and it is only the former that may be used in inductive reasoning. Natural kinds are usually interpreted realistically, following the Aristotelian tradition, and thus assumed to represent something that exists in the world independently of human cognition. When it comes to inductive *inferences*, however, it is not sufficient that the properties exist out there somewhere, but we must be able to represent the natural kinds in our minds if they are to be used in planning and decision making. What is needed to understand induction, as performed by humans, is a *conceptualistic* analysis of natural properties. It is one of the principal goals of this book to outline such an analysis.

We not only want to know how observational predicates should be combined in the light of inductive evidence, but, much more importantly, *how the basic predicates are established* in the first place. This problem has, more or less, been neglected by the logical positivists. Logical analysis, the prime tool of positivism, is of no avail for these forms of concept formation. There are several aspects of learning that are incompletely modeled on the symbolic level or not even possible to formulate. Fodor, who is one of the main defenders of the symbolic approach, claims that we cannot go beyond the basic concepts that we *already know*:

> What, then *is* being denied? Roughly, that one can learn a language whose expressive power is greater than that of the language that one already knows. Less roughly, that one can learn a language whose predicates express extensions not expressible by those of a previously available representational system. (Fodor 1975, 86)

The "extensions" expressed by predicates are the contents of the predicates, that is, the concept expressed by the predicates (for a presentation of extensional models of language, see section 3.2). In brief, the symbolic approach to concepts sustains no creative inductions, no genuinely new knowledge, and no conceptual discoveries.[50] To achieve this, we have to go below the symbolic level.

To sum up the criticism of the representational power of symbols, one may ask what is *cognitive* about purely formal operations on abstract symbols?[51] In my opinion, the symbolic paradigm has a narrow applicability. For many areas of representation and information processing, including semantic representation, it is positively misleading.

I do not claim that the symbolic paradigm is totally without value. It has given us insights into mathematical reasoning (but reasoning is not only logic). And if one tries to imitate natural language understanding, it may be necessary to use some linguistic structures, for example, to be able to analyze the grammar of the input (see, for example, Goldberg 1995). But even in this area we encounter problems when it comes to providing a *semantics* for the linguistic expressions. According to the symbolic approach, the contents of an expression in a natural language would be represented by an expression in Mentalese (see, for example, Katz and Fodor 1964). But this would basically be a *translation* from one language to another and it would not help us understand how the expression obtains its *meaning*.

2.3 Subconceptual Representations

2.3.1 Connectionism

For Locke and Hume, thinking consists basically in forming *associations* among "perceptions of the mind." This paradigm has since then been developed by British empiricists, American pragmatists (such as William James), and psychologists (Thorndike actually calls his version "connectionism").[52] Dellarosa (1988, 29) summarizes the central tenet of associationism as follows:

> Events that co-occur in space or time become connected in the mind. Events that share meaning or physical similarity become associated in the mind. Activation of one unit activates others to which it is linked, the degree of activation depending on the strength of association. This approach held great intuitive appeal for investigators of the mind because it seems to capture the flavor of cognitive behaviors: When thinking, reasoning, or musing, one thought reminds us of others.

During the last decades, associationism has been revived with the aid of a new model of cognition—*connectionism*. Connectionist systems, also called *artificial neuron networks* (ANNs), consist of large numbers of simple but highly interconnected units ("neurons"). The units process information in parallel (in contrast to most symbolic models where the processing is serial[53]). There is no central control unit for the network, but all neurons "act" as individual processors. Hence connectionist systems are examples of *parallel distributed processes* (Rumelhart and McClelland 1986).

Each unit receives "activity," both excitatory and inhibitory, as input, and then transmits activity to other units according to some function (usually nonlinear) of the inputs. The behavior of the network as a whole is determined by the initial state of activation and the connections between the units. The inputs to the network also gradually change the "weights" of the connections between units according to some *learning rule*. Typically, the change of connections is much slower than changes in activity values of the units.[54] The units have no memory in themselves, but earlier inputs are represented indirectly via the changes in weights they have caused. Several different kinds of connectionist models found in the literature can be classified according to their architecture or their learning rules (see, for example, Rumelhart and McClelland 1986, Beale and Jackson 1990, Zornetzer, Davis, and Lau 1990, Andy Clark 1993).

In brief, connectionist representations can be seen as a high-dimensional space of activities of neurons and connections between them. Sometimes this way of describing ANNs is called the "state space approach" in analogy with state spaces in physics. In contrast to (low-dimensional) conceptual spaces, the "dimensions" of an ANN are usually not possible to provide with an interpretation. It is possible to define similarity measures over the state space, so that the similarity of different states of the ANN can be compared. Such a measure is externally defined, however, and, unlike the similarity measures used on the conceptual level, is not explicitly represented by the system (see section 2.4).

2.3.2 Representations in Connectionist and Related Systems

According to connectionism, cognitive processes should not be represented by symbol manipulation, but by the *dynamics* of the patterns of activities in ANNs. Van Gelder (1995, 346) writes: "Rather than computers, cognitive systems may be dynamical systems; rather than computation, cognitive processes may be state-space evolution within these very different kinds of systems."[55] Here he focuses on how the cognitive processes are modeled. What processes are appropriate, however, depend on the way information is *represented* in an ANN.

Connectionist systems have become popular among psychologists and cognitive scientists since they appear to be excellent tools for building models of associationist theories. And artificial neuron networks have been developed for many different kinds of tasks, including vision, language processing, concept formation, inference, and motor control (see, for example, Beale and Jackson 1990, Zornetzer, Davis, and Lau 1990, Quinlan 1991, Kohonen 1995). Among the applications, one finds several that traditionally were thought to be typical symbol processing tasks. In favor of the ANNs, the connectionists claim that these models do not suffer from the brittleness of the symbolic models and that they are much less sensitive to noise in the input (Rumelhart and McClelland 1986, Andy Clark 1993). Furthermore, the learning mechanisms provide an answer to the question of how *new* properties can be discovered by a cognitive system.

What are the drawbacks then of using ANNs of the type described here for representing information? One ubiquitous problem is that such systems need a large training set to *learn* the relevant structures. Schyns, Goldstone, and Thibaut (1998, 15) write: "Only with great experience is the system able to categorize accurately. . . . The curse of dimensionality is such that unbiased machines designed to discover many types of new perceptual features flexibly will often need implausibly large training sets to achieve good categorizations."

As discussed in section 4.5, learning mechanisms are much quicker on the conceptual level. The reason ANNs learn so slowly is that they have a large number of learning parameters in the sense that all the weights between neurons are treated as *independent variables* that are slowly adjusted when the system is trained (compare the discussion in section 5.5.2) of Kohonen's self-organizing maps.

A fundamental epistemological problem for ANNs is that even if we know that a network has learned to categorize the input in the right way, we may not be able to describe what the emerging network represents. This kind of level problem is ubiquitous in applications of ANNs for learning purposes.[56] In this respect, it is similar to the outcome of multidimensional scaling processes. I argue in chapter 7 that the theory of artificial neuron networks must somehow bridge the gap of going from the subconceptual level to the conceptual and symbolic levels. We may account for the information provided at the subconceptual level as a dimensional space with some topological structure, but there is no general recipe for determining the *conceptual* meaning of the dimensions of the space.

An assumption that is implicitly made when constructing an ANN is that there is a given *domain* for the receptors of the network. The restriction to a particular domain turns out to confine the representational capacities of ANNs. In particular, a network cannot easily generalize what it has learned from one domain to another.

2.4 Conceptual Representations

A central question for any theory of representation is how concepts should be modeled. The main purpose here is to exhibit the advantages of focusing on the conceptual level and using conceptual spaces as a framework for representations for various problems in cognitive science, philosophy, and AI. My position, elaborated in chapters 7 and 8, is that the conceptual level should be placed *between* the symbolic and the subconceptual levels in terms of representational granularity.[57] Here, only brief remarks are made about how the conceptual level can avoid many of the representational problems encountered on the symbolic and subconceptual levels. The bulk of the book will deal with fleshing out a number of representational applications.

The dimensions are the basic building blocks of representations on the conceptual level. Humans and other animals can represent the qualities of objects, for example when planning an action, without presuming an internal language or another symbolic system in which these qualities are expressed. As a consequence, I claim that the quality dimensions of conceptual spaces are *independent* of symbolic representations and more fundamental than these. This is in contrast to the claims of Fodor (1975) and other defenders of a "language of thought."

About the problems of symbolic representations presented in section 2.2, it should be noted that conceptual spaces will solve the symbol grounding problem, at least when symbols refering to perceptual domains are considered. The perceptual domains that were exemplified in the previous chapter are tied to sensory input channels and hence what is represented in these domains has some correspondence with the external world. I am not defending a correspondence theory claiming that the structure of the external world corresponds to the structure of the represented world; I only demand that the representations in the perceptual domains to some extent are *constrained* by what is happening in the external world.

This point is elaborated in chapter 5 where I argue that symbols can be given meaning, and thereby be grounded, by being connected to various constructions in the conceptual spaces. Thus, to become meaningful, *the symbolic level depends on the conceptual.*

Conceptual spaces can also provide a better way of representing learning in general, and *concept formation* in particular, than what can be achieved on the symbolic level. Several dynamic aspects of concept formation will be treated in chapter 4. In addition, in chapter 6 it will be argued that many of the problems of induction created by the symbolic approach dissolve into thin air when analyzed on the conceptual level.

One notion that is severely downplayed in symbolic representations is that of *similarity*.[58] Judgments of similarity are central for a large number of cognitive processes. In particular, they can reveal the dimensions of our perceptions and their structures. On the conceptual level, the similarity of two objects can be defined via the distance between their representing points in a conceptual space as shown in section 1.6. On this topic, Aisbett and Gibbon (1994, 143) write:

> People are willing to rank simple objects of different shape and colour on the basis of "similarity". If machines are to reason about structure, this comparison process must be formalized. That is, a distance measure between formal object representations must be defined. If the machine is reasoning with information to be presented to a human, the distance measure needs to accord with human notions of object similarity. Since our perception of similarity is subjective and strongly influenced by situation, the measure should be tunable to particular users and contexts.

Palmer (1978, 270–272) introduces a distinction between *intrinsic* and *extrinsic* representation. Representation is intrinsic when the representing relation has the same inherent constraints as its represented relation. For example, if the age of a class of objects is represented by the height of rectangles, the structure of the represented relation (age) is intrinsic in the representing relation (height). In contrast, representing age by numbers is an extrinsic representation since the structure of the digit sequences does not have the same structure as the represented relation. Intrinsic representations exhibit the *same relations* as what they represent (see section 1.5). In contrast, extrinsic representations must be accompanied by a *rule* that specifies how the representation is to be interpreted—such a rule provides the "meaning" of the representation. Representations in connectionist systems are generally intrinsic, while in symbolic models they are, almost by definition, extrinsic.

On the symbolic level, atomic concepts are not modeled, just *named* by the basic symbols. Names of more complex concepts can then be constructed by compositions, logical or syntactical, of the simple names. Since the basic symbols are arbitrary, atomic concepts are represented totally extrinsically. (Some intrinsic relations among complex concepts can, however, be detectable from the composed symbols).

In contrast, the *relations* between different properties are intrinsically represented in conceptual spaces (as will be further detailed in the next chapter).[59] It is, for example, intrinsic in the representation of color space that yellow is closer to orange than to blue, since this follows from the geometrical relations between the regions. On the symbolic level, such relations must be extrinsically represented by special axioms or rules.

A particularly interesting case concerns how *similarity* is represented in the models on different levels. If represented at all, similarity can only be represented extrinsically, by rules or axioms, in a symbolic system. The possible similarities among the symbols themselves are not supposed to play any functional role for the system.

In a conceptual space, similarity is represented *intrinsically* via the distance measure with the aid of equations (1.7) or (1.8) in section 1.6.5. Because the functions in these equations are bijective, a similarity value determines a distance and vice versa. As will be seen in the following chapters, distances, and thereby similarities, play a key representational role in categorization and concept learning.

Goldstone and Barsalou (1998, 240–241) argue that similarity has a perceptual grounding:

> Overall similarity seems to be more efficiently processed by perceptual systems than amodal symbolic systems. First, the processes that allow simple features to be registered in parallel without a capacity limit are found widely throughout perceptual systems. For example, the features *red* and *horizontal line* can be detected simultaneously across an entire visual display . . . , whereas non-visual semantic features cannot be detected in parallel with unlimited capacity. . . . Second, perceptual systems often respond to multiple sources of information by blending them together without individuating the sources. . . . Amodal symbols are separately individuated, and thus require explicit combination of symbols in order to produce overall similarity responses.

An intriguing problem is in what way similarity is represented in ANNs. Hahn and Chater (1998, 205) argue that similarity is *not computed* at all in the networks:

> [T]hese networks neither compute similarity nor apply rules, because they do not involve matching to a stored representation of any kind. What representations could be held to be "matched" with the input pattern? ... The only candidate appears to be weight vectors, but these are not *matched*, i.e. brought into correspondence with, the input at all.
>
> ... [I]t is true that networks to some extent *depend* on similarity ... ; similar inputs will tend to produce similar outputs. This, however, is a causal story, due to similarity between inputs in the sense of 'overlap of input representations' and, thus, similar activation flow through the network. It is not due to the fact that similarity is being computed, any more than similar rocks producing similar splashes results from computation of similarity.

Their argument that similarity is not computed, however, does not entail that similarity is not *represented* in an ANN. For many ANNs, the *inner product* of two states of the network is often used, externally, by the modelers as a measure of the similarity of the states (Jordan 1986). Since the inner product depends on the connection weights between neurons, the value of the product will change as the network adjusts its weights during learning. Therefore, it can be said that similarity *becomes represented* intrinsically in an ANN when it has been trained with a number of instances.[60] Of course, the represented similarity will depend on the training set that has been presented to the network.

Another important feature of representations in conceptual spaces is that *information must be sorted into domains*. On the constructive side, the frame problem may be circumvented to a large extent if one keeps track of domain-relevant information. On the explanatory side, one can note that when we make an observation of an object or event it is located in space and time, the object has a particular color, shape, and etc so forth. And as argued in chapters 3 and 4, properties and concepts are intimately tied to a domain or a set of domains. Goldstone and Barsalou (1998, 232) claim: "Completely modality-free [domain independent] concepts are rarely, if ever, used even when representing abstract contents. In short, concepts usually stem from perception, and active vestiges of these perceptual origins exist for the vast majority of concepts."

Domains are thus ubiquitous in descriptions of cognitive processes. There is also ample support from neurophysiology and neuropsychology for domain specificity in the brain.[61] Barsalou (to appear, section 1.2.2) claims that there is little evidence that modality-free symbols exist in the brain. Knowledge about categories is grounded in sensory-motor regions of the brain since damage to a particular sensory-motor region destroys the cognitive processes of categories that use this region in the analysis of perceptions.

Neither symbolism nor connectionism provides any support for domain specificity (even though artificial neural networks in general presume that the domain of the inputs is given). It should be noted that in many semantic theories the notion of a domain is taken for granted, but no analysis is given. The conceptual level of representation will thus provide the underpinnings for this assumption.

Summing up the comparison among the three levels of representation, one can say that the conceptual level has a potential to solve many of the representational problems that are difficult to handle in models on the symbolic and subconceptual levels. Furthermore, symbolic representations presume a level which provides the meanings of the symbols. In chapter 5, I argue that the conceptual level is appropriate for this task.

In biological cognitive systems, the three levels apply to *one and the same* system. For example, we can describe the detection of visual features in terms of neural associations in the areas V1 and V2 of the visual cortex (subconceptual level); talk about topographic mappings in the superior colliculus among spatial representations from different sensory modalities (conceptual level); or talk about how damages in Broca's area block the production of certain grammatical features (symbolic level). On the other hand, in artificial systems the three levels are often implemented in *different* modules. An example of such a hybrid system is presented in section 7.5.

If one analyzes biological cognitive systems from an evolutionary point of view, the cognitive processes of the simplest animals can only be described, in a meaningful way, on the subconceptual level. For such organisms, models based on ANNs may indeed be the most appropriate. As a matter of fact, behaviorist learning principles can be successfully modeled by ANNs (for a survey see Balkenius and Morén 1998). For more advanced animals, in particular mammals and birds, it is clear that there are sophisticated mechanisms of concept formation and learning. In my opinion, these mechanisms are best modeled on the conceptual level (see the following section). On the symbolic level, I conjecture that only in humans can we possibly find cognition that is clearly based on symbolic representations in the sense that some forms of thinking are based on the manipulation of symbols in a rule-governed manner (compare Deacon 1997). It is debatable whether other primates can engage in symbolic thinking of this kind. Thus the applicability of the three levels represent a rough classification of the evolution of the cognitive capacities of animals. The mistake of the orthodox symbolic paradigm is to assume that the most advanced description of thinking can be applied to all forms of human thinking and all the way through the animal kingdom to the most primitive cognitive processes.

As yet another sign of the importance of the conceptual level, I conjecture that most of *scientific theorizing* takes place at this level. Determining the relevant dimensions involved in the explanation of a phenomenon is a prime scientific activity. Creating a new theory often involves *introducing a new domain* involving features that are not directly observable. And once the conceptual space, with its associated metric, has been established for a theory, *equations* that connect the domains can be proposed and tested.[62]

2.5 Connections to Neuroscience

The primary application of the theory of conceptual spaces is to function as a framework for representations. When the framework is complemented with assumptions concerning the geometrical structure of particular domains and how they are connected, one arrives at empirically testable theories. Some such empirical predictions are presented in chapters 3 and 4.

On the other hand, when constructing an artificial system for solving some cognitive task, the aptness of a particular form of representation cannot be decided merely on the basis of how similar problems are solved in biological agents. Nevertheless, evolution has been an efficient, albeit slow, problem solver. If nature uses geometrical representations on the relevant scale of granularity, this would comprise support for the theory of conceptual spaces. Hence, I consider data from neuroscience and psychology to be relevant when evaluating different ways of representing information in artificial systems.

An additional reason for relating conceptual spaces to data from neuroscience is that the information processing involved in various sensorimotor systems appears to be much more fundamental for the cognitive functioning of the human brain than the processes involved in symbolic manipulations. Consequently, I see it as an advantage for the theory of conceptual spaces that it can serve as an explanatory basis for many of the results of neuroscientific research on the representational capacities of human and animal brains. The symbolic paradigm is much weaker in this respect.

Historically, it can be noted that the first "geometrical" theory of sensorimotor control was proposed by Descartes (1664). Figure 2.1 sum-

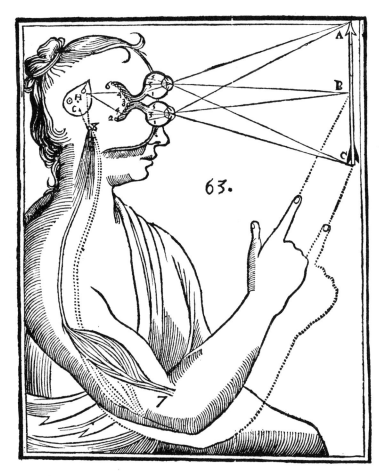

Figure 2.1
Descartes' topographic theory of sensorimotor control.

marizes the main components of his account (pages 180 to 183 in the French 1909 edition).

Descartes assigns the pineal gland (marked with H in figure 2.1) the role as the transformer of sensorial input to motor output. Since the pineal gland is where physical information is transformed to mental and vice versa, the intentional part of a movement is no problem for the Descartes's dualism. The intention comes from the soul and is used in combination with the information provided by the senses to determine the proper bodily movement. Note also that Descartes sketches a *topographic* theory of how the light that passes through the lens to the retina is transformed into patterns in the optic nerves. In figure 2.1, the points A, B, and C on the arrow correspond to the positions 1, 3, and 5, respectively, on the two retinas, which in turn correspond to the double set of nerve fibers 2, 4, and 6.

Among contemporary researchers studying the brain there is a tension between the representations presumed by philosophers and cognitive psychologists on the one hand and neuroscientists on the other. Zeeman (1977, 287) presents a possible way of resolving this tension:

> What is needed for the brain is a medium-scale theory. . . . The small-scale theory is neurology: the static structure is described by the histology of neurons and synapses. . . . Meanwhile the large-scale theory is psychology: the static structure is described by instinct and memory, and the dynamic behavior is concerned with thinking, feeling, observing. . . . It is difficult to bridge the gap between large and small without some medium-scale link. Of course the static structure of the medium-scale is fairly well understood and is described by the anatomy of the main organs and main pathways in the brain. . . . But what is strikingly absent is any well developed theory of the dynamic behavior of the medium-scale. . . .

As presented here, the theory of representations based on conceptual spaces is meant to be such a medium-scale theory.

In modern theories of the brain, a first thing to note is that the cortex abounds in topographic maps, whereby neighborhood relations at the sensory periphery are preserved in the arrangement of neurons in various "deeper" regions of the central nervous system.[63] For example, one finds "retinotopic" maps in the lateral geniculate nuclei that are arranged in six layers, each layer arranged in a topographic representation of the retina; there are "somatotopic" maps representing sensory positions on the body; and there are "tonotopic" maps which transforms the pitch dimension of a sound to a *spatial* dimension along the cochlea (compare figure 2.2). In these maps the orderly mapping of neurons with sound frequencies is preserved from the cochlea to the auditory cortex.

The topographic maps generate distinct *domains* of representation since most of them preserve the modularity of the senses. The underlying reason is that distinct types of receptor neurons are sensitive to different features of our environment and these features are kept distinct in the maps higher up in the projection system.[64]

Further support for my thesis that conceptual spaces are useful for understanding the representational structure of the brain can be gained

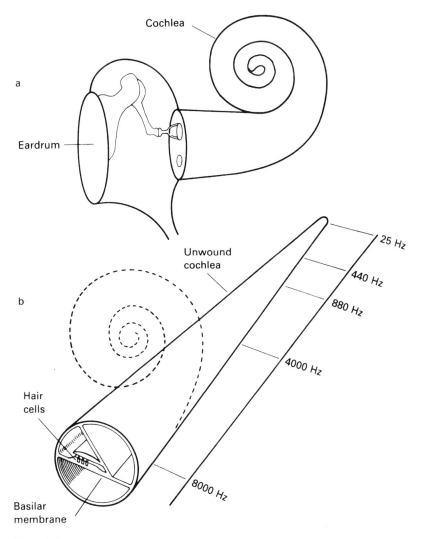

Figure 2.2
The coding of sound frequency in the human cochlea: (a) position of the cochlea relative
to the eardrum; (b) the "unrolled" cochlea (from P. S. Churchland 1986, 126).

from Gallistel (1990), who in his book on learning mechanisms in biological systems, devotes an entire chapter to "vector spaces in the nervous system." He writes (1990, 477):

> The purpose of this chapter is to review neurophysiological data supporting the hypothesis that the nervous system does in fact quite generally employ vectors to represent properties of both proximal and distal stimuli. The values of these representational vectors are physically expressed by the locations of neural activity in anatomical spaces of whose dimensions correspond to descriptive dimensions of the stimulus.

A proximal stimulus is the stimulus as it is perceived by the organism, while a distal stimulus specifies the stimulus in a coordinate system that is defined by the viewed object and is thus "detached" from the observer (compare Gärdenfors 1996a). Later in the chapter, Gallistel continues (1990, 501):

> The nervous system appears to be committed to a functional architecture in which the meaning of activity in a single unit is determined by the position of that unit relative to functionally specified anatomical axes. The brain uses a spatial scheme to represent combinations of stimulus properties, even when those properties are not spatial. The vectors by which the brain represents stimuli, like the vectors by which mathematicians represent them, are rooted in spatial considerations. In mathematics, these roots are historical; in the brain, they derive from a principle of functional architecture: what a unit represents is determined by where it is in an anatomical vector space (projection field).

As a first step in uncovering these brain representations, the dimensions of the perceptual spaces and motor spaces can be extracted by empirical neurophysiological and psychophysical research, as is witnessed, for instance, by the results on color perception.[65] And from an evolutionary point of view, the simplest hypotheses for the cognitive scientist is that *this geometrical mode of representation is also used for higher forms of mental processes.*[66]

According to this picture, symbolic representations would be rather exceptional and parasitic upon the geometrical ones. In brief, conceptual spaces would provide a more unified way of accounting for brain processes in general, and cognitive representations in particular, than would the symbolic paradigm. The idea is congenial to the general methodology of Pellionisz and Llinas (1980, 1125):[67]

> This view assumes that the brain is a "geometric object", that is to say, (1) activity in the neuronal network is vectorial, and (2) the

networks are organized tensorially: i.e. activity vectors remain invariant to changes in reference-frames. Understanding brain functions becomes, then, the establishment of the inherent geometric properties of the activity vectors and, more fundamentally, the determination of the properties of the multi-dimensional internal space (a frequency hyperspace) in which the vectorial transformations occur.

The following quotation from Gallistel (1990, 520) nicely sums up the view that the brain is a "geometrical object":[68]

In this chapter, we have surveyed electrophysiological and psychophysical evidence to the effect that spatial representations have a vectorial form in the nervous system itself. The nervous system's commitment to representing stimulus properties in vector spaces of modest dimensionality extends beyond the representation of spatial properties to encompass other stimulus properties, such as sound intensity, radial velocity, and spectral compositions. . . . The mathematical term *vector space*, for a coordinate system in which objects may be described by their positions along orthogonal descriptive continua, has an anatomical significance in the nervous system's approach to representation: vector spaces in the nervous system are quite literally spaces, or rather overlaid or interspersed planar areas.

2.6 Comparisons

One general thesis here is that a conceptual level of representation is needed as an alternative to the symbolic and connectionist representations that are in focus in current cognitive science. Conceptual spaces have been introduced as a suitable framework for representations on this middle conceptual level. There are several other theories in the literature that are related to my proposal. The purpose of this section is to compare my theory with three of these.

2.6.1 Harnad's Three-Level Theory

A three-level theory of cognitive representation has been suggested by Harnad (1987) as a way of analyzing problems of categorical perception. He calls his lowest level the *iconic* representation (IR), "being an analog of the sensory input (more specifically, of the proximal projection of the distal stimulus object on the device's transducer surfaces)" (Harnad 1987, 551). The IRs are analog mappings that "faithfully preserve the iconic character of the input for such purposes as same-different judgments, stimulus-matching, and copying" (552). This form of representation corresponds roughly to what I have dubbed here as the subconceptual level.

The middle level Harnad calls *categorical* representation (CR). This form of representation eliminates most of the raw input structure and retains what is invariant in the produced categorization: "Whereas IRs preserve analog structure relatively indiscriminately, CRs selectively reduce input structure to those invariant features that are sufficient to subserve successful categorization (in a given context)" (553).

This level appears to correspond to the conceptual level I use here. Unfortunately, Harnad says very little about how the categorization is accomplished, except that it is some kind of filtering process. It could perhaps be described as a "sorting level," where the more or less continuous input is classified as *discrete* phenomena that belong to a set of categories. Furthermore, he provides no account of the structure of the categorical representation, with the exception that he presumes that categorization to a certain extent is context dependent. I believe that it is a strength of the theory of conceptual spaces that their geometrical nature can provide mechanisms for concept formation and categorization, as presented in chapters 3 and 4. As a consequence, it has strong, and to a large extent testable, implications for categorization and concept formation.

The highest level in Harnad's triad is *symbolic* representation (SR), which obviously corresponds to the symbolic level presented here. He introduces a "description system" (554), the expressions of which assign category membership to experiences. In contrast to my proposal, the description system presumes that the CRs are already *labeled* by symbols: "Instead of constructing an invariance filter on the basis of direct experience with instances, it operates on *existing* labels, and constructs categories by manipulating these labels, in particular, assigning membership on the basis of stipulated rules rather than perceptual invariants derived from direct experience" (554).

Here it appears that Harnad is partly falling back on the classical Aristotelian tradition of concept formation (discussed in section 3.8). The upshot appears to be that CRs are hybrid between symbolic and nonsymbolic representations:

> Descriptions spare us the need for laborious learning by direct acquaintance; however, they depend on the prior existence of a repertoire of labeled categories on which the combinatory descriptions can draw. Hence *symbolic* representations (SRs), which are encoded as mental sentences, define new categories, but they must be grounded in old ones; the descriptive system as a whole must accordingly be *grounded* in the acquaintance system. (556)

The use of the metaphor "grounded" indicates that Harnad views the three representation forms as *separate* systems. Despite the differences pointed out here, the similarities between Harnad's view on representations and mine are indisputable. Since Harnad proposes his three kinds of representations as a tool for understanding phenomena of categorical perception, these similarities strengthen the links between concept formation and the analysis to be presented in chapters 3 and 4.

2.6.2 Two Other Theories

Another related theory is proposed by Mandler (1992), who discusses the relation between language learning and concept formation in infants. She contends that "image-schemas provide a level of representation intermediate between perception and language that facilitates the process of language acquisition" (1992, 587). Summing up her theory, she proposes that

> human infants represent information from an early age at more than one level of description. The first level is the result of a perceptual system that parses and categorizes objects and object movements (events). I assume that this level of representation is roughly similar to that found in many animal species. In addition, human infants have the capacity to analyze objects and events into another form of representation that, while still somewhat perception-like in character, contains only fragments of the information originally processed. The information on this next level of representation is spatial and is represented in analog form by means of image-schemas. . . . This level of representation also allows the organism to form a conceptual system that is potentially accessible; that is, it contains the information that is used to form images, to recall, and eventually to plan. A similar level of representation apparently exists in primates as well. . . . Humans, of course, add still another level of representation, namely, language. Whatever the exact nature of the step required to go from image-schemas to language, it may not be a large one, at any rate not as large as would be required to move directly from a conceptless organism to a speaking one. (1992, 602)

Mandler's theory is about how humans, or more precisely children, represent information, and, despite the title "how to build a baby," her paper is not about constructing artificial systems. Nevertheless, she emphasizes the spatial structure of the middle "conceptual" level, and she regards it as an ineluctable level in the process of language acquisition. Her focus on image schemas as belonging to the middle level accords well with what is presented in chapter 5, where image schemas are described in terms of conceptual spaces.

Again, the difference in comparison to the theory of conceptual space is that Mandler never spells out the geometrical or topological structures that are required. On the other hand, it is gratifying to see that she applies the *force dynamic* schemas (described by Talmy 1988 and others) when analyzing, for example, the concept of animacy.

Radermacher (1996) proposes a four-level architecture of cognition in artificial systems. At the surface, his program appears to be the same as the one pursued here: "Information processing in future robots should be organized on different levels of cognition, covering the handling of sensor streams, holistic processes (neural level), knowledge processing, and dealing with (mathematical) models" (1996, 10).

The first level of his model is the *signal* level that receives information from sensory systems and filters out "features" such as phonemes or line orientations. The second level is the *feature* level. Here features are aggregated "to arrive at the basic building blocks of level 3 of the hierarchy considered, namely concepts and notions as a higher level of representation, such as words in language understanding or objects in image analysis" (1996, 6). Level three deals with *knowledge processing* where the information content from level two is further interpreted and reduced, leading to symbolic concepts. Level four is the *theory* level, which concerns representing information in the form of formal theories or models, often using mathematical tools.

There appears to be no obvious mapping between the levels of this book and those proposed by Radermacher. The first two levels of his analysis cover what I call the subconceptual level. There is no clear correspondence with the conceptual level, but the third level appears to contain roughly the same items as the symbolic level of this book. The fourth level goes beyond the three levels that I have proposed. Radermacher puts emphasis on the notion of "features," which is a common notion within the theory of ANNs, but he neither considers the geometrical or topological structure of the features nor their domains.

2.7 The Jungle of Representations

The brain is a jungle of neurons, axons, and dendrites. Electric impulses travel between neurons along connections that wax and wane and die out. When trying to understand what is going on in a brain, we can describe the activities on different scales.

On a neuronal level, we can study mechanisms that make dendrites grow to establish new connections to other neurons, mechanisms that make connections grow stronger, mechanisms that make neurons fire more frequently, and so forth. We can simulate these processes in artificial neuron networks. (Or we can adopt an even more microscopic scale and study calcium channels, the role of transmitter substances, etc.)

But for many cognitive processes, for example concept formation or word recognition, the neuronal or connectionist scale is too fine-grained to be of explanatory or constructive value. And as Thom (1970, 1972) and Petitot (1995) point out, once we focus on the geometry of the emergent dynamics of cognitive systems, the details of lower levels are not so important.[69] We should therefore look for higher level organization among neurons, like for example topographic maps. Section 2.5 presented some evidence indicating that, on this scale, large regions of the brain can be seen as geometrical structures. As argued there, these structures correlate with the level of conceptual representations.

Finally, for some cognitive feats like language processing or logical reasoning, we may obtain the best model if we leave the neuronal perspective entirely and view the brain as a symbol processor. So far, we have a very shallow understanding of how such processes can be reduced to processes on a finer scale.[70]

In brief, depending on which cognitive process we are trying to explain, we must choose the appropriate explanatory level. There is no *passe-partout* perspective that allows us to understand everything going on the brain.

The picture becomes slightly different if one is in the constructive mode trying to build systems capable of performing cognitive tasks. In such a situation, it is often convenient to *combine* levels in the sense that one constructs different subsystems that work with representations on different levels and then makes each system communicate the results of its processes to other subsystems. For example, sensory input can be given a first analysis in an ANN, which then passes on the results to a conceptual systems that operates with geometrical representations in some low-dimensional vector space. The conceptual system can, in turn, cooperate with a symbolic system, in both a bottom-up and a top-down fashion. An example of this kind of three-level constructive system for object recognition is presented in section 7.5.

It is also possible, however, that higher levels of representation will *emerge* from systems working with subconceptual systems. For example, in the *schemata* analysis by Rumelhart, Smolensky, McClelland, and Hinton (1986), the "room" schemata emerge as "peaks" in the goodness-of-fit landscape generated by the forty room features they use. Another type of example, to be discussed in section 6.5, is Kohonen's self-organizing networks where the very architecture of the ANN together with the learning mechanism coerces the network to represent information in a low-dimensional topological space.

Something like a symbolic structure can also arise from a system that operates with representations on the conceptual level. In section 4.6, I show that *nonmonotonic inferences* will emerge from concept formation processes in conceptual spaces (see also Petitot 1995).

Thus, the interplay among the three levels of representation is a complicated matter. The aim of this chapter is to argue that, both for explanatory and constructive purposes, *all three levels are needed*. Unlike what is claimed by most adherents of the symbolic approch and some of the connectionists, there is no unique "right" level for cognitive science in its totality. A key message here is that the goals of cognitive science cannot be achieved using one level of representation only but one must exploit theoretical tools from all three levels.

In the following chapters, the focus is on representations at the conceptual level. The relations to the other levels, however, will not be forgotten. In particular, when treating induction in chapter 6 and computational processes in chapter 7, the role of these different levels is discussed in detail.

Chapter 3
Properties

This chapter is about the notion of a *property*. A central feature of our cognitive mechanisms is that we assign properties to the objects that we observe. This functions as a way of abstracting away redundant information about objects. Kirsch (1991, 163) says the following about the necessity of such a mechanism:

> This capacity to predicate is absolutely central to concept-using creatures. It means that the creature is able to identify the common property which two or more objects share and to entertain the possibility that other objects also possess that property. That is, to have a concept is, among other things, to have a capacity to find an invariance across a range of contexts, and to reify that invariance so that it can be combined with other appropriate invariances.

In this chapter I argue that conceptual spaces present an excellent framework for "reifying" the invariances in our perceptions that correspond to assigning properties to the perceived objects.

Within philosophical logic, properties have been analyzed as a part of more general semantic programs. I begin by discussing two of these analyses as they have been formulated within *extensional* and *intensional* types of semantics. I argue that the kind of model theory presumed in these traditions is not the right kind of framework for an analysis of properties. To accomplish this, I first introduce the standard extensional and intensional definitions of a property, which is formulated in terms of possible worlds. Then I present some of the philosophical problems these definitions lead to.

After this critical part, in a more constructive mode I show how conceptual spaces can be used for formulating new criteria of what a property is. The criteria are based on topological and geometrical notions such as *connectedness* and *convexity*. The criteria will be shown to elude the problems of the traditional approach. Furthermore, I argue that the criteria are useful for understanding *prototype effects* of properties and suitable for empirical predictions, which an analysis based on possible worlds is not. The theory of properties presented here is *conceptualist* in contrast to the realist theories of extensional and intensional semantics.

In most semantic theories or theories of concept formation, no distinction is made between *properties* and *concepts*. I propose, however, that properties should be seen as only a special case of concepts. Here, I use these notions in the following partly technical way: (1) A property is defined with the aid of a single dimension or a small number of *integral* dimensions forming a domain (as defined in section 1.8). For example the color space forms such an integrated domain.[71] (2) In contrast, a concept may be based on several *separable* subspaces. The general theory of concepts is developed in chapter 4. In chapter 5, I extend the analysis to a *cognitive semantics* that uses conceptual spaces in modeling the meaning of different kinds of words of a natural language. In natural language, the distinction between properties and concepts shows up in the distinction between adjectives and nouns. As will be argued there, adjectives normally refer to properties, while nouns refer to concepts.

A third relevant notion is that of a *category*. Sloman, Love, and Ahn (1998, 192) write: "Concepts and categories are, to a large extent, flip sides of the same coin. Roughly speaking, a concept is an idea that characterizes a set, or category, of objects." I take a *categorization* to be a rule for classifying objects. The rule is generated from the representation of one concept or a category of concepts (like the color concepts). Some examples of such rules are given in section 4.9. The result of applying a categorization rule will be a number of categories. In the model presented here, where (possible) objects are represented as points in conceptual spaces, a categorization will generate a partitioning of the space and a concept will correspond to a region (or a set of regions from separable domains) of the space.

3.2 Properties in Intensional Semantics

We begin with a fundamental ontological question: What *is* a property? I analyze two answers to this question; one deriving from intensional semantics and one based on conceptual spaces. Before diving into the philosophical intricacies of these theories, several everyday intuitions about what properties are should be noted. First, a property is something that objects can *have* in common.[72] If two objects both have a particular property, they are *similar* in some respect. Thus there are tight connections between similarity and properties—a connection discussed in sections 3.8 and 4.3. Second, for many properties, there are *empirical tests* to decide whether it is present in an object or not. In particular, we can often *perceive* that an object has a specific property.

These intuitions are not mirrored in the definitions of properties in the traditional semantic theories. In the classical *extensional* semantics, like in Tarski's model theory for first-order logic, a property is defined as *a set of objects*.[73] In other words, a property is identified with the set of objects that have the property; for example the meaning of "green" is the set of all green objects. Formally, this is done with the aid of a mapping from a language L to a model structure M, where each one-place predicate in L is mapped onto a subset of the objects in M. The intuition is that the model structure M represents "the world."

It became apparent to the logicians and semanticists, however, that many so called *intensional* properties did not fit this definition; a typical example is "small". An emu is a bird, but a small emu is not a small bird; hence, the property of being small cannot be identified by a set of "small" objects.

To handle the problems about intensional properties and other intensional concepts, the classical semantic theories were extended to so called *intensional semantics*.[74] Pioneers in this development were Kanger (1957), Kripke (1959), and Hintikka (1961). As an analysis of natural language, it reaches its peak with Montague (1974).

In intensional semantics, the language L is mapped onto a *set of possible worlds* instead of a single world. Possible worlds and their associated sets of objects are the only primitive semantic elements of the model theory. Other semantic notions are defined as *functions* on objects and possible worlds (see Lewis 1973 and Montague 1974). For example, a *proposition* is defined as a function from possible worlds to truth values. Such a function thus determines the *set of worlds* where the proposition is true. In this way, a proposition can be identified with a set of possible worlds. In traditional intensional semantics, this is *all* there is to say about the *meaning* of a proposition.

In this kind of semantics, a property is *something that relates objects to possible worlds*. In technical terms, a property can be seen as a many-many relation P between objects and possible worlds such that oPw holds just when object o has the property in world w.[75]

In intensional semantics, however, *functions* are prefered to many-many relations mainly because they are mathematically more elegant entities (Lewis 1973). There are two ways of turning the relation P into a function. First, it may be described as a *propositional function*, that is, *a function from objects to propositions* (see the function F_1 in figure 3.1).

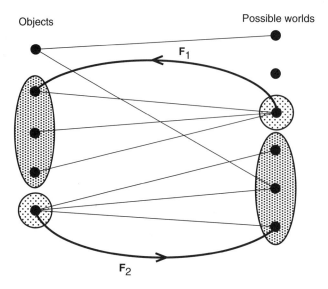

Figure 3.1
A property as a many-many relation between objects and possible worlds. F_1: "propositional" function mapping objects on propositions. F_2: "extensional" function mapping possible worlds on classes of objects.

Since a proposition is identified with a set of possible worlds, a property is a rule that determines a corresponding set of possible worlds for each object.

But we can also turn the table to obtain an equivalent function out of P; for each possible world w, a property will determine a set of objects that has w as an element of the many-many relation (see the function F_2 in figure 3.1). An equivalent definition of a property is that it is *a function from possible worlds to sets of objects*. This alternative definition shows the correspondence between the extensional and the intensional definition of a property because the value of the function representing a property is a set of objects as in the extensional case.

3.3 Criticism of the Traditional View of Properties

The standard definition of a property within intensional semantics, I contend, leads to a number of grave problems. First of all, the definition is highly counterintuitive since properties become very abstract things. Bealer (1989, 1) makes the following remarks: "How implausible that familiar sensible properties are functions—the color of this ink, the aroma of coffee, the shape of your hand, the special painfulness of a burn or itchiness of a mosquito bite. No function is a color, a smell, a shape, or a feeling."

The intensional definition is certainly not helpful for cognitive psychologists who try to explain what happens when a person *perceives* that two objects have the same property in common or, for example, why certain colors look similar. The fact that the definition is counterintuitive, however, is not a decisive argument. It may be argued that the abstract character of properties is merely a cosmetic feature of intensional semantics—as long as the semantics produces the right results, the technical form of the semantic concepts is not so important.

A related, but more serious problem for the traditional definition of a property is that it can hardly account for *inductive reasoning*. An inductive inference generally consists in connecting two properties to each other, as when one concludes that all living things have chromosomes. This connection is obtained from a number of instances of objects exhibiting the relevant properties. If a property is defined as a function from possible worlds to sets of objects (or equivalently as a function from objects to sets of possible worlds), then to determine which properties are instantiated by a particular object (or a set of objects), one has to determine which functions have the object (or the set of objects) as value in the *actual* world. Apart from problems concerning how we determine which, among the possible worlds, is the actual world, this rule is promiscuous in that it will give us too many properties.

As an example, consider Goodman's (1955) classical "riddle of induction." This puzzle starts from the fact that all emeralds examined up to now, having been identified by some criterion other than color, have been found to be green. Let us now call anything "grue" that is green before the year 2000 and blue after the beginning of the year 2000. Similarly, "bleen" means blue before 2000 and green thereafter.[76] This means that all emeralds examined up to now have been "grue." So why should we not expect that the property "grue" is as good as "green" when making inductive predictions about emeralds and other things?

Goodman (1955) calls the properties that can function in inductive reasoning "projectible." If the only thing we know about properties is that they are some kind of abstract functions, then we have no way of distinguishing natural and inductively projectible properties like "green" from inductively useless properties like "grue." What is needed is a criterion for separating the projectible sheep from the nonprojectible goats. Classical intensional semantics, however, does not provide such a criterion.[77] A closely related problem is that a definition of properties based on possible worlds will not make any empirical predictions possible, since predictions can only concern the *actual* world—what might happen in other worlds is of no interest for the experimenter.

A third problem with defining properties as abstract functions concerns the difficulty of expressing an *antiessentialistic* doctrine as has been pointed out by Stalnaker (1981). Antiessentialism is the doctrine that things have none of their properties necessarily. Stalnaker's aim is not to defend the doctrine, but to show that on the intensional account of properties it cannot be coherently expressed.

Some kinds of essential properties are unobjectionable also to an antiessentialist. These include any property that is necessarily an essential property of everything, like "being self-identical" or "being either human or nonhuman;" certain relational properties that are defined in terms of specific objects may be essential to that object, like "being the same age as Ingmar Bergman" which is essential to Ingmar Bergman. The problem for an antiessentialist is how to find a criterion that can distinguish between such innocent essential properties and the ontologically dangerous kinds of essential properties. Stalnaker (1981, 346) formulates the problem as follows:[78]

> In terms of this extensional account of properties (extensional in the sense that properties are defined by their extensions in different possible worlds), what corresponds to the intuitive distinctions between referential and purely qualitative properties, and between world-indexed and world-independent properties? Nothing. All properties are referential in the sense that they are defined in terms of the specific individuals that have them. . . . While one can, of course, make a distinction between essential and accidental attributes in terms of the standard semantical framework, one cannot find any independent distinctions corresponding to the intuitive ones needed to state a coherent version of the antiessentialist thesis. Thus there is no satisfactory way, without adding to the primitive basis of the semantical theory, to state the thesis as a further semantical constraint on legitimate interpretations of the language of modal logic.

Stalnaker (1981, 347) concludes: "[w]hat the standard semantics lacks is an account of properties that defines them independently of possible worlds and individuals. . . . [A] property must be not just a rule for grouping individuals, but a feature of individuals in virtue of which they may be grouped. . . ."

The final problem for the functional definition of properties is perhaps the most serious one. Putnam (1981) has shown that the standard model-theoretic definition of "property" that has been given here does not work as a theory of the *meaning* of properties. In proving this result, Putnam makes two assumptions about "the received view" of meaning: (1) the meaning of a sentence is a function that assigns a truth value to the sentence in each possible world; and (2) the meaning of the parts of a sentence cannot be changed without changing the meaning of the whole sentence.

Putnam's general proof is quite technical, but the thrust of the construction can be illustrated by his example (1981, 33–35). He begins with the sentence:

(1)   A cat is on a mat.

In (1) "cat" refers to cats and "mat" to mats as usual. He then shows how to give (1) a new interpretation, that is, a new mapping of the predicates to possible worlds. This alternative mapping is marked by putting a star on the words that refer to the new mapping. So (1) becomes:

(2)   A cat* is on a mat*.

The definitions of the properties cat* and mat* that Putnam uses for his argument make use of three cases (three classes of possible worlds):

(a)   Some cat is on some mat and some cherry is on some tree.

(b)   Some cat is on some mat and no cherry is on any tree.

(c)   Neither (a) nor (b) holds.

Here are Putnam's definitions:

(3) x is a cat* if and only if case (a) holds and x is a cherry or case (b) holds and x is a cat; or case (c) holds and x is a cherry.

(4) x is a mat* if and only if case (a) holds and x is a tree or case (b) holds and x is a mat; or case (c) holds and x is a quark.

Given these definitions, it turns out that the sentence (1) is true *in exactly those possible worlds* where (2) is true. Thus, according to the received view of meaning, these sentences will have the same meaning. In the appendix to his book, Putnam (1981) shows that a more complicated reinterpretation of this kind can be constructed that covers all the sentences of a language. He concludes that "there are always infinitely many different interpretations of the predicates of a language which assign the "correct" truth-values to the sentences in all possible worlds, *no matter how these 'correct' truth-values are singled out*" (1981, 35). Thus ". . . *truth-conditions for whole sentences* underdetermine reference" (*ibid.*). Again, the underlying reason is that there are *too many* potential properties if they are defined as functions from objects to propositions, that is, in terms of possible worlds and truth values. Cat* and mat* are just two examples from this large class.

Four different arguments have been presented here against the intensional definition of the notion of a property. The upshot is that there is something rotten in the kingdom of semantics. What is needed is a completely different way of defining properties. I argue that a cognitively oriented approach based on conceptual spaces will do the work.

3.4 Criteria for Natural Regions of Conceptual Spaces

My goal here is not to provide a universal description of all possible kinds of properties. I primarily want to pin down the properties that are, in a sense, *natural* to our way of thinking.

Philosophers are often less concerned with the cognitive aspects of properties. To evade some of the problems mentioned above, Lewis (1986, 59–60) introduces a distinction between an "abundant" and a "sparse" view of properties, where the abundant view corresponds to defining properties by functions, as described in section 3.2:

> Sometimes we conceive of properties as *abundant*, sometimes as *sparse*. The abundant properties may be as extrinsic, as gruesomely gerrymandered, as miscellaneously disjunctive, as you please. They pay no heed to the qualitative joints, but carve things up every which way. Sharing them has nothing to do with similarity. Perfect duplicates share countless properties and fail to share countless others; things as different as can be imagined do exactly the same. The abundant properties far outrun the predicates of any language we could possibly possess. There is one of them for any condition we could write down, even if we could write at infinite length and even if we could name all those things that must remain nameless because they fall outside our acquaintance. In fact, the properties are as abundant as the sets themselves, because for any set whatever, there is the property of belonging to that set. . . .
>
> The sparse properties are another story. Sharing of them makes for qualitative similarity, they carve at the joints, they are intrinsic, they are highly specific, the sets of their instances are *ipso facto* not entirely miscellaneous, they are only just enough of them to characterize things completely and without redundancy. . . .
>
> If we have the abundant properties (as we do, given set theory and *possibilia*) then we have one of them for each of the sparse properties. So we may as well say that the sparse properties are just some—a very small minority—of the abundant properties.

> We need no other entities, just an egalitarian distinction among the one's we've already got. When a property belongs to the small minority, I call it a *natural* property.

Lewis's position is ontologically *realistic*; the properties exist even if there are no agents, humans or otherwise, nor will there ever be any, that use the properties, or just "think" of them. His "abundant" properties are those that led to the problems presented in the previous section.

From the point of view of cognitive science the abundant properties are totally worthless. We, as cognitive agents, are primarily interested in the *natural* properties—those that are natural for the *purposes* of problem-solving, planning, memorizing, communicating, and so forth. These are the properties that can be used in inductive reasoning, the properties we can learn and the properties that get a foothold in natural language, in the sense that we give them names. By using conceptual spaces, I formulate here some cognitively motivated criteria for what characterizes a "natural" property and show that these criteria can avoid the conundrums of the traditional definition within intensional semantics.

Before formulating the criteria, let me repeat the characterization of a conceptual space presented in chapter 1. A conceptual space consists of a class $D_1, \ldots, D_n$ of quality dimensions. A *point* in the space is represented by a vector $v = \langle d_1, \ldots, d_n \rangle$ with one index for each dimension. Each dimension is endowed with a certain geometrical or topological structure. Now, how can we *represent* a property in such a space?

A first rough idea is to describe a property as a *region* of a conceptual space S, where "region" should be understood as a spatial notion determined by the topology or geometry of S. For example, the point in the time dimension representing "now" divides this dimension, and thus the space of vectors, into two regions corresponding to the properties "past" and "future." In contrast to the traditional definition in intensional semantics, this definition presumes *neither* the concept of an object *nor* the concept of a possible world.

To evaluate the proposal that a property corresponds to a region, one must determine more precisely what is meant by "region." As a start, I rely on the "region connection calculus" as presented in Cohn et al. (1997). The calculus is constructed from one primitive relation $C(X, Y)$ meaning that region X *connects with* region Y. The interpretation of this relation is that $C(X, Y)$ holds if X and Y overlap or if they merely "touch."[79] The only properties that are assumed of this relation is that it is reflexive, that is, $C(X, X)$, for all regions X, and that it is symmetric, that is $C(X, Y)$ if and only if $C(Y, X)$, for all regions X and Y.

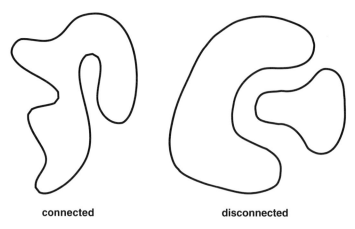

connected   **disconnected**

Figure 3.2
Examples of connected and disconnected regions.

Cohn et al. (1997) show how a number of relations can be defined from the relation $C(X, Y)$:

> X is a *part of* Y: $C(Z, X)$ entails that $C(Z, Y)$, for all regions Z.
> X *overlaps* Y: there is some region Z such that Z is a part of X and Z is a part of Y.
> X *partially overlaps* Y: X overlaps Y and neither is X a part of Y, nor Y of X.
> X is *externally connected to* Y: $C(X, Y)$ but X does not overlap Y.

I now formulate three criteria of increasing strength for what is required for a set to be a "region." The first criterion is the notion of connectedness, which can be defined as follows within the region connection calculus:[80]

DEFINITION 3.1   A region X is *connected*, if and only if, for all regions Y and Z such that $Y \cup Z = X$, it holds that $C(Y, Z)$. X is *disconnected*, if and only if X is not connected.

Figure 3.2 provides illustrations of connected and disconnected regions of R^2.

The second criterion depends on "betweenness" and on the possibility of identifying a "central" or "prototypical" point p in the region.

DEFINITION 3.2   A subset C of a conceptual space S is said to be *star-shaped with respect to point p* if, for all points x in C, all points between x and p are also in C.

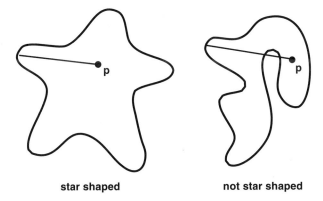

star shaped   **not star shaped**

Figure 3.3
Regions that are star-shaped and not star-shaped with respect to a point p.

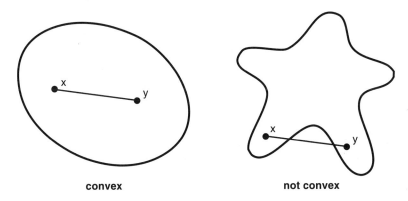

convex   **not convex**

Figure 3.4
Regions that are convex and not convex.

All star-shaped regions are connected, but the converse does not hold. Figure 3.3 provides an example of a star-shaped region and a region that is connected but not star-shaped (if betweenness is defined in the standard Euclidean sense).

The third and most powerful criterion of a region is the following, which also relies on betweenness:

DEFINITION 3.3   A subset C of a conceptual space S is said to be *convex* if, for all points x and y in C, all points between x and y are also in C.

All convex regions are star-shaped with respect to all points in the region (and thus connected), but the converse does not hold as is illustrated in figure 3.4 (again assuming the Euclidean sense of betweenness).

It should be noted that all three criteria on a region can be formulated using only the *betweenness* relation for the space S. As was seen in section 1.6, this is a rather weak assumption that demands very little of the underlying geometrical structure. Recall, however, that a set can be supplemented with several types of betweenness relations, which means that the properties of a region are not determined unless the relevant betweenness relation is specified. An example of the importance of this point will be given below.

3.5 Natural Properties

Each of the three definitions above can be used as a criterion for deciding whether a region of a conceptual space represents a natural property. Here, I mainly apply the strongest characterization based on the convexity of regions. This is the sharpest criterion that generates the greatest number of *empirical predictions*. An example of the empirical claims for the color space will be discussed below. As will be seen in sections 3.8 and 7.1, the proposal also has some treasurable computational characteristics.

Shepard (1987, 1319) provides an evolutionary argument that supports the convexity criterion. If an individual has had some experience with an object that had significant consequences for it, the individual should be able to decide which new objects are *sufficiently similar* to the old object that they are likely to have the same consequence. Such a class of similar objects is represented by a region in the individual's psychological space that Shepard calls a "consequential region":

> An object that is significant for an individual's survival and reproduction is never sui generis; it is always a member of a particular class—what philosophers term a "natural kind." Such a class corresponds to some region in the individual's psychological space, which I call a consequential region. I suggest that the psycho-physical function that maps physical parameter space into a species' psychological space has been shaped over evolutionary history so that consequential regions for that species, although variously shaped, are not consistently elongated or flattened in particular directions.

Although Shepard does not give any explanation of why evolution should prefer regions that are not oddly shaped, I believe that this can be defended by a principle of *cognitive economy*; handling convex sets puts less strain on learning, on your memory, and on your processing capacities than working with arbitrarily shaped regions.[81] This point is elaborated in section 3.9 and in chapter 4. Hence, I propose the following criterion that encapsulates one of the central ideas in this book:

CRITERION P   A *natural property* is a convex region of a domain in a conceptual space.

Criterion P only presumes that the notion of betweenness is meaningful for the relevant domains. Here, however, I mostly work with the stronger assumption that the domains we consider have a *metric* so that we can also talk about *distances* between points in the space (compare section 1.6.3).

Another way of expressing the criterion is that if some objects that are located at x_1 and x_2, in relation to some domain, both are examples of a property F, then any object that is located between x_1 and x_2 in the domain will also be an example of F. In connection with a discussion of prototype theory in section 3.8, I argue that this criterion has psychological validity. It should be noted that if the requirement in criterion P that the region be convex is replaced by a requirement of a star-shaped or a connected region, it will still be possible to make empirical predictions, but they will be less encompassing than those generated from criterion P.

Criterion P does not presume that one can identify sharp borders between properties, but it can also be applied to *fuzzy* properties or properties that are defined by *probabilistic* criteria. What convexity requires is that if two object locations x_1 and x_2 both satisfy a certain membership criterion, for example, they have a certain degree (or probability) of membership, then all objects between x_1 and x_2 also satisfy the criterion.

For instance, I conjecture that all *color terms* in natural languages express natural properties with respect to the psychological representation of the three color dimensions. In other words, the conjecture predicts that if some object o_1 is described by the color term C in a given language and another object o_2 is also said to have color C, then any object o_3 with a color that lies between the color of o_1 and that of o_2 will also be described by the color term C. It is well-known that different languages carve up the color circle in different ways, but all carvings appear to be done in convex sets.

But are the areas corresponding to natural color words truly convex? If we take "red" for instance, would not the corresponding region of the space spanned by the hue and chromaticness dimensions have a shape like the one depicted in figure 3.5? And this area is not convex since point b on the line between a and c is not within the region for red.[82]

To explain why I claim that basic color words correspond to convex regions of the color space, it should be noted that there is a subtlety

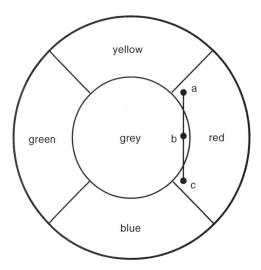

Figure 3.5
Possible counterexample to the convexity of color.

concerning the notion of "convex" in a circular space. When the Euclidean metric is used for defining distances in a space, the notion of betweenness as defined by definition B in section 1.6.3 means that b is between a and c if b lies on the *straight line* between a and c. In the two-dimensional case, this is equivalent to saying that if the three points have Cartesian coordinates (x_a, y_a), (x_b, y_b), and (x_c, y_c) respectively, then b is between a and c if there is some k, $0 < k < 1$ such that $x_b = kx_a + (1 - k)x_c$ and $y_b = ky_a + (1 - k)y_c$.

This characterization of the "line" between a and c, however, depends on the assumption that the Euclidean metric is used. Since the dimension of hue in the color spindle is circular, it is more natural to use *polar* coordinates to describe positions in the space. If we confine ourselves to the central color disk, generated by the two dimensions hue and chromaticness, a point can be described by two coordinates x and θ, where x is the distance from the center, that is, the co-ordinate for the intensity, and θ is the angle (with, say, 0 for focal red), that is, the co-ordinate for the hue. Given this representation, we can now define a notion of *polar betweenness* that is different from the one generated by the standard Cartesian coordinates. In analogy with the previous definition, let us say that a point $b = (x_b, \theta_b)$ lies between a point $a = (x_a, \theta_a)$ and a point $c = (x_c, \theta_c)$ if there is some k, $0 < k < 1$ such that $x_b = kx_a + (1 - k)x_c$ and $\theta_b = k\theta_a + (1 - k)\theta_c$. The "lines" generated by this polar betweenness relation will be "curved" (if seen with Euclidean glasses) as illustrated in figure 3.6.

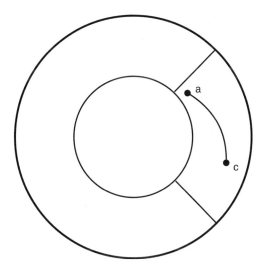

Figure 3.6
A "line" between a and c generated by the polar betweenness relation.

As a consequence, the convex regions determined by the polar betweenness relation, will not be identical with those generated by the Euclidean metric. As emphasized in section 1.6, there are several ways of defining a metric and the corresponding betweenness and equidistance relations on a space. Hence, depending on the choice of betweenness relation, different kinds of regions will be of interest when one looks at what counts as a natural property.

Strong support for the empirical conjecture on color terms can be found in Sivik and Taft (1994) (see also Taft and Sivik 1997 and Taft 1997).[83] Their study can be seen as a follow-up of the investigations of basic color terms by Berlin and Kay (1969) who compared and systematized color terms from a wide variety of languages. In Sivik and Taft (1994), they focus on Swedish color terms, while in Taft and Sivik (1997) color terms from Swedish, Polish, Spanish, and American English were compared.

Their method was to present subjects with various color samples and ask them how well, on a seven-graded semantic scale, the color corresponds to a particular color word. The means of the subjects' replies are calculated and the color samples that receive the same mean for a given color term can be plotted on "isosemantic" lines (Sivik and Taft, 1994, 150). In figure 3.7 an example is given of the lines for the Swedish "brun" ("brown") for a particular hue position, indicated in the color circle above the triangle. The triangle represents different degrees of blackness and chromaticness as explained in section 1.5. Dark shades

Brun (Brown)

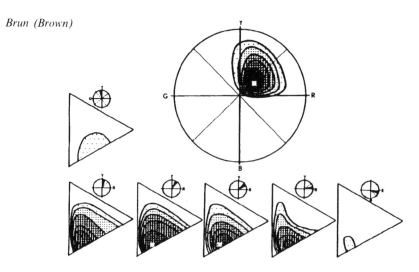

Figure 3.7
An example of isosemantic scales for "brun" ("brown") (from Sivik and Taft 1994, 155).

represent that subjects think that the color matches the term well, lighter shades that it matches less well.

Figures 3.8 and 3.9 give their results for one common color term, "röd" ("red"), and one less common, "olivgrön" (olive green). As can be seen, the regions marked by the isosemantic lines are all convex. Even though there is no sharp border for when a color is identified as red or olive green, it turns out that at *each* level of identification the structure is convex (both in the polar and the Euclidean senses).

This strong property holds for almost all the sixteen color words that Sivik and Taft have studied. The only potential counterexample where one can find a slight tendency to nonconvexity is for "blå" ("blue") as can be seen in the left-most triangle of figure 3.10. Here, a "bay" in two of the regions can be seen. This only applies, however, to the region that is most weakly identified as blue. Furthermore, since a limited number of subjects were used, the bay can perhaps also be explained as just a statistical deviation.

In contrast to the seemingly universal convexity of natural color categories, the reference of artificial color terms like Goodman's "grue" and "bleen" will not be a convex region in the ordinary conceptual space, as will be shown in section 6.3.1. Thus "grue" and "bleen" are not natural properties according to criterion P.

A programmatic thesis central to this book is that *most properties expressed by simple words in natural languages can be analyzed as natural*

Röd (Red)

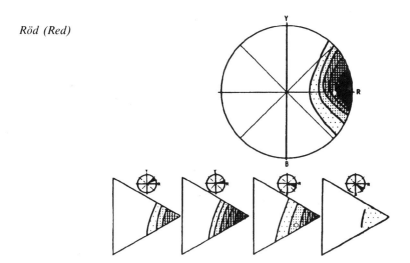

Figure 3.8
The isosemantic scales for "röd" ("red") (from Sivik and Taft 1994, 153).

Olivgrön (Olivegreen)

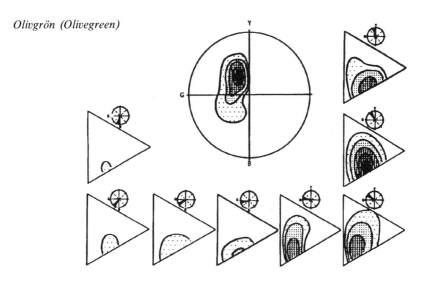

Figure 3.9
The isosemantic scales for "olivgrön" (olive green) (from Sivik and Taft 1994, 159).

Blå (Blue)

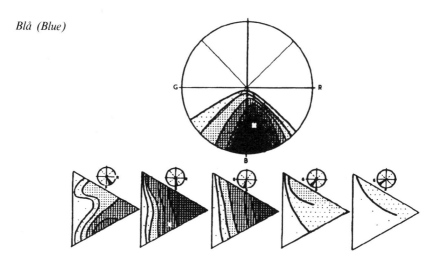

Figure 3.10
The isosemantic scales for "blå" ("blue") (from Sivik and Taft 1994, 154).

properties in the sense of criterion P. This thesis entails that the assignment of meanings to the expressions on the linguistic level is far from arbitrary. On the contrary, the semantics (and to some extent even the grammar) of the linguistic constituents is severely constrained by the structure of the underlying conceptual space. This thesis is one of the central tenets of the recently developed "cognitive" linguistics. The role of criterion P in semantics is illustrated in chapter 5.

Criterion P provides an account of properties that is independent of both possible worlds and objects. It should be emphasized, however, that I only view the criterion as a *necessary* but perhaps not sufficient condition on a natural property. The criterion delimits the class of properties that are fit for cognitive processes, but it may not be sufficiently restrictive.

Mormann (1993) criticizes criterion P, saying, among other things, that it is unnecessarily strong for many purposes. Instead he proposes the criterion that natural regions be connected as more suitable. He also introduces, however, another topological criterion of naturalness based on "closure structures" (Mormann 1993, 226–227).[84] The details of his general framework are not presented here, but only one example of a closure structure that he discusses (for a similar approach, see Fischer Nilsson 1999).

Let S be a conceptual space that is a Cartesian product of the quality dimensions D_1 and D_2, that is, $S = D_1 \times D_2$. For each region X of S, let "the closed set" $C(X)$ be the smallest "rectangle" of S that includes X, that is the smallest set $C_1 \times C_2$, where C_1 is a (connected) region in D_1

and C_2 is a (connected) region in D_2. It can be shown (Mormann 1993, Lemma 3.8) that the collection of all closed sets $C(X)$ generates a closure structure with the desired topological properties. Figure 3.11 illustrates a closed and a not closed set in this structure.

In my opinion a product structure of the kind given in the example above will be suitable for the case when the dimensions D_1 and D_2 are *separable* in the sense of section 1.8. The set of "rectangles" may be too sparse, however, for representing natural properties in a space that has integral dimensions, as, for example, the color space.

Mormann's (1993, 231) proposal is that we use closure structures of the general kind he considers to distinguish between "natural" and "not-so-natural" properties. It is easy to prove that the set of all convex regions of a conceptual space will form a closure structure.[85] Hence, Mormann's proposal has criterion P as a special case.

3.6 Reconsidering the Problems

Criterion P, I argue, eludes all the problems, as presented in section 3.3, that tainted the traditional definition of a property.[86] First of all, the criterion makes many properties *perceptually grounded*. Since many of the fundamental quality dimensions are determined by our perceptual mechanisms, there is a direct link between properties described as regions of such dimensions and perceptions. This means that criterion P (and its relatives) will be much more serviceable for cognitive scientists than the traditional definition. In the following sections, it will also be shown that there are close connections between the idea of describing properties in terms of convex regions in conceptual spaces and the *prototype theory* of categorization.

Second, as will be shown in chapter 6, describing properties in terms of conceptual spaces makes it much easier to understand how inductive inferences are made. I propose there that a fundamental criterion on induction is that only predicates denoting natural properties are sanctioned in the inferences. This criterion gives us a tool for separating projectible (that is inductively useful) properties from nonprojectible ones. In this way we cut down, in a nonarbitrary way, the abundant class of properties that will be available if properties are defined as functions from possible worlds to objects (among them the Goodman and Putnam type of properties). As has been exemplified for the color domain, this restriction creates ample opportunities for empirical predictions, something that is difficult to attain if the intensional definition is used.

Third, the problems for the antiessentialistic doctrine raised by Stalnaker now disappear. A property ". . . must be not just a rule for grouping individuals, but a feature of individuals in virtue of which they

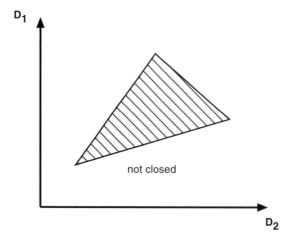

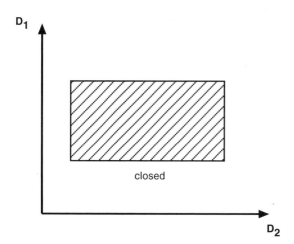

Figure 3.11
Example of closed and not closed sets in Mormann's closure structures (based on Mormann 1993, figure 7).

may be grouped" as Stalnaker (1981, 347) would like to see. The theory of conceptual spaces can be seen as an extension of what Stalnaker (1981) calls *logical space*. The main difference between his notion and mine is that he does not consider the role of the geometrical structure of the quality dimensions, and thus he can not talk about "convexity" and similar notions.

The following quotation from Stalnaker 1981, 348–349, presents his solution to the problem of expressing the antiessentialistic doctrine. By "location function" he means a function that maps the individuals (object) into a logical space.[87]

> It should be clear that every *property* (every region of logical space) determines a propositional function in the following way: given any property, the value of the corresponding propositional function, relative to a given possible world, will be the class of individuals that have the property in that possible world—the individuals that are located in that region of logical space by the location function that represents the possible world. Thus every property determines a unique propositional function and the correspondence is one-one: distinct properties never determine the same propositional function. But it is not the case that every propositional function corresponds to an intrinsic property, for the classes of individuals selected by a propositional function in the different possible worlds need not all come from the same region of logical space. Among the propositional functions, or properties in the broad sense, that do not correspond to regions of logical space are, of course, just those that the anti-essentialist wants to distinguish from full-fledged intrinsic properties. For example, referential properties such as *being the same weight as Babe Ruth* will clearly not correspond to regions of logical space.

Thus the possible worlds semantics *generated* from conceptual space semantics is rich enough to represent the distinctions needed to make sense of the appropriate kind of antiessentialism.

Fourth and finally, the problems that Putnam's theorem attests for the traditional definition of "property" dissolve into thin air under the new criterion. "Cat" presumably denotes a region of a conceptual space (relating to the class of possible animals, be they determined in terms of shape, biological functions, or whatever). This region would, at least partly, be determined by the perceptual features of cats (compare, for example, Marr and Nishihara's 1978 shape representations that will be presented in section 3.10). We cannot create a new natural property "cat*" by relating it to what facts are true in various possible worlds. The denotation of "cat*" as introduced by Putnam is indeed a propositional function since it is defined as a function from possible worlds to objects, but it is not a natural property in the sense of this book since it cannot be described as anything like a region of a conceptual space (compare the above quotation from Stalnaker). In my opinion this distinction accords well with a common-sense notion of a natural property. The role of "cat*" in various truth-functional constructions is totally irrelevant for whether it is a natural property or not.

3.7 The Relativism of Conceptual Spaces

Natural properties have here been defined in relation to a given conceptual space. But is not the choice of a conceptual space *arbitrary*? Since a conceptual space may seem like a Kuhnian paradigm, aren't we thereby stuck with an unavoidable *relativism*? After all, anyone can pick her own conceptual space and in this way make her favorite properties come out natural in that space.[88] More generally, for a domain of objects, there are several geometric structures that will generate different classes of natural properties. Which structure is the right one?

Mormann (1993, 1994) calls this the problem of "structural conventionalism." He compares it to geometrical conventionalism, which is "the thesis that the metrical structure of physical space is a matter of convention, that is physical space is *metrically amorphous* and may be metrically structured in many different ways, and all these metrical structures are on the same par." (1994, 248). Analogously, structural conventionalism claims that conceptual spaces are structurally amorphous.

Putnam (1975, 164–165) has criticized geometrical conventionalism as follows: "The conventionalist fails precisely because of an insight of Quine's. That is the insight that *meaning*, in the sense of reference, is a function of theory, and that the enterprise of trying to list the statements containing a term which are true by virtue of its meaning, let alone to give a list of statements which *exhausts* its meaning, is a futile one."

Mormann (1993, 236–237) generalizes this argument to structural conventionalism. He discusses a conceptual space C_o with different closure structures $ and $' (see section 3.5):

> Thus in the case of conceptual spaces the meaning of terms like "naturalness" of predicates, defined on C_o by the structures $ (or $'), is *not* exhausted by a short list of axioms . . . of a closure structure, rather it is a function of an extended net of empirical knowledge: that is, we do *not* fix the reference of the term natural predicate of C_o' by convention but by coherence.

The fixation of projectibility by coherence means that the task of determining which of the subsets of C_o represent natural predicates is not achieved by defining simple structures like closure or topological structures on C_o, rather it involves large parts of scientific (and cultural) background knowledge.

As an example of the background knowledge that may be involved, Mormann considers the color domain. The underlying neurological theory says that there are three types of color sensitive cells in the human eye that are adapted to blue, green, and orange, respectively (see figure 1.7). Furthermore, according to the theory, there is a systematic mapping among the relations between stimulations of the different kinds of retinal cells and the color perceptions of an individual. On the basis of such a mapping Mormann (1993, 237) argues as follows:

> Since according to the neurological theory of colour vision there are no Goodmanian cells (preferably stimulated by bleen or grue, respectively), the predicates "bleen" and "grue" are certainly more complicated, and are to be considered as contrived. In this way the symmetry between the traditional and Goodmanian predicates is broken. Hence, if we rely on a coherentist approach for fixing the meaning of "natural" this counts as strong evidence against the Goodmanian predicates—the traditional ones are far better entrenched in the global system of our conceptual framework.

As a result, the freedom in choosing a conceptual space is rather limited and thus the relativism inherent in this choice is not as problematic as it may first appear.[89]

As was noted in section 1.9, some quality dimensions are innate. This is the main reason why human beings, to a remarkable extent, agree on which properties are projectible, in particular if the properties are closely connected to what is provided by our senses. These are the properties that are named in language (compare Quine 1969, 123). For instance, different cultures show high agreement in identifying species of animals and plants, at least what concerns basic categories in the sense of prototype theory. It appears reasonable to assume that the psychological conceptual spaces of humans are, at least in their fundamental dimensions, close to identical. Mormann concludes (1993, 238–239):

> Even if we cannot exhaust the meaning of "natural" by imposing an all-embracing final structure on the conceptual space in question, we can approximate it step by step, thereby eliminating

more and more Goodmanian predicates of various degrees of sophistication.

This structural approach leads to a kind of "mathematical epistemology" based not on the unspecific and general framework of set theory but on specific frameworks of appropriate mathematical theories, e.g., topological and geometrical ones.

But even if such an agreement on the structure of a conceptual space exists, we must answer the question of why our way of identifying natural properties accords so well with the external world as to make our generalizations come out right. Peirce notes that "it can no longer be denied that the human intellect is peculiarly adapted to the comprehension of the laws and facts of nature" (1932, 474). Quine (1969, 126) formulates the problem in the following way: "[W]hy does our innate subjective spacing of qualities accord so well with the functionally relevant groupings in nature as to make our inductions tend to come out right? Why should our subjective spacing of qualities have a special purchase on nature and a lien on the future?"

The answer for me comes from evolutionary theory. Natural selection has made us all develop a conceptual space that results in inductions that are valid most of the time and thus promote survival.[90] Our quality dimensions are what they are because they have been selected to fit the surrounding world. In Peirce's words: "[T]here is a special adaptation of the mind to the universe, so that we are more apt to make true theories than we otherwise should be" (1932, 472). And Quine (1969, 126) says ironically: "Creatures inveterately wrong in their inductions have a pathetic but praise-worthy tendency to die before reproducing their kind."

Now, as indicated in section 1.9, not all of our quality dimensions have a genetic origin, but the agreement among the conceptual spaces of different individuals of our species is still high enough to produce very similar conceptions of, at least, the perceptual categories of the world.[91] As mentioned in section 1.9, another reason for this has been given by Freyd (1983), who argues that conceptual spaces may evolve as a representational form just because people have to share knowledge. The upshot is that rather limited freedom exists for humans in choosing a conceptual space for the most ecologically basic properties. The relativism that will occur only applies to the more advanced learned and culturally dependent quality dimensions.

A far-reaching consequence of this evolutionary account of conceptual spaces, however, is that *what we count as natural properties will depend on the ecological circumstances under which the spaces have evolved.* The psychological spaces of humans are attuned to the environment of thousands of years of hunting and gathering. Consequently, we cannot expect our intuitions about which properties are projectible to be successful in environments that wildly diverge from those present during our evolutionary history. The conclusion to be drawn is that we should only trust our capacities for inductive reasoning in situations that are "ecologically valid," to borrow a notion from Gibson (1979).[92] What should we do about the increasing proportion of artificial objects and situations that surround us?

This is where *science* enters on the scene. By introducing theoretically precise, nonpsychological quality dimensions, a scientific theory may help us find new properties that would not be possible to discover on the basis of our subjective conceptual spaces alone. A scientific breakthrough is often made when a new quality dimension or domain is introduced to a theory. Take, for example, the distinction between temperature and heat, which is central for thermodynamics, but which has no correspondence in human perception.[93] Equally important is Newton's distinction between weight and mass. This is the very first definition introduced in the *Principia*—without it his celestial mechanics would not have been possible.

The quality dimensions of scientific theories and their associated measurement procedures help us create new useful properties in environments that are completely different from those of our evolutionary cradle. Furthermore, the precise metrics of the scientific quality dimensions make it possible to formulate *functional laws* that in turn enable us to compute more sophisticated predictions (Galileo's laws of free fall have set the standard). Once a scientific conceptual space has been established, the formulation of such laws is a kind of *inductive inference*.[94] Clearly, such laws supersede generalizations of the form "all Fs are Gs." Such generalizations are the only possible inductive inferences on quality dimensions that just have a crude or rudimentary metric or merely classify objects. As Quine (1969) notes, it is a sign of mature science that notions of similarity become less and less important, being replaced by theoretically more sophisticated concepts (compare section 6.4). The development is away from "the immediate, the subjective, animal sense of similarity to the remoter sense of similarity determined by scientific hypotheses and posits and constructs" (1969, 134).

In this way science builds upon our more or less evolutionarily determined conceptual spaces, but in its most mature form becomes independent of them. Peirce (1932, 477) notes that this is a general trend of human thinking: "Side by side, then, with the well established proposition that all knowledge is based on experience, and that science is only advanced by the experimental verifications of theories, we have to place this other equally important truth, that all human knowledge, up to the highest flights of science, is but the development of our inborn animal instincts."

3.8 Connections to Prototype Theory

As we have seen, the delimitation of natural properties in terms of convex regions, that is criterion P, provides intuitively plausible solutions to the problems caused by the account within intensional semantics. Apart from this, the criterion derives independent support from the *prototype theory* of categorization developed by Rosch and her collaborators (see, for example, Rosch 1975, 1978, Mervis and Rosch 1981, Lakoff 1987).

The main idea of prototype theory is that within a category of objects, like those instantiating a property or a concept, certain members are judged to be more *representative* of the category than others. For example robins are judged to be more representative of the category "bird" than are ravens, penguins, and emus; while desk chairs are more typical instances of the category chair than rocking chairs, deck chairs, and beanbag chairs. The most representative members of a category are called *prototypical* members.

In the classical Aristotelian theory of concepts (Smith and Medin 1981), a concept is defined via a set of necessary and sufficient properties. Consequently, all instances of a classical concept thus have equal status. Another part of prototype theory, however, says that concepts show *graded membership*, determined by how representative the members are. It is well-known that some properties, like "red" and "bald," have no sharp boundaries and for these it is perhaps not surprising that one finds prototypicality effects. These effects have been found, however, for most concepts, including those with comparatively clear boundaries like bird and chair. Concept theories other than the prototype theory can also represent graded membership. Some such theories like "nearest neighbor" and "average distance" (Reed 1972, Nosofsky 1988b) are presented in section 4.9.

An intriguing illustration of how the prototypical structures determine categorizations is the phonetic identification of *vowels* in various languages. According to phonetic theory, what determines a vowel are the relations between the basic frequency of the sound and its formants (higher frequencies that are present at the same time). In general, the first two formants F_1 and F_2 are sufficient to identify a vowel. This means that the co-ordinates of two-dimensional space spanned by F_1 and F_2 (in relation to a fixed basic pitch F_0) can be used as a fairly accurate representation of a vowel. Fairbanks and Grubb (1961) investigated how people produce and recognize vowels in

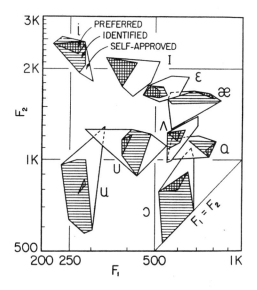

Figure 3.12
Frequency areas of different vowels in the two-dimensional space generated by the first two formants. Values in Hz. (From Fairbanks and Grubb 1961).

"general American" speech. Figure 3.12 summarizes some of their findings.

The scale of the abscissa and the ordinate is the logarithm of the frequencies of F_1 and F_2, respectively (the basic frequency of the vowels was 130 Hz). As can be seen from the diagram, the "preferred," "identified," and "self-approved" examples of different vowels form convex subregions (with focal regions) of the space determined by F_1 and F_2 with the given scales.[95] As in the case of color terms, different languages carve up the phonetic space in different ways (the number of vowels identified in different languages varies considerably), but I conjecture that each vowel in a language will correspond to a convex region of the formant space. This is another example of an empirical prediction generated from criterion P.

Prototype theory can also be used to provide a reasonable explication of the notion of *similarity* that is tightly connected to the notion of a property. Quine (1969, 119–120) argues that "natural kind" (corresponding to "natural property") is definable in terms of "similarity" and he proposes a precursor to the psychological prototype theory:

> One may be tempted to picture a kind, suitable to a comparative similarity relation, as any set which is 'qualitatively spherical' in this sense: it takes in exactly the things that differ less than so-

and-so much from some central norm. If without serious loss of accuracy we can assume that there are one or more actual things (*paradigm cases*) that nicely exemplify the desired norm, and one or more actual things (*foils*) that deviate just barely too much to be counted into the desired kind at all, then our definition is easy: *the kind with paradigm a and foil b* is the set of all things to which *a* is more similar than *a* is to *b*.

Quine notes that, as it stands, this definition of a kind is not satisfactory:

> Thus take red. Let us grant that a central shade of red can be picked as norm. The trouble is that the paradigm cases, objects in just that shade of red, can come in all sorts of shapes, weights, sizes, and smells. Mere degree of overall similarity to any such paradigm case will afford little evidence of degree of redness, since it will depend also on shape, weight, and the rest. If our assumed relation of comparative similarity were just comparative chromatic similarity, then our paradigm-and-foil definition of kind would indeed accommodate redkind. What the definition will not do is distill purely chromatic kinds from mixed similarity. (Quine, 1969, 120)

What causes the problem for Quine is that he does not assume anything like the notion of *domains* in conceptual spaces to help structuring the relations of similarity. If such a structure is given, however, we need not rely on actual objects as paradigm cases but can use *focal points* on a particular quality dimension, like the hue dimension, as a basis for comparing chromatic similarity. In a series of experiments, Rosch (1975, 1978) and others have been able to demonstrate the psychological reality of such focal colors. The shape, weight, and the rest of the qualities of objects will simply not be relevant for such comparisons.

Now, if the traditional extensional or intensional definition of a property is adopted, it is very difficult to explain the degrees of representativeness that prototype theory predicts. Either an object is a member of the class assigned to a property or it is not. Furthermore, all members of the class have equal status as category members. Rosch and her colleagues' research has been aimed at showing asymmetries among category members and asymmetric structures within categories. Since the traditional definition of a property does not predict such asymmetries, something else must be going on.

In contrast, when natural properties are defined as convex regions of a conceptual space, prototype effects are indeed to be expected. In a convex region one can describe positions as being more or less *central*. In particular, if the space has a metric, one can calculate the *center of gravity* of a region. For dense spaces, it can be shown that the center of gravity of a convex region always belongs to the region. This is not true in general for connected or star-shaped regions. For example, if color properties are identified with convex subsets of the color space, the central points of these regions would be the most prototypical examples of the color.[96] These would correspond to the focal colors identified by Rosch. This assumption is also supported empirically by the typicality patterns generated by Sivik and Taft (1994).

Even if different members of a category are judged to be more or less prototypical, it does not follow that some of the existing members must represent "the prototype" (see Lakoff 1987, chapter 2). If a category is viewed as a convex region of a conceptual space this is easily explained, since a central point of the region represents a possible object with the features that are most typical for the category, but such an object need not be among the existing members of the category.

3.9 Voronoi Tessellations of a Space

It is possible to argue conversely and show that if prototype theory is adopted, then the representation of properties as convex regions is to be expected, at least in metric spaces. Assume that some quality dimensions of a conceptual space S are given, for example the dimensions of color space, and that we want to partition it into a number of categories, for example color categories. If we start from a set of prototypes $p_1, \ldots, p_n$ of the categories, for example the focal colors, then these should be the central points in the categories they represent. If we assume that S is a metric space, the information about prototypes can be used to generate a categorization. To see this, assume that S is equipped with the Euclidean metric so that for every point p in the space one can measure the distance $d_E(p, p_i)$ from p to each of the p_i's (d_E is the Euclidean metric defined in section 1.6.3). If we now stipulate that p belongs to the same category as the *closest* prototype p_i, it can be shown that this rule will generate a partitioning of the space—the so called *Voronoi tessellation* (see Okabe, Boots, and Sugihara 1992 for an extensive treatment of such tessellations and their variants). An illustration of the Voronoi tessellation is given in figure 3.13.

The line between p_i and p_j is called the *bisector* of the two points and it is defined as the set of points x such that $d_E(x, p_i) = d_E(x, p_j)$. Each bisector divides the plane into two halves. The following lemma (see Okabe, Boots, and Sugihara 1992) brings out a crucial property of the Voronoi partitioning of a conceptual space, where the cell around a particular

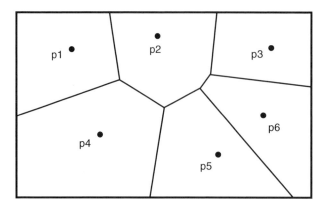

Figure 3.13
Voronoi tessellation of the plane into convex sets.

point p_i is generated by the intersection of all the bisector half-planes containing p_i:

LEMMA 3.1   The Voronoi tessellation based on an Euclidean metric always results in a partitioning of the space into *convex* regions.

Thus, assuming that a Euclidean metric is defined on the subspace that is subject to categorization, a set of prototypes will by this method generate a unique partitioning of the subspace into convex regions. The upshot is that there is an intimate link between prototype theory and criterion P. Furthermore, the metric is an obvious candidate for a measure of *similarity* between different objects according to equation (1.7) or (1.8). In this way, the Voronoi tessellation provides a constructive answer to how a similarity measure together with a set of prototypes *determine* a set of natural properties. In a more "dynamic" vocabulary, the prototypes can be seen as *attractors* and the Voronoi region associated with the prototype as its basin of attraction (see also section 7.2.1 below). Fenstad (1998, 16) gives the following example:

> [C]olor prototypes can be interpreted as a fixed set of patterns to be stored by a suitable attractor neural network. . . . In this case the prototypes are the attractors of the system and the concept of color corresponds to a domain of attraction in the energy surface of the system. This would give a reasonable dynamics for color perception. The correspondence between convex geometry and the dynamics of attractors is quite close; granted sufficiently regularity assumptions the claim is that the two accounts tell basically the same story. In this way we see a connection between grammar and mind—the link being geometry.

A Voronoi tessellation based on a set of prototypes is a simple way of classifying a continuous space of stimuli. The partitioning results in a *discretization* of the space. The prime cognitive effect is that the discretization speeds up *learning*. The reason for this is that remembering the finite prototypes, which is sufficient to *compute* the tessellation once the metric is given, puts considerably less burden on *memory* than remembering the categorization of each single point in the space. In other words, a Voronoi tessellation is a cognitively *economical* way of representing information about concepts. Furthermore, having a space partitioned into a finite number of classes means that it is possible to give *names* to the classes. As argued in chapter 4, however, psychological metrics are imprecise and often context dependent. As a consequence, the borderlines will not be exactly determined.[97]

For some category systems, the effects of a categorization are *amplified* by the perceptual systems so that distances within a category are perceived as being smaller and distances between categories are perceived as larger than they "really" are. This phenomenon is called *categorical perception* (see Harnad 1987 and the other articles in the same volume).[98]

The mechanism of categorical perception has been found in many kinds of categorization but has been studied in particular for phonetic systems (see, for example, Petitot 1989). Even though a set of sounds may be produced by an articulatory parameter that varies continuously (output variable), the auditory system perceives this variable in a categorical way so that when the articulatory parameter is varied along its scale, the perceived sound (input variable) appears to remain constant for a large interval and then suddenly jumps to a new sound that is relatively stable too. Figure 3.14 illustrates the functional relation between an articulatory parameter and the perceived sound.

Petitot (1989) applies Voronoi categorizations to explain some aspects related to the categorical perception of phonemes. In particular, he analyses the relations among the so called stop consonants /b/, /d/, /g/, /p/, /t/ and /k/. The relations among these consonants are expressed with the aid of two dimensions; one is the voiced-unvoiced dimension, the other is the labial-dental-velar dimension that relates to the place of articulation of the consonant. Both these dimensions can be treated as continuous. Figure 3.15 shows how Petitot represents the boundaries between the six consonants.

As an example of the information contained in this model, he points out (Petitot 1989, 68): "The *geometry* of the system of boundaries can provide precious information about the hierarchical relations that stop consonants maintain with each other. The fact that . . . the domains of /p/ and /d/ are *adjacent*, whereas those of /b/ and /t/ are *separated*,

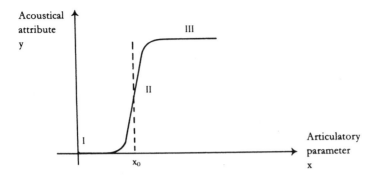

Figure 3.14
The relation between an articulatory parameter and the corresponding sound perception
(from Petitot 1989, 49).

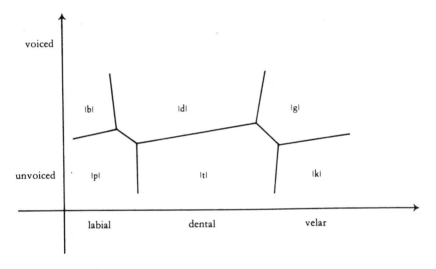

Figure 3.15
A Voronoi model of the boundaries of stop consonants (from Petitot 1989, 69).

indicates that the contrast between /b/ and /t/ is much greater than
that between /p/ and /d/."

Lemma 3.1 provides a connection between prototypes and convex
regions. The lemma heavily depends, however, on the assumption that
the appropriate metric for the space S is the Euclidean metric. As we
have seen in section 1.7, the *city-block metric* is sometimes more suitable, in particular if the dimensions of the space are not integral.

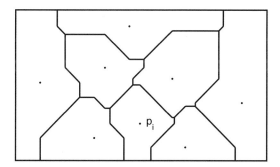

Figure 3.16
Voronoi tessellation based on the city-block metric (based on Okabe, Boots and Sugihara 1992, 187).

For the city-block metric d_C, the bisector defined as the set of points x such that $d_C(x, p_i) = d_C(x, p_j)$ is not always a straight line as in the Euclidean case. The Voronoi partitioning of the space generated by these bisectors will therefore be of a more complicated nature than the Euclidean metric. Figure 3.16 gives an illustration.

As can be seen from the figure, not all areas are convex if betweenness is defined as illustrated in figure 1.12. It is possible, however, to prove the following property with respect to the points p_i that generate the Voronoi tessellation (Okabe, Boots and Sugihara 1992, p. 187):

LEMMA 3.2 The Voronoi tessellation based on the city-block metric always results in a partitioning of the space into *star-shaped* regions with respect to the points p_i.

Thus we see that a set of prototypes within a given conceptual space will result in different partitionings of the space, depending on which metric is chosen. Yet another example of a Voronoi tessellation, based on a different kind of metric, is discussed in section 4.7.

This section has presented a number of criteria for natural properties. So, which of them is the "right" criterion? Partly, this appears to be an *empirical* question; for different quality dimensions, different assumptions concerning metrics and other geometrical properties are justified. For conceptual spaces that contain integral dimensions, the Euclidean metric is often warranted. If we make the additional assumption that, for each property, one can identify a prototype, lemma 3.1 shows that then the (strong) *convexity* assumption of criterion P is applicable. If the conceptual space consists of separable dimensions, the city-block metric appears to be empirically more motivated (see section 1.8). Again, if prototypes exist for the different properties, then a criterion of natural properties based on *star-shaped* regions follows from lemma 3.2. Finally, for domains where there is no natural metric and no prototype structure, a criterion of natural properties based on *connected* regions is perhaps the strongest that will be justified.

3.10 Higher Level Properties and Relations

3.10.1 Relations and Properties

The notion of a property has been analyzed as regions of a conceptual space. But apart from the direct methods of specifying regions of a space that have been used here, there are more sophisticated possibilities. The dimensions of a space can often be used to create new "higher order" dimensions. Let me illustrate the general idea by first showing how the idea of regions can be extended to binary *relations*.

A comparative relation like "longer than" is determined from the lengths of two objects. The length dimension can be represented by R^+, that is the positive half of the line of real numbers. Let $l(x)$ denote the length of an object x. We can then consider the space of all pairs of length values $\langle l(x), l(y) \rangle$, that is, $(R^+)^2$. In this space the relation "y is longer than x" can be identified with the region of all pairs such that $l(y) > l(x)$. This region turns out to be a convex subset of $(R^+)^2$ (see figure 3.17).[99] It is easy to see that this kind of analysis applies to all comparative relations where the generating dimension is isomorphic to R or R^+.

To give a less elementary example, consider "y is a (direct) heir of x." The relevant underlying conceptual space is the genealogical tree of social relations that is generated among the members of a society by

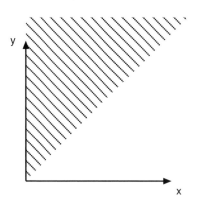

Figure 3.17
A geometric representation of "longer than."

combining links of the types "x is a child of y," "x is a parent to y," "x is married to y," "x is a sister or brother to y." If we fix a particular y we can look at the set $H(x)$ of all y which are (legal) heirs of x.

This set may vary a lot in different societies depending on various cultural factors. Even the structure of the genealogical tree may vary. For example, there are many cultures where no distinction is made between "mother" and "(maternal) aunt." Nevertheless, my conjecture is that $H(x)$ will be a convex set in most cultures in the sense that an individual z will not be counted as a heir of x unless all individuals y that are between z and x (in terms of the genealogical tree) are also considered to be heirs. For example, a grandparent will not be a heir unless the parents are also heirs or a niece unless the brother or sister is a heir.

As an alternative representation of kin relations, Joost Zwarts (personal communication) has proposed a two-dimensional scheme; one dimension is the number of steps "backward" in the genealogy, represented as the horizontal dimension in figure 3.18; the other is the number of steps "forward," represented as the vertical dimension.

Note that this representation makes "cousin" correspond to a convex region, unlike what would happen if we represent the concept in the genealogical tree. It would be interesting to investigate how this two-dimensional mapping treats kinship terms in other cultures.

A relation between two objects can be seen as a simple case of a *pattern* of the location of the objects along a particular quality dimension. There are also properties that can be seen as more general patterns that arise from relations among points located in a conceptual space. On the Cartesian space R^2 with the standard Euclidean metric, we can of course define regions as subsets of the space. But we can also introduce a new space of "shapes" that are *patterns* of points in the space. For example, let us consider the set of "rectangles." This set can be defined using the set of all quadruples $\langle a, b, c, d \rangle$ of points in R^2 that satisfy the condition that the lines ab, bc, cd, and ad form a convex

	0	1	2	3
0	I	mother	grandmother	great-grandmother
1	daughter	sister	aunt	(grand)aunt
2	granddaughter	niece	cousin	cousin
3	great-granddaughter	grandniece	cousin	cousin

Figure 3.18
Zwarts's two-dimensional representation of kinship (the figure only covers one gender).

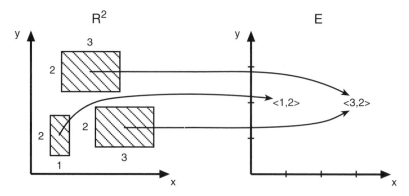

Figure 3.19
The mapping $\langle a, b, c, d \rangle \rightarrow (|ab|, |ac|)$.

polygon such that $a_x - b_x = c_x - d_x$ and $a_y - c_y = b_y - d_y$ (sides are pairwise equally long) and $|ad| = |bc|$, where $|ad|$ denotes the length of the line between a and d (diagonals are equally long). Let us partition this set of quadruples into equivalence classes by saying that two rectangles $\langle a, b, c, d \rangle$ and $\langle e, f, g, h \rangle$ are *identical* if $|ab| = |ef|$ and $|ac| = |eg|$. In this way we identify a rectangle by the *size* of its sides, independently of its *position* in R^2. Now let E be the set of all such equivalence classes. On E we can now define a distance function d as follows:

$$d(\langle a, b, c, d \rangle, \langle e, f, g, h \rangle) = \sqrt{\left(\left(|ab| - |ef|\right)^2 + \left(|ac| - |eg|\right)^2\right)}.$$

As a matter of fact, this measure corresponds to identifying a rectangle $\langle a, b, c, d \rangle$ with the point $(|ab|, |ac|)$ in R^2 as shown in figure 3.19. The space E of rectangles is therefore isomorphic to $(R^+)^2$ with the width and the length of the rectangle as the generating dimensions.

On E, we can now identify some regions that correspond to properties. For example, a *square* is a point $\langle |ab|, |cd| \rangle$ in E such that $|ab| = |ac|$. It is easy to show that this region is a convex subset of E (since this set will correspond to the line $x = y$ in E and a line is a convex set). On the right side of this line, that is, when $x > y$, one finds the set of all rectangles that are wider than they are high, which is also a convex set.

3.10.2 Shapes

So far, the examples of higher level properties and relations have been based on low-level perceptual or social domains. For more complex concepts like "bird" or "cat," it is more difficult to describe the underlying conceptual space (see section 4.2). If something like Marr and Nishihara's (1978) analysis of *shapes* is adopted, however, we can begin to see how such a space would appear.[100] As an example of a more advanced domain, here is a brief outline of their model.

Marr and Nishihara's scheme for describing biological forms uses cylinder-like modeling primitives as illustrated in figure 3.20. Each cylinder can be described by two coordinates (length and width). If we want, we can add dimensions describing the spatial orientation of the cylinder, for example, to describe whether it is horizontal or vertical.

Cylinders are combined by determining the angle between the dominating cylinder and the added one, as well as the position of the added cylinder in relation to the dominating one. Figure 3.20 provides an illustration of the cylinder-based representations. The details of the representation are not important in the present context, but it is worth noting that an object can be described by a comparatively small number of coordinates based on lengths and angles. Thus, the object can be represented as a vector in a high-dimensional space where most dimensions are constituted of spatial dimensions with a Euclidean metric while some dimensions represent the angles between cylinders (in polar coordinates). In this sense, the shape space is *supervenient* on the spatial and angular dimensions (just like the rectangles above are supervenient on the length dimension). The physical location of an object, say an animal, is, of course, described with the aid of the ordinary spatial dimensions.

The coordinates for the cylinders and their connecting points will generate a multidimensional space of shapes. Each particular cylinder shape will then correspond to a point in this space. It is easy to define an elementary betweenness relation for this space by comparing the values of each dimension separately (so that $\langle b_1, \ldots, b_n \rangle$ is between $\langle a_1, \ldots, a_n \rangle$ and $\langle c_1, \ldots, c_n \rangle$, if and only if b_i is between a_i and c_i, for all i). In this way one can, for example, create shapes between the "human" and the "ape" shape. It is possible to introduce a nontrivial metric on the shape space. For example, we can take the city-block metric over all the dimensions (possibly with different weights for the dimensions as in equation (1.5) or (1.6)). Intuitively, the "ape" shape is much more similar to the "human" than to the "horse" shape, which can be confirmed by this kind of metric (see also Aisbett and Gibbon's 1994 article discussed below).

In the multidimensional shape space one can then look at various regions, perhaps generated from prototypical animal shapes, and investigate their properties. Since Marr and Nishihara's simple cylinder figures already make it possible for us to identify a large class of animal shapes, it appears plausible that a lot of the contents of our concepts for animals comes from their shapes. Landau, Smith, and Jones (1998, 21) emphasize the role of shapes in early concept learning: "Our

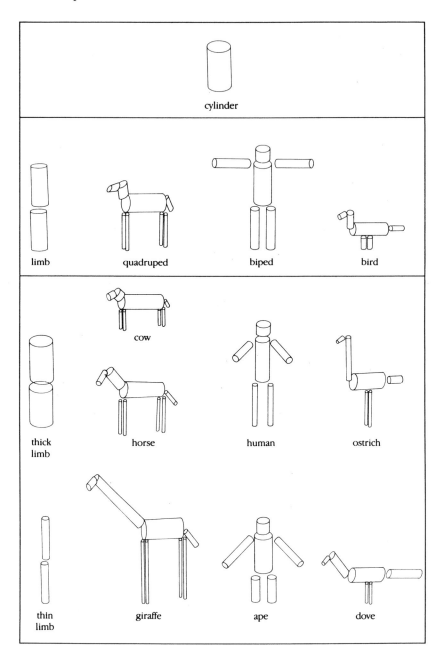

Figure 3.20
Representation of animal shapes using cylinders as modeling primitives (from Marr and Nishihara 1978).

view holds that, however the meanings underlying object names are ultimately characterized, shape similarity constitutes a critical bootstrapping mechanism operating to initiate learning of object names in young children by allowing them to identify category members in the absence of dense knowledge about the category."

For adults there are, of course, other dimensions involved in the animal concepts. (Some further aspects of this are developed in chapter 4). In natural language, however, nouns are often used on the basis of similar shapes. Naming at the basic level often ignores fundamental differences in other domains, while respecting shape similarities; we gladly say "teddy bear," "porcelain cat" and "plastic duck" about objects that have very little in common with the real animals except for their shape. In particular this "shape bias" applies when new words are learned (Jones and Smith 1993, 122–128).

The main factor preventing a more detailed analysis of shape space is the lack of knowledge about the relevant quality dimensions. The models developed by Marr and Nishihara (1978), Tversky and Hemenway (1984), Pentland (1986), Biederman (1987), Chella, Frixione, and Gaglio (1997) among others, are interesting attempts to solve the problem of how shapes are best represented.[101] Nevertheless, a lot remains to be learned about the geometrical structure of shape space and about the structure of the regions corresponding to the properties that we identify in this space.[102] The next chapter presents an experimental investigation of an idealized space of *shell shapes*, based on a three-dimensional conceptual space.

Aisbett and Gibbon (1994) develop a mathematical measure of the similarity of objects, where the judgments are supposed to be based on the shapes and colors of the objects. Their shape representations are much more sophisticated than Marr and Nishihara's (1978) cylinder models. Furthermore, the similarity measure they assume is *context sensitive*. Their model is "inspired by an attempt to treat physical and colour discontinuities as a human observer treats them . . ." (1994, 150). They make the following conjectures about how humans match objects:

> Firstly, humans seek to identify parts of one object as *uniquely* corresponding to parts of the other. Secondly, they will ignore parts of objects rather than force a fit between dissimilar objects. . . . Thirdly, . . . we believe humans are happy to match smooth regions onto piecewise smooth regions, but not vice-versa: it is not natural to "smooth out" creased areas to match them to smooth areas. Fourthly, humans are happy to collapse smooth regions onto parts of their boundaries, . . . (1994, 150–151)

On the basis of these assumptions, they define a distance function that is based on visual discontinuities (in shape as well as in color). This function combines visually prominent features of objects with a measure of geometrical distortions in their edges and surfaces.

3.10.3 Actions and Functions

This chapter's examples have all been of a static nature where the properties modeled do not depend on the time dimension. It is obvious, however, that a considerable part of our cognitive representations concern *dynamic* properties (see, for example, van Gelder 1995, Port and van Gelder 1995). If we, for the moment, consider what is represented in natural languages, *verbs* normally express dynamic properties of objects. Such dynamic properties can also be judged about similarities in a distinctive way: "walking" is more similar to "running" than to "throwing."[103]

An important question is how the meaning of such verbs can be expressed with the aid of conceptual spaces. One idea comes from Marr and Vaina (1982), who extend Marr and Nishihara's (1978) cylinder models to an analysis of *actions*. In Marr and Vaina's model, an action is described via differential equations for movements of the body parts of, say, a walking human (see figure 3.21).[104]

It is clear that these equations can be derived from the *forces* that are applied to the legs, arms, and other moving parts of the body. And as Talmy (1988) has convincingly demonstrated, a great deal of our understanding of verbs depends on the forces that are involved in the actions expressed by the verbs (compare section 5.5).

The upshot is that by adding force dimensions to a conceptual space, we may obtain the basic tools for analyzing dynamic properties. Scott Kelso's (1995) book presents a number of examples of self-organized patterns that emerge in dynamic systems. The forces involved need not only be physical forces, but can, by metaphorical extension, also be *social* forces.[105] Very little research has been directed toward this topic, however, so the details of the analysis will have to be left for the future.

Another large class of properties are the *functional* properties that are often used for characterizing artifacts. For example, Vaina (1983) notes that when deciding whether an object is a "chair," the perceptual dimensions of the object, like those of shape, color, and weight, are largely irrelevant or at least extremely variable. Since I have focused on such dimensions in my description of conceptual spaces, the analysis of functional properties is an enigma for my theory.

One possibility for analyzing these properties is to reduce them to the actions the objects "afford."[106] To continue with the example, a chair is prototypically an object that affords back-supported *sitting* for one

HUMAN

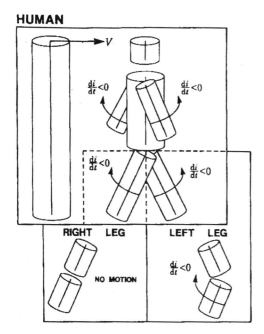

Figure 3.21
A representation of "walking" (from Marr and Vaina 1982, 509).

person, that is, an object that contains a flat surface at a reasonable height from the ground and another flat surface that supports the back. The actions involved in the affordance may then, in turn, be reduced to force dynamic patterns as was explained above. At this stage, however, the proposed strategy is little more than a programmatic statement. Hence, even if this path of analysis is long and to a large extent unexplored, functional properties can, in principle, be explained in the more basic properties that formed the starting point of this chapter.[107]

3.11 Conclusion

I have presented here a theory of properties that is based on conceptual spaces. In brief, a property is identified with a "well-behaved" region of a domain (consisting of integral dimensions). I have proposed three increasingly restrictive meanings of "well-behaved": connected, star-shaped, and convex. It is not possible to reduce this theory to any of the traditional philosophical theories since it heavily depends on the geometrical structures of the underlying domains. Several aspects of the prototype theory of concepts, however, can be explained with the aid of the theory of properties presented here.

As has been argued in section 3.3, traditional philosophical theories of properties do not give us the answers we intuitively expect. In addition to the criteria discussed earlier in the chapter, we can also return to Armstrong's desiderata presented in section 1.2. It can now be seen that the proposed theory of properties explains the phenomena that he brings out concerning the class of shapes and the class of colors:

> a. What colors have in common is that they are all represented as regions of the color *domain* and what shapes have in common is that they all correspond to regions of the (higher level) shape *domain*.
>
> b. While colors (shapes) have the color (shape) domain in common, they differ by being represented as *distinct* regions of the domain.
>
> c. Since the regions differ in how closely they are located (in terms of a distance function), shapes and colors "exhibit a resemblance order based upon their intrinsic nature" (Armstrong, 1978, 116).
>
> d. Colors and shapes form "a set of incompatibles" in the sense that the regions of a domain corresponding to different properties like "triangular" and "circular" or "red" and "blue" do not overlap (at least on the "basic level" of categorization).

Chapter 4

Concepts

Properties, which were the focus of chapter 3, form a special case of concepts. There, I defined this distinction by saying that a property is based on *one* domain (a subspace of integral dimensions), while a concept may be based on *several* domains (consisting of separable domains).

The distinction between properties and concepts has been obliterated in the symbolic as well as connectionist representations that have dominated the discussion in the cognitive sciences. In particular, this applies to representations in *logic*: both properties and concepts are represented by *predicates* in first-order languages. The predicates of a first-order language, however, correspond to several different grammatical categories in a natural language, most importantly those of adjectives, nouns, and verbs. The main semantic difference between adjectives and nouns is that adjectives like "red," "tall," and "round" usually, refer to a *single* domain and thus represent properties, while nouns like "dog," "apple" and "city" normally contain information about *several* domains and thus represent concepts.[108] Verbs are characterized by their temporal structure, which means that they essentially involve a time dimension. Even though it is difficult to formulate a generally valid rule, most "basic" verbs represent *dynamic* properties of domains.[109]

Using the notion of domains in conceptual spaces, one can in this way express the fundamental *semantic* differences between the most important grammatical categories. First-order languages do not appear to be sufficiently rich to make these distinctions in a systematic manner. The differences among the semantic representations of the major word categories are further developed in the cognitive semantics of section 5.5.

I provide an analysis here of concepts based on several domains. Even though the domains are assumed to be separable, the values of their dimensions may be correlated. Such correlations are also included in the concept representations. A significant feature of the chosen representation is that the *salience* given to various aspects of a concept may vary depending on the context. Thus the meaning of a concept is not static, but changes with the context in which it is used. Some further dynamic aspects of concepts show up when concepts are *combined*. The process of concept combination are analyzed in section 4.4.

We are not born with a fixed set of properties and concepts that we use to come to grips with the surrounding world. On the contrary, we constantly *learn* new concepts and *adjust* old ones in the light of new experiences. Section 4.5 outlines how the theory of conceptual spaces can explain some features of concept learning. This is also illustrated later in connection with the experiments on categorizations of shell shapes.

Since our applications of properties and concepts depend on context and earlier learning, it turns out that concepts exhibit a number of *nonmonotonic* features. Unlike the case in classical reasoning, new information may lead to the *withdrawal* of earlier conclusions or expectations even though the new information is consistent with the previous state of belief. Section 4.6 presents the different types of nonmonotonicity of concepts. The theory of concepts developed here will be used to explain these nonmonotonic effects.

In conclusion, the chapter presents a series of experiments on concept formation (presented in greater detail in Gärdenfors and Holmquist 1994). These experiments compared four different categorization rules. The rules presume that the stimuli to be classified can be modeled psychologically as points in a conceptual space. Two of the rules are based on the assumption that there are prototypical representatives of a concept, a third rule is a "nearest neighbor" model, and the fourth is based on "average distances" (Reed 1972), where distances are measured in the underlying conceptual space.

4.2 Modeling Concepts

4.2.1 Concepts with Features in Several Domains
The focus now is on the differences between single-domain properties and multi-domain concepts. As a paradigm example of a concept that is represented in several domains, consider "apple" (compare Smith et al. 1988). The first problem when representing a concept is to decide which are the relevant domains. When we encounter apples as children, the first domains that we learn about are presumably color, shape, texture, and taste. Later, we learn about apples as (biological) fruits, their nutritional value, and possibly some other dimensions. I do not require that a concept be associated with a closed set of domains.[110] On the contrary, this set may be expanded as one learns about further

aspects of a concept. The addition of new domains is often connected with new forms of *actions* that require attention to previously unnoticed aspects of concepts.[111]

The next problem is to determine the geometrical structure of the domains. The color domain can be represented by hue, chromaticness, and brightness and taste space presumably by the four dimensions sweet, sour, salty, and bitter, as seen in section 1.5. Other domains are trickier; it is difficult to be precise about the topological structure of "fruit space." Pomology—the biological categorization of apples— provides some notions, for example, the seed shapes and characters of the apple's flesh and peel. Some ideas about how "shape space" should be modeled were discussed in section 3.10 (following Marr and Nishihara 1978 and others). Textures could possibly be modeled using fractal theory (see, for example, Pentland 1986). It would be very cumbersome to give psychological support for a detailed presentation of the geometrical structures of the different domains. Instead, let me represent the "apple" regions associated with each of these domains by verbal means as shown in table 4.1.

When several domains are involved in a representation, some principle for how the different domains are to be *weighed* together must be assumed (compare equations (1.5) and (1.6)). To model this, I assume that the concept representation also contains information about the *salience* of the different domains.[112] One reason for this assumption is that the relative weight of the domains depends on the *context* in which the concept is used, as will be argued in the following section. If you are eating an apple, for example, its taste is more salient than if you are using it as a ball when playing with an infant, which would make the shape domain particularly prominent.

In section 1.6.5, the following equation was used to define a Euclidean distance measure, where the dimensions are weighted:

Table 4.1
Domains and regions in the representation of "apple"

Domain	Region
Color	Red-yellow-green
Shape	Roundish (cycloid)
Texture	Smooth
Taste	Regions of the sweet and sour dimensions
Fruit	Specification of seed structure, flesh and peel type, etc. according to principles of pomology
Nutrition	Values of sugar content, vitamins, fibers, etc.

$$d_E(x, y) = \sqrt{\Sigma_i w_i \cdot (x_i - y_i)^2}.$$ (1.5)

The weights w_i can be seen as *context-dependent* variables that represent the relative degree of salience assigned to different dimensions. In this model the distance between two objects x and y, and consequently their degree of similarity, is *not* constant but depends on changes in salience of the dimensions of the objects: similarity varies *both* with the magnitude of the difference between stimuli on the dimensions *and* with the dimension weights.[113]

The knowledge and interests of the user will also influence the salience weights. For example (following Bartsch 1996, 426), one can talk about taking different *perspectives* when using a concept. Taking a particular perspective means giving some domain particular attention. The salience of different domains determines which *associations* can be made and, to some extent, which *inferences* can be triggered by a particular use of a concept, as will be shown in section 4.7. In a context of moving furniture, for example, the weight dimension becomes highly prominent. Hence, the concept *piano* may lead to an association of *heavy*. In contrast, in a context of musical instruments, the weight dimension is much less important and an application of the concept *piano* will probably not become associated with *heavy* (Barclay et al. 1974).

In addition to salience effects, which means putting extra weight on an entire dimension, Goldstone (1994a) presents some empirical results that show subjects can be trained to become sensitized to certain *areas* of a dimension so that the perceived length of the area is increased in categorization tasks. The effect means that the metric of the dimension is changed locally, for example by "stretching" distances in a certain region. To borrow an example from Goldstone, suppose that objects are categorized by their length, and objects that are 1 or 2 cm belong to one category, while objects that are 3 or 4 cm belong to another. By attending to the gap between 2 and 3 cm, subjects will selectively highlight this difference so that, as a consequence, the perceived distance between 2 and 3 cm objects will become larger than the perceived distance between 1 and 2 cm (or between 3 and 4 cm). This selective attention will effect the similarity judgments of the subjects. Goldstone (1994a) also found "competition" for sensitization between dimensions so that dimension x is more sensitized when categorization depends only on dimension x than when it depends on both dimensions x and y. This kind of competition was stronger for separable than for integral dimensions.

Concepts are not just bundles of properties. The proposed representation of a concept also includes an account of the *correlations* between the regions from different domains that are associated with the concept.

In the "apple" example, there is a very strong (positive) correlation between the sweetness in the taste domain and the sugar content in the nutrition domain and a weaker correlation between the color red and a sweet taste. As shown in sections 4.7 and 6.6, there are several ways of modeling such connections in technical representations of concepts.

Condensing the previous considerations of salience and correlations results in the following general definition of concept representation:

CRITERION C   A *natural concept* is represented as a set of regions in a number of domains together with an assignment of salience weights to the domains and information about how the regions in different domains are correlated.

To give a more precise model of a particular concept, however, several aspects of criterion C must be specified in more detail. For example, the notion of a "region" can be made more exact by using one of the definitions from section 3.5, leading to more special kinds of concepts based on connected, star-shaped, or convex regions. Even though criterion C makes concepts partly context-dependent, it is rich in empirical predictions, as will be seen later in the chapter.

In this analysis of concepts, I have tried to bring in elements from other theories in psychology and linguistics. The kind of representation proposed in criterion C is on the surface similar to *frames* with slots for different *features* that have been very popular within the cognitive science as well as linguistics and computer science (from Minsky 1975 and on). My definition is richer since a representation based on conceptual spaces will allow me to talk about concepts being *close* to each other and about objects being more or less *central* representatives of a concept. My model combines frames with prototype theory, although the geometry of the domains will make possible predictions that cannot be made in either frame theory or prototype theory. Other related ideas about concept representation can be found in, among others, Langacker (1987, 154–166), Smith et al. (1988), Barsalou (1992), Holmqvist (1993), and Hampton (1993, 1998).

The main difference among these theories and the one presented here is that I put greater emphasis on the geometrical structure of the concept representations. For example, features in frames are often represented in a symbolic form. As will be seen in the following sections, the geometrical structures are cardinal in the analysis of combinations of concepts, learning, and the nonmonotonic aspects of concepts.

4.2.2 Essential Properties and the Theory-Theory of Concepts
Some models of concepts, presume a distinction between *essential* and *incidental* properties. This idea goes back to Aristotle's theory of

essences. In modern psychological theories (see for example Osherson and Smith 1981, Rips 1995), "core" properties are supposed to determine the meaning of concepts, while other "peripheral" properties (Kövescezs 1993) only have diagnostic value. The core is considered to be those properties that are essential to the concepts, while the peripheral properties do not determine whether something belongs to the concept or not, even though peripheral properties may be helpful in "identification procedures" (Osherson and Smith 1981). To repeat a classical example, "rational" and "animal" are essential properties of "human," while "featherless" and "bipedal" are peripheral. Sometimes the position is formulated as *perception* versus *conception*: perception delivers the peripheral properties, which may serve as cues for conception where the essential properties are represented.

This kind of psychological essentialism does not fit well with the instrumentalist cognitive epistemology of this book. A way out of the potential conflict is provided in the following quotation from Medin (1989, 1477), where he gives the following explanation of why people have a tendency to behave as if psychological essentialism is valid:[114]

> If psychological essentialism is bad metaphysics, why should people act as if things had essences? The reason is that it may prove to be good epistemology. One could say that people adopt an *essentialist heuristic*, namely, the hypothesis that things that look alike tend to share deeper properties (similarities). Our perceptual and conceptual systems appear to have evolved such that the essentialist heuristic is very often correct. . . .

In criterion C, the distinction between essential and core properties is not assumed. I believe that a theory of concepts can do without it. First of all, the present theory is conceptualistic. Human categorizations are based on how we represent things mentally, not on what ultimate physical properties they have. Hence, even if there were "real" essences in the world, they could not be allowed in theory. Locke formulated the idea elegantly in his *Essay*:

> Nor indeed can we rank and sort things, and consequently (which is the end of sorting) denominate them, by their essences; because we know them not. Our faculties carry us no further towards the knowledge and distinction of substances, than a collection of *those sensible ideas which we observe in them*. . . . When we come to examine the stones we tread on, or the iron we daily handle, we presently find we know not their make; and can give no reason of the different qualities we find in them. . . . A blind man may as soon sort things by their colours, and he that has lost his smell as

well distinguish a lily and a rose by their odours, as by those internal constitutions which he knows not. (1690/1959, book III,
chapter VI, 9)

Second, the role core properties play in essentialist theories of concepts can be taken over by the notion of salience.[115] A "core" (essential)
property of a concept is a property that belongs to a domain with a
high degree of salience, while a "peripheral" property is associated
with a domain with lower salience. Radical essentialism then corresponds to assigning extreme salience to some "essential" domains
when determining the content of a concept. I see no need, however, to
introduce any definite distinction between what counts as sufficiently
high or low degree of salience. Furthermore, the salience weights of
different domains vary depending on the context. Hence, what appears
to be a core property in one context may seem peripheral in another.
The problems philosophers and psychologists have had in identifying
the essential properties of various concepts is a symptom of the fact
that there is no sharp border between core and peripheral properties.
For example, Smith and Heise (1992, 244) describe how categorization
judgments depend on the task given to the subject:

> [A] demonstration that children perceive a bat and crow to be
> similar in a classification task and a crow and flamingo to be
> similar in the category induction task *need* not mean that children
> shifted from perceptual similarity to conceptual similarity when
> asked to make inductions. They may only have shifted the per-
> ceptual feature weights. Perceptual similarity may have played
> the key role in both judgments.

Some psychologist have criticized the prototype theory and other
similarity-based theories of concept formation and proposed a so-
called "theory-theory" of concepts (for example, Nelson 1974, Keil
1979, Murphy and Medin 1985, Rips 1989, Medin and Ortony 1989,
Gopnik and Meltzoff 1997). The basic idea is that concepts should
be thought of as embedded in knowledge that contains *theories* of
the world (Murphy and Medin 1985). These theories are supposed
to contain information on the origins and causes of category
membership—the "core" of the concepts. For this reason, the theory-
theory is closely related to theories of psychological essentialism: the
theories are about the essences of the concepts.

It would take too long to go into the details of the theory-theory or
of the battle with similarity-based theories of concepts. One weakness
of theory-theories, however, is that they hardly give any account of
how the assumed theories are represented in cognitive systems. And,

assuming that they are expressed symbolically, this would amount to putting the cart before the horse (compare the criticism of the symbolic approach in section 2.2.2). Furthermore, it is not clear *what* can count as a theory: if everything can, then the theory-theory is empty.[116] For one attempt to specify what a theory is in this context, see Gopnik and Meltzoff (1997, 32–41). I believe, however, that most of the features they claim are characteristic of theories could be accounted for on the basis of similarity as well, in particular, if dynamic conceptual spaces are considered.

Smith and Samuelson (1997, 165) summarize the criticism against the theory-theory as follows:

> First, there is no consensus as to what naive theories are, how they are mentally represented, or what kinds of knowledge are included. . . . Secondly, there is no well-formulated account of any natural category within this framework. Thus, once again, there is no demonstration that this kind of theory can actually do the job of explaining human category judgements. Thirdly, even amidst the vagueness of these accounts, naive theories clearly do not explain all the data. For example, they offer no account of why robins are psychologically better birds than blue jays.

Much of the criticism from theory-theorists against similarity-based accounts of concept formation has been based on the assumption that similarity is too general and that no constraints have been provided on what counts as a feature in analyses of similarity (Murphy and Medin 1985, 292). If similarity is connected to distances in conceptual spaces, as it is in this book, the criticism loses much of its force. Other accounts have presumed that similarity is purely perceptual (compare, for example, Rips 1989). Once some domains other than the basic perceptual dimensions are given higher salience weights, however, then there can be no simple perceptual account of similarity. For example, folk botany may classify plants according to the color or shape of the flowers and leaves, but after Linnaeus the number of pistils and stamens became the most important dimensions for botanical categorizations. And these dimensions are perceptually much less salient than the color or shape domains. Shifts of attention to other domains thus also involve a shift in overall similarity judgments. The general trend in the development of the categorizations of a domain is toward less dependence on perceptual similarity.[117]

For more advanced concepts, the perceptually grounded similarity can be transfered to abstract domains by metaphoric mappings. Such mappings will be studied in section 5.6.

Furthermore, I believe that most of the role that the theories are supposed to play in representations of concepts can be taken over by the dimensions or domains that are considered to have the highest salience. In many cases these domains may not be perceptual, but indeed correspond to what is conceived of as *theoretical entities* in science (discussed in section 6.4).[118] From this perspective, there may be no fundamental conflict between a similarity-based theory of the kind developed in this book and a theory-theory. In theories there is also similarity behind the scenes. Hahn and Chater (1997, 50) conclude: "Thus theory-based views demand a *better* account of similarity, rather than *no* account of similarity in explaining concepts."

4.3 The Role of Similarity in Concept Formation

4.3.1 Similarity as a Theoretical Construct

One of the most fundamental notions in the study of concept formation is that of similarity: concepts group together things that are similar. The notion of similarity, however, is also central to many other aspects of cognition like learning, memory, and perceptual organization. For example, Shepard and Chipman (1970) and Edelman (1996) go so far as to claim that representation is *representation of similarities*. By this they mean that representations need not be similar *to the objects* they represent. What is important is that the representations preserve the similarity relations between the objects they represent (compare section 1.5).

I focus here on the question of what role similarity plays in concept formation and categorization. The ultimate goal is to show how a theory of similarity can be used to explain why people and animals form the kind of concepts that they do.

Goodman (1972, 437) challenges the very meaningfulness of the notion of similarity. He says, "Similarity, I submit, is insidious. . . . Similarity, ever ready to solve philosophical problems and overcome obstacles, is a pretender, an impostor, a quack." He also states, "First, we must recognize that similarity is relative and variable, as undependable as indispensable. Clear enough when closely confined by context and circumstances in ordinary discourse, it is hopelessly ambiguous when torn loose" (1972, 444).

Goodman argues that there is nothing like overall similarity that can be universally measured, but we always have to say *in what respects* two things are similar. Similarity judgments will thus crucially depend on the context in which they occur. My interpretation of this point is that the degree of similarity between two things must always be determined relative to a particular *domain* (or dimension) as defined in section 1.8. Things are similar in color or size, or in any other domain, but they are not similar tout court.[119] The domain that is considered when a similarity judgment is made is often determined by the context of the judgment (Medin, Goldstone, and Gentner 1993).

A fundamental question about similarity that is often neglected is: what *kind* of quantity is similarity? Among the few who address the question, one can distinguish three major positions:

1. *Realism*: Similarity is something that exists objectively in the world, independent of any perceptual or other cognitive processes.
2. *Conceptualism, empirical entity*: Similarity is a cognitive magnitude that can be measured directly in subjects. This can be done, for example, by asking them "to rate the similarity or dissimilarity of stimuli on some scale or to judge which set of alternatives is most similar to some standard stimulus" (Medin, Goldstone, and Gentner 1993, 255).
3. *Conceptualism, theoretical entity*: Similarity is a cognitive magnitude that is used as a theoretical entity in *models* of categorization, concept formation, and so forth. If we follow Sneed's (1971) analysis of theoretical entities, similarity cannot be measured directly, but only determined *by applying* a theoretical model.[120]

In this book, I focus on cognitive phenomena. The question of whether things are inherently similar independent of any cognizing subject will, in general, be irrelevant to my concerns. Realism is thus put within brackets. The position adopted here is that similarity is best understood as a theoretical entity used in cognitive models. According to position 3, any measurement of similarity, direct or indirect, will be based on some assumptions concerning the properties of a similarity relation. Such assumptions come from a more or less explicit theoretical model.

What is, then, an appropriate theoretical model? Similarity data from direct or indirect measurements are usually interpreted as proximity data, giving information about the distance between objects in a conceptual space (Hahn and Chater 1997, 54). Multidimensional scaling is a typical technique for reconstructing spaces from similarity data (see section 1.7). The cognitive models that are studied here are based on conceptual spaces. Consequently, it will be assumed that similarity can be modeled by using the *distance* measures in the conceptual spaces. I will assume that similarity is a function of distance (and possibly some other factors) in a conceptual space. As described in section 1.6.5 (equations (1.7) and (1.8)), a common assumption in the psychological literature (Shepard 1987, Nosofsky 1988b, 1992, Hahn and Chater 1997) is that similarity is an exponentially decaying function of distance.

4.3.2 Similarity as Shared Properties

On the approach taken here, similarity and distances in conceptual spaces are intimately connected. Both equations (1.7) and (1.8), which spell out the connection, are bijective functions. Thus, one can go from a distance to a degree of similarity and vice versa. According to the construction of Voronoi tessellations in section 3.9, distances generate regions that represent properties. Because criterion C defines concepts as regions of conceptual spaces, similarity, in turn, can be used to define concepts.

There is, however, a contrary view of the relationship between concepts and similarity. According to this position, two objects falling under different concepts are similar because they have many *properties* in common. Thus, an apple and a pear are similar because they are both fruits that are juicy, sweet, green, have seeds, flesh, skin and contain vitamin C. Medin (1989, 1471) formulates four criteria for this view on similarity: (1) similarity between two objects increases as a function of the number of properties they share; (2) properties can be treated as independent and additive; (3) the properties determining similarity are all roughly the same level of abstractness; and (4) these similarities are sufficient to describe conceptual structure: a concept is equivalent to a list of its properties. According to this view, concepts can be used to define similarity. Hence, we face an apparent circularity.

Seeing properties and concepts, however, as more primitive than similarity leads to grim problems. A fundamental task for such an approach is to determine exactly what counts as a property. The problem is pressing because given only a moderate generosity, any two objects can be shown to share an infinite number of properties (Goodman 1972, Medin 1989). For example, a raven is like a writing desk (recall the Mad Hatter's question) because both are found above ground, both stand on legs, both are rotating around the sun, both weigh less than two tons, both are less than 100 meters long, both are avoided by earthworms, both ought to be made to shut up (Sam Loyd), and so forth.[121] If it is the number of shared properties that determines the similarity of objects, then any two objects will be arbitrarily similar. Restricting the problem to natural properties (in the sense of chapter 3) does not help—there are still arbitrarily many. To get out of this quandrum, one must be extremely careful in defining which properties to allow in a comparison and which to exclude. I know of no theory of properties that furnishes a satisfactory solution to this problem. Consequently, I see no way of defining similarity as the number of shared properties.

In support of this view, there are a number of findings that speak in favor of dimensional representations based on similarities in contrast to feature representations. Smith and Medin (1981, 121–123) present three types of results: (1) People can make fine discriminations about, for example, the size of objects, which implies that they have access to dimensionalized knowledge about the corresponding concepts. (2) Multidimensional scaling analyses consistently reveal dimensional properties. (3) In perceptual categorizations, like in Labov's (1973) experiment with container-like objects, subjects distinguish, for example, diameter-to-height ratios that are used in their categorizations (this experiment is be presented in section 4.5). Such ratios presume dimensional representations.

4.3.3 Tversky's Criticism of Similarity Determined from Distances

There are other kinds of attacks against the thesis that similarity can be modeled by using distances in conceptual spaces. This assumption has been heavily criticized by Tversky and his collaborators (Tversky 1977, Tversky and Gati 1982, Tversky and Hutchinson 1987). Since it is a core assumption for my theory, I must consider the criticism. The first two axioms on distances measures that were presented in section 1.6.3, can via equation (1.7) or equation (1.8) easily be translated to constraints on similarity (Hahn and Chater 1997, 58):

> D1 (identity): The similarity between any object and itself is at least as great as the similarity of any two objects.
>
> D2 (symmetry): The similarity between objects x and y is the same as the similarity between y and x.

The third axiom D3 (triangle inequality) is not so easily translatable since it depends on the exact form of the equation (1.7) or (1.8). The similarity between x and y, however, together with the similarity between y and z will constrain the similarity between x and y (Hahn and Chater 1997, 58–59).

The symmetry axiom (D2) has been the main focus of Tversky's attack against spatial models of similarity. In a number of experiments he and his colleagues have demonstrated that similarity judgments are often asymmetrical. For example, Tel Aviv is judged to be more similar to New York than New York is similar to Tel Aviv.

As an alternative to spatial models of similarity, Tversky (1977) proposed a set-theoretic model based on property matching or feature matching that can account for the violations of the distance axioms. Such a model is open to the criticisms of the previous subsection, however, since it assumes that similarity can be defined by shared properties.

Because Tversky assumes that the similarity of objects is determined from fixed sets of features for the objects, it appears that his criticism presumes that similarity is *not* dependent on context. A better way to explain the experimental results is by considering instead the cognitive *process* underlying the similarity judgments (Medin, Goldstone, and Gentner 1993, 258).[122] In criterion C, the *salience* of different dimensions play an important role. And as was noted in section 4.2, similarity judgments depend on the weighting of dimensions. When Tel Aviv is compared to New York, for example, other dimensions will be more prominent than when New York is compared to Tel Aviv. As Smith and Heise (1992, 242) formulate it: "[P]erceived similarity is the result of psychological processes and it is highly variable. The central process that changes perceptual similarity is attention. The perceived similarity of two objects changes with changes in selective attention to specific perceptual properties."

The different dimensions and their weightings in a comparison are determined by considering the properties of the domain that is in focus of the comparison. As explained in section 4.6.2, the conceptual space is "stretched" along the attended dimensions of the comparison.[123]

This mechanism can be used to explain the other violations of the distance axioms. In a brilliant experiment, Tversky and Gati (1982) showed that subjects make systematic violations of the triangle inequality. The violations occurred in cases where the stimulus dimensions were separable, in which objects x and y coincided on one dimension and y and z on a second dimension. In a series of MDS analyses, Tversky and Gati showed that a value of $n < 1$ in the Minkowski power model (see section 1.6) best fit the experimental data. For these values, the triangle inequality is not valid. As pointed out by Nosofsky (1992, 40), however, a plausible cognitive process model of the subject's similarity judgment is that subjects assign greater salience to those dimensions along which stimuli are more similar. Hence, subjects actively search for the ways stimuli are similar. Thus criterion C can also handle the alleged violations of the triangle inequality by using different patterns of salience weights for different comparisons.[124]

A different kind of criticism against geometric representations of similarity has been presented by Tversky and Hutchinson (1986). They contrast representations of objects in geometrical multidimensional spaces with descriptions of objects by common and distinctive features represented by clusters. On the basis of an analysis of a large number of data sets, they argue that perceptual data satisfy the geometrical approach, while what they call "conceptual" data are more appropriate for clustering representations.

In particular, they claim that "[t]he most striking discrepancies between the data and their multidimensional representations arise in semantic fields when the stimulus set includes a focal element (e.g., a superordinate category) that is the nearest neighbor of many of its instances" (Tversky and Hutchinson 1986, 3). For example, one data set contains twenty different fruits and the superordinate "fruit." In this set, it turns out that "fruit" is the nearest neighbor, in judged similarity, to eighteen of the fruits. Tversky and Hutchinson show that such similarity relations can never occur in any low-dimensional metrical space, but they can be adequately explained in a clustering diagram.

When judging similarities, however, it appears quite artificial to include a superordinate concept among a group of basic level concepts. If the superordinate concept is dropped from the group, the judged similarities between the basic level concepts fit much better with a low-dimensional geometrical space (Tversky and Hutchinson 1986, table 3, 11). Although the match is still not perfect, I believe that if the generalized Voronoi model that is presented in section 4.9 is used as the appropriate geometrical model, most of the remaining misfit can be accounted for. To some extent, Tversky and Hutchinson acknowledge this since they mention that the spatial density model of Krumhansl (1978), which is a model based on distances, can explain much of the problematic data (Tversky and Hutchinson 1986, 17). Even if Krumhansl's model is not the same as the generalized Voronoi model, the two models often result in closely related similarity measures. Although I have not worked out the empirical details of how the generalized Voronoi model would handle the data collected by Tversky and Hutchinson, my conclusion is that their data need not cause any fatal problems for geometrical models based on conceptual spaces.

4.4 Combining Concepts

4.4.1 The Primary Model
Our ability to combine concepts and, in particular, to *understand* new combinations of concepts is a remarkable feature of human thinking. Nobody has problem with grasping the meaning of combinations like *pink elephant*, *striped apple*, and *cubic soap bubble*, even if one never will encounter any object with these properties. An important criterion for a successful theory of concepts is that it should be able to explain the mechanisms of concept combination.

In standard uses of first-order logic, combinations of concepts are expressed by *conjunctions* of predicates. In extensional semantics (see section 3.2), the reference of the combination of two concepts is taken to be the *intersection* of the references of the two individual concepts. The reference of *red book*, for example, is the intersection of all red things with the class of all books.[125] It turns out, however, there are many everyday combinations of concepts that cannot be analyzed in this simplistic manner. For example, *tall squirrel*, *white wine*, and *stone lion* cannot be analyzed as intersections of extensions. Furthermore, as Hampton (1988) points out, taking intersections leads to the prediction that if something is *not* a D, then it is not a D-which-is-a-C. Subjects tend to deny that a screwdriver is a weapon, but in general affirm that a screwdriver is a weapon-which-is-a-tool.[126] These problems of concept combination were perhaps the main reason why logically oriented philosophers like Reichenbach and Montague turned to higher-order logic and intensional logic. As explained in section 3.3, however, these tools are heavy cannons that demolish the problems: the solutions are not at all natural.

The traditional form of prototype theory also has problems explaining combinations of concepts. An early proposal was to use fuzzy set theory to compute the prototype of a combination of concepts from the prototypes of its constituents. Osherson and Smith (1981) demonstrate, however, that this approach will lead to incorrect results for many types of combinations. But fuzzy sets need not be the only way of handling the problem. As shown in section 3.8, many aspects of prototype theory can be explained with the aid of conceptual spaces. Kamp and Partee (1995) try to circumvent these problems for the prototype theory by resorting to the notion of "supervaluations." But a straightforward application of their theory cannot handle examples like *striped apple* and *porcelain cat*.

In the literature there are still other attempts to model concept combinations (some of which are presented in section 4.4.2). All of them appear to have problems, however, with many everyday examples like *stone lion*. Here, I want to show that the criterion C presented in section 4.2 has the potential to handle combinations of concepts.

Suppose one wants to form the combination *CD* of two concepts *C* and *D*, where each concept is represented as a set of regions in a number of domains together with an assignment of salience weights to the domains according to criterion C. Note that in the linguistic expressions for the combination, the *order* of *C* and *D* is important: in English the word for *C* is taken to be a *modifier* of *D* (*D* is called the *head* of the combination). Thus *red brick* is a kind of brick, while *brick red* denotes a particular shade of red.

The most common case of concept combination is when *C* is a property (usually expressed by an adjective) and *D* is a concept (expressed by a noun). But there are also cases where both concepts are multi-domain concepts, usually expressed by nouns, for example, *iron cast* which can be contrasted with *cast iron*. Noun-noun combinations have been studied in some detail by, among others, Murphy (1988, 1990) and Wisniewski (1996).

As a first approximation, the general rule for the combination *CD* of two concepts *C* and *D* proposed here is that the region for some domain of the modifier *C* *replaces* the values of the corresponding region for *D*. It will turn out to be necessary, however, to account for further factors governing concept formation. Consequently, this rule will be amended below.

Let us first look at how the proposed rule applies to property-concept combinations and save the more complicated concept-concept combinations until later. To give a paradigmatic example, *green apple* denotes the concept where the color region of *apple* (which was illustrated as red-yellow-green in the frame in section 4.2) is replaced by the more specific region for green. In some cases *D* does not specify any value for the domain of *C*, in which case *C*-region is simply added to the corresponding domain of *D*. For example, the representation of *book* may not include any specified region of the color domain, so in *yellow book* the region for yellow is added to the representation of *book*.

If the region of *C* is *compatible* with the corresponding region of *D*, like in the two examples above, the result of combining *C* and *D* can be described as the *intersection* of the concepts, as is proposed in the classical logical theory. If the regions are incompatible, however, like in *pink elephant*, the region for *C* *overrules* that of *D* (which, in the case of *elephant*, presumably is the grey region of the color domain). In such a case *C* "revises" *D* and *CD* cannot be described by intersections. Such revisions will result in *nonmonotonic* effects of the contents of the concepts (see section 4.6).[127]

Even if the region for *C* is not strictly incompatible with that for *D*, modifying *D* by *C* may still lead to revisions of *D* because of the *correlations* between domains that are also part of the concept representation proposed in section 4.2. For example, in *brown apple*, modifying the color domain to the brown region may lead to a modification of the texture domain from smooth to shriveled (Smith et al. 1988, 523) since there is a strong correlation among apples between being brown and being shriveled. Similarly, in *wooden spoon*, the size region of the spoon will be changed from small to large when the material of the spoon is specified as wood (Medin and Shoben 1988).

Applying the proposed rule becomes more complicated for concept-concept constructions. Here, both concepts have values in several domains, leading to more difficult choices of which regions of *C* will overrule the corresponding regions in *D*. To borrow an example from Hampton (1997, 146), in *pet bird* the region of the "habitat" domain for *pet* is "domestic" while it is "in the wild"for *bird*. For this domain, *pet bird* inherits the region from *pet*. In contrast, the typical region in the "covering" domain for *bird* is "feathered" while it is "furry" for *pet*. In this case, *pet bird* inherits the region from *bird*. The general principle appears to be that if there is a conflict between two regions for the same domain, it is the region with the *highest degree of salience* that takes precedence.[128]

In some cases the regions of *C* may *block* some of the most prominent domains of *D*, leading to rather drastic changes of the concept *D*.[129] For example in *stone lion*, the representation of *stone* includes the property nonliving which is presumed by many of the domains of *lion*. These domains, like sound, habitat, behavior, and so forth, thus can not be assigned any region at all. By and large, the only domain of *lion* that is compatible with *stone* is the shape domain. Consequently, the meaning of *stone lion* is an object made of stone that has the shape of a lion.

Modifying concept *D* by another concept *C* cannot always be analyzed as a function of the representations of *C* and *D* only. Sometimes the modifier *C* functions almost as a metonymical construction, that is, an abbreviation of a longer phrase. For example, a *criminal lawyer* is usually not analyzed by taking the intersection of criminals and lawyers, but it is a lawyer who works with criminal cases (Hampton 1997, 137). An almost bizarre example is *topless district*. Here it is not the district that is topless, nor the bars in the district, nor the waitresses that work in the bars, but the dresses that the waitresses wear.

Wisniewski (1996) performed some empirical studies of how subjects interpret noun-noun combinations. He distinguishes between *property mapping*, where a property of the modifier *C* is assigned to the concept *D*; and *relation linking* where the combination is viewed as involving a relation between the two nouns. For noun-noun combinations, property mapping appears to be compatible with what is predicted by the model proposed here.

Examples of relation linkings are *honey bee* where the bee is the maker of the honey and *electric shock* where the electricity causes the shock (Wisniewski 1996, 435). In one of his studies Wisniewski showed that when the two nouns represent similar concepts, they are much more likely to be interpreted as property mapping. Relational linking appears to be based on the kind of metonymical construction noted above, where the modifier noun functions as an abbreviation for the relation holding between the two nouns in the combination (Wisniewski 1996, 441).

Conceptual spaces have their primary applications for domains based on perceptual dimensions. Hence, it is not easy to see how the functional relations involved in relation linking could be analyzed with the aid of the model presented here. Section 3.11 presented some ideas about how conceptual spaces could also cover functional and relational concepts. The theory is not very well developed in these areas, however, and it is therefore difficult, at this stage, to give an adequate account of relational linkings between concepts.

4.4.2 Comparisons with Other Theories

Smith et al. (1988) propose a frame-based model of concept combination that has many features in common with the one developed here. They distinguish a number of "attributes" (domains) for each concept and for each attribute a number of "values" (properties), where each value, like *red* or *green*, can have "salience values" (which generate a fuzzy membership in regions of the domain). Each attribute is also assigned a "diagnosticity" value that corresponds to the salience weights of the model presented in section 4.2, even though Smith et al. do not emphasize the context sensitivity of the diagnosticity value.

Their model can explain a number of the examples discussed above. Since they have no representation of the geometrical structure of the domains, however, my model will have greater explanatory and predictive power. For example, there is no mechanism in the model of Smith et al. that can handle the *stone lion* example above. On the other hand, they extend their model to cover concept combinations that include *adverbs*, which I do not treat here.

Holland et al. (1995, chapter 4.2) present a computer program called PI for concept formation and give some examples of how the program handles concept combination. Even though the system rule-based, and thus essentially a symbolic system, it uses a frame structure with different "slots" (domains). Since the representation employed by the system is based on (default or absolute) rules, it is difficult to see how a geometrical structure could be modeled. The program will also have problems in situations when the rules defining the concepts to be combined are in conflict with one another as in the *stone lion* example or in cases like *giant midget* and *midget giant* (Kamp and Partee 1995, 159). An advantage of their approach, however, is that the rule-generating mechanisms take into account expectations about the *variability* of concepts.

Kamp and Partee (1995) try to circumvent the problems for prototype theory presented by Osherson and Smith (1981) by applying the notion of "supervaluations" (van Fraassen 1969). But a straightforward application of the theory cannot handle the *striped apple* example, let alone *stone lion*. They "diagnose the case as crucially involving the dynamics of context dependence and argue that once the linguistic and nonlinguistic factors that affect the dynamic 'recalibration' of predicates in context have places for them in a enriched framework, the supervaluation approach can survive" (Kamp and Partee 1995, 131). They also propose that certain semantic processes involve the operation of several "modules" (1995, 181), which in their description play the role of the domains of the theory presented in this chapter. Their amendment of the supervaluation method, however, does not exploit any geometrical structures, so, again, the model proposed here is richer in structure.

Holmqvist (1993) develops a detailed theory that has many similarities to the one presented here. His analyses have much greater scope, however, than just covering concept combination since his goal is to develop a model of natural language processing. Nevertheless, the structures he presents for representing concepts and the corresponding mechanisms for combining concept are, in general, closely related to those proposed here. Like the other theories, he puts less emphasis on the geometrical structures of the concept representations than I do.

4.4.3 The Effect of Contrast Classes

To further motivate the geometrical approach to concept combination, I next turn to a kind of combination that cannot be handled properly by any of the theories considered in the previous section. The starting point is that, for some concepts, the meaning of the concept is often determined by the *context* in which it occurs. Since these phenomena are not accounted for by the general rule for concept combination that was proposed in section 4.4.1, this rule must be amended.

A typical example of context effects is that some properties cannot be defined independently of other properties. One simple example is the property of being *tall*. This property is connected to the height dimension, but cannot be identified with a particular region in this dimension. To appreciate this difficulty, note that a Chihuahua is a dog, but a tall Chihuahua is not a tall dog. Thus tall cannot be identified with a set of tall objects or with a tall region of the height dimension. The solution to the problem is this property presumes a *contrast class* given by some other property, since things are not tall in themselves but only in relation to some given class of things. Tallness itself is determined with the aid of the height dimension. For a given contrast class D, say the class of dogs, the region $H(D)$ of possible heights of the objects in D can be determined.[130] An object can then be said to be a tall D if it belongs to the "upper" part of the region $H(D)$. Technically, the property "tall" can be defined as a class of regions: for each contrast class D to which the height dimension is applicable, "tall" corresponds to the region of the height dimension that is the upper part of $H(D)$.[131]

The same mechanism can be applied to a number of other properties. It can sometimes result in rather odd effects. For example, the same stream of tap water can be described as "hot" if seen as water in general, but as "cold" if viewed as bath water. For the first contrast class, the region to which "hot" is applied is the full range of water temperatures, while in the latter case it is only the limited interval of bath water temperatures (see figure 4.1).

The effects of contrast classes appear also in many other situations. Consider the apparently innocent concept *red* (Halff, Ortony, and Anderson 1976). In the *Advanced Learner's Dictionary of Current English*, it is defined as "of the colour of fresh blood, rubies, human lips, the tongue, maple leaves in the autumn, post-office pillar boxes in Gt. Brit." This definition fits very well with letting *red* correspond to the standard region of the color space (see section 1.5). Now consider *red* in the following combinations:[132]

- Red book
- Red wine
- Red hair
- Red skin
- Red soil
- Redwood

In the first example, *red* corresponds to the dictionary definition, and it can be combined with *book* in a straightforward extensional way that is expressed by a conjunction of predicates in first-order logic (that is, intersecting the extensions). In contrast, *red* would denote *purple* when predicated of wine, *copper* when used about hair, *tawny* when of skin, *ochre* when of soil and *pinkish brown* when of wood. How can we then explain that the same word is used in so many different contexts?[133]

I do not see how this phenomenon could be analyzed in a uniform way using either possible worlds, a frame-based model, or any of the

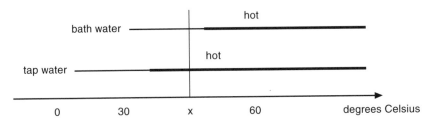

Figure 4.1
The meaning of "hot" in two different contrast classes.

other models discussed in the previous section, and I would challenge proponents of these theories to come up with a solution that is not ad hoc. I want to show here how the idea that *a contrast class determines a domain* can quite easily be given a general interpretation with the aid of conceptual spaces. For each contrast class—for example, skin color—one can map out the possible colors on the color spindle. This mapping will determine a subset of the full color space. The shape of this subset may be rather irregular. Now, if the subset is completed to a space with the *same geometry* as the full color space, one obtains a picture that looks like figure 4.2.

In this smaller spindle, the color words are then used in the same way as in the full space, even if the hues of the color in the smaller space do not match the hues of the complete space. Thus, "white" is used about the lightest forms of skin, even though white skin is beige,

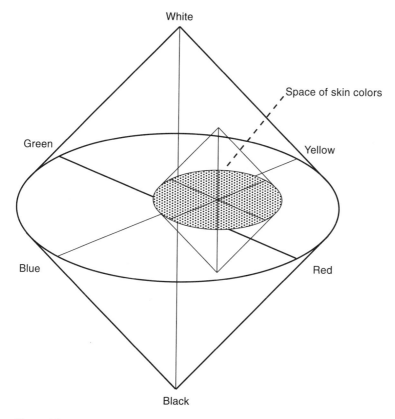

Figure 4.2
The subspace of skin colors embedded in a smaller color spindle.

"black" refers to the darkest form of skin, even though black skin is brown, and so forth. Note that the set of possible skin colors will not cover all of the small spindle, but certain skin color regions will be empty. There are, for example, no green people (but one can become green with envy or because of sickness).[134]

Given this way of handling contrast classes, I can now formulate a more precise version of the general rule for concept combination that was proposed above. The additional consideration is that the concept D in the combination CD determines a contrast class. This contrast class may then *modify* the domains to which the concept C is applied as is illustrated in the examples above. The final proposal thus becomes:

CONCEPT COMBINATION RULE   The combination CD of two concepts C and D is determined by letting the regions for the domains of C, confined to the contrast class defined by D, replace the values of the corresponding regions for D.

In the form presented here, the rule is not completely specified as a computational recipe. Once the underlying conceptual spaces, the regions for the concepts, and the positions of elements of various contrast classes are determined, however, the rule should not be difficult to implement in a program devoted to calculating combinations of concepts.

4.5 Learning Concepts

The fundamental cognitive role of concepts is to serve as a bridge between perceptions and actions. In the simplest case, where there is a direct coupling between perception and action, a concept can be seen as a *decision procedure* where the perception is categorized and the chosen category then determines a choice of action. This is the role of concepts in lower animals (and the only role behaviorists would accept). In humans and many of the higher animals, cognition is dominated by other more indirect modes that are not triggered by perceptions alone. In these cognitive processes, concepts have function in reasoning and in acting that is independent of perception.

We are, in general, not born with our concepts but they must be *learned*. The decision procedures that connect perceptions and actions must be created with the aid of the experience of the agent. To be useful, the procedures should not only be applicable to known cases, but should *generalize* to new situations as well.

The cost of generality is the increase of error. Decision procedures can be more or less successful. When a particular perception is sorted under a concept, this may be a miscategorization, which in turn leads the agent to choose the wrong action ("Pardon me," said the hedgehog and climbed off the scrubbing brush). If the agent realizes that it has made a mistake, it will adjust the application rules for the concept that led to the error. This is another aspect of concept learning. Here I outline how conceptual spaces can be used to model some of the fundamental aspects of how we learn concepts.

First note that if one is using symbolic representations, it is very difficult to model some of the important aspects of learning. Above all, the *similarity relations* between concepts, for example that "green" is closer to "blue" than to "red," is cumbersome to capture in a nonarbitrary way by symbolic representations. Connectionist models handle these problems in a better way (see, for example, Schyns 1991), but the representations formed in artificial neuron networks are in general difficult to interpret. One reason for this is that dimensions are normally not represented directly in connectionist systems. Furthermore, learning in connectionist systems is usually very slow.

An explanation of how *stimulus generalization* works may become complicated, for example, if the subconceptual approach is adopted. Stimulus generalization is the ability to behave in a new situation in a way that has been learned in other similar situations. The problem is how to know which *aspects* of the learning situations should be generalized. On the conceptual level of representation, the stimulus is assumed to be categorized along a particular dimension or domain. The applicability of a generalization can then be seen as a function (for example, a Gaussian function) of the *distance* from a prototype stimulus where the distances are determined with the aid of an underlying conceptual space.[135]

In the previous chapter, I briefly presented the prototype theory for concepts. This theory is not well suited, however, for explaining how learning of concepts functions. More precisely, even if prototype theory fares much better than the Aristotelian theory of necessary and sufficient conditions in explaining how people use concepts, the theory does not explain *how* such prototype effects can arise as a result of learning to use concepts. The theory can neither account for how new concepts can be created from relevant exemplars nor explain how the extensions of concepts are changed as new concepts in the same category are learned.

Let us then see how learning can be handled with the aid of conceptual spaces. Learning a concept often proceeds by generalizing from a limited number of *exemplars* of the concept (see, for example, Reed 1972, Hintzman 1986, Nosofsky 1986, 1988b, and Langley 1996). Adopting the idea that concepts have prototypes, we can assume that a typical instance of the concept is extracted from these exemplars. If the exemplars are described as points in a conceptual space, a simple rule that can be employed for calculating the prototype from a class of exemplars is that the ith coordinate p_i for the vector p representing the prototype is defined to be the mean of the ith coordinate for all the exemplars (Langley 1996, 99). The equation for the coordinates of a prototype p is thus

$$p_i = \Sigma_k x_{ik}/n, \tag{4.1}$$

where x_{ik} denotes the location of the n exemplars that fall under the concept associated with p. The prototypes defined in this way can then be used to generate a Voronoi categorization.[136]

Thus, a prototype is not assumed to be given a priori in any way but is completely determined by the experience of the subject. Figure 4.3 shows how a set of nine exemplars (represented as differently filled circles) grouped into three categories with the aid of equation (4.1) generate three prototypical points (represented as black crosses) in the space. These prototypes then determine a Voronoi tessellation of the space.[137]

The mechanism illustrated in figure 4.3 shows how the application of concepts can be *generalized* on the basis of only a few examples of each concept. The additional information required for the generalization is *extracted* from the geometrical structure of the underlying conceptual space required for the calculation of prototypes and for the Voronoi tessellation.

Furthermore, the concepts generated by such a categorization mechanism are *dynamic* in the sense that when the agent observes a new item x in a category, the prototype for that category will, in general, change somewhat, since the mean of the class of examples will usually change. For each dimension i, the effect Δp_i on dimension i of the stored prototype p can be calculated as

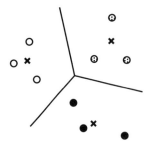

Figure 4.3
Voronoi tessellation generated by three classes of exemplars. The prototypes are represented by crosses.

$$\Delta p_i = (x_i - p_i)/(n + 1), \tag{4.2}$$

where x_i is the ith coordinate of the newly learned instance and $n + 1$ is the total number of instances (including the new one) in the class represented by the prototype p (see Langley 1996, 99–100).

Figure 4.4 shows how the categorization in figure 4.3 is changed by the addition of one new exemplar, marked by an arrow, to one of the categories. This addition shifts the prototype of that category, which is defined as the mean of the exemplars, and consequently the Voronoi tessellation is changed. The old tessellation is marked by hatched lines and the old prototype is marked by a thin cross.

This mechanism also explains some aspects of the overgeneralization that often occurs in concept formation. For example, when a child learns the word "dog" (or a "bow-wow" version of it) this notion will be applied not only to dogs, but to wolves, horses, calves, and so forth. Presumably, the child only masters a few prototypes in animal space and these prototypes are used to generate a partitioning of the entire space. Consequently, the child will overgeneralize a concept in comparison to its standard use. After all, communication functions better if the child has some word for any animal than if it has no word at all. When the child learns more prototypes for other animal concepts, however, it will gradually adjust an early concept to its normal use since its partitioning of the animal space will become finer.

The mechanism involving Voronoi tessellations that has been illustrated here is an example of *supervised* learning, where the learner is given feedback in form of names or other indications of the categories the different examples belong to. Learning mechanisms exist that can also pick up patterns from the environment without any error messages concerning the performance of the mechanism. All such mechanisms need is a large sample of training examples. These systems perform what is called *unsupervised* learning. A classic example of

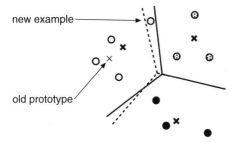

Figure 4.4
Change of Voronoi tessellation in figure 4.3 after adding a new exemplar.

unsupervised learning in ANNs is given by Hebb's rule (see Rumel-hart and McClelland 1986, 36–37). The rule is that if two units in the ANN are active at the same time, then the connection weight between these units is increased by some small amount; if one unit is active while the other is inactive, then the connection strength is decreased.

An established paradigm for unsupervised learning is the *clustering techniques* developed within the area of machine learning (for example, Michalski and Stepp 1983, Murtagh 1993, Langley 1996, Hulth and Grenholm 1998). Starting from a set of objects and some attributes that are used to characterize the objects, these methods often define a measure of similarity that is used for clustering the objects into disjoint categories. The general idea is that objects that are similar should be grouped together, but various criteria are used to determine the borders between the categories. The division is formed without any input concerning the "correct" categorization of the objects. The attributes that are used to define the similarity measure, however, are fed in by the programmer, in general as a list of atomic features (given a *symbolic* representation). Thus the potential geometrical structure of the features is normally not taken into account by the clustering program. Furthermore, the clusters generated by the program may be difficult to provide with a semantic interpretation, just like many categorization mechanisms based on artificial neuron networks.

4.6 Nonmonotonic Aspects of Concepts

Concepts play an important role in the generation of *inferences*. As Holland et al. (1986, 180) put it: "To know that an instance is a member of a natural category is to have an entry point into an elaborate default hierarchy that provides a wealth of expectations about the instance." Here, I show that the model of concepts presented above will generate expectations that result in different forms of *nonmonotonic reasoning*.

The deductive reasoning of traditional logic is *monotonic*: when proposition *A* can be infered from a set *S* of sentences, then *A* can be infered from any set that contains *S*. Everyday reasoning, however, which in general is based on assumptions about what is "normally" the case, is often nonmonotonic. For example, if I learn that Gonzo is a bird, then with the aid of the presumption that birds normally fly, I conclude that Gonzo flies. But if I obtain the additional information that Gonzo is an emu, this conclusion is no longer drawn.

Nonmonotonic reasoning is one of the hottest topics within AI.[138] Most of the research efforts however, have been concentrated on finding the appropriate *logical rules* that govern nonmonotonic reasoning. Thus, a propositional (symbolic) representation of the relevant knowledge is already presumed. On the basis of the arguments presented in chapters 1 and 2, to understand nonmonotonic reasoning I believe one must go below the symbolic level of representation.

An important point is that information about an object may be of two kinds: *propositional* and *conceptual*. When the new information is propositional, one learns new *facts* about the object, for example, that x is a penguin. When the new information is conceptual, one *categorizes* the object in a new way, for example, x is *seen as* a penguin instead of as just a bird. It is important to notice that describing information as propositional or as conceptual does not mean that these kinds of information are in conflict with one another. On the contrary, they should be seen as different *perspectives* on how information is described.[139] The propositional information falls under symbolic representations, in the sense of chapter 1, and it was there contrasted to conceptual representations, which belong to a different level of description.

The theory of nonmonotonic inferences has focused on propositions; hence it has been seen as a nonmonotonic *logic*. In the examples discussed in the literature, however, the great majority derive from the nonmonotonicity of *concepts*. For example, the *default rules* studied by Reiter (1980) and his followers have been seen as inference rules, although a more natural interpretation of "defaults" is to view them as *relations between concepts*. For instance, when something is categorized as a fruit, it will also, by default, be categorized as sweet, even though it is well-known that the category contains many exceptions that are not sweet.

It may be argued that no harm is done in focusing on the propositional side of nonmonotonicity since information about categorization can be quite naturally transfered to propositional information: categorizing x as an emu, for example, can be expressed by the proposition "x is an emu." This transformation into the propositional form, however, tends to suppress the internal *structure* of concepts. Once one formalizes categorizations of objects by *predicates* in a first-order language, there is a strong tendency to view the predicates as primitive atomic notions and to forget that there are rich relations among concepts that disappear when put into standard logical formalism. Indeed, the fact that the concept of an emu is a subcategory of "bird" is often represented by an explicit axiom in the form of a universal sentence "$(x)(Ex \rightarrow Bx)$." If the structure of concepts, however, were built into the predicates of the language themselves, such an axiom would be totally redundant. In fact, the inclusion relations between the regions and their domains will, in a sense, become *analytic* in a conceptual space.[140]

The literature contains one well-known theory of nonmonotonic inferences that focuses on conceptual relations, namely *inheritance networks* (see, for example, Touretsky 1986 and Makinson and Schlechta

1991). In the theory of inheritance networks, however, concepts are represented by (nonstructured) *points* and their relations by two kinds of links: "is-a" and "is-not-a." Since these links say nothing about the structure of concepts, this form of representation is far too meagre to handle the relations among concepts that are exploited in inferences, monotonic as well as nonmonotonic. In contrast, I submit that a theory of conceptual structure is necessary to understand different kinds of nonmonotonic inferences involving concepts.

To bring out the role of conceptual structure in nonmonotonic inferences, I show that there are several, albeit related, kinds of nonmonotonic inferences that appear in the use of concepts. In the following section, I explain some of these phenomena with the aid of conceptual spaces. Other aspects will be treated later in the book.

As a challenge to any theory about nonmonotonic inferences, I would like to point out the following nonmonotonic aspects of concepts.

Change from a general category to a subordinate.   This is the most well-known nonmonotonic aspect of concepts. When we shift from applying a "basic" category (a term borrowed from prototype theory) such as *bird* to an object to applying a "subordinate" category such as *emu*, we often give up some of the (default) properties associated with the basic category: a bird is normally small, sings, flies, and builds nests in the trees, while an emu has none of these properties.

Context effects.   Sometimes the mere *context* in which a concept is used may trigger different *associations* that lead to nonmonotonic inferences. Barsalou (1987, 106) gives the following example: "When *animals* is processed in the context of milking, *cow* and *goat* are more typical than *horse* and *mule*. But when *animals* is processed in the context of riding, *horse* and *mule* are more typical than *cow* and *goat*" (see also Roth and Shoben 1983).

Another example of how the context affects the application of concepts is the following by Labov (1973). He showed subjects pictures of objects like those in figure 4.5 to determine how the variations in shape influence the names the subjects use. But he also wanted to see whether the *functions* of the objects influence naming. In the "neutral" context, subjects were asked to imagine the object in somebody's hand. In a "food" context, they were asked to imagine the object filled with mashed potatoes; and in a "flowers" context, they were told to imagine the object with cut flowers in it.

Figure 4.6 shows the results, when the *width* of objects 1 to 4 (figure 4.6a) and *depth* of objects 1 and 5 to 9 (figure 4.6b) varied as is represented on the horizontal axes. The vertical axis represents the percentage of sub-

Figure 4.5
Cuplike objects (from Labov 1973).

jects that named the object with a particular word. As can be seen, the names for the objects were heavily influenced by the imagined context.

This example shows that even if the "prototypes" of two concepts such as *cup* and *bowl* remain unchanged, the context may change the *border* between the concepts. The food context makes certain properties more salient which results in changes within the psychological space (see the discussion of generalized Voronoi tessellations in section 4.9).

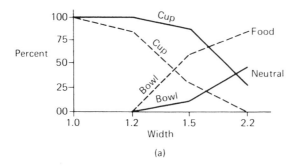

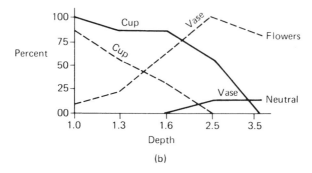

Figure 4.6
Context effects on the borders between concepts: (a) use of names "cup" and "bowl" in neutral and food contexts; (b) use of names "cup" and "vase" in neutral and flowers contexts (from Labov 1973).

Such changes may clearly have nonmonotonic effects on the use of the concepts.

The effect of contrast classes.   In section 4.4.2, I showed how the contrast class induced by a concept may influence the application of a modifying concept, for example, by embedding a color into a conceptual space that is generated by the contrast class. The embeddings into smaller conceptual spaces will naturally result in nonmonotonic effects. From the fact that x is a brown object and a person, for example, one cannot conclude that x is a brown person even though *person* is subordinate to *object*.

Metaphors.   Even more drastic combination effects occur in metaphorical (and metonymical) uses of concepts. For example, when we talk about a *red newspaper*, we do not expect it to be printed on red paper, only to express a certain political viewpoint. Or, take the combination *stone lion* that was analyzed in section 4.4. Knowing that something is a lion, usually leads to inferences of the form that it is alive, that it has fur, and so forth. In the combination *stone lion*, however, the only aspect of the object that is lionlike is its shape. One can not conclude that a stone lion has the other usual properties of a lion, and thus we see the nonmonotonicity of the combined concept. One can express the effect of the combination by saying that a stone object is metaphorically seen as a lion because the shape of an object, from a domain of nonliving things, maps onto the shape of a lion that belongs to a domain of living things. A more elaborate analysis of metaphors as mappings between domains is given in section 5.6.

The kind of conceptual change involved in varying contrast classes and metaphors corresponds to *revisions* of the concept, and thus the inferences involved in such uses of concepts parallel *belief revisions* that are modeled in propositional systems (Gärdenfors 1988a; for a comparison between nonmonotonic inferences and belief revision, see Gärdenfors and Makinson 1994).

Some different kinds of nonmonotonic aspects of concepts have been presented. These aspects are obviously interrelated even though it is difficult to spell out their exact connections. In the literature, however, the focus has almost exclusively been on what happens in the transition from a general category to a subordinate. The other aspects are equally important, I believe, and in need of a systematic investigation.

4.7 Concept Dynamics and Nonmonotonic Reasoning

By studying how the application of a concept changes dynamically when further information is provided to the agent, I now show how the analysis of concepts presented in section 4.2 can be applied to provide explanations for the nonmonotonic features of concepts. The analysis in section 4.4.2 already provides an account of the nonmonotonicity caused by varying contrast classes.

4.7.1 Change from General Category to Subordinate

If concepts are described with the aid of convex regions of a conceptual space in line with criterion C, prototype effects are indeed to be expected. In a convex region one can describe positions as being more or less *central*. If color concepts are identified with convex subsets of the color space, for example, the central points of these regions would be the most prototypical examples of the color.

Subordinate concepts may move away from the prototypes of the general concept and thus result in atypical properties. If the first thing I ever hear about the individual Gonzo is that it is a bird, I will, for lack of further information, naturally locate it in the conceptual space as a more or less prototypical bird, that is, at the center of the region representing birds as a subclass of animals. (The conceptual space needed to handle the concept of an animal may contain domains for shape, color, sound, behavioral variables, etc.). And in that area of the conceptual space, birds do fly. More precisely, almost all individuals who are located in the center of the bird region of animal space will also belong to the region of action space representing animals that fly. If I then learn that Gonzo is an emu, however, I must *revise* my earlier concept location and put Gonzo in the emu region, which is a subregion of the bird region, but presumably lies at the outskirts of that region. And in the emu region of action space none of the individuals fly.

This simple example only hints at how the *correlations* among different regions representing properties in one domain and regions representing properties in another domain can be used in understanding nonmonotonic reasoning. For this analysis, the geometrical structure of the regions in concepts is essential. A general inductive principle that underlies much human reasoning is that objects that are similar along some dimensions will also be similar along other dimensions. Such correlations will only be formulated in an ad hoc manner, if a symbolic representation of information is used where the similarity relations cannot be expressed in a natural way. I return to the correlations between domains in section 6.6.

A problem exists, however, with the mechanism for handling new information indicated by the example.[141] Suppose that robins are the most prototypical birds. If I first learn that Gonzo is a bird and then that it is a robin, I have indeed received new information. But, according to the proposal above, I will locate Gonzo at the same point in space both before and after the information that it is a robin. So how can the new information influence my reasoning? It appears reasonable that knowing that Gonzo is a robin should allow me to draw more default conclusions than when only knowing that it is a bird. A solution to this problem will be suggested in section 4.9.

4.7.2 *Change in Salience*
The main effect of applying a concept in a particular *context* is that certain domains of the concept are put into focus. In relation to the model based on criterion C that was presented in section 4.2, the context determines the salience of the domains. This results in a *dynamic* conceptual space, which in turn makes concepts and similarity judgments dynamic (see Smith and Heise, 1992, 242–248 and Jones and Smith 1993, 130–137).

Another effect of changes in context is that a change in the salience assigned to certain domains may result in a shift of the *borders* between different concepts. As was seen in the previous section, once the functionality was put in focus in Labov's study of the concept *cup*, the border between *cup* and *bowl* changed considerably. Such changes of borders naturally lead to nonmonotonic effects when the concepts are applied in different contexts.

This kind of change can be modeled mathematically with the aid of the Voronoi tessellations that were presented in section 3.9. When the distance between two points in a space is determined, the relative *scales* of the dimensions are important. A change in the salience weight assigned to a dimension can be described as putting more weight on the distances between objects on that dimension, that is, magnifying the scale of the dimension (compare section 4.2). In equations (1.5) and (1.6), this corresponds to changing the weights w_i.

Figure 4.7 (left) gives the positions of three objects in a two-dimensional space. Assume that weighted (city-block) distances between the positions are calculated as in equation (1.6), where $w_x + w_y = 1$, and the similarity between the objects are then determined via equation (1.7). If the weight w_x of the x-axis varies from 0 to 1 (while the weight w_y of the y-axis correspondingly varies from 1 to 0), then the degree of similarity between the three possible pairs of objects varies as in figure 4.7 (right). Conforming with the concept model of section 4.2.1, the weight w_x can be seen as the salience weight given to dimension x.

For another example, assume that we have a domain with two dimensions x and y, and three prototypical points p_1, p_2, and p_3, located as in figure 4.8a. Assume that distances are given by the Euclidean

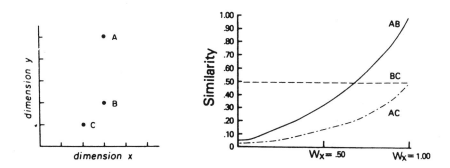

Figure 4.7
(left) Three objects represented in a 2-D space; (right) The similarity of pairs of objects as a function of the weight w_x of dimension x (from Smith and Heise 1992, 244).

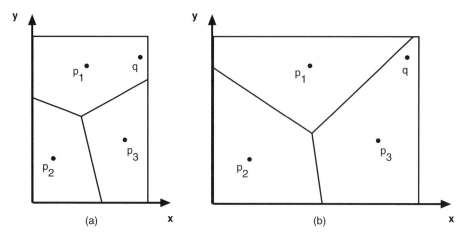

Figure 4.8
Changes in Voronoi tessellation as a result of a change of the scale of the x-axis.

metric. The Voronoi tessellation that is generated from these three points can then be determined. Now if the salience weight of the x-dimension is doubled, which means that the scale of x is multiplied by two, the resulting Voronoi tessellation will change the categorization of some points in the space as is shown in figure 4.8b. For instance, the point q will belong to the category associated with p_1 in the first case, but to the category associated with p_3 in the second. Similar changes would occur if the city-block metric was adopted instead of the Euclidean.

This phenomenon should be compared with Goldstone's (1994a) findings on sensitization between dimensions (presented in section 4.2). One of his results was that dimension x is more sensitized when categorization depends only on dimension x than when it depends on both dimensions x and y. The upshot is that categorization will, to some extent, depend on which dimensions are focused on in a particular context.

4.8 Objects as Special Kinds of Concepts

So far, the focus has been on using conceptual spaces as a tool for modeling concepts (with properties as a special case). It is also necessary, however, to consider how *objects* (or *individuals*, in the philosophical sense) can be represented in this framework. A straightforward way to represent an object is as a *point* in a conceptual space. Alternatively, a point in a conceptual space can be seen as a *vector* of coordinates, one for each dimension in the space. In this way, each (physical) object can be allocated a specific color, spatial position, weight, temperature, and so forth. *Abstract* entities have no location in space or time, so their underlying domains are different from those of physical objects.

If we assume that an object is completely determined by its set of properties (Leibniz' principle), then all points, specified for all domains in the conceptual space, can be taken to represent *possible objects*. On this account, a possible object is a *cognitive* notion that need not have any form of reference in the external world. This construction will avoid many of the problems that have plagued other philosophical accounts of possible objects. For example, a point in a conceptual space will always have an internally consistent set of properties. Since "blue" and "yellow", for example, are disjoint properties in the color space, it is not possible that any object will be both blue and yellow (all over). Consequently, there is *no need for meaning postulates* or their ilk (in the sense of Carnap) to exclude such contradictory properties.

Leibniz' law on the identity of indiscernibles obtains a special meaning in the present context: if two objects are assigned the same values in all dimensions of a conceptual space, the objects are identical within that space. Hence, if two objects are discernible, there is some dimension along which they differ.

In general, one will not know all the properties of an object. A more general representation that accounts for situations where we only have incomplete knowledge about the properties of the object is to use *partial vectors* (that is, points where the arguments for some dimensions are undetermined).

Representing objects as vectors (or partial vectors) in a conceptual space means that they are treated as a special kind of concept, that is, as concepts where all regions (or known regions) of the domains are reduced to points. According to this view there is no principal ontological difference between concepts and objects—objects are just very narrow concepts.

Another characteristic of physical objects is that they are *spatiotemporally continuous*: an object does not make any abrupt jumps in space. Modeling this characteristic requires that the space and time dimensions are always among the dimensions representing physical objects and that the trajectory of the object in space forms a continuous path over time. Consequently, an object is assumed to have a unique location even if it is not observed at the moment. This characteristic of object representation is, fundamentally, what lies behind the phenomenon of *object permanence* in Piaget's sense.

Following Stalnaker (1981, 347), one can define a function that maps the names of objects into points in a conceptual space and the predicates (properties and concepts) onto regions of the space. Stalnaker calls such a mapping a *location function* that would play the role of a so-called interpretation of a language in traditional logical semantics.[142]

One important contrast between location functions and the intensional semantics outlined in section 3.2 is that the analysis of objects, properties, and concepts proffered here does not presume the concept of a *possible world*. Different location functions, however, describe alternative ways that objects may be located in a conceptual space. Thus, these location functions may take the same role as possible worlds in intensional semantics. We can *define* the notion of a possible world as a possible location function. Should one need them (which I doubt), this can be done without introducing any new ontological primitives to the theory.[143]

4.9 Four Geometrical Categorization Models

The remainder of the chapter describes a series of experiments on concept formation that I performed in collaboration with Kenneth Holmqvist. Four models based on a geometrical approach to categorization are presented here, together with the experiments that were performed to test the models. These experiments are described in greater detail in Gärdenfors and Holmqvist (1994) (see also Gärdenfors 1992 and Johannesson 1996).

At the beginning of chapter 3, I drew a distinction between a *property*, which in this book is taken to be based on a single domain of integrated dimensions, and the more general notion of a *concept*, which may be based on several separable domains. I also defined a *categorization* to as a rule for classifying objects. The rule is generated from the representation of the relevant concepts. The result of applying a categorization rule is a set of categories. In this way, concepts generate classifications of stimuli. In the model presented here, where stimuli are represented as points in conceptual spaces and where concepts correspond to a set of regions from separable domains, a categorization will generate a partitioning of the space.

The particular space used in our experiments is a representation of *shell shapes*. One hypothesis tested is that a model based on conceptual spaces together with a categorization rule based on Voronoi tessellations can explain subjects' categorizations of shells. The Voronoi tessellation, however, is only one example of a categorization rule that can be formulated for the shell space. In general, a conceptual space can be seen as a geometrical framework for which several categorization rules can be formulated and tested. Three additional categorization rules for the shell space are introduced below. The question which our experiments addressed is which of these rules best explains how concepts are formed and how concepts change as a result of learning. There are several related studies in the psychological literature. Reed's (1972) investigation of classifications of Brunswick faces uses an approach that is similar to that of the current experiments, even if the "space" of faces has a very limited structure in comparison to the shell space presented below. Similarly, Ashby and Gott's (1988) investigations of decision rules for categorizing multidimensional stimuli are based on a methodology that shares many features with ours. Some further examples of studies of concept formation that utilize dimensional notions are Pittenger and Shaw (1975) on faces, Labov (1973) on cups, Nosofsky (1986) on semicircles, Shepard (1987), Nosofsky (1988a) on color, Smith and Heise (1992) on shape and color, Jones and Smith (1993) on shape, size and texture, and Goldstone (1994a) on brightness and size. An excellent survey of different mathematical models used in the area is given by Nosofsky (1992).

The theory of conceptual spaces will serve as the theoretical framework for the different categorization models. Since our experiments only concern the shape domain for shells, we can take as the starting point the following criterion from section 3.5:

CRITERION P   A *natural property* is a convex region of a domain in a conceptual space.

In support of criterion P, section 3.9 noted that, assuming we have a space with a Euclidean metric, a set of prototypes will generate a Voronoi tessellation of the space consisting of convex sets. By choosing the Euclidean metric, the dimensions of the space are regarded as *integral* (compare section 1.8). This assumption is, of course, not valid in general. However, our pilot studies, which will be described below, suggest that it is a reasonable premise for the shell space that is studied in the experiments.

In the experimental investigations, it is assumed that the prototype for a category is determined from the set of *exemplars* of the category that a subject has seen. As described in equation (4.1) in section 4.5, the rule employed for calculating the prototype from a class of exemplars is that the ith coordinate p_i for the vector representing the prototype is the mean of the ith coordinate for all the exemplars. These prototypes can then be used to generate a Voronoi tessellation of the space. Such a tessellation generated from a set $p_1, \ldots, p_n$ of prototypes results in the following categorization rule:[144]

PROTOTYPE VORONOI CATEGORIZATION (PV)   An object represented as a vector x in a conceptual space belongs to the category for which the corresponding prototype is the closest, that is, the p_j that minimizes the distance between x and p_j.

A drawback of the standard Voronoi tessellation is that it is *only* the prototype that determines the partitioning of the conceptual space. It is quite clear that for many natural categorizing systems, however, some concepts correspond to "larger" regions than others. For example, the concept "duck" covers a much larger variety of birds than "ostrich," even though both concepts are *basic level* concepts in the terminology of Rosch (1978), that is, they are both members of the same categorization of birds. In conformity with this, Medin (1989, 1472) states: "Prototype theory implies that the only information abstracted from categories is the central tendency. A prototype representation discards information concerning category size, the variability of the examples, and information concerning correlations of attributes. The evidence suggests that people are sensitive to all three of these types of information. . . ."

Furthermore, results on artificial categorization tasks by Fried and Holyoak (1984) suggest that subjects are indeed responsive to the variability of instances of different categories. Holland et al. (1995, section 8.2) present some empirical evidence that suggest that people's assessments of the variability of a properties effect their willingness to generalize from one or a few observations. For example, subjects were asked to imagine that they come to a distant island and encounter a person from an unknown tribe (Nisbett et al. 1983). The person was brown in color and obese. The subjects were asked what percentage of the tribe they expect to be brown and what percentage they expect to be obese. The subjects answered on average that more than 95 percent would be brown, while less than 40 percent would be obese. If the sample was three individuals from the tribe who all were brown and obese, the corresponding figures were 95 and 55 percent. The subjects' expectations about the variability of the members of the tribe on the properties in question clearly influenced their judgments of the percentages.

The question then arises whether there is some way of generalizing the Voronoi tessellation that can account for varying sizes of concepts in a categorization, but which will still result in a convex partitioning of the underlying conceptual space. As a matter of fact, such a generalization is possible. The standard Voronoi tessellation is based on the ordinary Euclidean metric, so that to determine the lines that form the tessellation, one solves equations of the form

$$\Sigma_i (p_i - x_i)^2 = \Sigma_i (q_i - x_i)^2, \tag{1}$$

where $p = (p_1, \ldots, p_n)$ and $q = (q_1, \ldots, q_n)$ are the vectors of two prototypical points in the conceptual space. Instead of saying that there is only a prototypical *point* for a particular concept, however, one can introduce the notion of a prototypical *area* and then determine a *generalized* Voronoi tessellation by computing distances from such areas instead. In relation to the earlier example, the prototypical area for ducks could then be taken to be larger than the corresponding area for ostriches. This idea is modeled by assuming that the prototypical area for a concept is described by a *circle* with centre $p = (p_1, \ldots, p_n)$ and radius c_p. By varying the radius, one can change the size of the prototypical area (for example, the c_p for ducks would be larger than that for ostriches).

To determine the generalized Voronoi tessellation, one then solves equations of the form

$$\Sigma_i (p_i - x_i)^2 - c_p = \Sigma_i (q_i - x_i)^2 - c_q. \tag{2}$$

It can be shown that for all choices of prototypical circles, this equation generates a set of straight lines that will partition the space into convex subsets.[145] The metric generated by this kind of equation will *not* be Euclidean. All points on the prototypical circle will have distance zero from the prototype and, as a consequence, points within the circle will have imaginary numbers as distances.

A simple illustration of a generalized Voronoi tessellation is given by the lines in figure 4.9. The prototype Voronoi tessellation generated from the centers of the circles, corresponding to the prototypes, is indicated by hatched lines.

Before the generalized Voronoi tessellation can be applied, the constants c_p must be determined. A natural choice is to define c_p as the magnitude of the *standard deviation* of the exemplars from the prototype.[146] This choice entails that the generalized Voronoi tessellation can be

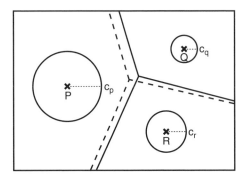

Figure 4.9
An example of a generalized Voronoi tessellation determined by the circles. The generalized Voronoi tessellation is represented by continuous lines and the prototype Voronoi tessellation by dashed lines.

completely determined from the coordinates of the exemplars of the different categories.

This method can be used to solve the problem on new information about typical objects that was presented in section 4.7.1. If I first learn that Gonzo is a bird and then that it is a robin, then the location of Gonzo in the space will not change if robins are prototypical birds. Since the standard deviation of birds is larger than that of robins, however, the generalized Voronoi circle associated with birds will be larger than that of robins. If we presume that the properties assigned nonmonotonically to an object are precisely those properties that *include* the assigned generalized Voronoi circle, then knowing that Gonzo is a robin will make it possible to draw more (default) inferences than when merely knowing that Gonzo is a bird.

The generalized Voronoi categorization can also be used to explain some alleged counter-examples to similarity-based accounts of concept formation. Rips (1989, 28–31) performed an experiment where subjects were asked to consider an object that was half-way between the size of an U.S. quarter and the smallest pizza they had seen. They then judged whether it was more likely to be a pizza than a quarter, whether it was more typical of a quarter or a pizza, and whether this object was more similar to a pizza than to a quarter (disjoint groups of subjects were asked the different questions). About 40 percent of the subjects reported that the object was more similar to a pizza, but 60 percent reported that it was more typical of a pizza and as many as 70 percent that it really was a pizza. From this and other similar experiments Rips concluded that categorization cannot be based on similarity judgments.

Smith and Sloman (1994) performed a couple of variations of Rips's experiment. In Rips's study, subjects were presented with a description of an object that mentioned only a single dimension, for example "an object 3 inches in diameter." Smith and Sloman (1994) call such descriptions "sparse." In one experiment, they used "sparse" descriptions of objects as well as "rich" that contained properties characteristic of the nonvariable category, for example, "a circular object with a 3-inch diameter that is silver colored." In contrast to Rips's results, they found that subjects' categorizations were based on similarity with both kinds of description. One difference between the experiments was that Rips's subjects were allowed to think aloud while making their categorization decisions. In a second experiment, Smith and Sloman (1994) also required subjects to think aloud. In this experiment, they found that categorization was not based on similarity with sparse descriptions of objects. With rich descriptions, however, categorizations were still based on similarity.

Given the mechanism of the generalized Voronoi categorization, however, Rips' result is not at all surprising. Similarity is judged on the *prototypes* of a quarter and a (small) pizza. But categorization takes *variability* into account: quarters do not vary at all in magnitude, while pizzas do come in different sizes.[147] Hence, the radius of the generalized Voronoi circle associated with pizza will be much larger than that of quarters (the latter is essentially zero). Consequently, it is in complete agreement with generalized Voronoi categorization that the unknown object is categorized as a pizza. When more dimensions are added, as in Smith and Sloman's rich descriptions, the variability effects may become smaller, which could explain the findings of their second experiment.

As noted in section 4.3.3, I believe that a similar argument concerning the variability of different concepts can be used to explain some of the data collected by Tversky and Hutchinson (1987) that appears problematic for geometrical models.

The generalized Voronoi tessellation corresponds to the following rule for categorization:

GENERALIZED VORONOI CATEGORIZATION (GV)   An object represented as a vector x_i in a conceptual space belongs to the category for which the corresponding prototypical circle is the closest.

Following Reed (1972), the results of the two Voronoi rules PV and GV will be compared to two other categorization rules:[148]

NEAREST NEIGHBOR CATEGORIZATION (NN)   An object represented as a vector x_i in a conceptual space belongs to the category to which the exemplar that is closest to x_i is included.[149]

AVERAGE DISTANCE CATEGORIZATION (AD)   An object represented as a vector x_i in a conceptual space belongs to the category to which x_i has the smallest average distance to the examples for the category.[150]

The AD rule is not identical to the PV rule. Nosofsky (1988b, 707) remarks that "when exemplar information is summed to form a prototype, information is lost concerning correlated values along individual component dimensions. . . ." This kind of correlation can be important in categorization (see section 6.6) and is, to some extent, preserved by the AD rule. Nevertheless, the four rules introduced here often result in very similar categorizations. As a consequence, it will sometimes become difficult to distinguish them in empirical tests about which rule best describes the behavior of subjects in classification tasks.

4.10 The Shell Space

Throughout all our experiments, we used depictions of *shell shapes* as stimuli. A shell normally grows in a spiralling way. According to Raup (1966), the shape of the shell is largely determined by three dimensions (see figure 4.10):

1. The rate E of whorl expansion that determines the curvature of the shell. The rate E, which is assumed to be a constant, is defined as the quotient e_{n+1}/e_n between the distance e_{n+1} of the central point to the generating axis and the distance e_n one revolution earlier. Small curvature results in densely spiralled shells, while a high curvature produces openly spiraled shapes.

2. The rate V of vertical translation along the coiling axis. The rate V is also assumed to be a constant. It is defined as the quotient v_{n+1}/v_n between the vertical distance v_{n+1} of the central point to the initial level on the generating axis and the corresponding distance v_n one revolution earlier. Having no vertical translation yields flat shells, while rapid growth results in elongated shapes.

3. The expansion rate R of the generating curve (the aperture) of the shell. The rate R, which is assumed to be constant, is defined as the quotient r_{n+1}/r_n between the radius r_{n+1} and the radius r_n one revolution earlier. Slow growth results in tube formed shells. Very rapid growth produces shells that look like those shown in

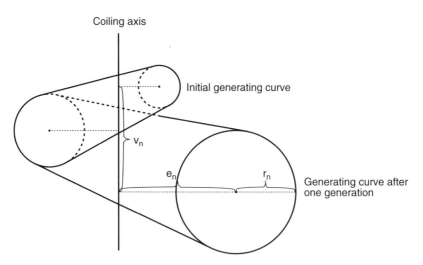

Figure 4.10
The three dimensions generating a shell shape.

figure 4.11c below. Our graphics program always used a circle as the aperture of the shell.

Figure 4.11 shows some examples of shapes that are produced by different combinations of values for the coordinates. All shell pictures here and in the following are generated by our program. The only input to the program are the three coordinates.

The three dimensions V, E, and R, span a space of possible shell shapes that is suitable for testing the four models of categorization described above. The conceptual space is defined, however, with the aid of three mathematical dimensions. As a preliminary step, it is

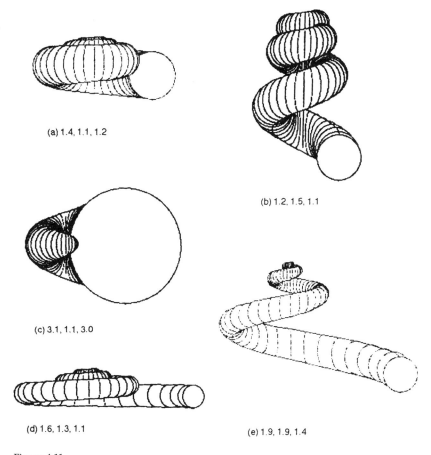

(a) 1.4, 1.1, 1.2

(b) 1.2, 1.5, 1.1

(c) 3.1, 1.1, 3.0

(d) 1.6, 1.3, 1.1

(e) 1.9, 1.9, 1.4

Figure 4.11
Some examples of shell shapes drawn by the graphics program together with their generating coordinates (rate of whorl expansion, vertical growth, growth of radius of aperture).

necessary to test the psychological validity of the hypothesis that our perceptions of shells also form a three-dimensional space. But even if the *phenomenal* shell space is three-dimensional, it does not follow that the metric of the space is the same as the mathematical coordinates used by the graphics program.[151] Before we can apply the four categorization models, it is necessary to establish the relevant psychological metric, the so-called scaling solution, of the shell space.

This methodology is supported by Shepard's (1987, 1318) recommendations for how psychological laws should be obtained:

> Analogously in psychology, a law that is invariant across perceptual dimensions, modalities, individuals, and species may be attained only by formulating the law with respect to the appropriate abstract psychological space. The previously troublesome variations in the gradient of generalisation might then be attributable to variations in the psycho-physical function that, for each individual, maps physical parameter space (the space whose coordinates include the physical intensity, frequency, and orientation of each stimulus) into that individual's psychological space. If so, a purely psychological function relating generalisations to distance in such a psychological space might attain invariance.

The three dimensions given by Raup's (1966) model are not the most natural ones from a perceptual point of view. We found that when estimating the vertical and horizontal growth rates of shells, subjects do not look at the center of the generating circle. Instead, they focus on its extreme points in the vertical and horizontal direction, loosely speaking the height and width of the shell. The vertical and horizontal expansion rates should instead be described by the following values:

$$V' = V + R - 1.$$

$$E' = E + R - 1.$$

Using the space generated by the dimensions V', E', and R, we wanted to check whether further transformations of the dimensions were necessary to obtain a satisfactory description of subjects' perceptions of shell forms. The transformations we tested for each of the dimensions were instances of Stevens' power law $d'(x) = w \cdot (d(x))^b$, where w is the weight of the dimension.[152] Since there were three dimensions (V', E', and R), we estimated the values of six parameters $w_{V'}$, $w_{E'}$, w_R and $b_{V'}$, $b_{E'}$, b_R. The optimal vector according to our analysis was (1, 1.55, 1, 1.72, 1, 0.99) which gave a correlation with subjects' average answers as high as 0.92.

These results strongly confirm our hypothesis that it is possible to identify an underlying perceptual space of shell shapes with sufficient accuracy. Since small changes of the optimal vector resulted in clearly smaller correlation coefficients, we decided to use the calibrated shell space that was generated by this vector in the main experiments.

There are several reasons why shell shapes constitute a useful domain for empirical investigations:

1. It is possible to generate a great number of fairly realistic shell shapes in a conceptual space that is built up from three dimensions.

2. The shells can easily be drawn by a graphic computer program where the only inputs are three coordinates in the shell space.

3. The pictures generated by our program are identified by the subjects as pictures of realistic 3-D shells. They are thus much more natural than most of the stimuli used in classification tasks in current cognitive psychology, for example, the dot-patterns (Posner and Keele 1968, Shin and Nosofsky 1992) or the semicircles with an additional radius (Nosofsky 1986, Ashby and Lee 1991). Not even the schematic faces used by Reed (1972) have a very high degree of "ecological validity" (Gibson 1979).

4. Even though test subjects recognize the object on the pictures as shells, they usually have no "prejudices" about how shells are actually categorized in biology in the sense that they have not already partitioned the shell space into categories. Consequently, in an experimental set-up, one can "create" new concepts for the subjects by showing appropriate shells, that is, more or less prototypical examples, in a desired region of the shell space. These newly learned concepts will then not be disturbed by prior categorizations of the space.

In the categorizations of the shells in our experiments, we assumed that only the shape domain is relevant. This is a simplifying assumption, since there may, of course, be other domains that influence the behavior of the subjects. The strong correlation between the values of the predictive model and the subjects' average answers, however, attest that other domains only have a marginal influence.

4.11 Experiments

The goal of the two main experiments was to evaluate the four categorization rules that were presented in section 4.9, that is, nearest neighbor categorization (NN), generalized Voronoi categorization (GV), prototype Voronoi categorization (PV), and average distance categorization (AD). The preliminary results from the pilot studies indicate that the best predictors are NN and GV.

The two main categorization experiments were based on different set-ups. In the first experiment, all the exemplars used to induce a category for a subject were visible on sheets of paper during the classifications of new test shells so that exemplars and test shells could be directly compared. We later assumed that such a setup would favor the NN model, which functions by comparing test shells to the exemplars. In contrast, the second experiment required subjects to *learn* the category from the exemplars presented on a computer screen. These exemplars were not shown when the new shells to be classified were presented.

4.11.1 Experiment 1

We expected that the closer a shell lies to a border between two categories in the psychological space, the more diversity we will find in the classification answers from the subjects. To model this intuition, we defined, for each of the four categorization models, a *predicted response frequency* for a given category x. Each of the four models provides a distance measure that determines the distance from the stimulus shell x to any category n. For PV, $d_{PV}(x, n)$ is the distance between x and the prototype for category n. For GV, $d_{GV}(x, n)$ is the distance between x and the prototypical circle for category n.[153] For NN, $d_{NN}(x, n)$ is the distance between x and the nearest shell in category n. For AD, $d_{AD}(x, n)$ is the average distance between x and the instances of category n.

If $d_M(x, n)$ is the distance function for one of the four models, we then define the predicted response frequency $p_M(x, n)$, the predicted number of times subjects will answer that the shell represented by x will belong to category n, by the following equation:

$$p_M(x, n) = d_M(x, n)^{-1} / \left(\Sigma_i d_M(x, i)^{-1} \right). \tag{4.3}$$

The main method of evaluating the predictive power of any of the four models is to compute the correlation between the predicted response frequency and the actual frequency.

The experimental data were classification judgments from the subjects. They first saw two (or sometimes three) groups of pictures of shells (three or four shells in each group). They were then shown a picture of a new shell and asked to classify this shell into one of the two (three) groups. In the trials where only two groups were involved, one sheet of paper with four exemplars of one group of shells, the "A-shells," was put on one side of a central sheet, and one sheet with four pictures of another group, the "B-shells," was put on the other side (the three sheets are presented simultaneously in figure 4.12). For each of the ten trials, between four and five pictures of test shells to be classified were then presented in a random order to the subjects.

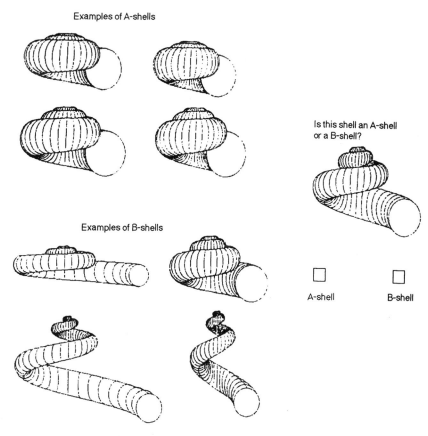

Examples of A-shells

Is this shell an A-shell
or a B-shell?

Examples of B-shells

☐   ☐
A-shell   B-shell

Figure 4.12
Example of classification of shells. Subjects were asked to check one of the squares.

In three of the ten trials, there were examples of three groups, "A-shells," "B-shells," and "C-shells." The purpose of these trials was to study the effects of adding a new category to a classification trial. For each test shell in all of the trials, the subjects were required to make a two-alternative (or three-alternative) forced choice decision, indicating whether the shell on the middle sheet was an A-shell or a B-shell (or a C-shell).

For each test shell x, let $f(x, A)$ be the actual frequency of subjects that classified x as an A-shell. For each model M among the four we studied, this number was compared to the predicted answer frequency $p_M(x, A)$. For each model, we computed the average squared sum of errors $\text{SSE} = \Sigma_x(p_M(x, A) - f(x, A))^2/n$, where n is the number of test shells involved. The smaller the SSE-value is for a model, the better is its predictive capacity.

The results suggest that NN has the best predictive power, while GV has the worst; however, the differences were not significant at the 5 percent level (t-test).[154] It should be remembered that we selected test shells that were close to the border lines between the categories that were generated by the four different models. One hypothesis that we formed at this stage concerned the case when the classification is a border-line case, in the sense that the test shell is perceived to be as similar to the A-shells as to the B-shells. In this case we predicted that subjects tend to focus on the A- or B-shells that are most similar to the test shell, which means that they employ the NN model so that the other models would not be applicable.

On the trials having variants with three categories, the results strongly support that the relations between the A- and B-category remained stable after the addition of the C-shells.

In experiment 1, the subjects could *see* the different examples of A- and B-shells during all trials. This is an advantage for the NN model since it benefits from visible examples. An easily accessible strategy (which may be unconsciously used by the subjects) is that to classify a test shell as an A- or a B-shell, a subject identifies the example among the *displayed* A- and B-shells that is *most similar* to the test shell and then classifies the test shell according to this example.

4.11.2 Experiment 2

In the second experiment, the shells were presented on a computer screen and not on paper sheets. The experiment was run in two phases. First, examples of A- and B-shells (and sometimes C-shells) were presented to the subjects and they were trained to *remember* the exemplars so that they could be correctly classified. The purpose of this identification learning was to induce the subjects to create some form of internal representation of the two (or three) categories.[155] Hence, the similarity judgments necessary for the NN model could not be based on direct visual information.

Only after this phase was completed could the subject see and classify new test shells in the same way as in experiment 1, but now the test shells were presented alone on the computer screen without the presence of the exemplars from the learning phase. Our hypothesis was that since this experimental setup blocked the visual availability of the different examples, we would obtain a better evaluation of the predictive power of the four categorization models, in particular the results of GV and NN.

In the learning phase, the subjects were instructed to determine what kind of shell was shown (without seeing the original pictures). The response time of the subject was measured by the program. The subject was informed by the program whether or not the response was correct. The identification learning procedure continued until the subject showed an error rate of less than 10 percent.

In the test phase, the subjects were presented with a series of test shells that were always different from the example shells. The subjects were asked to classify the test shell as one of the two (or three) categories that had been studied in the learning phase. Again, the response time was measured.

We hypothesized that the "naturalness" of a class of examples would be reflected in the difficulty of learning to correctly classify these examples in the first phase of a trial. To operationalize this we measured several variables, including *learning rounds*, which were defined as the number of presentations of the example shells that had to be made before a subject passed the 90 percent correctness level, *learning time*, which is the time a subject spent studying the screen with the two or three classes of examples before pressing the "ready" button, and *learning errors*, which were defined as the total number of classification errors during the learning phase. Apart from these three learning variables, we also measured *classification time*, which is the time it took for a subject to classify a test shell as an A- or B-shell (or C-shell) after it was presented on the screen.

First of all, when evaluating the results, the predictive accuracy of the models should be compared. This was done by calculating the average squared sum of errors (SSE) values for each trial.

The predictive power of the models was quite good. Out of the 34 test examples, PV made the same classification prediction as the majority of the subjects in 25 cases, GV in 26 cases, NN in 30 and AD in 22 cases. These figures should be seen as high since we have deliberately chosen test examples that are "difficult" in that they represent border cases for the categorization rules.

Our general hypothesis was that NN performed better than GV when the categorizations were "unnatural," that is, when the examples of a category were spread out over a large area of the shell space (like the B-shells in figure 4.10). Thus, the results of the models should be compared to the performance measures that were introduced above. The correlations among the three learning variables above were very high. Each of these will thus function as a reliable indicator of the difficulty for the subjects in forming the categorizations from the learning examples presented to them.

A central result of our investigation is the correlations between the SSE of GV and NN, which can be seen as measures of the predictive powers of the two models, and the performance values. The results suggest that there is a general negative correlation between how "natural" the concepts to be learned in the classifications trials are and the degree of misfit of PV, NN, and AD. Thus, these models have a smaller misfit when the trials are unnatural. The converse is true of GV which handles the "natural" concepts better, although the correlations are not quite as strong in this direction.

The general conclusion to be drawn from the two experiments is that none of the four models is superior overall to the others in explaining the subjects' classifications in all situations. In the process of testing the models, however, we have discovered that the difficulty in forming new categories and remembering them can vary enormously. We have used a number of performance measures (learning rounds, learning time, learning errors, and classification time) that serve as good indicators of the difficulty of forming a category from some exemplars. The strong correlations between these measures support their validity.

If the "naturalness" of a categorization trial is taken into account, a clearer pattern in the performance of the four models can be seen. If the exemplars used to generate a category form a "natural kind" so that categorization is "easy," then the GV model is the best predictor of the test results. On the other hand, if categorization is "unnatural," as measured by the indicators used above, then the NN model appears to perform best.

Summing up, the experiments have shown that the shell space is an example of a conceptual space that can become a rich source for investigations of human concept formation. The stimuli that are generated by the graphics program have a high degree of "ecological validity" (in the sense of Gibson 1979) compared to other kinds of stimuli that have been used in categorization experiments. Perhaps the most important finding of our experiments is that the level of "naturalness" of categorization, as measured by the indicators we have identified, has been shown to play an important role in the performance of the models.

Chapter 5

Semantics

5.1 What Is a Semantics?

5.1.1 Questions for a Semantic Theory
Everybody agrees that semantics concerns the relation between the words or expressions of a language and their meanings. But when it comes to explicating this relation, opinons soon diverge. As a consequence, there is a long-standing philosophical dispute concerning the meaning of "meaning." The semantic relation can, however, be studied from several perspectives. The aim here is not to settle the debate, but to structure it around four basic questions that a theory of semantics should be able to answer:

1. What are meanings? (the ontological question)
2. What is the relation between linguistic expressions and their meanings? (the semantic question)
3. How can the coupling between linguistic expressions and their meanings be learned? (the learnability question)
4. How do we communicate meanings? (the communicative question)

On the ontological question, a first division concerns whether semantics is *referential* or not—whether there are some kinds of objects that are the meanings of linguistic expressions. Within modern philosophy of language, one can find two fundamentally different referential answers to the ontological question, one *realist* and one *cognitive* (or *conceptualist*).[156] In the realist approach to semantics, the meaning of a word or expression is something out there *in the world*. According to the cognitivist answer, meanings are *mental entities*—things in the head. This chapter outlines how the theory of conceptual spaces can be used as a basis for a cognitive semantics.

Within the philosophy of language there is also a *functionalist* tradition of meaning that is nonreferential. An excellent survey of this tradition is given by Harder (1996, chapter 4). Perhaps the most well-known proponent of this view is the later Wittgenstein, who in

Philosophical Investigations (1953) defended a view that is often summarized by the slogan "meaning is use." Harder (1996, 101) provides this more precise account of the functionalist notion of meaning: "The (linguistic) meaning of a linguistic expression is its (canonical, proper) communicative function, i.e. its potential contribution to the communicative function of utterances of which it forms part."

He relates this definition to the position of the later Wittgenstein:

> The definition that equates the meaning of a word with its function (rather than with the representational content itself) updates Wittgenstein's famous dictum about meaning as use in two ways. First, it explicitly filters off accidental aspects of the use of an expression; secondly, it avoids the antimentalistic stance: the mental element is necessary, but does not in itself constitute meaning—meaning needs to be understood as communicative potential for the speaker. (Harder 1996, 105)

By explicitly defining meaning as communication, however, the functionalist tradition makes meaning a part of *pragmatics* rather than part of a narrower semantic theory. There is no immediate conflict between a functionalist position and the cognitivist theory that will be focused on here. Even though I agree with the functionalists that part of the meaning of some expressions is only determined in the context of its use, I want to argue that for many kinds of expressions a semantic meaning can be modeled independently of its communicative use.[157]

Why is the ontological status of meanings so important? Apart from its long-standing philosophical bearings, a different kind of motivation comes from the constructive aims of cognitive science. When building robots that are capable of linguistic communication, the constructor must decide at an early stage how the robot grasps the meaning of words. A fundamental methodological decision is whether the meanings are determined by the state of the world or whether they are based on the robot's internal model of the world. I view only the latter option as a viable alternative.[158]

5.1.2 A Classification of Semantic Theories

For the referential types of semantics one needs to account for *how* linguistic expressions are related to their meanings. Realist semantics comes in two flavors: *extensional* and *intensional*. These positions have been presented in section 3.2 in connection with the analysis of properties. In the extensional type of semantics, the constituents of the language become mapped onto a "world." Names are mapped onto objects, predicates are mapped onto sets of objects or relations between objects, and so forth. By *compositions* of these mappings, sentences are mapped onto truth values.

The main objective of this kind of semantics is to formulate *truth conditions* for the sentences in the language. Such conditions are supposed to determine the meaning of the expressions in that they specify the way the world should be constituted if the sentences of the language are to be true. By specifying truth conditions, one intends to describe the semantic *knowledge* of competent speakers. A consequence of this approach is that the meaning of an expression is *independent* of how individual users understand it. The first developed theory of this type is Frege's semantics, but it acquires a more precise form in Tarski's theory of truth. Schematically, the semantic mapping can be illustrated as in figure 5.1.

The extensional theory of reference implicit in this kind of semantics was soon found to be wanting as an account of several phenomena in natural languages. To handle some of these problems, so-called *intensional* semantics was developed by logicians and linguists. In this brand of semantics, the set of linguistic expressions is mapped onto a set of *possible worlds* instead of only a single world (compare section 3.2). The goal of intensional semantics is still to provide truth conditions for the sentences. The meaning of a sentence is taken to be a *proposition* that is identified with a set of possible worlds: the set of worlds where the sentence is true. The setting can be illustrated as in figure 5.2.

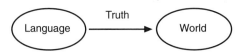

Figure 5.1
The ontology of extensional semantics.

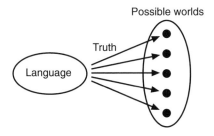

Figure 5.2
The ontology of intensional semantics.

As an alternative to possible worlds semantics, *situation semantics* was developed during the 1980s (see, for example, Barwise and Perry 1983). Instead of mapping the linguistic expressions onto a set of possible worlds, they were connected to "situations." Situations consist of a number of "facts" that are built up from relations among individuals. Instead of a truth value, a fact contains a "polarity value" that expresses whether the fact holds in the situation or not. Situations are *partial* descriptions of the world (Barwise 1981). Consequently, situation semantics is also a branch of realist semantics. The general structure is illustrated in figure 5.3.

We next turn to the conceptualist (alias cognitive) approach to the semantic question which will be the focus of this chapter. The core idea is that meanings of linguistic expressions are *mental entities*—meanings are elements of the cognitive structure in the heads of the language users.[159] Language itself is seen as part of the cognitive structure and not an entity with independent standing. The framework of cognitive semantics can be illustrated as in figure 5.4.

A semantics is described as a mapping from the expressions to a conceptual structure. This mapping can be seen as a set of *associations* between words and meanings—associations that have been established when the individual learned the language. According to this view, language represents a conceptual structure, but it does not directly represent the world (see below).

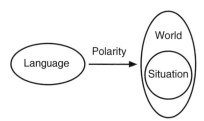

Figure 5.3
The ontology of situation semantics.

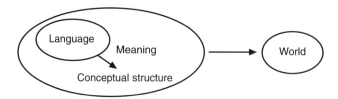

Figure 5.4
The components of cognitive semantics.

A special case of such a mapping is Jackendoff's "conceptual semantics" where the mapping between the linguistic expressions and the conceptual structure is seen as a cognitive version of the model-theoretic semantics developed by Tarski or Kripke (see Jackendoff 1990, 12–13). For Jackendoff, the meaning relation is described by traditional truth conditions, with the exception that the referents of the linguistic expressions are mental representations instead of entities in an external world. In principle, this does not put his position in conflict with the one proposed here. As argued in section 5.5, however, it is difficult to combine truth conditions with the idea that the semantic mapping consists of associations between words and meanings. Furthermore, Jackendoff does not exploit any geometrical structure of the mental representation.

Since both linguistic expressions and their meanings are in the head of an *individual*, a semantics for a language is primarily connected to a single speaker (or listener). Prima facie, this appears to be an enigma for the cognitive approach to semantics: meanings are things that are *common* to the language users. A possible solution to this problem, which is essentially the communicative problem, is outlined in sections 5.9 and 5.10. The idea is that the conceptual structures of different individuals will become *attuned* to each other, otherwise linguistic communication will break down. Thus, for practical purposes, cognitive linguists often write as if every (adult) speaker of a language is endowed with the same conceptual structure.

Interestingly enough, something very much like a conceptualist theory of semantics is found in Aristotle's *De Interpretatione*. The following is an excerpt from the first paragraph of E. M. Edghill's translation: "Spoken words are the symbols of mental experience and written words are the symbols of spoken words. Just as all men have not the same writing, so all men have not the same speech sounds, but the mental experiences, which these directly symbolize, are the same for all, as also are those things of which our experiences are the images."

Aristotle makes a distinction between "mental experiences" and the "things" of which the experiences are "images." Furthermore, spoken or written words refer to the mental experiences and not to any external reality. He assumes, however, that the mental experience of all speakers is the same. This is not obvious for a cognitive theory of semantics since individual conceptual structures, and thereby meanings, may be very different prima facie.

De Saussure (1966) also proposes a conceptualist analysis of the signification relation. The following excerpt from the first paragraph of his first chapter illustrates this:

[F]or some people a language, reduced to its essentials, is a nomenclature: a list of terms corresponding to a list of things. . . . This conception is open to a number of objections. It assumes that ideas already exist independently of words. . . . It does not clarify whether the name is a vocal or psychological entity. . . . Furthermore, it leads one to assume that the link between a name and a thing is something quite unproblematic, which is far from being the case. None the less, this naive view contains one element of truth, which is that linguistic units are dual in nature, comprising two elements. . . .

[T]he two elements involved in the linguistic sign are both psychological and are connected in the brain by an associative link. This is a point of major importance.

A linguistic sign is not a link between a thing and a name, but between a concept and a sound pattern.

Like Aristotle, de Saussure appears to assume that the linguistic sign—the link between a concept and a sound pattern—is the same for all users of a language.

5.1.3 The Relation between the Conceptual Structure and the World

In figure 5.4 the nature of the relation between the conceptual structure and the world is left unspecified. We have a strong sense that some of our utterances have a fit to reality. The question then is what *is* the relation between the conceptual structure and reality according to cognitive semantic theories? There is no unique answer to this question, but here I adopt a *pragmatic* account.[160] The appropriate question on the relation between the conceptual structure and the world is whether a conceptual structure is *viable* or not. Having a viable conceptual structure means that one is able to solve the essential problems when acting in the world.

Via successful and less successful interactions with the world, the conceptual structure of an individual will adapt to the structure of reality. It must be emphasized, however, that this does not entail that the conceptual structure *represents* the world.[161] Take color vision, for example, where Thompson (1995, 29) defends a pragmatic view of conceptual structures:

[T]he biological function of colour vision is not to detect surface reflectance, but rather to generate a set of colour categories that have significance for the perceptual guidance of activity. In my view, the categories that give structure to colour perception are indeed modes of *presentation* in visual perception, but they are not modes of *representation*, at least not in the typical computationalist [realist] sense, because colour perception does not represent something that is already present in the world apart from perceivers; rather, it presents the world in a manner that satisfies the perceiver's adaptive ecological needs. . . .

The *epistemological* question of the relation between the conceptual structure and the world must be kept separated from the *semantic* question of the relation between linguistic expressions and the conceptual structure. Grasping the meanings of linguistic expressions is a combination of having the right associations from the words to a conceptual structure and having a viable conceptual structure. A person who has severe misunderstandings of the meanings of the words of a language will, by the failures of his plans or his attempts to communicate, be forced to revise either his semantic mapping or his conceptual structure.

In particular, our conceptual representation of *space* must be well attuned both to our perceptions of space and the way we express spatial structures in language. As Bryant (1997, 240) points out this is important ". . . because of the need to coordinate action in space on the basis of perceptual and linguistic information. In other words, one must move given what one has seen, but also given what one has been told. Effective coordination of action depends on having a representational format that can incorporate both kinds of information and extract the abstract, amodal structure of the environment."

This chapter attempts to show how the conceptual structure required for a cognitive semantics can be modeled with the aid of conceptual spaces. To start, I discuss whether words or sentences form the building blocks of a semantics. Then, in section 5.2, I outline some of the main tenets of cognitive semantics as it has developed during the last years. This position will be contrasted with the extensional and intensional semantics, but my goal is not primarily to criticize these kinds of semantics.[162] In the following sections, the semantic model is then applied to some problems in lexical semantics, including a theory of metaphors. The last part of the chapter treats the communicative question, arguing that semantics cannot be seen as purely intramental (and individual), but that a certain *social* component, in the form of a linguistic power structure, is also required.

5.1.4 Lexical Meaning versus Truth Conditions
Even though cognitive linguists often deny that there is a sharp distinction between lexicon and syntax, the emphasis of the studies within cognitive semantics has been on *lexical meaning* rather than on the meaning of sentences. Hence most of the analyses concern relations

between words and representations of *concepts*, for example, the "image schemas" developed by Langacker (1987), Lakoff (1987), and Talmy (1988). Such schemas are abstract pictures constructed from elementary topological and geometrical structures like "container," "link," and "source-path-goal." A common assumption is that such schemas constitute the representational form that is common to perception, memory, and semantic meaning. In contrast, traditional semantic theories within philosophy have focused on logical operators—for example, quantifiers—and *sentences* have been the main units of analysis. Consequently, these two semantic traditions often talk past each other.

Within philosophical logic, the focus has been on sentences. In section 3.3, I presented Putnam's theorem that can be taken to show that the traditional truth-functional accounts of meaning do not work. It appears that the point of Putnam's theorem was anticipated, in an informal way, by Quine.[163] Assuming a traditional truth-functional account of semantics, Quine writes (1979, 165):

> What were observational were not terms but observation sentences. Sentences, in their truth or falsity, are what run deep; ontology is by the way.
>
> The point gains in vividness when we reflect on the multiplicity of possible interpretations of any consistent formal system. For consider again our standard regimented notation, with a lexicon of interpreted predicates and some fixed range of values for the variables of quantification. The sentences of this language that are true remain true under countless reinterpretations of the predicates and revisions of the range of values of the variables.

The moral that Quine draws from this, however, is not that there is something wrong with truth-conditional semantics (as I suggest). He prefers to retain the truth conditions and acknowledges that reference is indeterministic:

> Perhaps our primary concern belongs with the truth of sentences and with their truth conditions, rather than with the reference of terms. If we adopt this attitude, questions of reference and ontology become incidental. Ontological stipulations can play a role in the truth conditions of theoretical sentences, but a role that could be played as well by any number of alternative ontological stipulations. The indecisiveness of ordinary language toward questions of reference is the more readily excused. (1979, 165)

I do not agree. I maintain that a cognitive approach to semantics requires that meaning be separated from truth conditions. The meaning of an expression is a conceptual structure (with its own ontology) that must be determined *before* the correspondence with the world, that is, truth conditions, can be discussed. In the analytic philosophy of language emanating from Frege, it has been taken for granted that sentences are the principal carriers of meaning, as witnessed in the quotation from Quine above.[164] Within model theory itself, however, this has not been the case, since the "interpretations" of a formal language have been built up from assignments of meanings to names and predicates. In addition to rejecting truth-functional semantics, I believe that the semantics of *words* in general should be given primacy to a semantics of *sentences*. A completely atomistic approach to meanings, however, cannot be upheld: the meaning of many verbs, for instance, is inseparable from the syntactic context in which they appear.[165]

The root of the problem is that within analytic philosophy, language has been seen as an *abstract* system, preferably formal and rule-based, that exists independently of its users and of other cognitive functions.[166] In contrast, a cognitive approach to semantics puts language in the heads of the users and connects it to perception, memory, action, and mental representation in general. It is, indeed, *we* that give meaning to language.

5.2 Six Tenets of Cognitive Semantics

According to the cognitive view, semantics is a relation between linguistic expressions and a cognitive structure. The main proposal here is that the appropriate framework for the cognitive structure is a conceptual space. Some general aspects of using conceptual spaces as a foundation for a cognitive semantics are discussed here. In particular, I want to show that conceptual spaces provide an appropriate *ontology* for such a semantics.

A programmatic presentation of cognitive semantics in the form of six tenets is presented here, together with some comments (see also Gärdenfors 1996c). The approach of a cognitively oriented semantics will be contrasted with the more traditional realist cum symbolic view. Prime examples of works in the cognitive tradition are Lakoff's (1987) and Langacker's (1987, 1991a, 1991b). Related versions of cognitive semantics can be found in the writings of Johnson-Laird (1983), Fauconnier (1985), Talmy (1988), Rudzka-Ostyn (1988), Sweetser (1990), Holmqvist (1993), Allwood and Gärdenfors (1999), and many others. There is also a French semiotic tradition, exemplified by Desclés (1985) and Petitot (1985, 1992, 1995), that shares many features with the American group. Jackendoff's (1983, 1987a, 1990, 1997) "conceptual semantics" shows some similarities, but he tries to marry it to a

Chomskian style of syntax. In the following sections, I give some examples of how the cognitive approach to semantics can be merged with the theory of conceptual spaces.

I   Meaning is a *conceptual structure* in a cognitive system (not truth conditions in possible worlds).

The prime slogan for cognitive semantics is *meanings are in the head*. More precisely, a semantics for a language is seen as a mapping from the expressions of the language to some cognitive entities. Harnad (1987, 550) says that ". . . the meanings of elementary symbols must be grounded in perceptual categories. That is, symbols, which are manipulated only on the basis of their form (i.e., syntactically) rather than their 'meaning,' must be reducible to nonsymbolic, shape-preserving representations."

This thesis puts cognitive semantics in contact with psychological notions and makes it possible to talk about a speaker "grasping" a meaning (compare Jackendoff 1983). As noted in the previous section, a consequence of the cognitivist position that puts it in conflict with many other semantic theories is that no reference to reality is necessary to determine the meaning of a linguistic expression. Jackendoff (1987a, 123) says, "The buck stops here: expressions at the level of conceptual structure simply *are* the meanings of utterances." A related point is that the truth of expressions is considered to be secondary since truth concerns the relation between a cognitive structure and the world. To put it tersely; *meaning comes before truth*.

Sometimes Fodor's (1975) "language of thought" hypothesis is grouped with cognitive semantics, but the two should be kept strictly separated. There are some superficial similarities, though: Fodor also uses mental entities to represent linguistic information. This is his "language of thought" which is sometimes also called "Mentalese." According to Fodor, this is what speakers use when they compute inferences (according to some internal set of rules) and when they formulate verbal responses (translated back from Mentalese to some appropriate natural language). The mental entities constituting Mentalese, however, form a symbolic *language* with syntactic structures governed by some recursive set of rules. And when it comes to the *semantics* of Mentalese, Fodor still is a realist and relies on references in the external world as well as truth conditions (see Fodor 1975, 79–84).

II   Conceptual structures are *embodied* (meaning is not independent of perception or of bodily experience).

Since the cognitive structures in our heads are connected to our perceptual mechanisms, directly or indirectly, it follows that *meanings are*, at least partly, *perceptually grounded.*[167] Jackendoff (1983, 16–18) formulates this as "the cognitive constraint":

> There must be levels of mental representation at which information conveyed by language is compatible with information from other peripheral systems such as vision, nonverbal audition, smell, kinesthesia, and so forth. If there were no such levels, it would be impossible to use language to report sensory input. We couldn't talk about what we see and hear. Likewise, there must be a level at which linguistic information is compatible with information eventually conveyed to the motor system, in order to account for our ability to carry out orders and instructions.

Following Johnson (1987) (and also Lakoff 1987, Clark 1997, Zlatev 1997, Bailey et al. 1998) it is appropriate to go even further and say that meanings are *embodied*, that is, the conceptual structures are tied to bodily experiences and to emotions. Conceptual spaces are well suited for modeling the perceptual and embodied aspects of semantics since many basic dimensions have a grounding in perception or kinaesthetics.

The second tenet is also in conflict with traditional realist versions of semantics which claim that since meaning is a mapping between the linguistic expressions and the external world (or several worlds), meaning has nothing to do with perception. The relation between language and perception will be discussed further in section 5.5 in connection with the learnability question.

III   Semantic elements are constructed from *geometrical* or *topological* structures (not symbols that can be composed according to some system of rules).

Instead of being a symbolic system, with syntactic structure like Mentalese, the conceptual schemes that are used to represent meanings are often based on spatial or force dynamic constructions. As will be seen in the following sections, conceptual spaces function very well as a framework for representing such semantic elements.

In particular, there is a strong similarity between the domains of a conceptual space as defined in section 1.8 and the domains as used in Langacker's (1987) semantic theory. The following quotation concerning his notion strongly supports this thesis:

> What occupies the lowest level in conceptual hierarchies? I am neutral in regard to the possible existence of conceptual primitives. It is however necessary to posit a number of "basic domains," that is, cognitively irreducible representational spaces

or fields of conceptual potential. Among these basic domains are the experience of time and our capacity for dealing with two- and three-dimensional spatial configurations. There are basic domains associated with various senses: color space (an array of possible color sensations), coordinated with the extension of the visual field; the pitch scale; a range of possible temperature sensations (coordinated with positions on the body); and so on. Emotive domains must also be assumed. It is possible that certain linguistic predications are characterized solely in relation to one or more basic domains, for example time for (BEFORE), color space for (RED), or time and the pitch scale for (BEEP). However, most expressions pertain to higher levels of conceptual organization and presuppose nonbasic domains for their semantic characterization. (Langacker 1987, 5)

IV   Cognitive models are primarily *image-schematic* (not propositional). Image-schemas are transformed by *metaphoric* and *metonymic* operations (which are treated as exceptional features on the traditional view).

The main metonymic operations are *pars pro toto*, where a part represents a whole as in "there are twenty heads in the class room," and *toto pro pars*, where a whole represents a part as in "Paris announces shorter skirts."

The most important semantic structure in cognitive semantics is that of an *image schema*. A common assumption is that such schemas constitute the form of representation common to perception, memory, and semantic meaning (compare tenet II). Image schemas have an inherent spatial structure. Lakoff (1987) and Johnson (1987) argue that schemas such as "container," "source-path-goal," and "link" are among the most fundamental carriers of meaning. They also claim that most image schemas are closely connected to *kinaesthetic* experiences.

As an example of an image schema, consider Langacker's (1991b, 22) depiction of "across" in figure 5.5. According to Langacker, the meaning of "across" is a "complex atemporal relation" where one object, the *trajector* (the small circle in figure 5.5) is located in different relations to another elongated object, the *landmark* (the thick rectangle in figure 5.5). First, the trajector is outside the landmark, then it is inside, and finally it is on the other side. The image schema contains two domains: a *time dimension*, marked by the horizontal arrow at the bottom of figure 5.5, and *two spatial dimensions*, indicated by the thin rectangle that is repeated five times in different stages of the crossing. Note that the geometrical notions presumed in this schema are "elongated," "outside," "inside," and "the other side," which are quite weak in the sense that they do not presume that the space has a metric.

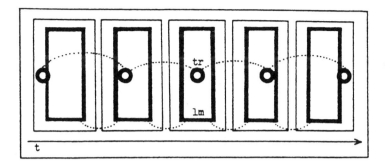

Figure 5.5
An image schema for "across" (from Langacker 1991b, 22).

Neither Lakoff nor Langacker, who use the notion extensively, give a very precise description of what constitutes an image schema. Zlatev (1997, 40–44) argues that the notion is used in different ways by different cognitive semanticists. The most condensed account I have found comes from Gibbs and Colston (1995, 349), who define image schemas as "dynamic analog representations of spatial relations and movements in space." Unlike Lakoff and Langacker, who focus on the spatial structure of image schemas, this definition puts the dynamics of the representations in focus.

My proposal is that a more precise account of what constitutes an image schema can be given with the aid of the theory of conceptual spaces. The image schemas are often just *topological* structures. A "container", for example, is a closed border that separates space into "inside" and "outside." An object such as a cup may count as a container even though is it not physically closed. Cognitively, the rim surface of the cup functions as part of the border (see Herskovits 1986 for a discussion of how the border is determined). In the following section, I give some examples of how the topological and geometrical structures of conceptual spaces are helpful in modeling lexical meanings.

The writers within cognitive linguistics present lists of image schemas but never any analysis of which schemas are possible and which are not. A developed theory of images schemas should present a principled account of what constitutes a schema. A fascinating proposal in this direction is that of Thom (1970, 232) who claims that any basic phrase expressing an interactive process can be described as one out of sixteen fundamental types. Among these types one finds "begin," "unite," "capture," and "cut." The sixteen types are derived from some deep mathematical results on "morphologies" within catastrophe theory. Even if there are excellent mathematical reasons why there are exactly sixteen types of interaction, it is not obvious that they correspond neatly to cognitive representations, although such a correspondence would be very gratifying.

An image schema is a conceptual structure that belongs to a particular *individual*. When the authors within cognitive linguistics write about them, however, they are often presented as structures that are common to all speakers of a language. In most situations this is a reasonable assumption for several reasons. One is that since basic image schemas are supposed to represent perceptual and other bodily experiences, the very fact that humans have similar constitutions make it likely that our representations are very similar. Furthermore, if the image schema corresponding to a particular expression is markedly different for two individuals, it is likely that this will lead to problems of communication. A desire for successful communication will therefore lead to a gradual alignment among the members of a linguistic community of the image schemas as well as their underlying conceptual spaces. This process will be further discussed in sections 5.6 and 5.7.

Metaphors and metonymies have been notoriously difficult to handle within realist semantic theories. In these theories such linguistic figures have been treated as deviant phenomena that have been ignored or incorporated via special stylistic rules. In contrast, they are given key positions within cognitive semantics. Not only poetic metaphors but also everyday "dead" metaphors are seen as central semantic features and are given systematic analyses. One of the first works in this area was Lakoff and Johnson (1980). Analyses of different kinds of metaphorical expressions have since then become one of the trademarks of cognitive semantics (see, for example, Brugman 1981, Tourangeau and Sternberg 1982, Indurkhya 1986, Lakoff 1987, 1994, Sweetser 1990, Broström 1994, and Gärdenfors 1996b, 1996c). Metaphors will be analyzed with the aid of conceptual spaces in section 5.4.

Metaphors and metonymies are primarily seen as *cognitive* operations, and their linguistic expression is only a secondary phenomenon. They are analyzed as *transformations* of image schemas. Such transformations involve operations on spatial structures. In line with this, Lakoff (1987, 283) puts forward what he calls the "spatialization of form hypothesis" which says that the meanings of linguistic expressions should be analyzed as spatial image schemas plus metaphorical mappings. For example, many uses of prepositions, which primarily have a spatial meaning, are seen as metaphorical when applied to other domains (see, for example, Brugman 1981 and Herskovits 1986).

v *Semantics* is primary to syntax and partly determines it (syntax cannot be described independently of semantics).

This thesis is anathema to the Chomskian tradition within linguistics. Within Chomsky's school, grammar is a *formal calculus*, which can be described via a system of rules, where the rules are formulated independently of the meaning of the linguistic expressions. Semantics is something that is added, as a secondary independent feature, to the grammatical rule system. Similar claims are made for pragmatic aspects of language.

Within cognitive linguistics, semantics is the primary component (which, in the form of conceptual representations, exists before, both phylogenetically and ontogenetically, syntax is fully developed).[168] The structure of the semantic schemas puts constraints on the possible grammars that can be used to represent those schemas. Petitot (1995, 232), who is building on a proposal from Thom, formulates the idea very clearly (see also Dixon 1982, 8):

> One of our main theses is that syntactic structures linking participant roles in verbal actions are organized by universals and invariants of a topological, geometric, and morphological nature. This thesis is deeply akin to the work . . . concerning the central cognitive role of spatial and temporal Gestalten or image schemas. Actually, we will show how constituent structures can be retrieved from the morphologial analysis of perceptual scenes.

Later on, he puts the position in stark contrast to the Chomskian symbolic theory:

> The formal universals, which are not characterizable within the theory of formal grammars, need not necessarily be conceived of as innate. They can be explained by *cognitive* universal structures. . . . Insofar as these structures are not symbolic but of a topological and dynamical nature, there exists in syntax a *deep iconicy*. At this level, semantics and syntax are inseparable: syntax is no longer an independent and autonomous linguistic dimension. (Petitot 1995, 256)

Since the cognitive analysis focuses more on speech acts rather than on free-floating sentences, the meaning of the modals is partly determined by a *pragmatic* analysis, and thus it does not provide just a semantics in the sense of philosophical logic. Traditionally, semantics concerns the meaning of expressions, while pragmatics concerns their use (but compare section 5.4.3 below). But if the meanings of certain expressions, like the modal verbs studied in Talmy (1988) and Winter and Gärdenfors (1995), cannot be determined without recourse to their use, the traditional distinction between semantics and pragmatics may not be sustainable.

There is also a sense in which semantics to some extent not only determines syntax but also the *logic* of the language. If the meanings of the predicates are determined by a mapping into regions of a conceptual space S, it follows from the geometrical structure of different domains that certain statements will become *analytically* true in the sense that they are independent of empirical considerations. For example the fact that comparative relations like "earlier than" are *transitive* follows from the linear structure of the time dimension and is thus an analytic feature of this relation (analytic-in-S, that is).[169] Similarly, it is analytic that everything that is green is colored, since "green" refers to a region of the color domain, and that nothing is both red and green (all over), since these words refer to disjoint regions of the color domain.

Analytic-in-S can thus be defined on the basis of the topological and geometrical structure of the conceptual space S together with the partitioning into regions for concepts.[170] Since different conceptual spaces, however, do not have the same underlying geometrical or topological structure, they will yield different notions of analyticity.[171]

The Chomskian tradition within linguistics has been dominated by syntactic studies. Since grammars are represented by formal rules, they are suitable for computer implementations. This kind of work has, to be sure, been the main focus of computational linguistics.

Within cognitive semantics, computer friendly representations are much rarer. Implementing the diagrammatic representations of Langacker's and Lakoff's image schemas are tough challenges for a programmer. One notable exception is Holmqvist (1993, 1994, 1999), who develops implementable representations of image schemas and other concepts from the cognitive linguists. To some extent, he is inspired by Langacker's compositional image schemas and Lang's spatial models (see Lang, Carstensen, and Simmons 1991), but he extends their formalisms to much richer computational structures in particular *superimpositions* of image schemas.[172] In his (1994) he also utilizes an old idea of Behaghel to generate grammatical structure from the valence expectations of different lexical items. The result is something that looks like a rule-governed syntax, albeit there is no single explicit syntactic rule in the system. Also Regier's (1996) and Zlatev's (1997) implementations of spatial expressions take some steps in this direction. The upshot is that much of syntax is semantically motivated.[173]

vi   Concepts show *prototype* effects (instead of following the Aristotelian paradigm based on necessary and sufficient conditions).

The prototype theory of concepts was presented in section 3.8. Within cognitive semantics, one attempts to account for prototype effects of concepts (Lakoff 1987). A concept is often represented in the form of an image schema and such schemas can show variations just like birds and chairs. As we have seen, prototype effects are difficult to model using traditional symbolic structures: the predicates that are used in most formal representations are supposed to have a precise denotation and graded membership must be represented in an *ad hoc* fashion.

5.3 Analyses of Some Aspects of Lexical Semantics

Here and in the following sections, I turn to lexical aspects of *natural* languages. I have no ambition of providing a comprehensive analysis of the semantics of the lexical items of a language, but I will focus on some areas where the theory of conceptual spaces has immediate applications. I intend to show that geometry and topology are useful tools when analyzing meanings. The basis for the lexical analyses is the following fundamental semantic thesis (L for "lexical"):

L: Basic lexical expressions in a language are represented semantically as natural concepts.

Here, "basic" should be taken in the sense of prototype theory (as discussed in sections 3.8) and "natural concept" in the sense of section 4.2—being represented by a convex region of a conceptual space (or, as a weaker claim, as connected or star-shaped regions). It is still rather unclear how far the applicability of this thesis ranges. It can be given further content by being specified to the following grammatical categories:

LA: Basic adjectives are represented semantically as natural properties.

Recall that a property is a concept only represented in one domain (see section 3.1).[174]

LV: Basic verbs are represented semantically as dynamic natural concepts.

By a dynamic concept, I mean a concept that involves the time domain (see section 3.9).

LN: Basic nouns are represented semantically as multidomain, nondynamic natural concepts (see section 4.2).

Apart from these word classes, *prepositions* have been studied extensively within cognitive semantics (for example, Herskovits 1986, Lakoff

1987, Bowermann 1991, Landau and Jackendoff 1993, Zwarts 1995, Regier 1996, Zlatev 1997, Zwarts and Winter 1998, Helmantel 1998). The basic semantic function of prepositions is to express *spatial relations*, but they also have obtained a number of metaphorical and metonymic extensions.[175] A neurolinguistic connection is brought forward by Landau and Jackendoff (1993), who propose that there are two distinct cognitive systems for *objects* the "what" system, and for *places* the "where" system. These systems are connected to two different pathways of the visual cortex. The separation of the systems result in a separation between a *nominal* and a *prepositional* system in language.[176]

The criteria LA, LV, and LN should be seen as programmatic theses, and they will presumably have numerous counterexamples. Nevertheless, they contain the embryo for a *semantic foundation for word classes* based on conceptual spaces.[177]

On thesis LA, it was argued in section 3.5 that most properties expressed by simple words in natural languages correspond to connected (or star-shaped or convex) regions. I predict that there is no language, for example, that has a single color word for the hues denoted by "green" and "orange" in English (and which denotes no other colors), since such a word would represent two disjoint areas in the color space. Theoretically, the analysis presented in chapter 3 thus directly provides a cognitive semantics for all words that express (basic) properties. An impediment is that for many words in natural languages that denote properties, we have only vague ideas, if any at all, about what are the underlying conceptual dimensions and their geometrical structure.

As an example of thesis LV, consider an image schema representing the verb "leave." In the theory of image schemas, developed by Lakoff (1987) and Langacker (1987) among others, "leave" would be analyzed as a *dynamic process* where the thing departing, the *trajector*, follows a *path* from the inside to the outside of the neighborhood of the presumed point of departure, the *landmark*. This process is depicted in figure 5.6. Several verbs like "sit" and "support" do not not express any movement, but they can nevertheless be described as dynamic since they involve *forces* (acting and counteracting) in a nontrivial way.

The horizontal dimension is the time dimension and the vertical is a spatial dimension representing *distance* from the landmark rather than any particular spatial direction. The core of the meaning of "leave" is a change in the spatial relation of the trajector to the landmark, going from closeness to being distant. Thus the scheme is basically topological, representing a change in the spatial relation of the trajector to the

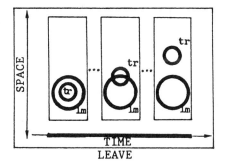

Figure 5.6
An image-schematic representation of "leave" from Langacker (1988, 96). The object departing is the trajector tr which is leaving the landmark lm.

landmark and going from inclusion (or closeness) to separateness (and being distant).[178]

Technically, the meaning of "leave" can be represented as *the set of all paths* of a trajector that fulfil this general condition. Even though I have no precise definition of betweenness for paths, it appears reasonable to claim that this set is *convex*, in the sense that for any two paths p and q representing a departure from a point x, any path in between p and q will also represent a departure from x. It is thus a (dynamic) natural concept in conformity with LV.

For an example involving another domain, consider "shout." Shouting is represented as a dynamic process involving primarily a path within the *loudness* dimension. Again, I would predict that the set of all such paths representing shouting is a convex set. In this case where the paths run along the time dimension (they are bijective functions), it is easy to define betweenness: path p is between paths q and r, if and only if $q(t) \le p(t) \le r(t)$, for all points of time t (or $r(t) \le p(t) \le q(t)$).

A more action oriented cognitive model of verb meanings has been proposed by Bailey et al. (1998). The key notion is that of an *executing schema* (which replaces image schemas). These schemas represent actions that are executed and they contain information about the movements and postures of different body parts as well as information about the object that is interacted with (if any). Bailey et al. (1998) describe a simulated agent based on executing schemas that can learn to label actions (hand motions) and to carry out similar actions.

As a paradigmatic example of LN one can take the analysis of "apple" from section 4.2. Nouns do not merely denote physical objects that are located within a limited spatial region—consider, for example, "thunder," "family," and "language," let alone more abstract nouns.

Rather, a noun typically denotes a phenomenon that shows a number of *correlations* in a number of domains. Thus, nouns are represented by clusters in the conceptual space (see also section 5.8.2). Not all clusters of correlations that exist, however, will be named by nouns in a language—an important factor is whether the correlations have a (potential) pragmatic significance, that is, whether they are helpful in choosing the right actions.

So far, I have given only a few examples of how the theses LA, LV, and LN can be applied (for the distinction between LV and LN, see also Thom 1970, 244). A gargantuan amount of lexical work remains to substantiate these theses.

The thesis L can also be applied to other word classes. An elegant geometrical semantics for *locative prepositions* has been developed by Zwarts (1995).[179] Even though he does not refer to conceptual spaces explicitly, it is obvious that his analysis can be directly rephrased within the theory of the present book.

The locative prepositions discussed by Zwarts are the following:

in front of	in back of/behind
above	below
over	under
next to/beside	between
inside	outside
in/on/at	near

A locative preposition, for example, "in front of," combines with a noun phrase, for example, "the castle," that refers to a spatially located object. The basic idea is that the preposition maps the reference object to a *region* that is related to the object (this criterion is also put forward by Jackendoff 1983, and by Landau and Jackendoff 1993, 223). Zwarts proposes to analyze this region as a set of *vectors* emanating from the reference object.[180] The interpretation of "Oscar is in front of the castle" can be illustrated as in figure 5.7, where the marked area represents the region in front of the castle and v is one of the vectors starting from the castle and ending at o which is Oscar's position.[181]

Zwarts studies *closure* and *continuity* properties of the vector regions representing prepositions. He studies *closure under vector addition*, for example, which is defined by the condition that if v and w are both vectors in the region representing a preposition, then $v + w$ also belongs to the region. Among the locative prepositions listed above, this property is satisfied by "in front of," "behind," "over," "under," "above," and "below," but not by the remaining prepositions.

Another closure property operation is *closure under shortening*, which means that if v is a vector in the region representing a preposition, then

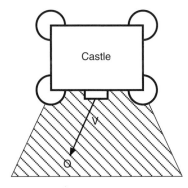

Figure 5.7
The set of vectors denoting "in front of" in relation to the castle.

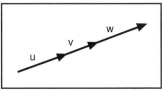
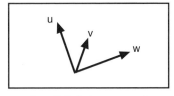

v is linearly between u and w   v is radially between u and w

Figure 5.8
Two senses of "between" for vectors.

$k \cdot v$ is also in the region, for any k such that $0 < k < 1$. It turns out that *all* the prepositions in the list above satisfy this condition. He calls these *simple* prepositions, in contrast to *modified* prepositions like "far behind," "just behind," and "three meters behind." So Zwarts proposes the following universal about the semantics of the class of locative preposition he is considering:

UNIVERSAL 1   All simple locative prepositions are closed under shortening.

Another universal about locative prepositions can be identified using the notion of "betweenness" for vectors. There are two basic definitions of this relation for vectors. One is that a vector v is *linearly between* u and w; the other is that v is *radially between* u and w (compare section 3.5). The two senses of "between" are illustrated in figure 5.8. In both cases it is assumed that all three vectors have the same starting point.

We can then say that a set R of vectors is *linearly (radially) convex*, if and only if for all u and w in R holds that if v is linearly (radially) between u and w, then v also belongs to R.[182] Using these concepts,

Zwarts can now formulate the following two universals that exploit these geometrical notions:

UNIVERSAL 2   All simple locative propositions are linearly *and* radially convex.

UNIVERSAL 3   All locative prepositions (including the modified ones) are linearly *or* radially convex.

Recall criterion P in chapter 3 which said that a natural property is a *convex* region of a conceptual space. Convexity is defined with the aid of "between" but, as shown in section 3.5, there may be several notions of betweenness for a set of points that belong to a conceptual space. Universal 2 can be rephrased as saying that, independently of whether we define convexity as linear or radial betweenness, all simple locative prepositions will be natural properties according to criterion P. Correspondingly, universal 3 says that any locative preposition, simple or modified, will be a natural property in at least one of the two types of betweenness. Zwarts (personal communication) also notes that all the regions associated with locative prepositions are *symmetric* along at least one axis.

Elegant as it appears, Herskovits (personal communication) has pointed out some problems for Zwarts' analysis (see also Zlatev 1997). She writes:

> supporters of the region view generally assume, without checking or justifying it, that the meaning of a prepositional phrase is fully "reducible" to a region; that is, this region depends strictly on the preposition, the landmark, and sometimes an observer; and a uniform relation of inclusion relates the target to this region. In other words the spatial expression is true iff the object is in such a region.

She then gives the following arguments against this position:

1. Many spatial prepositions such as "on," "against," "upon," and "on top of" require *contiguity* between objects. This notion is not reducible to a region.
2. The region is *context-dependent*. This context-dependence also involves environmental characteristics beyond a frame of reference (see Herskovits 1986).
3. Such a region can be defined; inclusion in it is necessary but not sufficient. Examples:
  • "On": requires support also.
  • "Throughout," "about," "over" (covering): besides being included in the region, the target must be distributed over or extended all over it.

• "Alongside": a flower bed alongside the fence must have its length parallel to the fence.
• The static senses of the motion prepositions all present problems; a cable over the yard must extend beyond the yard's edges; a path along the ocean must be approximately parallel to it; and so forth.
• "Among": the target must be commensurable with the objects in the landmark.
4. Such a region is definable, but applicability is not uniform within it—there is context-dependence involving more than a frame of reference here, too.

Herskovits' arguments show that the semantics of prepositions is not a simple matter. While I cannot go into a detailed discussion of the issue here, the example of "on" shows that just a spatial region is not sufficient to determine the meaning of the preposition. The region that is "on" a table (or a box) in its normal position is not the same as the region when the table (or the box) is turned upside down. To analyze this phenomenon, something like Talmy's (1988) force dynamics is required, taking the gravitational direction into account. The object that is "on" must be supported from below. Thus the force dimension is also required for modeling the meaning of "on."

For linguistic concepts on a more abstract level, it appears that some kind of spatial contiguity constraints can be identified. Bickerton (1990, 44–46) gives the example of words that are used to express the abstract concepts of "existence," "location," "possession," and "ownership." The main difference between the semantics of "possession" and "ownership" is that the former but not the latter involves spatial contiguity. Different languages use different verbs to express these concepts. In English "be" is used for existence, location, and ownership, while "have" is used for possession. Bickerton suggests that the contiguity relations of the four abstract notions can be represented as shown in figure 5.9.

He claims (1996, 45) that "no language has turned up that uses the same verb for 'location' and 'possession' but a different verb (or verbs)

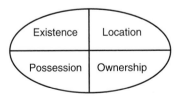

Figure 5.9
Spatial relations between some abstract lexemes.

for 'existence' and 'ownership,' or that has the same verb for 'existence' and 'ownership' but a different verb (or verbs) for 'location' and 'possession.' "

Even though the geometrical structure of the space for these abstract notions may not be very elaborate, Bickerton's argument holds that the meaning of the verbs correspond at least to connected regions of the space.

A more advanced example of a spatial structure in a grammatical category has been proposed by Broschart (1996). He presents a geometrical model of *case relations* that is suggested to work across languages. One dimension of the model (the horizontal axis in figure 5.10) is the "closeness to the frame of comparison." This measure of closeness should be seen as the relation between an "observer" (who functions as a landmark) and an object (the trajector) within a "perceptual field" where the "perceptions" may only be imagined. This cognitive closeness varies from (1) *identity*, followed by (2) *concomitance*, which implies some form of contact, followed by (3) *possession*, which requires control but not contact, (4) *separation* of the objects, and then finally (5) *localization* in relation to some (not necessarily spatial) frame of comparison. The other dimension (the vertical axis in figure 5.10) is "transfer" which goes from the *agent* of a situation, who is the source (normally in control of the transfer), via a neutral (noncontrol) state to the *patient*, who is the goal. Broschart shows how the cases of different languages can be mapped onto the conceptual space spanned by these two dimensions.[183]

In languages like English and German, cases are often expressed by prepositions. Simplifying Broschart's model slightly, the meanings of a large class of prepositions can be mapped onto the two-dimensional space as shown in figure 5.10.

Since there are only a few distinctions along the two axes, the geometrical structure of the space is rather meagre. Nevertheless, the areas representing the prepositions appear to conform to Criterion P, forming roughly convex regions.

Another example involving prepositions is provided by Bowermann and Pedersen (1992) (see also Bowermann and Choi, to appear). In a cross-linguistic study involving thirty-eight languages, they investigated how native speakers described situations of containment, support, attachment, adhesion, hanging, and so forth. In particular, they studied the following six spatial situations: (1) support from below (for example, cup on table), (2) clingy attachment (band-aid on leg), (3) hanging over/against (picture on wall), (4) fixed attachment (handle on door), (5) point-to-point attachment (apple on twig), and (6) full inclusion (apple in bowl) (compare figure 2 in Bowermann and Choi, to appear).

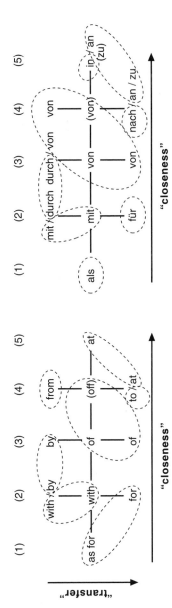

Figure 5.10
Map of English and German prepositions (based on Broschart, 1996, 21).

Different languages use different spatial expressions to express these kinds of situations. For example, in English (1)–(5) are covered by "on" and (6) by "in," and in Dutch, the prepositions used are "op" for (1)–(2), "aan" for (3)–(5), and "in" for (6). Despite considerable variation in the languages investigated, the spatial situations were not categorized in arbitrary ways. All of them appear to be constrained by an underlying dimension that orders the spatial situations from (1) to (6). For example, in no language did Bowermann and Pedersen find a term that was used for (1) and (5), but not (3). In all the languages studied, the regions along the axis from (1) to (6) covered by a spatial term form convex sets in conformity with criterion P.

In this section, some examples have been given of how various aspects of conceptual spaces can generate a new kind of semantic analyses of lexical meanings. The examples have been chosen from different levels of grammatical abstraction. They do not provide a developed theory of lexical semantics. Rather, the examples should be seen as programmatic snapshots, indicating some directions that may prove fruitful for more thorough analyses.

5.4 An Analysis of Metaphors

As a way of filling out tenet IV within a cognitive semantics based on conceptual spaces, let us look at the way metaphors work. In the mainstream of formal grammars and semantic theories, metaphors have been treated as an aberrant linguistic phenomenon that at best can be incorporated via special rules (compare Johnson and Malgady 1980). The view within cognitive semantics is that metaphors should be treated on par with all other semantic processes, or perhaps even as one of the central cognitive features of language. Lakoff (1994, 203) says, "The generalizations governing poetic metaphorical expressions are not in language, but in thought: they are general mappings across conceptual domains. . . . In short, the locus of metaphor is not in language at all, but in the way we conceptualize one mental domain in terms of another."

5.4.1 The Spatial Analysis
The core hypothesis here is that *a metaphor expresses an identity in topological or geometrical structure between different domains*. A word that represents a particular structure in one domain can be used as a metaphor to express the same structure in another domain. Lakoff (1994, 215) expresses a closely related position in his *invariance principle*: "Metaphorical mappings preserve the cognitive topology (that is, the image-schema structure) of the source domain, in a way consistent

with the inherent structure of the target domain."[184] In this way one can account for how a metaphor can *transfer information* about one conceptual domain to another. Incidentally, this analysis fits well with the etymological root of "metaphor" which derives from the Greek μετα + φερειν (to carry)—literally "to carry across."

As a simple example, let us consider the expression "the peak of a career." The literal meaning of *peak* refers to a structure in physical space, namely the vertically highest point in a horizontally extended (large) object, typically a mountain. This structure thus presumes two spatial dimensions, one horizontal and one vertical (see figure 5.11a).

A career is an abstract entity without location in space. So how can a career have a *peak*? What happens when we metaphorically talk about the peak of a career is that the same geometrical structure is applied to a two-dimensional space that consists of the *time* dimension (of the career), which is mapped on the horizontal spatial dimension, and a dimension of *social status* (see figure 5.11b). The latter dimension is usually conceived of as being vertical: we talk about somebody having a "higher" rank, "climbing" in the hierarchy, and so forth (see Lakoff and Johnson 1980).[185]

For another example, let us consider temporal expressions that derive from the spatial *length* dimension, like "longer," "distant," "in front of," and "forward." Here the structure underlying the length dimension is transfered to the time dimension. Since we can identify the corresponding structure on the conceptual time dimension, we know what the words mean as expressions about time. The usual use of the length dimension is to refer to the most salient direction of the two-dimensional surface we are usually moving on. The default

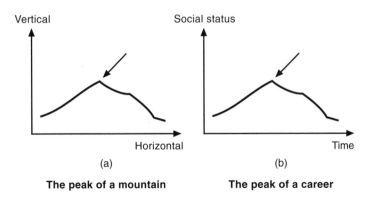

(a)   (b)

The peak of a mountain   The peak of a career

Figure 5.11
The literal and a metaphorical meaning of "peak."

direction of this dimension is determined by the speaker's front and back (this can be altered by the communicative context). Length is represented by a geometrical structure that is isomorphic to the real line, where we, for the present purposes, can take the zero point to represent "here."

In our (modern Western) conceptual space, the time dimension has the same structure as the real line. According to the hypothesis about how metaphors work, we can use some of the words we use to talk about length when we want to say something about time. In support of the hypothesis it can be noted that we speak of "longer" and "shorter" intervals of time, and of a "distant" future.

I propose that the length dimension is more fundamental than the time dimension and expressions like "longer," "distant," and "in front of" are thus used metaphorically for the time dimension.[186] This may be difficult to see since these expressions about time are so idiomatic in our language that we no longer think of them as metaphors. There are *two* mappings of space onto time (see Lakoff and Johnson 1980). In one the speaker is conceived as moving along the time axis: given this mapping, we say that we have some tasks "in front of" us, that some events are "behind" us, and that we are looking "forward" to doing something. In the other mapping *time* itself is seen as moving along a line. For example, when we say that Easter Sunday "follows" Good Friday or that New Year's Eve comes "after" Christmas, it is as if events are on a moving train and, consequently, a later event is "coming after" an earlier one.

This is a paradigmatic example of how a study of the basic metaphors of a language can reveal the geometrical structure of the underlying conceptual domains. Another linguistic category that has many metaphorical uses is the class of *prepositions*. Words like "in," "at," "on," "under," and so forth primarily express spatial relations and, when combined with nonlocational words, they create a "spatially structured" mental representation of the expression. Herskovits (1986) presents an elaborated study of the fundamental spatial meanings of prepositions and she shows how the spatial structure is transfered in a metaphoric manner to other contexts. A sentence like "We meet *at* six o'clock" provides a further illustration of the dependence of temporal linguistic expressions on spatial dimensions (Herskovits 1986, 51). Here "six o'clock" is seen as a point on a travel trajectory and the locational preposition "at" is used in the same way as in "The train is at the bridge."

A very common type of metaphor uses *shapes* of things as vehicles (the "legs" of a table, the "hands" of a clock, the "mouth" of a river, the "peak" of a career, etc.). In the account given in section 3.10, shapes are higher level properties, generated from the spatial dimensions and, as such, the space of shapes has its own geometrical structure.[187]

The general idea of how metaphors work can be illustrated by a diagram as shown in figure 5.12. A linguistic expression E originally denotes a particular structure in relation to a domain D_1 (sometimes called the *vehicle* of the metaphor). When E is used metaphorically about another domain D_2 it expresses that the same structure can be found also in this domain (the *subject* or *tenor* of the metaphor).

The reference of E can be a higher level shape structure (as in section 3.10) which is applied to a more abstract domain. The foot of a person, for example, can be transfered to the foot of a mountain. Sometimes the metaphor E is *creative* for the hearer in that the conceptual structure expressed by E has no corresponding structure in the D_2 of the hearer. Accepting the metaphor as valid means that the hearer adds the structure expressed by E to the domain D_2 (such new connections are indicated by the thicker line between some of the nodes in D_2 in figure 5.12). A recent example is when certain computer programs were named "viruses." This metaphor from a biological domain created a new way of looking at the programs and it suddenly opened up for expressions like "invasive" viruses, "vaccination" programs, and "disinfecting" a hard drive.

Given metaphors as mappings between domains, the "death" of a metaphor can be explained as a result of incorporating the structure of the mapping into the target domain itself. Thus when the structure which is the reference of E comes to be seen as one of the "natural" structures of D_2 by the speakers of the community, the metaphorical mapping loses its function and the metaphors generated by the mapping die. Sometimes, even the original meaning of E in D_1 is lost and only the metaphorical meaning survives. (How many remember the original meaning of touchstone or scapegoat?)

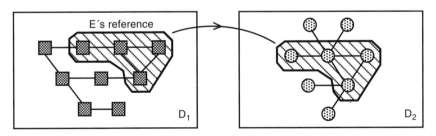

Figure 5.12
Mapping of metaphorical structure from one domain to another.

5.4.2 Relations to Other Cognitive Theories of Metaphors

Lakoff and Johnson (1980) analyze several networks of metaphors. In line with the description above, they argue that the introduction of a new metaphor creates relations of a new kind within the tenor domain. These relations are not "objective," but once one domain has been connected to another via a metaphor, this connection may serve as a generator for new metaphors based on the same kind of relations. Lakoff and Johnson avoid talking about similarities, but it appears that new metaphorical relations usually lead to a (contextual) change in the similarity relations within the tenor domain.

A closely related point is raised by Tourangeau and Sternberg (1982). Their "domains-interaction" view is based on the observation that "metaphors often involve seeing in a new way not only two particular things but the domains to which they belong as well. . . . Metaphors can thus involve whole systems of concepts" (214). *A metaphor does not come alone*—it is not only a comparison between two single concepts but it also involves an identification of the structure of two complete domains.[188]

Tourangeau and Sternberg's analysis is obviously congenial to the present one. They even use the notion of "dimension" when spelling out their view:

> In interpreting a metaphor, we see one concept in terms of another by construing features or dimensions that apply within the domain of the first concept (the subject or tenor of the metaphor) as somehow parallel to those that apply within the domain of the second concept (the vehicle); further tenor and vehicle are asserted to have similar values on these corresponding dimensions. (Tourangeau and Sternberg 1982, 215)

Tourangeau and Sternberg do not interpret "dimension," however, as a geometrical or topological concept; on the contrary, they assume that "the meaning or structure of concepts uses semantic networks . . . as the chief representational device" (219). This representation means that the two domains that a metaphor relates "include the same skeleton of semantic relations, represented as labelled arrows" (1982, 420). It appears that their use of "labelled arrows" makes their representation of a symbolic form. This mode of representation misses much of the content of metaphors which, in my opinion, is better captured by comparing the topological or geometrical structure of the underlying domains (their examples of semantic networks on pages 220–221 do not appear to tell us much about the meaning of any metaphors). Indurkhya (1986) also interprets metaphors as mappings between different domains, but, again, the geometrical structure of the domains are not exploited.

Verbrugge (1980, 95) notes that "[m]etaphoric processes are not solely dependent on language as a source of activation or medium of expression. Perceptual experiences can be metaphoric—for example, recognizing a familiar object in the guise of a cloud, or recognizing a familiar ocean-wave undulation in a field of grain."

According to the present proposal, this feature of metaphoric processes is easily explained: because perception produces mental representations of objects in a conceptual space, these representations can be used for metaphoric transfers in precisely the same way as the mental representations generated by linguistic inputs.[189]

As a wild speculation, I would like to suggest that what happens in *synesthesia* (for example seeing colors when listening to music) is a kind of "automatic" transfer from one domain to another.[190] In contrast, ordinary metaphors involve a creative "discovery" of similarity in topological or geometrical structure.

Another feature pointed out by Tourangeau and Sternberg (1982), but without satisfactory analysis, is the *asymmetry* of metaphorical comparison. We frequently use expressions based on the space dimension metaphorically, for example, the time dimension as in "yesterday's party is behind us." On the other hand, it is much more difficult to use expressions from the time dimension metaphorically for the spatial dimensions.[191] For instance, if I want to express that the mirror is behind me, I would hardly be understood if I said "The mirror is in the past."

The explanation of the asymmetry of metaphorical comparisons is that the domains of a conceptual space are *partially ordered* in how fundamental they are. The spatial dimensions probably form the most fundamental domain since they appear very early in the development of a child which, in turn, can be explained by their importance in the course of evolution.[192] (This could form an explanation why prepositions are primarily spatial.) And the reason for the asymmetry of metaphors is that they always carry information from a more fundamental domain, for which the geometrical structure is well established conceptually, to a less fundamental domain for which the structure is not yet completely determined. For example, we often use optic terminology when describing our mental capacities: "a bright mind," "a brilliant idea," "a transparent argument," and so forth.

Tourangeau and Sternberg (1982, 241) are on the right track in their analysis of the asymmetry of metaphors when they introduce a distinction between "earlier" and "later" dimensions "in terms of their order of appearance in, say, a multidimensional scaling or factor analysis." The distinction is the correct one, but the ordering should be determined from considerations of ontogeny, that is the cognitive development of individuals (along the same lines as Piaget's research).

These considerations can only indicate the general direction of a systematic analysis of metaphors. In spite of the simplicity of the examples used here, I hope they show that an analysis of metaphors as similarities of geometrical structures between domains is a promising program.

5.4.3 Contrast Classes, Pragmatics, and Metaphors

In section 3.5, I proposed that properties correspond to "natural" regions (connected, star-shaped, or convex regions) of a conceptual space. The situation is more complicated than this, however, since the meaning of a word is often determined by the *context* in which it occurs. In section 4.3.2, I showed that the meaning of "red" depended on the underlying *contrast class*. "Red" was presented in the following contexts:

- Red book
- Red wine
- Red hair
- Red skin
- Red soil
- Redwood

One way to get around the effect of contrast classes, for someone who wants to defend a more classical approach to properties, would be to say that it is only in "red book" that the word is used in its proper (extensional) meaning, while in the other cases it is used as a *metaphor*. Broström (1994, 101–102) discusses this proposal. She says:

> Given that the same color term clearly has a different reference in each domain, that would seem to give us every ingredient of metaphor. Still we hesitate to call this metaphor. Why? The most reasonable answer is that the color terms aren't used so much to refer to particular colors as to maintain the color *contrasts* between different referents. Every "domain" is thus a contrast class, to which we apply color terms of maximal distinctiveness.

Nevertheless, the process of applying different contrast classes for the same word is closely related to that of metaphorical uses of a word. According to my suggestion above, a word that represents a particular structure in one domain can be used as a metaphor to express a similar structure about another domain. Now, in the case of contrast classes, one set of dimensions is not mapped onto *another* set but the conceptual space is mapped onto a *subspace* of itself retaining the same geometrical structure (compare figure 4.2).

Another thing to notice about color terms is that not all words will be used, but only those that are "basic" in the sense of Berlin and Kay (1969). On this point, Broström (1994, 102) writes:

> The "late" color terms will seldom be used since they are only needed to contrast with the early ones—"lilac" is only needed if "blue" has already been used (thus the rarity of the categorization "lilac flowers"). If we regard the reference and meaning of color terms as relative rather than absolute, we avoid the conclusion that we are dealing with metaphor. There is no understanding in the prototypical metaphorical sense involved. We do not understand Caucasian skin as though it were paint white, we just call it "white" to distinguish it from other ethnic skin colors, such as "black", "yellow", or "red".

Berlin and Kay (1969) presented a partial ordering of color words depending on how common they are as basic terms in different languages. The ordering is (1) black and white (dark and light); (2) red; (3) blue and yellow; (4) green; (5) brown, (6) purple, pink, orange, and grey. In general, color terms that are first employed within a contrast class follow this scheme, but the rule is not without exceptions. For example, the basic distinction among wine colors in English and French is between "white" and "red" (which is really pale yellow and purplish red). "Black" wines are rare in these languages (but the wines from Cahors in France are often called "vins noir"). There is "vin jaune" (for example, Château-Chalon) and "rosé" (and even a "rosé gris") in France. Note that the Portuguese "green" wine ("vinho verde") does not refer to the color of the wine, but to the fact that the grapes are not quite ripe when they are picked (there is a "green" red wine as well as a "green" white wine). This terminology, however, is far from universal. In Spanish and Portuguese, the basic distinction is between "colored wine" and "white" wine. In Catalan, the names are "black" wine and "white" wine, in full conformity with Berlin and Kay's scheme.[193]

It is not only color terms that appear in different contrast classes. As shown in section 4.3.2, the same phenomenon can appear with most adjectives. For example, the same stream of tap water can be described as "hot" if seen as water in general but as "cold" if seen as bath water; a "large" Chihuahua is a "small" dog, and so forth.

Do problems relating to the variety of contrast classes really belong to semantics? Since contrast classes are often determined by the context rather than by linguistic markers, should this kind of problem perhaps be classified as part of *pragmatics*? The proper classification of the contrast class phenomenon is not a serious problem since I do not believe that one can draw a sharp borderline between semantics and pragmatics.

In defending a functionalist approach to semantics, Harder (1996) criticizes the cognitivist position for not being sufficiently comprehensive:

> As a starting point, let me reemphasize that if it were not for the mental skills, meaning could not exist, but neither could other intelligent coordinated activities: put meaning inside the head, if you like, but then football goes with it. (1996, 105)

> The point is that over and above the conceptual dimension which linguistic meanings tend to have, there is a another dimension of the meaning of a word which in certain cases is the only one: the meaning of the event of using it. Words like *hello* fit directly into a pattern of life (including experiential qualia) without requiring conceptual mediation—just like alarm calls. (1996, 78)

For certain types of expression, I agree that the pragmatic use is a dominant factor of their meaning. This view is perfectly compatible, however, with the position that, for a large class of linguistic expressions, their conceptual structure is an inevitable component of their meaning.

The analysis of the role of contrast classes is a good example of the interplay of semantic and pragmatic elements. The basic semantic meaning of "red" is given as a region of the (original) color spindle. The contrast class, which is pragmatically given, then determines a restricted color spindle (as described in section 4.3.2) which determines the contextual meaning of "red." Sometimes, the contrast class that is relevant for a word is marked by a head noun in the language (see section 4.4) and sometimes it is implicit in the context of the speech act (see, for example, Clark 1992, 370–371).

I thus agree with Jackendoff (1987b, 97) that there is no formal distinction of level between semantics and pragmatics. Traditionally, semantics concerns the meaning of expressions while pragmatics concerns their use. But if the meanings of certain expressions cannot be determined without recourse to their use, the traditional distinction between semantics and pragmatics may not be sustainable.

Broadly speaking, one can find two conflicting views on the role of pragmatics in the study of language (compare Gärdenfors 1998, and Winter 1998):

1. In mainstream contemporary linguistics (dominated by the Chomskian school), syntax is viewed as the primary study object of linguistics; semantics is added when grammar is not enough; and pragmatics is what is left over (context, deixis, etc.).
2. The other tradition (which connects to several other disciplines like anthropology, psychology, and situated cognition) turns the study program up-side-down: actions are seen as the most basic entities; pragmatics consists of the rules for linguistic actions; semantics is conventionalized pragmatics (Langacker 1987, section 4.2); and finally syntax adds markers to help disambiguate when the context does not suffice.

This book clearly champions the second view.

5.4.4 Can Domains Be Separated?
The analysis of metaphors presented here presumes that the domains used in the representation of concepts can be identified and separated. If not, it appears meaningless to talk about mapping from one domain to another. Some authors have questioned, however, whether we can find *boundaries* between domains that are sharp enough to make such an analysis viable. For example, Engberg Pedersen (1995, 114–115) writes:

> The issue here is whether there are some processes of categorization based on analogy which distinguish themselves by occurring across boundaries that are special in that they constitute domain boundaries. Do domain boundaries have a cognitive reality that distinguish them from other boundaries such as the boundary between one token (the child's leg) and another token (the father's leg), the boundary between very dissimilar tokens (the child's leg and the dog's leg), the boundary between a token and a type (legs in general), the boundary between requests (*dus* as a request for juice) and classifications (*dus* as a classification of a liquid), etc.? In the gradual acquisition of the full range of meanings of a word—or an interrelated set of words—it is hard to see some boundaries as domain boundaries in any other sense than as a post-hoc classification.

Broström (1994, 27–28) provides the following example: "If when looking at a dog, I think of his *face*, is that the result of metaphorical categorization? When looking at a caterpillar? Or, to recast the question in domain terms, does the concept of a face belong to the domain of the human body, to the more general domain of animate bodies or to a domain of intermediate scope, say mammalian bodies?"

Her general analysis follows:

> Now, even if the concept of a domain may be a useful approximation, as is the term "metaphor" itself, it does not provide us with an explanation of the difference between litera [literal meaning] and metaphor. The reason why is that it is not possible to individuate domains, to tell one domain from another, independently of establishing which expressions are literal and which metaphorical. Domain boundaries are not clearer than the boundary between litera and metaphor. The original problem—when is a categorand sufficiently different from its category to warrant the term "metaphor"—is merely recast in other terms: when is a categorand sufficiently different from its category to warrant the positing of a domain boundary? Unfortunately, rewriting the problem of delimiting metaphor as the problem of delimiting domain boundaries is also misleading, since it supposes the traditional misconception that there is a qualitative difference between litera and metaphor. (Broström 1994, 26)

For explanatory purposes (in the sense of section 1.1) it is not necessary, and also undesirable, to require a uniquely identifiable domain for the "literal" meaning of an expression. Natural language allows for considerable vagaries here. The examples provided by Engberg Pedersen and Broström show convincingly that the traditional distinction between literal meaning and metaphor is impossible to uphold. For constructive purposes, however, I would recommend that domains be kept separated to simplify the representational structures.

But if a domain cannot be specified for the meaning of a linguistic expression, how then can one identify the image schema that is supposed to be the meaning of the expression? The answer is that even though image schemas in Lakoff's and Langacker's theories are described in the context of a given domain, it does not matter very often if the domain of the image schema is varied to some extent. The key aspects of the image schema are the geometrical and topological structures expressed by the schema, and they can generally be preserved under extensive variations of the domain. For example, in the analysis of "red" in section 4.3.2, the different contrast classes led to *restrictions* of the color domain, while the geometrical relations between the color words were preserved also in the restricted domains.

In comparison, in the examples provided by Engberg Pedersen (1995) and Broström (1994), one encounters domain *expansions*. When a child extends the meaning of "leg" from its own leg, to human legs, to animal legs, and to the legs of tables, the domain of application for the word is constantly changing. A similar process occurs when one extends the meaning of "face" from a human face, to a dog's face, to a caterpillar's face, and to the face of a clock or a car or a mountain. When expanding domains in this way, it is, as in the contrast class example, often impossible to draw a nonarbitrary boundary between a domain that covers the literal meaning of an expression and a domain that is clearly metaphorical. The upshot is that there is no sharp distinction between literal meaning and metaphor. This is compatible with the assumption that, for any word, there is a fundamental semantic meaning component in the form of a topological or geometrical structure.

5.5 The Learnability Question

The learnability question, posed at the beginning of the chapter, concerns how a person can comprehend the meanings of a language. It is commonplace that language is *conventional* in the sense that the connections between most of the linguistic expressions and their meanings are arbitrary (de Saussure 1966). Consequently, the semantics of a language has to be *learned* by individual speakers. This comprises a problem for semantic realism since, if there is a semantic mapping between a set of linguistic expressions and a world (or several possible worlds or a partial world), such a mapping does not tell us anything about how individual users can "grasp" the meanings determined by the mapping. Thus the realists owe us an answer to the learnability question.

Realists tend to eschew the learnability and communicative questions, however, by driving a wedge between semantics proper and psychological and sociological analyses of the use of language. In this tradition, meanings are taken to be objective, publicly available entities and the purpose of semantics is to explicate "truth" as a relation between linguistic expressions and reality. Thus Lewis (1970, 19) states: "I distinguish two topics: first, the description of possible languages or grammars as abstract semantic systems whereby symbols are associated with aspects of the world; and second, the description of the psychological and sociological facts whereby a particular one of these abstract systems is the one used by a person or population. Only confusion comes of mixing these two topics."

For the cognitivist approach, the learnability question has a simple answer: a person grasps the meaning of an expression by connecting it to a cognitive structure. For a cognitive answer to the learnability question, however, it does not suffice to say that we associate perceptual representations with linguistic representations. It is necessary to account for *how* the associations are formed. How can we, for example,

explain that we can talk about what we see and hear? As Jackendoff
(1987b, 90) notes, it is a problem of translation: "[T]o talk about what
we see, information provided by the visual system must be translated
into a form compatible with the information used by the language
system. So the essential questions are: (1) What form(s) of information
does the visual system derive? (2) What form of information serves
as the input to speech? (3) How can the former be translated into the
latter?"

Conversely, we can create pictures, mental or real, of what we read
or listen to. A central hypothesis of cognitive semantics is that our
memories are mentally represented in the *same conceptual form* as the
meanings of words.[194] If we can create an understanding of how the
semantics links are learned, we can translate back and forth between
the visual form of representation and the linguistic code.[195]

Children who are exposed to a language very quickly learn to pick
out the relevant phonological patterns of what they hear. In this way
they learn the structure of the symbolic representations of the linguistic expressions, that is, the sound patterns that comprise the words. As
a second component, they will organize their perceptual inputs into
concepts, presumably using some form of conceptual space as a framework (see, for example, Jones and Smith 1993).[196]

Now, if a child hears a word at the same time as some perceptual
stimuli is noted, a link will be formed between the mental representation of the world and the concepts triggered by the stimuli. This con-
forms with de Saussure's (1966) statement that "the two elements
involved in the linguistic sign are both psychological and are connected
in the brain by an associative link" (see section 5.1.2). Consequently,
a theory of learning based on *associations* will construe the coupling
between a linguistic expression and its cognitive meaning as just
a special case of general learning. A deeper understanding of this
process, however, is still wanting and the details of how the associations are formed must be elided here. Even though traditional (more
or less behaviorist) theories of learning deal with associations between
stimuli and responses and not with mental constructs, some of the techniques of this tradition can presumably be used when investigating
how the semantic associations are learned.[197]

Could not a semantic realist give the same answer to the learnability question? Instead of forming an association between words and
concepts, the language user could perhaps learn associations between
sounds and things in the world. Essentially, this appears to be what the
behaviorists aim at.

Such a connection between reality and a sound pattern, however,
always goes *via* a mental concept. There is nothing in the external world

that can "carry" an association between a thing and a sound, but this coupling must take place *within* a cognitive system: the brain is the carrier of the connections between concepts and sound patterns. As a consequence, one cannot learn associations between things in the world and sounds without first having the relevant *concepts*. In brief, a realist answer to the learnability question presumes the cognitivist answer.

Even if an associationist story could be told for the required relation between sounds and things in the world, there are other insurmountable problems for a realist account of the learnability problem. Within a language there are infinite possibilities of refering to things or events that do not exist, will only exist in the future, and will never exist, but are only figments of the imagination. How could an associative link to the world function in these cases? Realists hardly try to answer this question. An answer to the learnability quesiton, however, from intensional semantics that presumes associative links between sounds and entities in merely "possible" worlds would be riddled with problems. How would such links be physically realized? How could one *learn* something about a nonactual world?

In conclusion, realist brands of semantics have serious problems with the learnability question. These problems become particularly tangible if we consider the task of constructing a robot able to learn the meaning of new words that have no immediate reference in the environment of the robot. For example, Fenstad (1998) argues that for a question-answering system a list of symbolic items or a data base (in symbolic form) may be sufficient. But he says that the problem will be completely different if we want to build a system that combines speech and vision: "The difficulty lies with the conceptual module. Meaning can no longer be reduced to a list or a data base; to succeed we need geometry" (1995, 8). Of course, spelling out the mappings from an actual natural language to a cognitively realistic conceptual space is a herculean task.

5.6 Communicating Referents

Some examples have been given of how the semantics of different parts of a language can be modeled using conceptual spaces. A fundamental assumption of this analysis, however, has been that the conceptual structure belongs to some *individual* language user: the meanings of words reside in the heads of individuals.

On the other hand, it is also obvious that language is a *social* phenomenon. So how can individual conceptual structures become social? If each person can mandate his own cognitive meaning, how can we then talk about *the* meaning of an expression? And how can someone be *wrong* about the meaning? If cognitive semantics with its emphasis on individual conceptual structures is correct, why do we not have Babel?

The communicative question, posed at the beginning of the chapter, is how can it be established that we talk about the same things? Firstly, it should be noted that realist theories of semantics have no problem with this question: since the meanings of the words are out there in the world, we will talk about these things as soon as we speak the same language, that is, as soon as we share a mapping from linguistic expressions to the world. Even if this answer is elegant in principle, however, it adds to the burden of the learnability question for realist theories of semantics. The question becomes: how can you know that you have learned the *right* mapping of the language to the world?

In contrast, the communicative question is a genuine problem for cognitivist theories of semantics. In this section, I address the problem of how we can communicate about objects (partly following Winter and Gärdenfors 1998). In the following section, I counter a philosophical attack, due to Putnam and Burge, against the very possibility of a cognitivist semantics.

5.6.1 Freyd's Analysis

To start my analysis of communication about objects, I cite a theoretical scenario proposed by Freyd (1983). Her main theme is that knowledge, by the fact that it is *shared* in a language community, imposes *constraints* on individual cognitive representations. She argues that the structural properties of individuals' knowledge domains have evolved because "they provide for the most efficient sharing of concepts," and she proposes that a dimensional structure with a small number of values on each dimension will be particularly "shareable."

According to Freyd, the description of an object C—say a certain car—in terms of two other known objects, A and B—say a tomato and another car—can result in a distortion of the hearer's representation compared to the speaker's, as shown in figure 5.13. C's properties will be understood by the hearer as being aligned with those of A and B. For example, C may be thought of having the same color as A and the same shape as B.

This shareability process is continuous: the interplay between individual and social structures is in eternal coevolution. The effects are magnified when communication takes place among many individuals. Freyd hypothesizes that over time the mechanism will create a *grid* of fairly stabilized and discrete values on a few dimensions, as shown in figure 5.14.

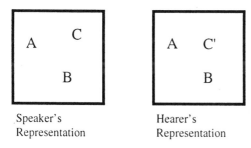

Speaker's
Representation

Hearer's
Representation

Figure 5.13
Distortion of hearer's representation. After Freyd (1983).

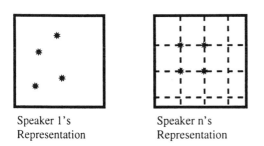

Speaker 1's
Representation

Speaker n's
Representation

Figure 5.14
The conceptual grid created by communication. After Freyd (1983).

Freyd's approach is suggestive: using previously known landmarks to communicate about other objects makes the mental representation of the new object more similar to the representations of the old ones. Her approach assumes that the *dimensions* are given in advance. But her account does not answer the question of how speakers choose which dimension (or domain) to use when communicating.

I want to insert Freyd's approach into a broader developmental setting where three levels of abstraction in referential communication are distinguished.[198] As will be seen, dimensional structures only emerge on a rather high level of abstraction. Furthermore, the kind of adjustment of mental representations described in Freyd's model will facilitate the processes of abstraction.

5.6.2 Three Levels of Abstraction: From Object to Cluster to Dimension
The starting assumption is that each object perceived or communicated about is represented cognitively as a point in a conceptual space as was described in section 4.8. Different individuals may structure their spaces differently, so there may be no immediate way of comparing them.

The properties of the objects may be changing, which means that the points representing them move around in the conceptual space as shown in figure 5.15. Furthermore, objects come into existence and disappear, which means that points come and go in the representing space.

Now suppose each individual in a communicative dyad has his own set of points in his private conceptual space. Also assume that the paradigmatic communicative situation is one where the speaker wants to use language to make the hearer identify a particular object.[199]

At the lowest level of abstraction, this communicative task is achieved by *names*. A name picks out a particular object in the conceptual space. In figure 5.16, this identification is shown by encircling the representation of an object. If both participants associate the same name with the same object (independently of differences in how they are represented cognitively), then the hearer can identify the object that the speaker intends.

This communicative mechanism only works, however, when both speakers are *acquainted with* the named object and have associated the same name with it. Furthermore, the mechanism depends on a *stable context* in the sense that entities exist in the presence of the speaker and the hearer long enough for a name to be established (by deixis or some similar pragmatic mechanism).

In the light of these assumptions, we should ask: how can objects that are not suitable for naming be identified? To answer this question, we must enter the second level of abstraction within the set of points

Figure 5.15
Points move around in the conceptual space.

Figure 5.16
A name singles out a unique referent.

in a conceptual space. A fundamental fact about the world around us is that it is *not random*. Properties of objects tend to go together. Furthermore, our minds appear predisposed to detect such correlations (see section 6.6).

A likely explanation of this capacity is that our perceptions of natural objects show correlations along several dimensions and, as a result of evolutionary pressures, we have developed a competence to detect such correlations. As Smith and Heise (1992, 252) note:

> If we imagine multiples of local and dimension-wide distortions of the similarity space—distortions resulting from real-world correlations between specific properties, from co-relations between material kind and kind of motion, eyes and texture, eyes and kind of motion, shape and motion, and so on—then what emerges is a bumpy and irregular similarity space that *organizes itself into multiples of categories at multiple levels* in context dependent ways.

In the conceptual spaces, correlations show up as *clusters* of points. Such a cluster is marked by a circle in figure 5.17.

A paramount feature of clusters is that they, unlike single objects, will remain *stable* even when objects change their properties somewhat or when new objects come into existence or old ones disappear. Thus, clusters are much more reliable as references of words than are single objects. Furthermore, even if two individuals are not acquainted with the same objects within a cluster, their representations of the cluster may still be sufficiently similar to be matched. For this to happen, it is sufficient that we interact with the same kinds of objects and have shared sociocultural practices.

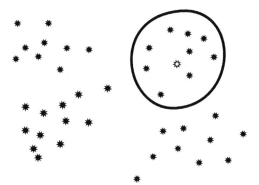

Figure 5.17
A noun corresponds to a cluster of correlated properties.

The prime linguistic tool for refering to a cluster is a *noun*. Rather than refering to the entire cluster, a noun refers to an object that functions as a stand-in for the cluster. This stand-in object, marked by a white star in figure 5.17, can be identified as the *prototype* of the cluster. This mechanism explains why nouns (noun phrases) have basically the same grammatical function as names. By using a noun, the speaker indicates that she is talking about one of the elements in the cluster, by default a prototypical element, which is often sufficient for the hearer to identify the appropriate object in the context.

A fundamental difference between objects and prototypes, however, is that there are, in principle, an infinite number of possible individuals (with different combinations of properties) while we typically work with a small number of clusters and their representing prototypes. This mechanism thus results in a *discretization* of the space (compare Petitot 1989, 27). As discussed in section 3.9, this process is related to the phenomenon of categorical perception. Such a discretization is also necessary for a finite language.

As explained in section 3.8, the prototype need not be any of the objects anyone has encountered. It is represented as a central point in the cluster associated with a noun, but no existing object needs to be located there. Nevertheless, since different regions of the space are correlated with different properties in other domains, the prototypical object will, by default, be assigned a number of properties (see section 4.7). For example, a bird is normally small, sings, flies, and builds nests in the trees. These properties form the *expectations* generated by the mention of a noun.

Among the objects represented in the conceptual space of an individual, there may be several layers of clusters, depending on how finely one wants to partition the space. There tends to be a privileged way of clustering the objects, however, that will generate the *basic categories* in the sense of prototype theory (see, for example, Rosch 1978). This is the set of clusters that provides the most "economic" way of partitioning the world. What is "economic" depends, among other things, on the *practices* of the members of the community. Economy goes hand in hand with learnability: the basic categories are also those that are first learned by children.

5.6.3 Adjectives and Dimensions

Basic level nouns partition the conceptual space only in a rather coarse way. Using nouns presumes that the communicators are *acquainted with the same clusters*, which is a much less severe assumption than that they are acquainted with the same individuals. In some communicative contexts, however, even this presumption delimits the communicative capacities. One example of such a context is when the speaker and hearer face a class of objects that all fall under the same noun and the speaker needs to identify one of the objects in the class but has no name for it. This is where the third level of abstraction becomes necessary.

A fundamental strategy to distinguish objects *within* a category that has been determined by correlated properties is to identify a feature that does *not* covary with other properties of the category. This is the basic mechanism for generating the *dimensions* of communication, or more generally, the *domains*. For example, the color of an object often does not covary with other properties. In figure 5.18, the color dimensions are indicated (in one dimension only) by different shades of grey.

Domains that are singled out by this process will be expressed by *adjectives* in natural language (see also Givón 1984). For example, to identify a particular block among a set of toy blocks, one can say "the red block" (color domain) or "the big block" (size domain). In identification tasks, adjectives are usually only used in combination with nouns (compare concept combinations in section 4.4).

This mechanism provides a rationale for Freyd's model presented above. The thesis that adjectives are more abstract tools for communication than names and nouns is supported by data from children's language, as seen in the following quotation from Smith (1989, 159):[200]

> [T]here is a *dimensionalization* of the knowledge system. . . . Children's early word acquisitions suggest such a trend. Among the first words acquired by children are the names for basic categories—categories such as *dog* and *chair*, which seem well organized by overall similarities. Words that refer to superordinate categories (e.g., *animal*) are not well organized by overall similarity, and the words that refer to dimensional relations themselves (e.g., *red* or *tall*) appear to be understood relatively late. . . .

Social interactions will generate a need for representations where the dimensional structure is represented by a small number of values on each dimension. As a matter of fact, dimensional adjectives often come in polarity pairs: heavy-light, tall-short, and so forth. In this way, the

Figure 5.18
Adjectives single out dimensions.

combinations of values on different dimensions generate a *grid* over the conceptual space as was argued by Freyd (compare figure 5.14). When communicating about objects, the grid, with its corresponding combinations of adjectives, will generate a class of *communicable references*. Meanings outside this class cannot be easily shared in communication since they are not directly codable.

It should also be noted that representational availability of a domain usually precedes explicit *awareness* of the domain. This means that even if a domain is exploited in linguistic communication, the communicators are often not able to *refer* to the domain itself. Such a capacity would presume an even higher level of abstraction than the three levels discussed here. To support this position, note that children learn to use color words before they can engage in abstract talk of color in general. A related phenomenon from children's language is that adjectives denoting contrasts within one domain are often used for other domains. Thus, three- and four-year-olds confuse "high" with "tall," "big" with "bright," and so forth (Carey 1985).

Here, I have modeled an abstraction process on communication about referents based on the requirement that knowledge be sharable, showing that geometrical structures are likely to emerge. This stance leads to a chicken and egg problem: are conceptual spaces prerequisites for successful communication or are they emergent results of successful communication? The answer, it appears to me, is "both." As discussed in section 1.9, the dimensions in conceptual spaces have several origins. This section has added yet another: communication is a catalyst for geometrically structured meanings (see also Deacon 1997). The communicative question is: how do we communicate meanings? In my opinion, the emergence of sharable spaces provides a clue to the answer. Some do not accept this kind of answer, however, as will be seen in the following section.

5.7 Can Meanings Be in the Head?

A heavy attack against the coherence of cognitivist semantics has been launched by Putnam (1975, 1988). He claims that, for principled reasons, meanings cannot be in the head. His argument starts from the following assumptions about meaning and mental representations, all of which are accepted by the cognitive semanticists (Putnam 1988, 19):

> 1. Every word the speaker uses is associated in her mind with a certain mental representation.
> 2. Two words are synonymous (have the same meaning) just in case they are associated with the *same* mental representation by the speakers who use those words.

3. The mental representation is what the word refers to, if anything.

Putnam claims that these three conditions cannot be simultaneously satisfied. The reason is that we "cannot individuate concepts and beliefs without reference to the environment" (1988, 73). A central part of his argument can be illustrated by the following example (Putnam 1975, 226–227):

> Suppose you are like me and cannot tell an elm from a beech tree. We still say that the extension of "elm" in my idiolect is the same as the extension of "elm" in anyone else's, viz., the set of all *elm* trees, and that the set of all beech trees is the extension of "beech" in both of our idiolects. Thus "elm" in my idiolect has a different extension from "beech" in your idiolect (as it should). Is it really credible that this difference in extension is brought about by some difference in our *concepts*? My *concept* of an elm tree is exactly the same as my concept of a beech tree (I blush to confess). (This shows that the identification of meaning "in the sense of intension" with *concept* cannot be correct, by the way). . . . Cut the pie any way you like, meanings just ain't in the *head*!

Realists would claim, therefore, that meanings must refer to something noncognitive (for a related argument see Burge 1979). The lesson to be learned from Putnam's argument is not that cognitive semantics is impossible, but that it has forgotten about the *social structure* of language. In Gärdenfors (1993a), I argue that the social meanings of the expressions of a language are indeed determined from their individual meanings—the meanings the expressions have for the individuals, together with the structure of *linguistic power* that exists in the community. In contrast to Putnam, I claim that no reference to the external world is needed to handle the problem he presents.

The linguistic powers concern who is the master of meaning—who decides on what is the correct meaning of an expression in a society. There are two basic types of power structures: oligarchic and democratic.[201] An *oligarchic* (or *dictatorial*) power structure emanates in a society where the social meanings are determined by a group of linguistic *experts* writing dictionaries, encyclopaedias, handbooks on the proper use of the language, and so forth. When a member of such a society is in doubt about the meaning of a locution, he would rely on the judgments of these experts.

In contrast, a *democratic* power structure appears in a society where linguistic meaning is identified with "common usage." In a society with this power structure, a dictator or a small group of speakers cannot, by themselves, change the meaning of an expression; for this, the consent of almost all language users is mandatory. This is analogous to prices in a free market—a single agent cannot decide to change the price of a good but the price *emerges* from their collective interactions.

Similarly, the social meaning of a language emerges from individual meanings. The concept of an emergent feature of a collective system is a fairly old idea within cybernetics perhaps best illustrated by Wiener's (1961) famous example of the "virtual governor." Consider a system that consists of a network of AC generators. Each generator has a built-in regulator that controls its speed so that it deviates very little from 60 Hz at any time. A generator in isolation, however, does not give a very steady 60 Hz output. Remarkably, when a large number of such generators are interconnected, they behave much more stably. This "mutual entrainment" of the generators is an example of *self-organization*. Out of the mutual entrainment emerges a virtual governor that is an *equilibrium* property of the entire system viewed as having *causal effects* on the individual generators in the system.

In a sense, *conventions* function as virtual governors in a society. Successful conventions create equilibrium points, which, once established, tend to be stable. The convention of driving on the left-hand side of the road will force me to "get into step" and drive on the left. The same applies to language: a new member of a society will have to adjust to the language adopted by the community. The meaning of the linguistic utterances emerges from the individuals' meanings. Language, in the sense of "la langue," thus has no existence independent of the individual generators and their connecting structure of linguistic power.

I do not claim that all parts of the semantics of a language are governed by the same power structure. A more realistic description is to say that a language is a conglomerate of several *sublanguages*, each with its own conditions of mastery. The semantics of the language of lawyers is determined by criteria different from those of the language of entomologists; which in turn are different from the canons used for slang expressions. For lawyers' and entomologists' expressions, the power structures may very well be oligarchic, while the use of slang is a more democratic business. In support of this, it appears as if hedges like "technically" can be used for expressions governed by an oligarchic power structure, but not for those that are determined democratically: "Technically, a spider is not an insect" is correct, but "Technically, a hooker is a prostitute" sounds odd.[202]

Putnam (1975, 227–229) describes something very much like an oligarchic power structure in his hypothesis about the "division of linguistic labor." This hypothesis maintains that every linguistic community "possesses at least some terms whose associated "criteria" are known only to a subset of the speakers who acquire the terms, and whose use by the other speakers depends upon a structured cooperation between them and the speakers in the relevant subsets." (228)

He claims that this hypothesis accounts for the failures of the assumptions that knowing the meaning of a locution is just a matter of being in a certain psychological state and that the meaning of a term determines its extension. Putnam's argument for this is that "[w]henever a term is subject to the division of linguistic labor, the "average" speaker who acquires it does not acquire anything that fixes its extension. In particular his individual psychological state *certainly* does not fix its meaning; it is only the sociolinguistic state of the collective linguistic body to which the speaker belongs that fixes the extension." (229)

The last remark indicates that Putnam thinks of the fixation of social meaning in much the same way as in my analysis. For a given individual, the "sociolinguistic state" is accounted for in the form of metaknowledge about the use of words. On this metalevel Putnam knows that beeches and elms are different, since he understands that the words "beech" and "elm" refer to different things, although he does not know in which way. It appears that he misses the possibility of *democratic* power structures, however, which is a different way of determining social meaning.[203]

As an alternative to looking at social structures only, one could describe the inside of Putnam's head more specifically. Since he knows that "elm" and "beech" mean different things, even though his immediate (visualized or image-schematic) representations of the concepts are identical, he has somehow *internalized* the social structure in the form of metaknowledge about concepts. He is aware that there are social forces that decide words mean different things. And if Putnam's communication at some point hinges on the difference between the concepts, he knows that he *could* find out the applicable social meanings of the words.

Humpty Dumpty said: "When *I* use a word, it means just what I choose it to mean—neither more nor less." He misses that using a language is playing a *game*. We make successful moves in the game when we *coordinate* our expressions so that when I assign a meaning to an expression I utter (or write) you assign the same meaning when you hear (or read) it. If we all were Humpty Dumpties, I would never know whether you mean the same thing by the expression as I do.

In games in general and language in particular, the players want to coordinate their actions so that they reach an *equilibrium point*. For those not familiar with game theory, an equilibrium is a set of *strategies*, one for each individual in the game, in which an individual does as well as he can given the strategies of the others. In the present context, a strategy is a way of assigning meanings to the elements of the language, that is, an individual semantics. A situation where the set of individual semantic mappings are identical would be an equilibirum since then the speakers would achieve a maximal degree of communication. Such a perfect match between the individual semantic mappings, however, is never achieved. What makes semantics intersubjective is this mutual coordination of meanings. Hence, I advocate a form of "sociocognitive" semantics.[204]

A noteworthy consequence of such a game-theoretic perspective on semantics is that one cannot say the individual meanings of linguistic expressions come first and then generate a social semantics. Rather, there is a perpetual *interplay* between the individual semantic mappings and the emerging social semantics. The semantic equilibrium point in a language group is constantly renegotiated and it is moving slowly over time.

In a more recent book, Putnam (1988) also discusses "conceptual role" semantics (this is his term for a cognitivist form of semantics), in particular in relation to *natural-kind terms*. He argues that the meaning of such terms cannot be given by their conceptual roles only, but "once we have identified a word as a natural-kind term, then we determine whether it is synonymous with another natural-kind term primarily on the basis of the extensions of the two words" (1988, 50). Here, *extension* is the set of things in the world that the word applies to. So natural-kind terms presume a *realistic* component for their semantics according to Putnam.

But, how do we *know* when something is a natural-kind term? Putnam (1988, 50) is aware of the problem:

> Some words which were intended to be natural-kind terms turn out not to refer to natural kinds. "Phlogiston" was intended to be the name of a natural kind, but it turned out that there was no such natural kind. And similarly for "ether" and "caloric." In these cases it does seem that something like conceptual role is the dominant factor in meaning, for obvious reasons; we don't want to say that the words "ether" and "caloric" and "phlogiston" are synonymous just because they have the same (empty) extension. . . . Indeed the conceptual role theory comes closest to being true in the case of words with an empty extension.

In this quotation, however, he appears to rely on some form of *realist essentialism*. If "phlogiston" could turn out not to be a natural-kind term, so can "water" and "gold," unless one assumes that natural kinds exist *independently* of language and cognition. This is the kind of essentialist assumption Putnam needs to argue against the conceptual approach. But this is putting the cart before the horse: he assumes that a term is defined by realist notions to show that it cannot be given a purely conceptual meaning.

One can conceive of a form of "conceptualistic essentialism" where certain properties are considered essential to a natural kind, but where properties are interpreted in a conceptualistic way, as in this book. Such a position would be compatible with the idea of certain dimensions being more attended to than others as described in section 4.2.2.[205] Then the determination of the salience that makes certain properties essential can be seen as part of the linguistic power structure.

In brief, I claim that there is no linguistic meaning that cannot be described by cognitive structures together with sociolinguistic power structures.[206] Semantics per se does not need external objects. In opposition to Putnam, I claim that the meaning of natural-kind terms like "gold" and "water" *do* change because of changes in the linguistic power structure. Orwell's "Newspeak" is a fictitious example of this phenomenon. I believe that this kind of meaning change is common in science in connection with scientific revolutions. For example, as Kuhn (1970) points out, before the Copernican revolution "the earth" *meant* something that did not move, and before Einstein "mass" was something that was a constant of an object.[207]

5.8 Conclusion: The Semantic Program

In this chapter, I have tried to summarize, and to some extent defend, the foundations of cognitive semantics, and I have presented the skeleton of a lexical semantics based on conceptual spaces. This kind of semantics has been contrasted with the more traditional extensional and intensional types. Using the notions from the theory of conceptual spaces, I have tried to show how the tenets of cognitive semantics presented in section 5.3 can be given some significant content.

The cardinal semantic hypothesis for cognitive representations of words has been thesis L, which states that basic lexical expressions in a language can be represented semantically as natural concepts. I have tried to support this hypothesis by analyzing some examples from different lexical categories. In spite of these examples, however, L remains more a programmatic thesis than a well-supported law. An immense amount of arduous lexical labor is required before this can be achieved.

My analysis presumes the central canon of cognitive semantics: meanings are mental entities. The referents of words are identified with conceptual structures in people's heads. This position has been attacked by several researchers, notably Putnam (1981, 1988) and Burge

(1979) who claim that a conceptualist approach to semantics, *mentalism* as they call it, is doomed to fail.

I believe that their diagnosis is wrong. I have argued that the social meanings of the expressions of a language are indeed determined from their individual meanings together with the structure of linguistic power that exists in the community. People have private meanings, but to succeed in communication, they gradually calibrate their semantic structures and mappings. In contrast to Putnam, I claim that no other reference to the external world is needed to handle the problem he presents.

My "sociocognitive" position can be summarized as follows: meanings are not in the head of a single individual, but they *emerge* from the conceptual structures in the heads of the language users together with the linguistic power structure. Even if Putnam cannot distinguish beeches from elms, they are distinguished in the emergent social semantics. So when he says that he knows that their meaning of "elm" and "beech" are distinct, he knows that their *social* meanings differ.

Considered as a theory about the meaning of linguistic expressions, however, cognitive semantics is still rather undeveloped. Its most detailed applications have been areas where language is tightly connected to perception, as for example in spatial prepositions. Cognitive semantics has also offered new insights into the mechanisms of metaphors. Its strength lies mainly in the analysis of lexical items, even though there are interesting attempts to explain syntactic features by cognitive means (for example, Langacker 1987, Holmqvist 1993, 1994, 1999). There are, however, areas where traditional semantics is strongly developed and where cognitive semantics is still weak, for example, in analyses of negation and quantifiers.[208]

Chapter 6
Induction

One of the most impressive features of human cognitive processing is the ability to perform *inductive inferences*. Without any perceived effort, we are prepared, sometimes with overwhelming confidence, to generalize from a very limited number of observations.

We do not perform inductive inferences, however, in an arbitrary manner. Peirce (1932, 476) notes that there are certain forms of *constraints* that delimit the vast class of possible inferences:

> Nature is a far vaster and less clearly arranged repertory of facts than a census report; and if men had not come to it with special aptitudes for guessing right, it may well be doubted whether in the ten or twenty thousand years that they may have existed their greatest mind would have attained the amount of knowledge which is actually possessed by the lowest idiot. But, in point of fact, not man merely, but all animals derive by inheritance (presumably by natural selection) two classes of ideas which adapt them to their environment. In the first place, they all have from birth some notions, however crude and concrete, of force, matter, space, and time; and, in the next place, they have some notion of what sort of objects their fellow-beings are, and how they will act on given occasions.

Here, Peirce hints at an *evolutionary* explanation of why "the human intellect is peculiarly adapted to the comprehension of the laws and facts of nature" (1932, 474). In Quine's (1969, 125) words: "To trust induction as a way of access to the truths of nature . . . is to suppose, more nearly, that our quality space matches that of cosmos."

In this chapter, I use conceptual spaces to develop a theory of constraints for inductive inferences. The focus is on the problem of *projectibility*—the problem of which properties and concepts may be used in induction.

The constructive goal of cognitive science in general, and artificial intelligence in particular, is to provide computational models of different aspects of human cognition. So how can we mechanize induction? How can we even hope to capture the ease and assurance of the human inductive competence in a model confined by the thoroughness and precision of computation?

It is commonplace that induction is going from single observations to generalizations. This statement loses its air of triviality if one takes seriously the question of how an *observation* is represented. It is surprising that this question has received very little attention within the philosophy of science.[209] The leitmotif of this chapter is that there is no unique way of characterizing an observation. According to the forms of representation discussed in chapters 1 and 2, I distinguish three levels of accounting for observations:

> 1. *The symbolic level*: This way of representing observations consists of describing them in some specified language. The language is assumed to be equipped with a fixed set of primitive predicates and the denotations of these predicates are taken to be known. As will be argued in the next section, the symbolic approach is a central part of logical positivism.
> 2. *The conceptual level*: On this level observations are not defined in relation to some language but characterized by an underlying conceptual space. Induction is seen as closely related to concept formation. According to the conceptual perspective, the concepts formed by inductive inferences show prototype effects in contrast to the symbolic perspective which presumes Aristotelian concepts.
> 3. *The subconceptual level*: Observations are here characterized by inputs from sensory receptors. The observations are thus described as occuring before conceptualization. The inductive process is conceived of as establishing connections among various types of inputs. One currently popular way of modeling this kind of process is to use artificial neuron networks.

The main objective here is to argue that depending on which approach to observations is adopted, thoroughly different considerations concerning inductive inferences will be brought into focus.[210] In my opinion, a multitude of interconnected aspects of inductive reasoning exist and nothing can be identified as *the* problem of induction. Here, I distinguish among the following four questions on inductive processes:

> 1. *Which concepts* (properties) may be used in inductive generalizations? (This is Goodman's 1955 "problem of projectibility.")

This question arises from the puzzles for induction that have been proposed within the philosophy of science by Goodman, Hempel, and others.

2. How can one *generalize* from single observations to general laws?

Section 4.5 treated this question on the conceptual level as the problem of how concepts are learned. Related problems also occur, however, on the other levels.

3. How can *inferences* be made from limited information about an object?

As shown in chapter 7, what is meant by "inference" depends on the level of representation that is in focus. In one form, this is just question 2.

4. Which *connections* can be established between different domains?

Unlike the first three questions, this one addresses the problem of how new relations among properties or concepts from different domains can be discovered. The notion of a domain has not played any central role on the symbolic approach to representation, so this question is most important on the conceptual and subconceptual levels. On the symbolic level, the corresponding problem is to formulate *laws*, typically in the form of universal sentences or expressions of conditional probabilities.

The four question are heavily interrelated. They emphasize different aspects, however, of what has been lumped together under the heading "inductive reasoning." These questions receive different interpretations depending on which of the three levels is in focus. There is no canonical way of studying induction. What is judged to be the salient features of the inductive process depends to a large extent on the level of representation and on which question is addressed. I now turn to a discussion of inductive processes on each of the three levels.

6.2 The Symbolic Level

6.2.1 Logical Positivism and Its Enigmas
For the logical positivists, the basic objects of study were sentences in some more or less formal language, as described in section 2.2. Very often the language was a version of first-order logic where the atomic *predicates* were supposed to represent "observational" properties.

The main tool used when studying the symbolic expressions was logical analysis. In its purest form logical positivism allowed only this tool. A consequence of this methodology, which is important here, was that all observational predicates were treated in the same way since there were no logical reasons to differentiate among them. For example, Carnap (1950, section 18B) requires that the primitive predicates of a language be *logically independent* of each other.[211] In contrast to this position, the properties *within* a domain (on the conceptual level) cannot be independent, since they are mutually exclusive. If something is green, for example, it can be small or big but it cannot at the same time be red.

Inductive inferences were important for the logical positivists, since such inferences were a cardinal component in their verificationist program. It soon became apparent, however, that their approach resulted in paradoxes. The most well-known are Hempel's (1965) "paradox of confirmation" and Goodman's (1955) "riddle of induction." To see the problems for logical positivism, I present brief recapitulations of these paradoxes.

Hempel's paradox of confirmation deals with the problem of what observations would count as inductive support for a general law. Suppose we are interested in a law of the form $(x)(Rx \rightarrow Bx)$ (for example, "all ravens are black"). The most obvious confirming instances are sentences of the form $Ra \& Ba$ (black ravens). The general law, however, is logically equivalent to $(x)(\neg Bx \rightarrow \neg Rx)$. For symmetry reasons, the observations confirming this law are of the form $\neg Ba \& \neg Ra$ (nonblack nonravens). But if this is true, we can confirm the law that all ravens are black by gathering green apples, blue suede shoes, and red herrings. This is obviously counterintuitive.

Goodman's puzzle, which was presented in section 3.3, starts from the universal sentence that all emeralds (examined up to now) are green. The property "grue" is defined as something that is green before the year 2000 and blue after the beginning of year 2000. Similarly, "bleen" means blue before 2000 and green thereafter. According to this definition, all emeralds examined up to now have been grue. So why should we not expect that the inductive inference that all emeralds are grue is as valid as the apparently more natural inference that all emeralds are green? This is an enigmatic case of question 1 in the previous section.

Note that it does not help to say that "green" is a *simpler* predicate than "grue" because it does not involve any reference to a particular point of time. It is true that "grue" can be defined by "green" and "blue" and a time reference, but it is equally true that "green" can be defined as "grue before the year 2000 and bleen thereafter." So from a purely logical point of view, "green" and "grue" are perfectly symmetrical as predicates. And the logical point of view is the only one that counts within the methodology of orthodox logical positivism which is based on symbolic representations. As Goodman and Hempel have shown, however, such a purist position results in paradoxes about induction.

We do not expect "grue" and "bleen" to be successful in inductive inferences. Even if we have a Goodman-type predicate, however, that succeeds in some inductive generalization, we do not count it as projectible. This point can be illustrated by the property "whack" which is defined as "white in Europe and black in Australia." The inductive generalization "All swans are white" is false, but the generalization "All swans are whack" is much more successful. The predicate "whack" may even be used in further successful generalizations like "all aboriginals are whack." Still, at the present state of knowledge, we would hesitate to include "whack" among the projectible predicates. Were we to find some underlying reason, however, why things should be black in Australia while white in Europe, the situation might change.

Apart from these problems, there are some others of a closely related nature. First imagine that we have examined a large number of Fs (brown bears, say) and found all to be Gs (for example, hibernating). We then tend to form the inductive conclusion that all Fs are Gs. But suppose that all examined Fs are also incidentally Hs (for example, found outside the Abisko National Park in Lapland). Then the inference that all things that are F and H are G has at least as strong support as the original inference (compare Goodman 1961).

Again there is no logical reason to differentiate among the predicates in the antecedent of the universal sentence, saying for example that F is a simpler predicate than F & H. We may as well start from a predicate K meaning F & H and a predicate L meaning F & $\neg H$ and then define F as $K \vee L$.

Second, suppose again that a large number of Fs have been found to be Gs. If none of the objects examined have been an H (a reindeer, say), then the observations support the general sentence "all things that are Fs or Hs are Gs" (all bears and reindeers are hibernating) equally well as "all Fs are Gs." For similar reasons as given above, logic alone is not sufficient to distinguish between these generalizations.

Finally, imagine that all examined instances of F have been found to be G and all instances of H have been found to be K, where F and H are properties belonging to different domains, and so are G and K. Why do we find "all Fs are Gs" and "all Hs are Ks" to be better generalizations than "all Fs or Hs are Gs or Ks" which has a larger class of support than each of the two separate generalizations? Again, traditional inductive logic within the symbolic paradigm would tell us that the latter generalization is the more valid one.

If we use logical relations alone to determine which inductions are valid, the fact that all predicates are treated on a par induces *symmetries* that are not preserved by our understanding of the inductions: "raven" is treated on a par with "nonraven," "green" with "grue," F with $F \vee H$ and so forth. What we need is a nonlogical way of distinguishing these predicates that may be used in inductive inferences from those that may not.[212] This is the problem for induction formulated in question 1 in the previous section.

There are several suggestions for such a distinction in the literature. Goodman calls the predicates that may be used in inductions "projectible." This is only a name of the problem, not a solution. Goodman's step toward a solution is his notion of "entrenchment": a new predicate in a developing theory may result in several successful inductions and in this way becomes entrenched. This is a kind of "second-order" induction. As Quine (1969, 129) puts it: "We newly establish the projectibility of some predicate, to our satisfaction, by successfully trying to project it. In induction nothing succeeds like success."

Another idea is that some predicates denote "natural kinds" or "natural properties" while others do not, and it is only the former that may be used in inductions. There is a strong tendency among philosophers to give the notion of "natural kind" a realistic interpretation, that is, natural kinds are claimed to exist in the external world independently of anyone thinking about them. This is in contrast to the treatment of properties and concepts in this book, which is *conceptualist* in depending on human (or animal) cognition for their construction.

A third notion is that of "similarity." Quine (1969, 117–123) discusses the relation between "similarity" and "natural kind" (see section 3.8). He rejects several attempts to define similarity relations or natural kinds in logical or set-theoretical terms. For instance, let us look at an attempt, adapted from Carnap, which says that a set is a natural kind if all its members are more similar to one another than to any one thing outside the set. Goodman (1966, 162–164) has shown, however, that this construction does not work. Quine concludes that the notions of similarity and natural kind are fundamental to our thinking, while they are completely alien to logic and set theory. In philosophy, "similarity" is often given a realistic interpretation too, as exemplified by Lewis's writing, for example his (1973).[213]

Thus the strict methodology of logical positivism succumbs to the problems of characterizing notions like "projectible," "natural kind" and "similarity." As shown by the paradoxes above, these problems are central to the task of distinguishing acceptable inductive inferences from unacceptable ones (compare Stegmüller 1973, 507–510). It should also be obvious that the problem of defining "projectible" is intimately related to the problem of identifying law-like sentences.

6.2.2 An Example from Machine Learning

Within cognitive science and artificial intelligence, another requirement on a distinction between projectible and nonprojectible predicates is that it should be suitable for being implemented in a computational process. Thus, the problem of projectible inductions, like so many other problems within AI, is basically a problem of representing information.

Now, if we want a computer program to perform inductions based on natural concepts, it is not sufficient that they exist out there somewhere, but we need some way of specifying them in computational expressions. For this reason, a *conceptual* analysis of natural kinds is much more serviceable for AI than a realistic one.

The most common type of representation within the AI tradition, however, is *symbolic* in the sense that it is based on a set of rules or axioms together with a database. In this representation, the "facts" in the database correspond to observations. The rules and the database are combined with the aid of a theorem prover or some other inference mechanism to produce new rules or facts. The basic and the derived "knowledge" are then the material on which a planning or problem-solving program can operate.

The propositional (symbolic) form of representation used in mainstream AI is thus well suited to the positivist tradition. And when implementing inductive inference mechanisms on a computer, this has been the dominant methodology. A rather typical example of the symbolic perspective within AI is the chapter on induction in Genesereth and Nilsson (1987). The inductive problem they address is how to generalize from single observations to general statements (question 2 in the previous section). They assume (1987, 161–162) that there is a set Γ of sentences that constitutes the *background theory* and a set Δ of data sentences (which is to be generalized). It is required that Γ does not logically imply Δ (otherwise the data sentences would give no new information). They then define a sentence ϕ to be an *inductive conclusion* if and only if ϕ is consistent with $\Gamma \cup \Delta$ and the hypothesis ϕ *explains* the data in the sense that $\Gamma \cup \{\phi\}$ logically entails Δ.[214]

Genesereth and Nilsson (1987, 165) view inductive inferences as problems of *concept formation*: "The data assert a common property of some objects and deny that property to others, and the inductive hypothesis is a universally quantified sentence that summarizes the conditions under which an object has that property. In such cases, the problem of induction reduces to that of forming the *concept* of all objects that have that property."[215]

They define a *concept-formation problem* as a quadruple $\langle P, N, C, \Lambda \rangle$, where P is a set of positive instances of a concept, N is a set of negative instances, C is a set of concepts to be used in defining the concept, and Λ is a language to use in phrasing the definition.

Consider the problem of identifying a class of cards, for example, from a regular card deck. The language for problems of this kind of problem is taken to be a standard first-order language with a set of basic predicates like "numbered," "face," "odd," "jack," "four," "red," and "spade." The set P consists of those cards we know belong to the class and N consists of the cards we know are not members of the class. The "conceptual bias" C determines which among the basic predicates are allowed to be used in forming the inductive rule determining the class. For example, only "numbered," "face," "black," and "red" may be allowed when describing the rule, so that "bent" and "played with the left hand," among others, are excluded. Λ, finally, is the "logical bias" that restricts the logical form of the rule that determines the class. For instance, only definitions consisting of conjunctions of basic predicates may be allowed.

Using the notion of a concept-formation problem $\langle P, N, C, \Lambda \rangle$, Genesereth and Nilsson develop an algorithm for performing inductive inferences satisfying the constraints given by C and Λ. A central notion in their construction is that of the "version space" for the concept-formation problem that consists of all rules satisfied by all the positive instances in P but by no instance in N. The algorithm works by pruning the version space as new positive and negative instances are added. In the interpretation of the results, the reference of the basic predicates is taken for granted. The result of the algorithm is a logical combination of these predicates. Thus, the reference of the concepts that are generated is restricted by the references of the basic predicates and the reference of these never change. Consequently, the algorithm never results in any radically new concepts.

Even though AI researchers have had some success in their attempts to mechanize induction (see, for example, Michalski and Stepp 1983, Genesereth and Nilsson 1987, Pearl 1988, and Langley 1996), it appears that their methodology suffers from the same problems as the symbolic level in general. The enigmas of induction that have been unearthed by Goodman, Hempel, and others are also applicable to the induction programs in mainstream AI.

Trying to capture inductive inferences by an algorithm also highlights some of the general limitations of the symbolic perspective. The programs work by considering the applicability of various logical combinations of the atomic predicates, but the *epistemological origins* of these predicates are never discussed. Even though AI researchers are not actively defending the positivist methodology, they are following it implicitly by treating certain predicates as observationally, or at least externally, given. The fact that the atomic predicates, however, are assumed as granted from the beginning means that much inductive processing has already been performed.

I agree with Genesereth and Nilsson (1987) that symbolic induction is *one form* of concept formation, but their sense of concept formation is much too narrow. We not only want to know how observational predicates should be combined in the light of inductive evidence but, much more importantly, *how the basic predicates are inductively established* in the first place. This problem has, more or less, been swept under the rug by the logical positivists and their programming followers in the AI tradition. Using logical analysis, the prime tool of positivism and AI is of no avail for these forms of concept formation. In brief, the symbolic approach to induction sustains no creative inductions, no genuinely new knowledge, and no conceptual discoveries. To achieve this, we have to go below the symbolic level.

6.3 The Conceptual Level

According to the conceptual perspective, induction is seen as closely related to *concept formation* as developed in chapter 4. The essential role of induction is to establish *connections* among concepts or properties *from different domains*. As seen in the previous section, the traditional way of handling predicates in a symbolic language treated all of them symmetrically. Thus the notion of a domain seldom plays a role in symbolic representations.[216] Here, I argue that the theory of conceptual spaces provides an answer to question 1: *Which concepts* (or properties) may be used in inductive generalizations? In particular, I propose a solution to Goodman's problem.

6.3.1 Induction and Natural Properties

Let us approach the problem by considering how *observations* are identified on the conceptual level. In the present context, an observation can be defined as *an assignment to an object of a location in a conceptual space*. For example, the observation that is described on the symbolic level as "*x* is yellow" is represented on the conceptual level by assigning *x* a point in the yellow region of color space. Since natural languages only divide the color domain into a finite number of categories, the information contained in the statements that *x* is yellow is much less precise than the information furnished by assigning *x* a location in color space. In this sense, the conceptual level allows much richer instruments for representing observations than the symbolic level.

Here is a look at how Goodman's predicate "grue" can be modeled in a conceptual space. Given the standard representations of colors as presented in section 1.5, "green" and "blue" are natural properties according to criterion P, while "grue" and "bleen" are not. "Grue" presumes two dimensions, color and time, for its description.

To model the predicate, we can consider the cylindrical space that is generated by taking the Cartesian product of the time dimension and the hue dimension (the color circle). This cylinder is depicted in figure 6.1. In this space, "grue" would not represent a convex region but rather be discontinuous at the point on the time dimension representing the year 2000.

Carnap (1971, 70–76) excludes Goodman-type predicates by distinguishing between "locational" and "nonlocational" attributes. "Grue" denotes a locational attribute since it refers to a particular temporal location. Carnap's solution appears rather ad hoc, however, since it does not explain, for example, why a nonlocational predicate like "green or orange" is not regarded as projectible.

Mormann (1993, 230–231) suggests a different solution to Goodman's riddle based on the closure structures that were presented in section 3.5. The underlying conceptual space is again the "time-color" cylinder of figure 6.1. Simplifying Mormann's construction, a closed set is a region A multiple B (a Cartesian product) where A is a segment of the time dimension and B a segment of the color circle. In a sense, the closed sets are all the "rectangles" of the time-color cylinder. Mormann proposes the criterion that a natural property on the time-color cylinder is such a closed set. On this criterion, "green" and "blue" are again natural properties while "grue" and "bleen" are not.

Let us next take a brief look at the concepts that occur in Hempel's (1965) paradox of confirmation. As a matter of fact, "nonblack" corre-

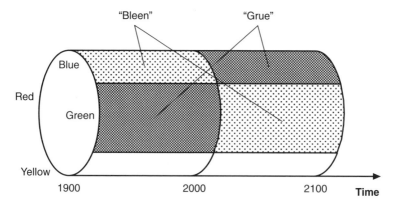

Figure 6.1
The regions of "grue" and "bleen" on the "time-color" cylinder.

sponds to a convex region of the color space since any color between two nonblack colors is also nonblack. I have no firm intuitions on whether "nonblack" is projectible or not. "All nonblack bodies reflect some light" appears to be a completely acceptable generalization. The concept "nonraven," however, would be difficult to count as a natural concept according to criterion C of section 4.2. The class of all objects that are nonravens belong to many unrelated domains. Hence, it would be extremely tricky to specify the associated regions in a way that satisfies criterion C.

Nolan (1994, 134–137) points out that grue-like predicates can not be *learned* in the normal way of learning a language. This idea fits well with my emphasis on natural properties. Given a conceptual space, it is much easier to learn a predicate that corresponds to a natural region of the space, than learning something that corresponds to an irregular subset of the space. For example, one can follow the learning mechanism specified in section 4.5: by observing some instances of a property, one forms a prototype by equation (4.1) and this prototype can then be used for generating a Voronoi categorization. The only things that need to be *remembered* by the agent are the prototypes for the different properties.

In relation to the other problems for the symbolic approach discussed in section 6.2.1, note that even if both F and H denote natural properties, the disjunction $F \vee H$ need not denote a natural property.[217] And if F is a natural property, but H is not, then $F \& H$ need not be a natural property. If both F and H are natural properties, however, the conjunction F and H will also be natural. This conclusion holds independently of whether "natural property" is interpreted as "region that is star-shaped with respect to the point p" or "convex region" (see section 3.4). The intersection of two connected regions, however, need not be connected.[218]

Even if predicates like "grue" and its ilk do not correspond to natural properties in our standard conceptual space, it is conceivable that such predicates would correspond to natural properties in some other conceptual space, where, consequently, our predicates "green" and "blue" would denote nonnatural properties. In other words, what counts as a natural property depends on the underlying conceptual space. This form of relativism was treated in section 3.7 where it was connected to evolutionary processes (see also Gärdenfors 1993b).

6.3.2 Comparison with Carnap

In Carnap's later writings one finds some ideas that go against his earlier views on inductive logic and which come quite close to the theory presented here. To explain the difference between his earlier position and the newer one, he introduces a distinction between *pure* and *applied* inductive logic Carnap (1971, chapter 4). The crucial difference is that in pure inductive logic, the language is described in an abstract way *without* any interpretation of the nonlogical constants, while in applied inductive logic, the language is interpreted.

In agreement with question 1 of section 6.1, he says that it is one of the tasks of applied inductive logic to "lay down requirements that primitive attributes and relations must fulfil to be admissible as primitive concepts in an object language . . ." (1971, 70). This means, among other things, that "[w]e specify for each family the modality on which it is based (e.g., color), the attribute space (color space), and the chosen partition of this space. We define a suitable metric for the attribute space, i.e., a distance function based on similarity relations. Furthermore, we give as much information about the regions of the partition as seems relevant for inductive logic" (Carnap, 1971, 69–70).

Here, the distinction between "attribute space" and "partition" corresponds to the distinction between the domains and the regions of the domains that have been discussed in previous chapters. Carnap's position thus appears close to the theory presented in this book; however, there are differences. One is that he never proposes convexity or any other criterion for partitioning the space into "natural" regions. A more fundamental difference is that even if he notes that the similarity comparisons sometimes can be expressed in terms of a metric (1971, 79), he never takes such a metric as a fundamental notion. On the contrary, he assumes that the "phenomenological" assumptions ("B-principles") that cannot be formulated in the object language L are expressed in the metalanguage that is used to talk about the models and propositions of L and the inductive functions defined on L. This means that he never abandons the ideal that all knowledge should be expressed symbolically, although he relegates some of the information to a metalanguage.

As examples of the "phenomenological" assumptions that Carnap discusses, one can mention the following (Carnap 1971, 78):[219]

> 1. "The colors Green and Blue are incompatible, that is, they cannot occur simultaneously at the same place."
> 2. "Green is *similar* to Blue."
> 3. "Green is *more similar* to Blue than to Red."

Carnap (1971, 79) says the following about such assumptions:

> There are many controversies among philosophers about the logical nature of statements of these kinds, whether they are analytic or synthetic, and about their epistemological nature, whether they are known a priori, that is, independently of factual experi-

ence, or a posteriori, on the basis of experience. At least the simpler ones . . . may be counted as phenomenological. Statements of this kind were regarded by Husserl as synthetic-a-priori. In the Vienna Circle we regarded them likewise as a priori, but analytic. . . . For years now, however, my friends and I tend to a more cautious attitude with respect to the epistemological question. We think that so far no satisfactory explication has been given for the concepts of a priori versus empirical (a posteriori) knowledge.

A consequence of the theory presented here that if we assume that the meanings of the predicates are determined by a mapping into a conceptual space S, criterion C (see section 3.5) and the topological structure of different quality dimensions entail that certain statements will become *analytically true* as argued in section 5.2, tenet V. The "phenomenological" assumptions that Carnap formulates are validated by the very structure of the space and need not be added as metalinguistic constraints. Different conceptual spaces will yield different notions of analyticity, however, which leads to a form of *relativism* that would be foreign to a classical notion of analyticity (compare section 3.7).

6.4 The Role of Theoretical Concepts

As another sign of the importance of the conceptual level, I claim that most of *scientific theorizing* takes place at this level. Determining the relevant dimensions involved in the explanation of a phenomenon is a prime scientific activity. And once the conceptual space for a theory has been established, theories, in the form of *equations*, that connect the dimensions can be proposed and tested. Again, it has been a myth of the symbolic paradigm that scientific theories consist of sets of sentences, most importantly in the form of "laws." Unfortunately, it is a myth that has dominated philosophy of science during most of the twentieth century.

Now a defender of the symbolic form might protest and say that, certainly, equations like Newton's second law or Boyle's law for gases are symbolic expressions and that science can not do without such expressions. Granted, equations are very useful constructs, but this does not mean that their *mode of representation* is symbolic. The equations are symbolic only on a metalevel. Most scientists (and students) using the equations perform *calculations* with the aid of them; that is, they treat the variables of the equations as variables over particular dimensions with a certain mathematical structure (typically that of the real line). Very few people outside philosophy departments treat the equations as symbolic expressions in the sense that they are part of a formal system with axioms and inference rules. Thus, the main use of equations is on the conceptual level of representation and not on the symbolic.

If my diagnosis that the equations used in science are not part of a formal symbolic system, then one must ask what *is* their role in scientific thinking? This question has received very little attention in the psychological studies of science. It appears to me that the symbolic equations are not, as such, elements of the internal cognitive process, but they function as *external devices* that are, literally, *manipulated*. The equations serve as a scaffold for the scientific thinking (compare Clark 1997). When it comes to how the contents of the equations are represented mentally, I conjecture that the conceptual level is the appropriate level of description. We thus find an interesting *interplay* between an external symbolic mode of representation and an internal conceptual form. If this is right, the use of written equations is an example of "situated cognition."

Now, if scientific theories are seen as representations on the conceptual level, one must raise the fundamental question: where do the dimensions and their geometry come from? In particular, what is the process that introduces *new domains* that have no direct correspondence in perceptual mechanisms? This problem is closely related to the problem of the origin of *theoretical concepts* in scientific theories. New domains are introduced by theoretical concepts, and these domains often become highly salient. As a matter of fact, it appears that theoretical "concept" is a misnomer, since what is introduced is a *theoretical domain*, which then generates a number of new concepts. Some prime examples of such domains from the history of science are Newton's dimension of mass, Mendel's principles of the genetic constitution, and Rutherford's atomic structure.

The conceptual space of Newtonian particle mechanics is, for example, based on scientific (theoretical) quality dimensions and not on phenomenal (psychological) dimensions. The quality dimensions of this theory are ordinary space (3-D Euclidean), time (isomorphic to the real numbers), mass (isomorphic to the nonnegative real numbers), and force (3-D Euclidean space). Once a particle has been assigned a value for these eight dimensions, it is fully described as far as Newtonian mechanics is concerned. In this theory, an object is thus represented as a point in an eight-dimensional space.

When creating this theory, Newton introduced the distinction between "weight" and "mass."[220] That distinction is nowadays ubiquitous in physics even though there is only scant sensory support for it.

"Mass" functions as a theoretical magnitude in the theory, since it can only be determined by indirect methods. According to Sneed's (1971) characterization, theoretical terms are exactly those that cannot be measured without applying the theory *itself*—in this case Newton's three laws.[221] Without going into details, I believe that similar principles apply also to many of our psychological concepts. When we decide whether somebody is, say, trustworthy, we have to go by the observable behavior of the person and then apply our "theory" of trustworthiness.

According to mainstream philosophy of science (see, for example Popper 1959), the introduction of theoretical concepts involving new domains is not a problem of induction but belongs rather to the "context of discovery." Within the philosophy of science, it has in general been thought to be futile to construct a mechanistic procedure for generating scientific discoveries of this kind. When considered as a cognitive process, however, the problem may not be so hopeless, and it could be seen as a form of induction. For example, both multidimensional scaling (see section 1.7) and Kohonen's self-organizing maps (to be described in section 6.5.2) are methods for generating new dimensions that organize apparent unstructured data.

I believe that the problem of the introduction of theoretical terms within scientific theories is basically the same as understanding what causes a new domain to be added in a phenomenal conceptual space. Thus I propose that the introduction of theoretical terms in science is analogous to the psychological introduction of new domains in conceptual development. This kind of process could be used to explain why a child appears to be a little scientist, as argued by Gopnik and Meltzoff (1997).

Hence, in analogy to theoretical concepts, psychological domains that are not perceptually salient, but appear during conceptual development, can be seen as introducing the "essential" ("core") properties of a concept as discussed in section 4.2.2. In the terminology of the model presented there, a high salience is assigned to the dimensions of the representation that are not directly perceptual. Along these lines, Hampton (1997) distinguishes between "deep" similarity and "surface" similarity. Judgments of deep similarity depend not only on superficial perceptual features but also on other properties that we ascribe objects. Thus he writes: "[S]imilarity should be broadened to encompass a range of semantic information that goes well beyond the perceptual appearances of objects. When this is properly understood, it is clear for example why whales should not be fish" (1997, 108).

But introducing new theoretical terms and thereby expanding the number of domains for a concept means that representations of concepts become more complicated. From the point of view of cognitive economy, one must therefore ask: what are the benefits of theoretical concepts? The short answer is that they allow *new predictions*. Even without Newtonian mechanics, for example, we can observe the motion of physical bodies. One can even formulate "observational" laws, like Galileo's law of free fall. It is only when we introduce the mass of an object as a constant magnitude associated with the object, however, that we can predict how the object will move under different circumstances, as for example when the object is moved to the moon. To follow Hampton's (1997) distinction, "deep" theoretical notions *unify* the "surface" features of objects.

Another way of expressing the cognitive economy of theoretical terms is that a theoretical magnitude can *correlate more strongly* with the surface features than these features correlate with each other and thereby the theoretical dimension increases the coherence of a cluster of surface features. In section 5.8, I argued that the existence of clusters in a multidimensional space is an important factor in the development of nouns and their references in communication. Hence, if the introduction of a new dimension considerably improves the clustering of a set of objects, it may lead to a substantial improvement of communication about these objects.

Another topic on theoretical concepts is that within many areas there is a marked difference between how lay people apply concepts and how scientists treat them. Whales used to be categorized as fish, for example, while zoologists now tell us that whales are not fish but mammals. I believe that this can be analyzed as a difference in the *relative salience* of the domains involved in the whale concept. Formerly, the shape domain and maybe some of the behavioral dimensions of whales, like swimming in the sea, were more attended to than the physiological domain, which for the modern zoologist is the main factor when categorizing whales among the mammals. This kind of change in salience thus results in a *recategorization* of the class of animals of the kind discussed in section 4.7.2.

One type of development of a scientific theory consists in realizing that a particular domain of a concept is more important for a coherent categorization of a class of phenomena than the domains considered to be the most prominent by lay people, as exemplified by the recategorization of whales. For another example, this is what happened when Linneaus discovered that focusing on the number of pistils and stamina of flowers resulted in a more adequate categorization of flowers than by merely looking at the color, shape, and medical domains as was done in folk botany. In this kind of change of a theory, the underlying conceptual space remains fixed—it is just the saliences of the domains that are shifted.

A more drastic change is when one scientific theory is replaced by another. I believe that for most of the "paradigm shifts" discussed by Kuhn (1970), a *shift in the underlying conceptual space* is involved.[222] I do not see any principal difference between this kind of change, however, and the change involved in the development of a child's conceptual space. Introducing the distinction between "height" and "volume" when you are about five years old (Piaget) is the same kind of phenomenon as when Newton introduced the distinction between "weight" and "mass."

Another tenet of Kuhn's paradigm shifts is that observations are "theory-loaded" and will be interpreted differently after a change of paradigms (Hanson 1958). For example, planets are seen as freely falling bodies in Newton's mechanics, in contrast to being locked in a circular (or elliptical) orbit as in the Ptolemaian system. The same phenomenon appears to occur in child development: once a child has learned "conservation" in the Piagetian sense, a liquid will be *seen* as maintaining a constant volume when poured from one glass to another.

I believe that many aspects of the "theory-loadedness" of observations can be explained with the aid of conceptual spaces. The world is "seen" through the glasses of a conceptual space. This is supported by the ways in which judgments of perceived similarities change as a result of a shift in conceptual spaces. To repeat the example above, in Newton's mechanics the movement of the moon is judged to be similar to that of a stone that is thrown while it was of a different nature in the older system. In the model of concepts presented in chapter 4, this shows up both by the addition of new (theoretical) domains when a new theory is introduced and by changes in the salience of old domains.

6.5 The Subconceptual Level

6.5.1 Observation versus Perception

Within science, the introduction of a new theoretical dimension is a discovery that cannot be generated by mechanical methods. When it comes to human learning and concept formation—the cognitive aspects—however, the prospects for understanding the genesis of conceptual spaces may not be so hopeless since there are some models of how such spaces are formed. The topic here is to consider inductive processes below the conceptual level.

On the most basic modeling level, an observation is what is *received* by our sensory organs. In this sense, an observation can be identified with the reactions of a set of *receptors*. For human beings, these inputs are provided by the sensory receptors, but one can also talk of a machine making observations of this kind via some measuring instruments serving as receptors. The receptors provide "uninterpreted" data in the sense that the information is not assumed to be processed in any way, neither in a conceptual framework nor in the form of some symbolic expression.

Within the philosophy of science, a distinction between *perception* and *observation* is sometimes made. As Shapere (1982, 507–508) points out, the term "observation" plays a double role for the traditional philosopher of science. He writes:

> On the one hand, there is the *perceptual* aspect: "observation," as a multitude of philosophical analyses insist, is simply a special kind of perception, usually interpreted as consisting in the addition to the latter of an extra ingredient of focussed attention. . . . On the other hand, there is the *epistemic* aspect of the philosopher's use of "observation": the *evidential* role that observation is supposed to play in leading to knowledge or well-grounded belief or in supporting beliefs already attained.

This distinction parallels the one between phenomenal and scientific interpretations of conceptual spaces introduced in section 1.4. Within the empiricist tradition of philosophy of science, the two uses of "observation" have been confounded. In modern science, however, it is obvious that it is the epistemic aspect of observation that is of importance. As Shapere (1982, 508) formulates it:

> Science is, after all, concerned with the role of observation as evidence, whereas sense-perception is notoriously untrustworthy. . . . Hence, with the recognition that information can be received which is not directly accessible to the senses, *science has come more and more to exclude sense-perception as much as possible from playing a role in the acquisition of observational evidence*; i.e., it relies more and more on other appropriate, but dependable, receptors.

An important question in this context is: how do we distil sensible information from what is received by a set of receptors? This is question 3 from section 6.1 formulated on the subconceptual level. An adjoining question concerns how the levels of representation can be related to each other: how do we make the transition from the subconceptual to the conceptual and the symbolic levels? These questions expose the kinds of inductive problems that occur on the subconceptual level.

The prime problem is that the information received by the receptors is too rich and too unstructured. What is needed is some way of transforming and organizing the input into a mode that can be handled on the conceptual or symbolic level. This basically involves finding a more *economic* form of representation: going from the subconceptual to the conceptual level usually involves a *reduction of the number of dimensions* that are represented (see section 7.1.4).[223]

There are several methods for treating this kind of problem. In section 1.7, *multidimensional scaling* (MDS) was outlined. For example, in Shepard's (1962a, 1962b) MDS algorithm, the input data is assumed to contain information about the relative distances between n points in some unknown space. The distances between the points are not expressed in metrical terms, but only given as a rank order of the $n(n-1)/2$ distances between the n points. Any such rank order can be represented in a space of $n-1$ dimensions. Shepard's algorithm starts out from a representation in such a space and then successively reduces the dimensionality until no further dimensions can be eliminated without a substantial disagreement between the rank order generated by the metric assignment and the original rank order. For many empirical areas the initial data can be reduced to a space with two or three dimensions.[224] These dimensions can then function as a basis for concept formation according to the theory presented in section 4.2.

6.5.2 Generalizing within a Domain with the Aid of Artificial Neuron Networks

In this section, a different method than MDS for reducing the dimensionality of representation will be outlined. The mechanisms for the method are based on *artificial neuron networks* (ANNs). In an ANN, the receptors and the information they receive can be identified with a set of *input neurons* and their *activity values*. This set of values will be called the *input vector*. In real applications there will be a large number of input neurons which means that the dimensionality of the input vector will be very high.

The ANN model I outline here is based on Kohonen's (1988, 1995) *self-organizing maps*. The purpose of the method is to *reduce the representational complexity* of the input in an efficient and systematic way. Thus the proposed method can be seen as a way of answering question 2 from section 6.1 on the subconceptual level. The distinguishing property of these maps is that they are able to describe the topological and similarity relations of the signals in the input vector, exploiting something like a conceptual space with a small number of dimensions.

Kohonen's goal in using the maps is not limited to inductive inference but representation of information in general. He writes:

> Economic representation of data with all their interrelationships is one of the most central problems in information sciences, and such an ability is obviously characteristic of the operation of the brain, too. In thinking, and in the subconscious information processing, there is a general tendency to compress information by forming *reduced representations* of the most relevant facts, without loss of knowledge about their interrelationships. (Kohonen 1988, 119)

A self-organizing map is an ANN that consists of an input vector connected to an output array of neurons. In most applications, this array is one- or two-dimensional, but in principle it could be of any dimensionality. The essential property of the network is that the connections between the neurons in the array and the learning function are organized in such a way that similarities occuring among different input vectors are, in general, *preserved* in the mapping, in the sense that input vectors with common features are mapped onto *neighboring* neurons in the output map. The degree of similarity between two input vectors is determined by some (intrinsic) *distance* measure (see section 2.4).

The mapping from the input vector to the array preserves most topological relations while reducing the dimensionality of the representation space. Preserving the topology means that points closely related in the high-dimensional space are mapped onto closely related points in the low-dimensional space. Since dimensionality is reduced, this entails that regions of the high-dimensional space are mapped onto points in the low-dimensional space. This mapping can be seen as a form of *generalization* and hence as an answer to question 2 of section 6.1. The low-dimensional "feature map" that results as an output of the process can be identified with a conceptual space. The mapping is *generated* by the network itself via the learning mechanism of the network. A drawback of the method is that, in practice, it takes quite a large number of learning instances before the network stabilizes enough so that further changes can be ignored.[225]

The mechanism is best illustrated by a couple of artificial examples taken from Kohonen (1988). In figures 6.2 and 6.3 the input vectors were assumed to be uniformly distributed over a triangular area. In the network represented in figure 6.2, the output array was one-dimensional, that is, the output neurons were arranged along a line.

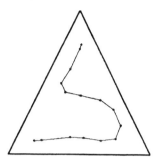

Figure 6.2
Distribution of weight vectors on a linear array of neurons (from Kohonen 1988, 135).

The number of neurons on this line is fixed. Any input from the triangular space results in some activities in the neurons in this line.

Figure 6.2 shows the *inverse* mapping of the input vectors. This means that each output neuron in the one-dimensional array is mapped onto the point in the triangular area that caused the highest activity in the output neuron. These points are represented as dots in figure 6.2 and the lines between them maps the order of the output neurons in the one-dimensional array. If this set of points is used to generate a Voronoi partitioning, the resulting tessellation areas will consist of those points that are mapped onto the corresponding point in the linear array. The mapping preserves relations of similarity, and, furthermore, there is a tendency of the line trying to "cover" as much space as possible, in the sense that the distance between any point in the map and the line is as small as possible.

In figure 6.3, the corresponding network contains an output array that is two-dimensional with the neurons arranged in a square. Figure 6.3 again shows the inverse mapping, indicating which neurons in the input space produce the greatest responses in the output square. Again, the inverse mapping represents a deformation of the output array that preserves topological relations as much as possible.

Figure 6.4 shows an example of how the network self-organizes dynamically in learning a mapping. The initial values of the mapping were selected so that there was a random mapping from a circular region of the input triangle to a linear array of output neurons. The network was then fed with a number of input vectors randomly selected from the full triangle. The sequence of figures indicates how the mapping has improved over time, where the numbers below the figures represent the number of learning trials. It should be noted that the learning procedure is very slow.

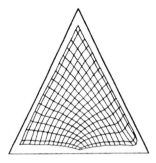

Figure 6.3
Distribution of weight vectors on a rectangular array of neurons (from Kohonen 1988, 135).

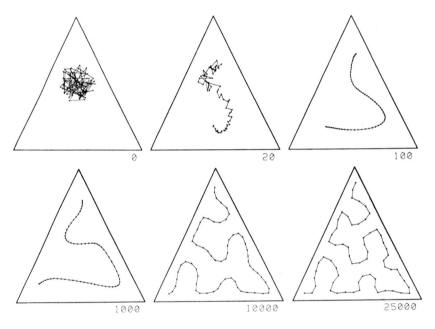

Figure 6.4
Distribution of weight vectors during the ordering process (from Kohonen 1988, 136).

These examples are artificial in that we know the distribution of input vectors in advance which furthermore is of low dimensionality. In real applications, the dimensionality of the input space is high and its topology is unknown. It can be proved, however, at least when the output array is one-dimensional, that, in the limit (after infinitely many learning instances), the mapping will preserve as much as possible of the topological structure of the input space.[226]

6.6 Correlations between Domains

Kohonen's self-organizing maps are one way of modeling how the geometric structure *within* a domain can be created from information on the subconceptual level. There is another kind of inductive process that is more typical, however, namely the process of establishing *correlations* between properties from *different* domains (question 4 in section 6.1). On the symbolic approach, the outcome of inductive generalizations is typically a universal sentence of the form "all *Fs* are *Gs*," where F and G are properties that belong to different domains (or, alternatively a probabilistic statement saying that a certain proportion of the *Fs* are *Gs*).

If we turn to human abilities to detect clusters of properties, we are, in general, extremely poor at performing *abstract* correlation assessment tasks (Nisbett and Ross 1980, Kornblith 1993, 96–100).[227] Work by Billman (1983) and Billman and Knutson (1996), however, indicates that humans are quite good at detecting correlations that cluster *several dimensions*, in spite of our limitations in detecting isolated correlations among variables.[228] A plausible explanation of this phenomenon is that our perceptions of "natural" objects do show correlations along multiple dimensions, and, as a result of natural selection, we have developed a competence to detect such clustered correlations. In brief, we are better at learning concepts than learning scattered correlations among properties.

When investigating correlation learning, Billman used a technique called *focused sampling* both in her computer models and in her and Heit's study of human subjects (Billman and Heit 1988). In this process, the material consists of a large class of objects, each of which is characterized by a large number of properties. Because of the large number, a complete survey of the objects and the corresponding properties is impossible both for a computer and a human. Correlations must therefore be detected from samples of the objects. Rather than performing a random search, focused sampling preferentially selects those objects that have properties already proven to be connected. So if properties C and D have been found to correlate, objects with these properties are more likely to be studied. If C and D correlate with a further property

E, this technique will reinforce itself and rapidly detect clusters of properties that correlate. As Billman and Heit (1988, 593–594) note, this technique is successful only under certain assumptions:

> Focused sampling benefits learning only when the structure to be learned is consistent with the bias that focused sampling assumes. It does not benefit rule learning if the structure of input does not afford intercorrelated features. If regularities are scattered through the system, predictions that a feature will be used in additional rules because it is used in one will not be sound. However, psychologically natural categories typically provide the correlational coherence assumed by focused sampling. Within a domain, if a feature participates in one regularity it is likely to participate in others. For example, singing predicts having feathers, flying and living in trees.

In line with this, Holland et al. (1995, 183–184) formulate the hypothesis that the *basic level* categories of prototype theory (Rosch 1975, 1978) are characterized by distinctive clusters of correlated properties. If valid, this hypothesis would provide a potent underpinning for that part of prototype theory. As argued in section 5.6.2, clusters of correlated properties considerably streamline *communication* concerning objects, in particular when the communicators have only partial knowledge of the objects (compare Winter and Gärdenfors 1998).

A different tradition of investigating inductions involving concepts rather than properties concerns so-called *categorical inductive inferences*. Osherson et al. (1990) studied two types of inductive arguments: general, where the conclusion concerns a class that is superordinate to those of the premises, and specific, where the class of the conclusion is on the same categorical level as the premises. An example of a general argument is:

> Grizzly bears love onions
> Polar bears love onions
> ———————————————
> All bears love onions

And an example of a specific argument is:

> Robins use serotonin as a neurotransmitter
> Bluejays use serotonin as a neurotransmitter
> ———————————————————————
> Geese use serotonin as a neurotransmitter

Osherson et al. (1990) investigated thirteen qualitative patterns on how subjects judge the confirmation strength of such inductive arguments. For example, the inference

Robins use serotonin as a neurotransmitter
Bluejays use serotonin as a neurotransmitter
_____

Sparrows use serotonin as a neurotransmitter

was considered stronger than the inference

Robins use serotonin as a neurotransmitter
Bluejays use serotonin as a neurotransmitter
_____

Geese use serotonin as a neurotransmitter

The underlying reason is that robins and bluejays resemble sparrows more than they resemble geese. Relations of similarity are thus important for our judgments of the validity of inductive inferences.

Osherson et al. present different kinds of empirical evidence to support the patterns of confirmation that they have identified. The model they put forward claims that the confirmation assigned to categorical inductive inferences "varies directly with the following two variables: a = the degree to which the premise categories resemble the conclusion category; and b = the degree to which the premise categories resemble the members of the lowest level category that includes both the premise and conclusion categories" (1990, 189–190).

This model is challenged by Sloman (1993). Instead of a category-based model, he proposes a feature-based one. Every category in the inductive arguments is described by a vector of real number from the [0, 1] interval. Sloman calls each coordinate of the vector a "feature," but in the present context they may as well be called "dimensions." He says that these features "represent a large number of interdependent perceptual and abstract attributes. In general, these values may depend on the context in which categories are presented" (1993, 237).

To explain the patterns of confirmation that were investigated by Osherson et al. (1990), Sloman (1993) develops a connectionist model. Using this model, he is able to explain ten of the previous patterns and three new ones not treated by Osherson et al. He also presents empirical support for the new patterns. According to Sloman's model, the strength of an inductive argument can be determined as the proportion of features in the conclusion category that are also included in the premise categories. In the simplest case there is only one premise "all Ps are Q" and a conclusion of the form "all Cs are Q." The premise category P can be represented by a vector $F(P)$ of feature values and the conclusion category C by a corresponding vector $F(C)$. In the single-premise case of Sloman's model, the strength of the inductive argument is measured by the value $F(P) \cdot F(C) / |F(C)|^2$, where $F(P) \cdot F(C)$ can be seen as a measure of the overlap of the features of P and C, and $|F(C)|^2$ seen as a measure of the magnitude of the conclusion category vector.[229]

Sloman (1993, 275) points out two major differences between his model and that of Osherson et al. (1990). First, the model of Osherson et al. relies on *two* factors: (1) the similarity between premise categories and the conclusion category, and (2) the similarity between the premise categories and the members of the lowest level category that includes both the premise and conclusion categories. In contrast, Sloman's model only uses *one* factor, that is the similarity between the premise categories and the conclusion category as encoded by the weights of the corresponding feature vectors. Second, the model of Osherson et al. presumes that we can accurately identify the lowest level category that includes both the premise and conclusion categories. Such an identification, however, is often problematic. Sloman asks: "What is the lowest level category that includes ducks, geese and swans? Is it birds, water-birds, web-footed birds?" (1993, 275). Sloman's model requires no category structure but only a set of features for each category to predict the strength of an inductive argument. This aspect also makes Sloman's model computationally simpler. Both models have considerable success in their empirical predictions, but the two differences presented here speak in favor of Sloman's model as the cognitively more realistic one. The studies of categorical inductive inferences, however, are so far rather limited. More empirical data covering a larger range of inferences are needed before a judgment of the validity of a model can be reliably made.

The empirical results presented here show that humans have powerful abilities to detect multiple correlations among different domains. In relation to the constructive goals of cognitive science, it appears advisable to aim at reconstructing such a capacity in artificial systems designed for concept formation (compare Holland et al. 1986).

In the theory of conceptual spaces, this kind of inductive process corresponds to determining *mappings* between the different domains of a space. Using such a mapping, one can then determine correlations between the regions of different domains. The correlation between two properties F and G, expressed on the symbolic level by a universal statement of the form "all Fs are Gs," would then just be a special case. More generally, the process can be used to generate the conditional probabilities needed by Bayesian reasoning and decision making (see Gärdenfors 1996e). Such correlations also generate the nonmonotonic inferences discussed in sections 4.5 and 4.6.

There are several ways of mathematically modeling the process of learning the correlations between different domains. I will not attempt to give a survey here, but only illustrate the techniques by way of an example. Christian Balkenius and I performed some experiments with a system that implements this kind of inductive inferences.[230] The system is based on ANNs that utilize Kohonen's (1988) self-organizing maps. The overall architecture of the inductive network is depicted in figure 6.5. The input receptors are divided into a small number of subsets (in the figure there are two such subsets). The purpose of this division is to group together receptors that contain information about "the same" domain, so for example, visual receptors belong to one group, auditory receptors to another, and so forth. When the network is applied, the decision about how the set of receptors should be grouped must be made by the user. But this is about the only thing she has to decide. Except for some parameter settings, the network then performs the rest of the inductive inferences.

The input vectors are next mapped onto one Kohonen map each. Figure 6.5 depicts these as one-dimensional lines, but they may as well be two- or three-dimensional spaces. In the figure, there are only two Kohonen maps, but there may be more than two depending on how the input receptors are grouped into domains. One of the maps may be a purely classificatory space, representing "names" of the categories that are identified by the network (compare Schyns 1991 and the system developed by Chella, Frixione, and Gaglio (1997) that will be presented in section 7.5).[231]

The Kohonen maps are then paired by asymmetric connections between the neurons in the two maps. The connections are total in the sense that each neuron on one map is connected to all neurons on the other map. The learning rule for these connections functions in such a way that the strength of the connection (that is the weight w_{ij}) between a neuron x_i on one map and a neuron y_j on another reflects the conditional probability (estimated from the learning examples) that y_j be activated given that x_i is activated.[232] The connections vary between –1 and

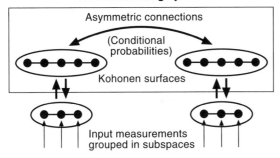

Figure 6.5
Architecture of the experimental inductive neural network.

+1 and obtain the extreme values only when x_i and y_j are never and always, respectively, activated together. In a sense, the network performs *implicit* computations of the inductive statistics.[233]

Once the learning phase has been completed, relating input receptors to Kohonen maps and these maps to each other, it is then possible to use the network to classify new objects. By feeding the system with a *partial* input vector—for example, the values for one of the domains—the network can then compute the *expected* values for all the other receptors and the expected locations in all the Kohonen maps. (This is a form of "vector completion" discussed in section 7.2.) In this way the network *guesses* the unknown properties of the object it has only received partial information about. The network is thus able to *generalize* from earlier experience and make inductive inferences using the connections between the different Kohonen maps.[234] The system thus provides an answer to the question of how *inferences* can be made from limited information about an object (question 3 in section 6.1).

6.7 Conclusion: What Is Induction?

Induction has been called "the scandal of philosophy." Unless more consideration is given to the question of how the relevant information is to be represented, I am afraid that induction may remain a scandal of AI and cognitive science as well. The traditional problems for the logical positivists' analyses of induction have arisen because they confined themselves to narrowly symbolic representations of information and to logical tools for analyzing the information.

Where on the three levels described here is real induction be found? The answer is nowhere and everywhere. The main thesis of this chapter is that there are several kinds of inductive processes. The processes can be classified with the aid of the four questions that were formulated at the beginning of the chapter. Depending on which level observations are interpreted and on the inductive question in focus, different ways of generalizing the observations become relevant. Traditional philosophy of science has concealed these distinctions by neglecting the conceptual and subconceptual levels. For a complete account of the different problems of induction, all three levels must be mustered.

As stated in chapter 1, I do not view the three levels as being in conflict with each other. They should rather be regarded as three *perspectives* on observation and induction that complement each other. Even though all three perspectives are necessary to provide a complete picture of different kinds of inductive processes in science and in everyday life, the conceptual level has a special status for several reasons. First, scientific laws and theories are mainly formulated under the assumption of an underlying conceptual space with a specific set of dimensions. Second, the conceptual level provides the *semantics* for the expressions on the symbolic level (as was argued in the previous chapter). Finally, the information expressed on this level serves as a comprehensive summary of all that reaches sensors of different kinds at the subconceptual level. Since research on inductive processes during this century has focused on the symbolic level, I propose that the conceptual level should be given much more attention in the future.

Chapter 7

Computational Aspects

7.1 Computational Strategies on the Three Levels

A central aspect when evaluating the merits and drawbacks of different forms of representations is how they are *used* in cognitive processes. This problem occurs for biological processes as well as for artificial ones. Within contemporary cognitive science, computer simulations have become a standard tool for investigating various kinds of cognitive processes. Such simulations are based, however, on many different methodologies. The choice of implementation methodology to a large extent depends on the level at which the process is represented.

This chapter focuses on the constructive goal of cognitive science (compare section 1.1). The aim is to evaluate how amenable various kinds of representations are for computer implementations of cognitive mechanisms. In this section, I outline some of the standard computational strategies that are used on the three different levels of representation. I first give a brief account of the classical symbolic (Turing machine) computations. Next, I turn to vector calculations and clustering techniques that are the typical tools of the conceptual level. Finally, some computational aspects of ANNs will be discussed. The remainder of the chapter is devoted to comparisons among the different kinds of computations. I also discuss how computations on the different levels can be connected to each other.

7.1.1 Symbolic Computations
The symbolic approach to information representation is intimately connected with the classical view of computation. On this view, computations are defined by the Turing machine paradigm.

If we look at the methods used in the "symbol crunching" of traditional AI, a clearly dominating feature of the algorithms is that they implement some form of *rule following*. The rules can be logical axioms as in an automated theorem prover, they can be syntactic rules as in a parsing program, or they can be of a cognitively more general type as in the ACT* (Anderson 1983) and SOAR (Newell 1990) architectures.

Since the rules often are applied iteratively, methods for handling *recursive procedures* become central elements of computer programs within the symbolic tradition.[235] As a matter of fact, a mainstream position in mathematical logic and (Chomiskian) linguistics is that the proper theory of thinking is *nothing but* recursion theory.

When theories of theorem proving or sentence parsing are implemented in a computer, the program must be able to efficiently handle *tree-like structures*. This, in turn, entails that the computational methods require some smart heuristics for *searching* the tree structures. Consequently, using symbolic representations will lead to a focus on searching methods.

Symbolic representations and Turing machine computability go hand in hand. According to Church's thesis everything that can be computed with symbols can be computed on a (universal) Turing machine. I argue that this is not all there is to computation, however, because the thesis builds on the assumption that *all information is symbolically represented* (this argument is expanded in section 7.4). And this is exactly what is being questioned by the connectionist and the conceptual approaches to information representation.

And when it comes to the *meaning* of the expressions that appear in the computations, most adherents of the symbolic paradigm are semantic *realists*: for them the "meaning" of a predicate or a sentence is determined by mapping it to the external world (or, to make it even more remote from a cognitive system, to a plethora of possible worlds). Meanings are put *outside* the computer; the world (and the mapping) is assumed to exist independently of any relation to a cognitive subject (compare Stewart 1996). A clear example of this position is given by Fodor (1981, 231): "If mental processes are formal [symbolic], then they have access only to the formal properties of such representations of the environment as the senses provide. Hence, they have no access to the semantic properties of such representations, including the property of being true, of having referents, or, indeed, the property of being representations of the environment."

Fodor realizes that his position creates some problems: "We must now face what has always been the problem for representational theories to solve: what relates internal representations to the world? What is it for a system of internal representations to be semantically interpreted?" (1981, 203). These problems arise for the symbolic paradigm because it presumes a realist semantics that presumes external representations (compare chapter 5).

The realist view on the semantics of the symbols is one reason why it is difficult to explain how the meanings of the predicates *change* during the cognitive development of an agent. Semantic realists are more or less obliged to assume that the meanings of symbols are fixed. In a sense this view is inherited from the model theory of mathematical logic. For mathematical concepts, however, one never has the problem of adapting concepts to new encounters with reality.[236]

7.1.2 Conceptual Computations

Turning next to computations on the conceptual level, the central representing structures are conceptual spaces, consisting of a number of domains with certain geometrical or topological structures. The basic representational elements of a conceptual space are *points*. Mathematically, points in dimensional spaces can be seen as *vectors*. Thus, calculations on the conceptual level to a large extent involve *vector calculations*, using matrix multiplications and so forth. The geometrical properties of the vectors confer their basic representational capacities.

For example, the *learning algorithms* that are appropriate for representations on the conceptual level heavily exploits the vectorial representation. By using the distances provided in conceptual spaces, different numerical *threshold criteria* can be used in classification tasks (see, for example, Langley 1996, chapter 3, for a presentation of such criteria). In particular, *linear* and *spherical* threshold units have been studied. To classify an object using a linear threshold one multiplies the dimension values of the vector representing the object by the weights of the dimensions, sums the products, and checks whether the result exceeds the given threshold. This corresponds to using a (hyper-)plane in the conceptual space to classify the objects. The Voronoi rule presented in section 3.9 is an example of such a linear threshold criterion. In a spherical threshold criterion all objects falling within a certain distance from a given point p are classified in the same category as p. This corresponds to using (hyper-)spheres in the space to sort the objects. Threshold criteria of these types obviously exploit the geometrical structure of the conceptual space, particularly because they rely on distances.

One methodological feature that clearly distinguishes the conceptual level from the symbolic is that *similarity* plays a central role on the conceptual level. Similarity between objects or properties will be represented by *distances* in spaces. Such a notion of a distance is difficult to model in a natural way in a symbolic system. In a connectionist system, distances may appear as an emergent feature, but are difficult to represent directly on a neuronal level (unless built in, as in Kohonen systems).

Once distances between objects are represented, one can group objects according to the relative distances between them. In particular, *clusters* of objects are very useful when studying concept formation processes (compare sections 5.6.2 and 6.6). Within the area of machine learning, there is a flourishing tradition on algorithms for identifying clusters (see, for example Michalski and Stepp 1983, Murtagh 1993, Langley 1996, Hulth and Grenholm 1998).

When going from the input stages of a system (biological or artificial) to more advanced levels, *coordinate transformations* are often involved. Coordinate transformations are paradigm examples of vector calculations. For example, following Marr (1982) and Gallistel (1990), one can make a distinction between a *viewer centered* (proximal) representation, which is specified relative to the viewer, and an *object centered* (distal) representation, which specifies locations in a coordinate system defined by the viewed object. The change of representation involves a coordinate transformation.[237] Representation on the subconceptual level is often viewer centered while it is object centered on the conceptual level.

It is true that coordinate transformations can be represented via equations and thus, in principle, be handled by symbolic representations. In a traditional AI system, this was the only mode available and it still has many defenders. It appears preposterous, however, to assume that the brain solves symbolic equations when, for example, coordinating eye movements with hand movements. P. M. Churchland (1986b, 290–291) argues that the general process works as follows:

> I therefore propose the hypothesis that the scattered maps within the cerebral cortex, and many subcerebral laminar structures as well, are all engaged in the coordinate transformation of points in one neural state space into points in another, by the direct interaction of metrically deformed, vertically connected topographic maps. Their mode of representation is state-space position; their mode of computation is coordinate transformation. . . .

An important consequence of this way of performing a coordinate transformation is that it will be performed in a very small number of steps: activity at one point in the input space will be sent directly to the "transformed" point in the output space. Topographic mapping is a more *direct* form of computing coordinate transformations than are symbolic calculations.[238] The radical question that now presents itself is whether the brain computes *anything* on the symbolic level.

Here a defender of the symbolic paradigm might object and say that since conceptual representations are, nevertheless, dependent on calculations, this form of representation is still following rules. One must make a distinction, however, between *rule following* and *rule describable* behavior (see, for example, Hahn and Chater 1998, 203–204). In symbolic systems, the processes are rule following in the sense that the symbolic rules—for example, in a computer program—affect the behavior of the system. In contrast, even though the vector calculations of a conceptual system or the learning process of an ANN may be described by symbolic equations or rules, there need be nothing in the *architecture* of these systems that corresponds to these rules—they have no causal effects.[239] To illustrate the point by an example from physics: even though the movement of a pendulum is following Galileo's law and thereby is describable by a mathematical rule, the rule itself is not represented in the pendulum—there is nothing in it that "follows" the rule.

As seen in section 2.5, Gallistel (1990) argues that the nervous system can also be seen as exploiting the representational capacity of vector spaces. He writes:[240]

> The term *vector space*, which refers to the space defined by a system of coordinates, has a surprisingly literal interpretation in the nervous system. The functional architecture of many structures that process higher-level sensory inputs is such that anatomical dimensions of the structure correspond to descriptive dimensions of the stimulus. There is reason to think that this correspondence is not fortuitous; rather, it is a foundation for the nervous system's capacity to adapt its output to the structure of the world that generates its inputs. (1990, 477)

Braitenberg (1984, 39–40) shows that by exploiting the connectivity of neurons it is possible to represent 3-D or 4-D vector spaces and so forth, using only a 2-D surface of the kind that one finds in cortex. He says the following about the "vehicle" which is his artificial cognitive system: "The point I want to make is the special virtue of networks as opposed to solids. Once you have decided to represent space by discontinuous, discrete points within the vehicle, you can represent 'neighborhood' by means of lines connecting the points. This gives you the freedom to mimic all sorts of spaces, including spaces that human mind cannot imagine" (1984, 40).

This idea is illustrated in figure 7.1, where it is shown how a 2-D surface of neurons can support a 1-D, 2-D, or 3-D topology by exploiting different systems of connections among the neurons. Hence it is not primarily the physical layout of the neurons that determines the computational topology but *the pattern of connections*. In principle, it is possible to represent topologies of any dimensionality on a 2-D surface of neurons.

Another economic aspect of vectorial representations is that they may be suitable for *sharing* knowledge between agents. This has been argued convincingly by Freyd (1983):[241]

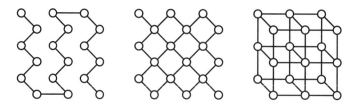

Figure 7.1
Different topologies implemented on the same 2-D pattern of neurons (based on Morasso and Sanguineti 1996, 291).

It is easier for an individual to agree with another individual about the meaning of a new "term" (or other shared concept) *if* that term can be described by (a) some small set of the much larger set of dimensions upon which things vary; and (b) some small set of dimensional values (or binary values as on a specific feature dimension). Thus, terms are likely to be defined by the presence of certain features. At the same time, children are learning to pay attention to those features or values on dimensions since they want to be able to learn about the existing shared knowledge structure. . . .

Over time one could expect mutually held domains of terms to have a dimensional structure that emphasized discrete values along a small number of dimensions. Thus, the presence or lack of a feature would be a useful way to define a number of terms. Indeed, one would expect that of all the possible dimensions available for categorizing real objects or abstract ideas, people would tend toward isolating a few dimensions that they can apply to a number of knowledge domains to ease the problems of agreeing on the meaning of new terms." (1983, 197–198)

Summing up on computations on the conceptual level, it is clear that (low-dimensional) vectorial representations open up for a programming methodology that is quite different from the focus on recursion and searching in computations on the symbolic level. Vectorial calculations allow efficient implementations of the mechanisms for concept formation, induction, and learning that have been discussed in previous chapters.

7.1.3 Associationist Calculations

The computational methodology of connectionism is quite different from that of the symbolic and conceptual approaches. As is argued by, for example, Smolensky (1988, 1991) and van Gelder (1995), connectionist systems can be seen as special cases of *dynamic systems*. A dynamic system can in general be described by a set of possible states of the system and a dynamics for these states—for example, a set of differential equations—that describe how the system changes from one state to another (as a function of the input). For example, in an ANN the states are the possible vectors of neuron activity and the dynamics is determined by the weights of the connections, the firing rules for the neurons, and the learning rule—the rule for how the weights are changed as a result of learning in the ANN.

Van Gelder (1995, 371) notes that the following three properties are special for ANNs among the class of dynamic systems:

1. ANNs are *high-dimensional* since they typically contain hundreds of neural units, each corresponding to a dimension of the state space.

2. ANNs are *homogenous* in the sense that they are constituted by units that all have the same basic form (a single equation describes the behavior of every unit in the network).

3. ANNs are *neural* in the sense that the units adjust their activation values as a function of their total input (the weighted sum of the activities of other units).

The computations performed by connectionist systems are of a different nature than Turing machine computations. It is common to point out that neural computing is *distributed* and *parallel* instead of sequential as in a Turing machine. More important, what goes on in a network can be described as a combination of a *fast* process of spreading of activities among the neurons and a *slow* learning process of adjusting the weights of connections among the neurons (see the following section). Even though each single neuron can be described as following a simple rule for its firing (normally a function of the sum of its inputs) and some rule for updating its weights, this is *not* an example of rule following in the sense described above. In biological systems, a rule is always intrinsically represented (see section 2.4).

Different kinds of *pattern recognition* or *pattern transformation* are important for connectionist systems, even though it is difficult to specify a uniform computational method for the many different kinds of artificial neuron networks.[242] Patterns can then be represented on the conceptual level, like the shapes discussed in section 3.10. The patterns are not determined by a set of explicit exact rules as in symbolic systems but rather decided by various kinds of *approximations* and *optimizations*.[243] Another important aspect, distinguishing ANNs from the Turing machine paradigm of symbolic representations, is that all these decisions are made at a very *local* level—there is no central processing unit in an ANN.

An ANN can also be seen as a multidimensional representation where the activity of *each neuron* is considered to be a dimension. This way of looking at ANNs is sometimes called the *state space* approach (P. M. Churchland 1986a, 1986b, Foss 1988). It is a special case of what in physics is called the *phase space* approach to a system. P. M. Churchland (1998) points out, however, that for some ANNs the "content" of a state is not determined by the position of the state in relation to the axes of the multidimensional state space, but to its position in relation to the *other contentful points*. Hence, any linear shift of coordinates of the state space for such an ANN should not affect its content (compare Edelman 1996).

7.1.4 Reduction of Dimensions: From Subconceptual to Conceptual Representation

When the behavior of an ANN is regular enough to be viewed from the conceptual perspective, the representational space on this level is usually of a *low dimension*. In going from the subconceptual level to the conceptual, a considerable *reduction of the number of dimensions* represented takes place. On the conceptual level, the irrelevant information has been sorted out, while the activation vectors describing the state of an ANN contain a lot of noise and other redundancies from the input.[244]

Another way of describing such a reduction of dimensions is to say that the multidimensional input to an ANN (or to a sensory organ) is *filtered* into a (small) number of domains. Schyns, Goldstone, and Thibaut (1998, 15) write (see also Petitot 1995, 237):

> Complex supercised categorization problems in high-dimensional spaces would be simplified if it were possible to reduce the dimensionality of the input. Several linear and nonlinear dimensionality reduction techniques have been designed to achieve this goal. Underlying dimensionality reduction is the idea that information processing is divided into two distinct stages. A first stage constructs a representation of the environment and a second stage uses this representation for higher level cognition such as categorization and object recognition.

The methods of multidimensional scaling that were presented in section 2.6 result in this kind of dimension reduction as do the Kohonen networks of section 6.5.2 (see also Schyns 1991). In the latter, *the very architecture* of the surfaces sets up a low-dimensional space on which a distance function may be defined.

Reduction of dimensions provides a new kind of answer to question 2 of section 6.1: how can one *generalize* from single observations to general laws. In this context, the observations are the inputs to the subconceptual level, while the "laws" are connections between domains on the conceptual level. (The laws are obviously not extrinsically represented).

Neurophysiological processes are also often described as dimension reductions.[245] Churchland and Sejnowski (1992, 171) give the following example of the transition between the two levels of computations:

> Consider, for example, that 3-D information is implicitly carried (one might say buried) in the output from the retinal ganglion cells. How can the information be extracted and made usable? An efficient and fast way to do this is to distribute and redistribute the information, to convolve the representations through the living matrix of synapses, until it shows up on our recording electrodes as a cell tuned to stimulus velocity in a specific direction, or to an illusory boundary, or to a human face. Topographic mapping then is a means whereby vector coding can bring to heel the problem of assembling relevant information. As Kohonen's 1984 model showed, in a competitive learning net, the system will self organize so that nearby vectors map onto nearby points of the net, assuming that the connections are short range. That the brain avails itself of this organization is not so much a computational necessity as a wiring economy. Far from being inconsistent with topographic mapping, vector coding exploits it.

In accordance with this, Schyns, Goldstone, and Thibaut (1998, 15) also note:

> ... the existence of low-dimensional somatosensory maps in cortex clearly demonstrates that brain structures are particularly adept at reducing high-dimensional inputs to lower-dimensional representations. ... Furthermore, there is now growing support for the notion that these natural processes of dimensionality reduction are flexible, allowing different types of reorganizations of cortical maps following different forms of sensory deprivation.
> . . .

Another method to reduce dimensionality is *vector averaging* where the activities of a large number of neurons are averaged to a single representation in a dimension of a conceptual space. Churchland and Sejnowski (1992, 233–237) discuss this computational technique and argue that there are neural mechanisms, for example in the motor cortex, that exploit vector averaging.

Yet another method is the technique of using *principal components* in ANNs, which exploits redundancies in input data (see, for example, Schyns, Goldstone, and Thibaut 1998, 15, and Schyns 1991, 471–472). If the dimensions of the input data are correlated, principal component analysis finds a number (determined by the user) of orthogonal directions in the dimensions of the input data which has the highest variation. Thus the first principal component is the spatial direction in the data set that has the highest variation and is thus the maximally "explanatory" dimension.

The process is not without drawbacks, however, Schyns, Goldstone, and Thibaut (1998, 15) make the following comment:

> In general, however, the featural interpretation of principal components is often difficult because orthogonal directions of highest variance have little connection to the best projections for categorization. That is, there are no *psychological* constraints on the principal components. Principal components need not be spatially or topologically coherent (perceptual constraints), or summarized by a single explanation (conceptual constraints).

As was pointed out at the end of section 2.3.2, this is a general problem when converting representations on the subconceptual level to conceptual structures. Even if we, for example, know that an ANN will generate Kohonen spaces that end up with an appropriate mapping, we may not be able to "describe" *what* the emerging dimensions represent. This kind of level problem is ubiquitous in applications of ANNs for learning purposes. Similar problems occur within multidimensional scaling where the technique of *property vector fitting* is often used as a way of "interpreting" the dimensions generated by MDS (compare section 1.7 and Jones and Koehly 1993, 110–112). A system that is suitable for practical purposes must somehow bridge the gap of going from the subconceptual level to the conceptual level. One such system, constructed by Chella, Frixione, and Gaglio (1997), is presented in section 7.5.

A problem of a different nature is that in the transition between levels one faces a double interpretation of "vector" that is a source of equivocation. On the one hand, there are the low-dimensional vectors on the conceptual level and, on the other, the high-dimensional state space vectors representing activities in the ANN. It is important to separate the two uses of "vector" when discussing computational aspects of cognitive processes. (The same double interpretation applies to the notion of a "state space.")

7.1.5 The Necessity of Conceptual Computations
Even if the advantages of representations on the conceptual level are considerable in comparison to symbolic representations, a defender of the connectionist approach may question whether the conceptual level

is needed. Could it not be that artificial neuron networks are sufficient to solve the representational problems? After all, there are several kinds of networks—for example, Kohonen networks—where information is represented in a dimensional structure very much like it would be represented in a conceptual space. Furthermore, biological cognitive systems are indeed neural.

It is true that ANNs learn about similarities but, in general, they do so very slowly and only after exorbitant training. The main reason for this is the high dimensionality of ANNs (see, for example, van Gelder 1995, 371). The dilatoriness of the learning is a result of each connection weight being adjusted *independently* of all the others. In addition to this, the adjustments are normally done in very small steps to avoid instabilities in the learning process. Since the vectorial representations of conceptual spaces have a much lower dimensionality and hence much *fewer parameters* that must be estimated, learning different kinds of patterns can be speeded up considerably by exploiting the conceptual level. This is an aspect of the *learning economy* of conceptual representation that is often neglected. In brief, using conceptual spaces facilitates learning in artificial systems.

One way of making learning in ANNs more efficient is to build in *structural constraints* when setting up the architecture of a network. One can reduce the dimensionality of the learning process by making neurons *dependent* variables (see section 2.3.2). Adding structural constraints, however, often means that some forms of information about the relevant domains or other dimension generating structures are added to the network. Consequently, this strategy presumes the conceptual level in the very construction of the network. Nosofsky (1992, 49) argues that in the future such influence from the conceptual level on connectionist systems will become important:

> One direction likely to be pursued will involve the use of similarity scaling to constrain connectionist/distributed models of perception and cognition. The recent explosion of studies that demonstrate the potential power of connectionist models is slowly giving way to efforts to test these models rigorously on their psychological validity and predictive, quantitative accuracy. An impediment to developing rigorous tests is that there is often no associated theory of stimulus representation in these models.[246]

Even though he is not always consistent (see section 7.3), Smolensky (1988, 223) writes as if the cognitive representation takes place only on a conceptual level: "[C]onnectionist cognitive architecture is intrinsically two-level: semantic interpretation is carried out at the level of patterns of activity while the complete, precise, and formal account of mental processing must be carried out at the level of individual activity values and connections. Mental processes reside at a lower level of analysis than mental representations."

If "patterns of activity" are defined by conceptual spaces (as in section 3.10), Smolensky's position comes very close to the one defended here. Sometimes he fails, however, to distinguish this kind of pattern from symbolic structures (compare section 7.3).

7.2 Conceptual Spaces as Emergent Systems

7.2.1 "Fast" and "Slow" Features of a System

In physical systems one often finds descriptions of "slow" and "fast" aspects of dynamic processes. A well-known example from statistical mechanics is the slow changes of temperature as a different perspective on a complex system of fast-moving gas molecules. Another example is catastrophe theory (Thom 1972), which is an entire mathematical discipline devoted to investigating the qualitative properties (in particular the "catastrophes") of the slow manifolds generated by a dynamical system. For example, Petitot (1989) exploits catastrophe theory to derive some of the topological properties of phonetic space (which is the slow manifold in a phonological system).[247] Many other researchers in the cognitive sciences, however, work with related notions, for example, Amit (1989) P. M. Churchland (1989), Pellionisz and Llinas (1982, 1985), Port and van Gelder (1995) and Scott Kelso (1995).

Cognitive systems are dynamical systems (Petitot 1992, 1995, Port and van Gelder 1995). Conceptual spaces, as such, are not. The analogy to make in the context of the relation between the symbolic, conceptual, and the connectionist computational paradigms is that connectionism deals with the fast behavior of a dynamic system, while vectorial (and even symbolic) structures may *emerge* as slow features of such a system.[248]

The behavior of dynamical systems can often be described economically by their *attractor points*, that is, the stable points that the systems ends up in after having been perturbed by some input. From this perspective, a conceptual space can be seen as the set of attractor points of an underlying dynamical system, for example an ANN, and thus the conceptual space is a way of summarizing the behavior of the system.[249] Petitot (1995, 234–235) writes:

> [I]n the morphodynamical paradigm the conceptual contents of mental states and their semantic correlates are no longer

identified with labels for symbolic ordering. *Their meaning is embodied in the cognitive processing itself.* More precisely, it is identified with the *topology* of the complex attractors of the underlying neural dynamics, and the mental events are identified with sequences of bifurcations of such attractors. The basic analogy is with thermodynamics, phases, and phase transitions.

Let me elaborate on the double interpretation for the case when the system is an ANN. Pictorially, the fast behavior of an ANN are the "associations" between the neurons in the network—the transmissions of the activity within the network. The slow process can be described as that the ANN is locating minima in a "cognitive dissonance function" (which can be identified as maxima in Smolensky's (1986) harmony functions, as will be seen below). Sometimes, the slow dynamics of an ANN is represented as the set of attractor points or "resonant states" of the system (see, for example, Rumelhart and McClelland 1986). Van Gelder (1998, 621) makes the same point in relation to more general dynamic models of cognition: "Dynamicists . . . understand a state geometrically, in terms of its position with respect to other states and features of the system's dynamical landscape such as basins of attraction."

The stabilization in attractor points can, for many ANNs, be described with the aid of the so-called *harmony function* (see Smolensky 1986). Mathematically, this function assigns an "energy" value to a state s of the network (a state is defined as the set of all activation values of the neurons). The formula is:

$$H(s) = \Sigma_{ij} s_i s_j w_{ij}. \tag{7.1}$$

Here s_i and s_j are the activity values of neurons i and j, respectively, and w_{ij} is the weight of the connection between neurons i and j. The energy function is defined in such a way that the dynamics of the ANN strives to maximize the harmony of the state of the network. If a network stabilizes in an attractor state, it has reached a (local) maximum of the harmony function. $E(s) = -H(s)$ is often called the *energy function* of the network. Thus maximal "harmony" corresponds to minimal "energy."

If the ANN is sufficiently regular in its behavior, the set of attractor points will form a low-dimensional hyper-surface in the high-dimensional state space of the ANN. Under certain conditions, this surface can be interpreted as a conceptual space. In such cases, we have a very elegant way of explaining how the conceptual level of representation emerges from the subconceptual.

7.2.2 Emergent Inferences

When a dynamical system is fed information that represents the observed features of an object as input, the attractor points of the system can be seen as a description of what further properties of the object are to be *expected*. This kind of process often occurs in ANNs (see, for example, Balkenius and Gärdenfors 1991). A large class of ANNs are *resonant* systems in the sense that, for any input activity vector, the activity of the ANN will, after some time, stabilize in an attractor state. For example, all ANNs with symmetric connections between pairs of neurons are resonant systems.

Since the input vector is often only partial, in the sense that only certain dimensions of the object are represented, the ANN calculates a *vector completion* in that the vector given by the attractor state represents the expected values of the unobserved dimensions. If the features of the input vector are "incoherent" according to what has been learned by the ANN, the system may change the values of the observed dimensions to what it expects; thus it may "correct" the observed value.

In Balkenius and Gärdenfors (1991) it is shown that the slow behavior of many networks, corresponding to the attractor states, can be described as the results of the network performing *inferences* in a precisely defined sense and with a well-defined logical structure. It turns out the these inferences are, in a very natural way, *nonmonotonic* (compare section 4.5).

In comparison, Smolensky sees the activities of a connectionist system as performing inferences even on the *subconceptual* level. This point is made very clearly in Dellarosa's (1988, 29) commentary:

> It is a belief of many cognitive scientists (most notably, Fodor 1975) that the fundamental process of cognition is inference, a process to which symbolic modelling is particularly well suited. While Smolensky points out that statistical inference replaces logical inference in connectionist systems, he too continues to place inference at the heart of all cognitive activity. I believe that something more fundamental is taking place. In most connectionist models, the fundamental process of cognition is not inference, but is instead the (dear to the heart of psychologists) activation of associated units in a network. Inference "emerges" as a system-level interpretation of this microlevel activity, but— when representations are distributed—no simple one-to-one mapping of activity patterns to symbols and inferences can be made. From this viewpoint, the fundamental process of cognition is the activation of associated units, and inference is a second-order process.

Hence, Smolensky is wrong in talking about "nonmonotonic inferences" on the subconceptual level, since there are no inferences on this level; claiming this confuses levels of representation and is basically a kind of category error.[250] As is argued in Balkenius and Gärdenfors (1991), however, he is right in that the inferences that emerge on the symbolic level from the subconceptual processes are fundamentally nonmonotonic.

7.3 Smolensky's Treatment of Connectionism

It is worthwhile comparing the three levels of representing information presented in this book with Smolensky's (1988) distinction between the subsymbolic and symbolic levels in the context of connectionist models. In a later article (1991, 203), he states the difference between connectionism and symbolic representation as follows (see also his 1988, hypothesis 8, 6): "The connectionist systems I will advocate hypothesize models that are not an *implementation* but rather a *refinement* of the Classical symbolic approach; these connectionist models hypothesize a truly different cognitive architecture, to which the Classical architecture is a scientifically important approximation."

Smolensky also rebuts the argument that, in principle, one type of system can be *simulated* by a system of the other kind. First, he argues, connectionist models cannot be "merely implementations, for a certain kind of parallel hardware, of symbolic programs that provide exact and complete accounts of behavior at the conceptual level" (1988, hypothesis 10, 7) since this conflicts with the connectionist assumption that neural networks cannot be completely described on the symbolic ("conceptual") level (1988, hypothesis 8c, 6–7). Second, even if a symbolic system is often used to implement a connectionist system, "the symbols in such programs represent the activation values of units and the strength of connections" (1988, 7), and they do not have the conceptual semantics required by the symbolic paradigm. Thus the translated programs are not symbolic programs of the right kind.

Smolensky's "subsymbolic level" corresponds closely enough to what is called the subconceptual level in this book. He confounds, however, the symbolic and conceptual levels. He even uses the two names: "I will call the preferred level of the symbolic paradigm the *conceptual* level and that of the subsymbolic paradigm the *subconceptual* level" (Smolensky 1988, 3). The reason for the confusion is simple: he is committing himself to so-called "high church computationalism" by "limiting consideration to the Newell/Simon/Fodor/Pylyshyn view of cognition" (1988, 3). One of the central tenets of the symbolic approach is what Smolensky (1988, 5) formulates as hypothesis 4b:

"The programs running on the intuitive processor are composed of elements, that is, symbols, referring to essentially the same concepts as the ones used to consciously conceptualize the task domain."

He then gives the following reason for calling the symbolic level "conceptual":

> Cognitive models of both conscious rule application and intuitive processing have been programs constructed of entities which are *symbols* both in the syntactic sense of being operated on by symbol manipulation and in the semantic sense of (4b). Because these symbols have the conceptual semantics of (4b), I am calling the level of analysis at which these programs provide cognitive models the *conceptual level*.

As I have shown earlier, however, there is a well-established tradition within cognitive science where the conceptual level of this book is given independent standing. Even though he fails to identify it as a separate level, Smolensky is well aware of the "vectorial" approach involved in conceptual spaces, as can be seen from this quotation: "Substantive progress in subsymbolic cognitive science requires that systematic commitments be made to vectorial representations for individual cognitive domains. . . . Unlike symbolic tokens, these vectors lie in a topological space in which some are close together and others far apart" (Smolensky 1988, 8).

As can be seen, he is aware that the symbolic approach has difficulties with representations of distances and similarity. He even recognizes the importance of establishing a connection between the subconceptual and the conceptual levels:

> Powerful mathematical tools are needed for relating the overall behavior of the network to the choice of representational vectors; ideally, these tools should allow us to *invert* the mapping from representations to behavior so that by starting with a mass of data on human performance we can turn the mathematical crank and have the representational vectors pop up. An example of this general type of tool is the technique of *multidimensional scaling* (Shepard 1962), which allows data on human judgments of similarity between pairs of items in some set to be tuned to vectors for representing those items (in a sense). The subsymbolic paradigm needs tools such as a version of multidimensional scaling based on a connectionist model of the process of producing similarity judgments. (Smolensky 1988, 8)

I conclude that Smolensky's binary distinction between the symbolic and the subsymbolic level is insufficient. All three levels of representing information that have been presented in this book are needed to give an adequate description of the various cognitive processes that are encountered in the biological realm as well as in the artificial.

It is often claimed that the symbolic and the associationist/connectionist paradigms are *incompatible*. Some of the most explicit arguments for this position have been put forward by Smolensky (1988, 7) and Fodor and Pylyshyn (1988). Smolensky argues that, on the one hand, symbolic programs requires linguistically formalized precise rules that are sequentially interpreted (hypothesis 4a in his paper); and, on the other hand, connectionist systems cannot be given a complete and formal description on the symbolic level (hypothesis 8).

I do not agree that the symbolic and the connectionist modes of representation are incompatible. The relation between the symbolic and conceptual levels on one side and the connectionist (subconceptual) level on the other is rather, as described in the previous section, that connectionism deals with the fast behavior of a dynamic system, while the conceptual and symbolic structures may emerge as slow features of such a system.[251]

7.4 Not All Computation Is Done by Turing Machines

The different perspectives on computing that are discussed here are not only applicable to neural networks. Also the behavior of a traditional computer with a von Neumann architecture can be given a "subconceptual" interpretation and need not be seen as merely symbol crunching. The subconceptual perspective is adopted when one describes the dynamic properties of the physical processes driving the computer; for example when describing the electric properties of transistors. This is the perspective that one must adopt when the computer is defective, in which case the processing on the symbolic level does not function as expected (compare Dennett 1978, chapter 1).

A consequence of the fact that one can adopt multiple perspectives on all kinds of computing devices is that every ascription of symbolic processing to some system is an *interpretation* of the activities of the system. The Turing paradigm of computation neglects this distinction since a computer is thought to uniquely identify some Turing machine; and, clearly, Turing machines are described on the symbolic level.[252] The reason this identification works is that traditional computers are constructed to be "digital," that is, on the subconceptual perspective the outcomes of the electronic processes are very robust with respect to disturbances (so that particular currents can be identified as either 1s or 0s) and the behavior of the "logical" gates is predictable. The identification may break down, however, as soon as the computer is malfunctioning.

It follows that the notion of "computation" can be given two meanings. The first, and to many the only meaning, is computation on the symbolic level in the sense that is made precise by "Turing computable." According to Church's thesis this kind of computation is all there is *on the symbolic level.* The other sense of computation only becomes apparent when one adopts a conceptual or subconceptual (connectionist or more general associationist) perspective. From this perspective "computation" means "processing representations," where the representations have a fundamentally different structure compared to those on the symbolic level described in section 7.1. And processing on this level does not mean "manipulating symbols" but must be characterized in other ways. Some kinds of processing of representations on the conceptual and subconceptual levels generate structures that can be interpreted meaningfully on the symbolic level. Many kinds of processes, however, cannot be interpreted on the symbolic level as performing any form of Turing computation. For instance, the notion of "analog" computation only makes sense on the conceptual and subconceptual levels (Sloman 1971). Hence, the class of computational processes on these levels is much wider than the class of processes corresponding to Turing computations. Church's thesis does not apply to these senses of "computation."

Even if artificial neuron networks can be simulated by Turing machines, it does not mean that they perform the same kind of computations as Turing machines do (compare Smolensky's arguments in the previous section). On this point, Harnad (1990) writes:

> Connectionist networks can be simulated using symbol systems, and symbol systems can be implemented using a connectionist architecture, but that is independent of the question of what each can do *qua* symbol system or connectionist network, respectively. By way of analogy, silicon can be used to build a computer, and a computer can simulate the properties of silicon, but the functional properties of silicon are not those of computation, and the functional properties of computation are not those of silicon.

In addition to Harnad's point, there are other aspects where a connectionist system differs from the system simulated by a Turing machine. A computationally important feature is that the *complexity* of the computations may be incomparable. For example, the edge-detection processing of an image in an artificial connectionist retina may take place in a few (massively parallel) steps, while a Turing machine will need thousands of (sequential) steps to simulate the process. If the retina is doubled in size, this will not markedly change the number of steps in the connectionist system, but it will multiply the number of steps performed by the Turing machine.[253]

7.5 A System for Object Recognition

Chella, Frixione, and Gaglio (1997) have constructed an interesting example of a computational architecture for some tasks within artificial vision that utilizes all three levels of representing information.[254] Their architecture is summarized in figure 7.2.

The three levels of representation are constructed with the aid of five computational blocks. Block A receives digitized images as input and gives as output a $2\frac{1}{2}$-D description of the input image according to

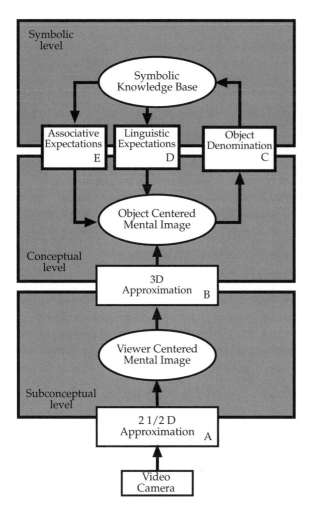

Figure 7.2
The general architecture of a three-level vision system (based on Chella, Frixione, and Gaglio 1997).

Marr's (1982) model. This can be seen as a representation on the sub-conceptual level.

Block B builds, on the conceptual level, a scene consisting of a combination of 3-D geometrical primitives. The geometrical primitives are based on "superquadrics" (see Pentland 1986) that can be described in a 5-D shape space by three parameters and two "form factors" (compare the analysis of shapes in setion 3.10). The spatial position of a primitive building block is then coded by a set of six coordinates consisting of three center coordinates and three orientation parameters. Each geometrical primitive is thus described by an eleven-dimensional vector. The algorithms in block B estimate these coordinates from the data given on the subconceptual level. A *scene* is a collection of such estimated primitives. For example, a scene may contain as primitives models of the handle and the head of a hammer. Consequently, a scene can be described by a set of *vectors* in a conceptual space that combines information about the shape and location of objects.

The computational links between the conceptual and the symbolic levels are bidirectional in the system: the conceptual level functions as the semantic domain for the symbols, and the symbolic level generates *expectations* that control the *focus of attention* in the scenes that are created on the conceptual level. This system has the effect of scanning the information contained in the scenes in an effective way.

Block C maps the conceptual level to the symbolic level by proposing a categorization of the objects modeled on the conceptual level. For instance, it can suggest that two geometric primitives identified on the conceptual level forms the handle and head of a hammer and thus introduce a symbolic representation "hammer" of the combination. Objects are represented on the symbolic level by a version of the KL-ONE system (Brachman and Schmoltze 1985). Block D uses symbolic expectations to drive the focus of attention of the visual system. If, for example, "computer screen" is identified from the conceptual level, the knowledge representation on the symbolic level will generate an expectation that a "keyboard" will be found in the scene, which then will function as a top-down constraint on the conceptual level. Block E, finally, is responsible for the associative mode of the focus of attention. This mode connects different kinds of objects via a Hebbian learning mechanism, so if a hammer has often been present together with a sickle in the scenes seen by the system, then the next time a hammer is seen the focus of attention tries to find a sickle, too.[255] The expectation systems in blocks D and E are both implemented by attractor ANNs (Hopfield 1982).

As can be seen in figure 7.2, the system of Chella, Frixione, and Gaglio combines bottom-up and top-down processes in the identification of objects. The symbolic level is used to generate "expectations" of what to look for on the conceptual level. The system is an excellent example of how the three different levels of representation can *cooperate* and *complement* each other in an artificial system that is performing a cognitive task. An implementation of variant of the system in a robot is presented in Chella, Frixione, and Gaglio (to appear).

7.6 Conclusion

This chapter has attempted to show that, depending on which level of representation is adopted, different kinds of computational processes will become relevant. On the symbolic level, searching, matching of symbol strings, and rule following are central. On the subconceptual level, pattern recognition, pattern transformation, and dynamic adaptation of values are some examples of typical computational processes. And on the intermediate conceptual level, vector calculations, coordinate transformations, as well as other geometrical operations are in focus. Of course, one type of calculation can be *simulated* by one of the others (for example, by symbolic methods on a Turing machine). A point that is often forgotten, however, is that the simulations will, in general, be computationally *more complex* than the process that is simulated. So, when constructing artificial systems, one will consequently improve efficiency by exploiting computations on different levels of representation.

Chapter 8

In Chase of Space

8.1 What Has Been Achieved?

This book has been an investigation into the geometry of cognitive representations. One of its main messages is that when analyzing representations in cognitive systems, one should distinguish three levels of representation: the subconceptual, the conceptual, and the symbolic. It has also been suggested that the three levels should take different roles in the construction of artificial cognitive systems.

Most of the analyses in the previous chapters have been devoted to cognitive problems that can be treated using geometrical and topological representations on the conceptual level. My ambition has been rather comprehensive since I have tried to apply the conceptual level of analysis to widely varying areas within cognitive science.

I have provided analyses of properties and concepts. The distinction between the two notions has been neglected in the literature. A key notion has been that of a *natural property* which is defined in terms of well-behaved regions of conceptual spaces—a definition that cardinally involves the geometrical structure of the various domains.

I have suggested new ways of modeling concept formation, nonmonotonic inferences, and inductive reasoning. I have tried to clarify how these processes are related. For these problem areas, I have also shown how different considerations become relevant depending on whether one focuses on the symbolic, the conceptual or the subconceptual level.

Another major theme has been a cognitively based semantic theory. I have defended a conceptualistic view of semantics where the meanings of linguistic expressions are cognitive structures rather than entities in the external world, let alone entities in merely possible worlds. I have also emphasized the connections between perceptual and linguistic representations. My position is not purely cognitive, but rather "sociocognitive," since I do not claim that meanings are entirely in the head of single individuals, but they *emerge* from the conceptual structures in the heads of the language users together with the linguistic power structure.

The framework connecting all these themes has been the theory of conceptual spaces. I hope the results that have been presented, even if they sometimes are merely programmatic, justify the claim that conceptual spaces and, more generally, a conceptual level of representation ought to play a central role within cognitive science.

After having been dominant for many years, the symbolic approach was challenged by connectionism (which has nowadays been broadened to a wider study of dynamical systems). For many purposes, however, the symbolic level of representation is too coarse, and the connectionist level too fine-grained to be manageable. In particular the limitations show up in models of learning. On the symbolic level, it is never explained how the basic concepts are learned. It is true that the connectionist models handle this problem but they do it at a cost—they learn much more slowly than humans do. I believe that the conceptual level is the right level to formulate models of learning.

In relation to the two goals of cognitive science, I submit that the conceptual level will add significantly to our explanatory capacities when it comes to understanding cognitive processes, in particular those connected with learning, concept formation, and language understanding. I believe that from the constructive point of view, the conceptual level will be very advantageous for many applications, in particular within robotics. Furthermore, by making explicit the three levels and their interrelations, a unified view of representations in cognitive science might emerge.

The borderline between constructive and explanatory uses of conceptual spaces is not sharp. When constructing the representational world of a robot, for example, it is often worthwhile to take lessons from how biology has solved the problems in the brains of humans and other animals. Conversely, the construction of an artificial system that can successfully solve a particular cognitive problem may provide clues to how an empirical investigation of biological systems should proceed. For example, the development of our understanding of visual processes in the brain has been influenced by some of the computational models that have been proposed within artificial vision. Consequently, there can be a spiraling interaction between constructive and explanatory uses of conceptual spaces.

In the remainder of this concluding chapter, I first bring forth some aspects of the connections among the three levels that summarizes much of the constructions developed in the previous chapters. Second, I argue that a predominant obstacle for the further development of a theory of conceptual spaces is a lack of an appropriate *methodology* for studies of representations on the conceptual level.

8.2 Connections among Levels

Depending on the perspective adopted, one and the same biological system can be seen as both an associationist mechanism and as a conceptual space which, in turn, sometimes provides a grounding for a symbolic system. Thus, by changing from one perspective to the other, conceptual representations and symbolic inferences can be seen as *emerging* from dynamic processes in a connectionist system.[256] The pivotal point is that when we are studying a cognitive system in the explanatory mode there is no need to distinguish among two or three kinds of systems—the different perspectives can be adopted on a single information processing system. In constructive applications, the three perspectives aid us in selecting the right kind of representation for a particular cognitive modeling task. In such a context, it is often natural to work with an architecture that exploits cooperating systems functioning on different levels of representation. Such *hybrid systems* have become quite popular among cognitive scientists. A particularly illustrative example of such a use of the three levels is the model of artificial vision proposed by Chella, Frixione, and Gaglio (1997) which was discussed in the previous chapter.

In brief, the conceptual level can be seen as a *bridge* between the two other levels.[257] In biological systems, the dimensions of a conceptual space often emerge from self-organizing neural systems. This generally involves a reduction of dimensionality from that of the subconceptual level. When going from the conceptual to the symbolic level, the symbolic structures can be seen as emerging from the structure of the conceptual spaces. For example, the tessellations of a conceptual region induced by different categorization mechanisms, like those studied in chapter 4, provide the disjoint regions that are assigned as the *meanings* of basic symbols. This position is defended by Petitot (1995, 234):

> The Chomskyan thesis that ignorance of the physical basis of mental structures forces one to restrict syntactic theory to a mere formal description of competence need not be accepted. Even if one does not know the neurophysiological implementation of this competence, one can nevertheless hypothesize that there are *dynamical processes underlying performance* and that the formal structures of competence *emerge* from them.
> ... [T]he conceptual contents of mental states and their semantic correlates are no longer identified with labels for symbolic ordering. *Their meaning is embodied in the cognitive processing itself.* More precisely, it is identified with the *topology* of the complex attractors of the underlying neural dynamics. ...

The representations on the three levels occur at different *scales* of resolution: a high-dimensional vector on the subconceptual level is reduced to a low-dimensional structured vector on the conceptual level; and a symbol just summarizes the information contained in a region of a domain of a conceptual space by refering to the prototypical element of the region (compare the jungle analogy in section 2.1 where peoples' movements could also be described on different scales).[258]

In Chomskian linguistics and much of functionalist philosophy, the symbolic structures are thought of as having an independent standing. According to Dixon (1982), Petitot (1995), and several of the cognitive linguists, however, much of the syntactic relations emerge from structures on the conceptual level. Schyns (1991, 503) argues that such connections between levels are unavoidable: "[S]ymbols either have the status of indicators of knowledge or facilitators of concept extraction. In both cases, they are ultimately grounded on conceptual knowledge."

Although his methodology is not exactly the same as the one presented here, Kohonen's (1995, 73) account of different kinds of representation strikes a similar tone:

> The possibility that the representation of knowledge in a particular category [domain] of things in general might assume the form of a feature map [conceptual space] that is geometrically organized over the corresponding piece of the brain has motivated the series of theoretical investigations reported in this book. The results thereby obtained have gradually led this author into believing that one and the same general functional principle might be responsible for self-organization of widely different representations of information. Furthermore, some results indicate that the very same functional principle that operates on a uniform, singly-connected, one-level medium is also able to represent *hierarchically related data*, by assigning different subareas of a homogenous medium to different abstract levels of information. The representations over such maps then resemble [symbolically represented] *tree structures* that are obtained by conventional taxonomic and clustering methods. . . .

As noted in section 7.1.2, another aspect that distinguishes the three levels is that the representation on the subconceptual level is often *viewer centered*, while it is *object centered* on the conceptual level (compare Chella, Frixione, and Gaglio 1997). On the symbolic level finally, the representations have become *amodal*, since there is nothing in the symbolic structures themselves that distinguishes the different domains.[259] In contrast, the low-level quality dimensions of conceptual spaces are more or less tied to perceptual mechanisms.

8.3 Conclusion: The Need for a New Methodology

As presented in this book, the theory of representations based on conceptual spaces is more a research program than a well-developed theory. The theory is full of gaps. How can it be elaborated?

The main factor preventing a rapid advancement of different applications of conceptual spaces is the *lack of knowledge* about the relevant quality dimensions. It is slightly discomforting to read that Locke already formulated the problem in his *Essay* in 1690:

> [M]en are far enough from having agreed on the precise number of simple ideas or qualities belonging to any sort of things, signified by its name. Nor is it a wonder; since it requires much time, pains, and skill, strict inquiry, and long examination to find out what, and how many, those simple ideas are, which are constantly and inseparably united in nature, and are always to be found together in the same subject. (1690/1959, book III, chapter VI, 30)

It is almost only for perceptual dimensions that psychophysical research has succeeded in clearly identifying the underlying geometrical and topological structures (and, in rare cases, the psychological metric). For example, we still have only a very sketchy understanding of how we perceive and conceptualize things according to their shapes. Psychophysics, however, is not the only entry to the dimensions. As indicated in chapter 5, metaphors, as they occur in everyday language, can give clues to the structures we ascribe to more abstract domains. Again, a lot of empirical work is needed before these clues can be developed into a systematic understanding of such domains.

To attain a mature theory of conceptual spaces a new *research methodology* is also requisite. The symbolic tradition has fairly well established methodologies involving various kinds of symbol manipulation techniques in different areas. Within connectionism the situation is not so settled, but there are several paradigms for constructing, testing, and evaluating ANNs. On the conceptual level, vectorial representations are not unknown; people from rather different research areas such as perception, machine learning, and cognitive semantics have been working with dimensions, distances, and vectors. Even though there are methodological precursors like Suppes et al. (1989) and Petitot (1992), however, the conceptual level ought to be much more strongly identified as a separate type of representation.

There are a number of fundamental methodological questions that ought to be addressed:

- How does one find out how dimensions are structured?

I have outlined some techniques for identifying the structure of conceptual space, such as psychophysical measurements, multidimensional scaling, and Kohonen networks. It would be advantageous, however, to have an overarching theory for this problem.

- Which are the best dimensions, the best topology, the best metric to be used for representing a particular cognitive process?

On this question, Austen Clark (1993, 147) notes:

Metric assumptions are . . . treacherous. Distances are monotonically related to similarities, but there is no presumption that sums or ratios of distances are interpretable. There may be no common unit to express distances along different axes. Instead, the "space" of multidimensional scaling is the sparse and empty sort found in graph theory and branches of topology. It is a representation of the order intrinsic to sensory judgements, and is discovered, not postulated.

As so often happens in science, a breakthrough in a representational problem area comes when a set of interpretable dimensions is found that creates order in the similarity and classificatory judgments of people. When the dimensions are found, one can dig deeper into the details of their topological and geometrical structure.

When the structure of the dimensions of a particular domain is unearthed, often fruitful research follows. For example, the development of the vowel space that was presented in section 3.8 started from the discovery of the dimensional role of the different formants in describing the data. This discovery has led to a wealth of new results in phonetics and to a deeper understanding of the speech process (see, for example, Fairbanks and Grubb 1961, and Petitot 1989, Kuhl et al. 1997).

- How are levels of representation connected?

This is perhaps the least understood question. Only in a few cases, like when the set of attractor points form a regular (hyper-)surface, as described in section 7.2.1, do we have a principled account of the connections among levels.

- What is the dynamics of representations in conceptual spaces? How are different kinds of learning best modeled?

Only occasionally, such as when discussing the learning of concepts using Voronoi tessellations, have I touched upon the dynamic processes involving conceptual spaces. This is obviously an area that deserves much more thorough treatment.

· How do we create the right emergent structures in ANNs?

Engineering complex systems that generate interesting emergent structures is an extremely difficult task. It has taken nature many millions of years of evolutionary processes to achieve such systems. In most artificial systems that operate with different levels of representation, the connections are added explicitly by the programmer, like in the systems of Chella, Frixione, and Gaglio (1997, to appear). By adding constraints on the conceptual level, one can reduce the number of degrees of freedom in the learning on the subconceptual level, which hopefully speeds up the learning process.

· How should one model structural representations, such as shapes consisting of connected parts?

In section 3.10, I presented some first attempts to model shape spaces. When it comes to shapes consisting of several parts, however, we still have a very fragmentary understanding of the structure of the underlying conceptual space (Tversky and Hemenway 1984).

· What is the role of action concepts and functional concepts in the research program?

In section 3.10.2, I sketched how actions and functional concepts could be analyzed with the aid of (dynamic) conceptual spaces. These kinds of concepts are very important for a general theory of concepts. Much ground-breaking work remains, however, before the sketches can be turned into something substantial.

Despite all these methodological lacunas and all the caveats, I believe that once the conceptual level is focused on, the research program offers exciting prospects. Thus, those who want to contribute to the research program should start hunting for the hidden conceptual spaces. First, as presented in section 2.5, the rapid development of neuroscience may generate new insights into the structure of our cognitive processes. And, as argued there, good reasons exist for viewing representations in the brain as geometrical objects. Successful conceptual models will also give feedback to the neuroscientific investigations in the form of predictions to be tested. Another ground is that efficient computer programs for learning, induction, and concept formation depend on finding apt representations on the conceptual level. Finally, these representations contain the meanings of linguistic expressions. Even if results on the structure of conceptual spaces may not be easily forthcoming, they are sure to have repercussions in many areas of cognitive science.

In the heyday of logical positivism and good old-fashioned AI, when the symbolic approach was the only game in town, the war call was:

"go out and axiomatize!" Later, connectionists propagated a more pragmatic methodology: "let the networks pick up what structure there is by training, training, and training!" I believe that neither approach gives a complete description of our cognitive processes. To understand the structure of our thoughts and to be able to build artificial systems with similar cognitive capacities, we should aim at unveiling our conceptual spaces.

Notes

Chapter 1

1. An extreme position is held by Brooks (1991) who argues that representations are not needed at all (see also Freeman and Skarda 1990). For a forceful rebuttal of his position, see Kirsch (1991).
2. See, for example, Fenstad (1998) for a survey of the representational forms used within semantics.
3. Since all levels may be identified in one single system, they may as well be called *perspectives*.
4. Even though Armstrong belongs to a realistic tradition of concept theories, the desiderata that he presents are also applicable to the conceptualistic approach of this book.
5. The perception of the spatial dimensions is also partly generated by other senses like touch and stereo hearing.
6. In traditional philosophy, following Descartes and Locke, a distinction between "primary" and "secondary" qualities is often made. This distinction corresponds roughly to the distinction between "scientific" and "psychological" dimensions to be presented in the following section.
7. Compare Austen Clark (1993, 112–114) who gives an account of how dimensions are based on differentiative attributes.
8. It is interesting to note, however, that during a period of phlogiston chemistry, scientists considered negative weights to evade some of the anomalies of the theory (see Kuhn 1970).
9. In section 6.4, the conceptual space of Newtonian mechanics is briefly considered. This is a prime example of a scientific conceptual space.
10. Quine (1969, 127) makes the point very succinctly: "Color is king in our innate quality space, but undistinguished in cosmic circles. Cosmically, colors would not qualify as kinds."
11. It appears to be assumed that this interval is closed, which means that there is a maximal phenomenal color intensity.
12. A similar point is made by P. M. Churchland (1998, 8) with respect to representations in neural networks: "A point in activation space acquires a specific semantic content not as a function of its position relative to the constituting *axes* of that space, but rather as a function of (1) its spatial position relative to all of the *other content-ful points* within that space; and (2) its causal relations to stable and objective *macro-features of the external environment*." See also Edelman (1996).
13. The importance of the "second-order relation" underlying representations will be illustrated in connection with concept formation in section 4.4.3.
14. In this connection, Saunders and van Brakel (1997, 177) point out the following problem for any attempt to match the scientific dimensions of color with the

phenomenal: "There is strong evidence that between retina and cortex, processing of wavelength is intricately mixed with luminosity, form, texture, movement response, and other environmental change. It is sometimes suggested that the value of colour vision is to pick up survival information from the environment. But why pick up *colour*? Answers could be: because colour contributes to object recognition; or: it contributes to identifying edible fruits, and so on. However, to arrive at the conclusion that the fruit is ripe, or over there, there is no unique need for colour. . . ." This quotation underscores the importance of maintaining the distinction between the scientific and the phenomenal interpretation of quality dimensions.

15. See, for example, Gabrielsson (1981, 20–21).

16. For further discussion of the structure of musical space, see Shepard (1982), Krumhansl and Kessler (1982), and Gärdenfors (1988b, sections 7–9).

17. See Schiffman (1982, chapter 9) for an exposition of some such theories.

18. Readers who find mathematics boring, or at least overrated, can skip the formal details of this section and rely on the intuitive meanings of the notions. Readers who want to know more about the relevant mathematics can consult Borsuk and Szmielew (1960) and Suppes et al. (1989, chapter 12).

19. It may be necessary to point out that these axioms belong to the *metatheory* of "between." Hence, even if the metatheory uses the symbolic form of representation, it says nothing directly about how betweenness itself is represented. As a matter of fact, most uses of betweenness relations in this book concern representations on the conceptual level.

20. Birkhoff (1967, 42–43) studies the notion of betweenness in *lattices* and formulates a set of axioms that entail B1–B4. A technical difference is that he allows that if b is between a and c, then b and c may be identical points. Goodman (1966) presents a phenomenal definition of betweenness based on "matching" rather than on similarity. He proves that the defined relation satisfies many of the basic properties of betweenness. See Austen Clark (1993, 81–83) for a discussion of Goodman's proposal.

21. For another nonstandard example of a "line," see the discussion of polar coordinates in section 3.5.

22. Let us say that point b is between point a and line L, in symbols $B(a, b, L)$, if there is some point c on L such that $B(a, b, c)$. Similarly, L is between a and b, in symbols $B(a, L, b)$, if there is some point c on L such that $B(a, c, b)$. Then if a, b, and c are three points that do not lie on any line, the *plane* through a, b, and c can be defined as the set of all points d such that $B(a, d, L_{bc})$ or $B(b, d, L_{ac})$ or $B(c, d, L_{ab})$ or $B(d, a, L_{bc})$ or $B(d, b, L_{ac})$ or $B(d, c, L_{ab})$ or $B(a, L_{bc}, d)$ or $B(b, L_{ac}, d)$ or $B(c, L_{ab}, d)$ (Borsuk and Szmielew 1960, 58). Again, we are not guaranteed that such a plane will look like a plane from Euclidean geometry.

23. For readers with some background in mathematical analysis, it may be interesting to know that it possible to formulate an axiom of continuity *only* using the notion of betweenness (Borsuk and Szmielew 1960, 151):

> B6: For any sets X and Y of points, if there exists a point a such that $p \in X$ and $q \in Y$ implies $B(a, p, q)$, then there exists a point b such that $p \in X\text{-}b$ and $q \in Y\text{-}b$ implies $B(p, b, q)$.

24. Proof: (i) From $E(a, b, c, d)$ and $E(a, b, b, a)$, it follows by E3 that $E(c, d, b, a)$. From this, together with $E(c, d, e, f)$, it follows by E3 again that $E(b, a, e, f)$. From $E(b, a, a, b)$ and $E(b, a, e, f)$, it follows by one more application of E3 that $E(a, b, e, f)$. (ii) From $E(a, b, c, d)$ and $E(c, d, d, c)$, it follows immediately by (i) that $E(a, b, d, c)$.

25. See Suppes et al. (1989, section 12.2.6) for more details on Minkowski geometries.

26. See Kruskal and Wish (1978) and Jones and Koehly (1993) for presentations of the techniques and methodology of multidimensional scaling.

27. See Kruskal (1964) or Jones and Koehly (1993, 100–101) for a definition of the stress function.

28. This is often expressed as looking for a "knee" in the curve mapping stress as a function of n.

29. See Jones and Koehly (1993, 110–112).

30. It is sometimes difficult to maintain a sharp distinction between the two types. Garner (1974) has argued that there is a continuum of dimension integrity rather than a dichotomy.

31. A qualifying remark is that in cases of *synesthesia*, color may not be separable from other dimensions (Cytowic 1995). Maybe synesthesia could be defined as a set of perceptual dimensions that are separable for ordinary people, but which are integral for the synesthetic.

32. *Timbre* would then become a higher level domain of a tone (in the sense of section 3.10), since the timbre of a tone can be identified with a pattern of harmonics of the fundamental tone with varying degrees of loudness.

33. In this context, it is worthwhile to consider Johnson's (1921, chapter XI) old distinction between "determinables," corresponding to *domains*, and "determinates," corresponding to *regions* of domains. He writes: "[W]hat have been assumed to be determinables—e.g., color, pitch, etc.—are ultimately *different*, in the important sense that they cannot be subsumed under some one higher determinable, with the result that they are incomparable with one another; while it is the essential nature of determinates under any one determinable to be comparable with one another. The familiar phrase 'incomparable' is thus synonymous with 'belonging to different determinables,' and 'comparable' with 'belonging to the same determinable' ..." (1921, 175). The notion of a "region" of a domain will be extensively analyzed in section 3.4. Also compare Carnap's (1971) distinction between "attribute space" and "partition" discussed in section 6.3.2. In relation to Armstrong's (1978, 116) characteristics, as presented in section 1.2, a determinable is what a class of colors or a class of shapes have in common.

34. In particular, Gallistel considers how bees use their mental maps in solving navigational tasks. As the following quotation (Gallistel 1990, 139) indicates, the behavior is surprisingly intelligent (given the miniscule size of the bee's brain): "[B]ees use their terrain map in evaluating the message contained in the dance of a returning forager. Instead of simply taking that dance as a set of flying instructions, they take it as the specification of a point on a terrain map that the foragers share. When the point specified is not in terrain where forage could be found, the message is ignored."

35. It is impossible to draw a sharp distinction between innate and learned quality dimensions, since many sensory dimensions are structurally prepared in the neural tissue at birth but require exposure to sensory experiences to fixate the exact geometrical structure of the mapping.

36. See also Smith (1989, 159).

37. Smith and Sera (1992) have studied the development of the polar structure of dimensions. One of their conclusions is that "comprehension of dimensional terms is temporarily related to change in cross-dimension similarities and in the magnitude marking of dimension poles. The perceived similarity between big and loud and the ability to pick the louder object as "more" happen at the same developmental time as children understand the words *loud* and *quiet*" (1992, 132).

38. I do not claim that my typology of the origins of quality dimensions is exclusive, since, in a sense, all culturally dependent dimensions are also learned.

39. Lakoff's (1987, 283) "spatialization of form hypothesis" suggests, however, that all domains can be grounded, via metaphoric and metonymic mappings, in the

domain of sensory 3-D space. For a discussion of metaphoric mappings, see section 5.6.

40. P. M. Churchland (1989, 234) formulates this point as follows: "People react to the world in similar ways not because their underlying weight configurations are closely similar on a synapse-by-synapse comparison, but because their *activation spaces* are similarly partitioned." Also see P. M. Churchland (1998, 29) where he makes a similar point in relation to "conceptual similarity" for artificial neural networks.

Chapter 2

41. This is in parallel with Smolensky's (1988) distinction between symbolic and sub-symbolic representations, except that I add conceptual representations as an intermediary level.

42. To some extent, this analogy is inspired by Waddington's (1957) dynamic landscapes.

43. Barcan Marcus (1987) names this position "the language centered theory of belief." It is also closely related to what Palmer (1978) calls "propositional representation" and what Smolensky (1988, 3) calls "the symbolic paradigm." Lakoff's presentation of "objectivism" (1987, xii–xiii) also encompasses a linguistically oriented version of the symbolic paradigm.

44. Compare Pylyshyn (1984, 29): "[T]o be in a certain representational state is to have a certain symbolic expression in some part of memory."

45. Here I am referring to the traditional sequential kind of computer programs with "explicit" symbol representations and not to parallel distributed processing that may use "intrinsic" representations (compare Palmer 1978). This distinction is discussed in section 2.3.2.

46. This is in contrast to so-called "situated" or "embodied" cognition (Clark 1997). For the notion of a detached representation see Gärdenfors (1995, 1996a).

47. Tirri (1991, 62) says: "In practice one of the most difficult issues in the design of an expert system is the question of attribute selection for knowledge representation. As any real world process has infinitely many attributes, the problem is how to choose such a small attribute set for the knowledge base that it would be descriptive enough for the modeling purposes. This problem is present especially when machine learning methods (either neural or symbolic, decision tree based ones such as ID3) are used for knowledge acquisition."

48. A similar point is made by Hutchins (1995, 363) who in his criticism of the symbolic approach says: "The physical-symbol-system architecture is not a model of individual cognition. It is a model of the operation of a sociocultural system from which the human actor has been removed."

49. Fenstad (1978) was aware of the problems quite early, and he had, in my opinion, the right diagnosis. He writes the following about the model theory of intensional semantics: "But lexical rules or meaning postulates give only part of the answer. It is equally important to enrich the structures of the domains. And to 'enrich' means to give more *geometric structure* to the interpretations" (1978, 337).

50. Petitot (1992, 41) expresses the limitations of symbolic naturalism as follows (my translation): "The propositionalist direction of the symbolic cognitivism is fundamentally limited. . . . As it stands, this approach is *incompatible* with any *naturalistic* thesis, *because there are no symbolic forms in the external or internal nature. At the very most, geometrical and dynamical forms can exist*. Thus, any naturalization of mind, lan-

guage, and meaning presupposes a revolution in the conception of the formal that is inherited from the formalism within logic."

51. See Stewart (1996, 313).

52. Associations are treated in a special way by the behaviorists. Since they shun mental notions, their stimulus-response pairs replace the traditional associations, but such pairs function in a similar way.

53. The distinction between serial and parallel processing is not, in itself, pivotal for the representational powers of a model.

54. The distinction between "fast" and "slow" dynamics of a network is discussed in section 7.2.

55. Later he continues: "[I]t may be that the basically computational shape of most mainstream models of cognition results not so much from the nature of cognition itself as it does from the shape of the conceptual equipment that cognitive scientists typically bring to bear in studying cognition." (1995, 358). For further arguments, see van Gelder (1995, 378–380). See also van Gelder (1998).

56. For example, see the comments by Schyns, Goldstone and Thibaut (1998, 15) on the use of "principal components."

57. This is in accordance with Petitot (1992, 49, my translation): "*[T]he morphological is a middle term between the physical and the symbolism*: it has a physical origin (emergent), although it is not material, it is not formal, although it is not symbolic (it is *topologically and geometrically* formal, but not logically formal)."

58. Quine (1969, 117) says about similarity that we "cannot easily imagine a more familiar or fundamental notion than this, or a notion more ubiquitous in its application. On this core it is like the notions of logic: like identity, negation, alternation, and the rest. And yet, strangely, there is something logically repugnant about it. For we are baffled when we try to relate the general notion of similarity significantly to logical terms."

59. Since the theory of conceptual space is presented in a linguistic form in this book (what else can be done?), the *metatheory* is symbolic. This may be source of confusion unless one is clear about when the theory is used and when it is talked about.

60. Churchland and Sejnowski (1992, 169) make a related point even though they write about an "activation space" in an ANN: "An activation space will also be a similarity space, inasmuch as similar vectors will define adjacent regions in space. This means that similarity between objects represented can be reflected by similarity in their representations, that is, proximity of positions in activation space. Similarity in representations is thus not an accidental feature, but an intrinsic and systematic feature. It is, consequently, a feature exploitable in processing. Nearby vectors can cancel small differences and highlight similarities, thereby allowing the network to generalize as well as distinguish."

61. Karmiloff-Smith (1992) points out that the fact that the brain organizes information in a domain-specific way does not entail that the brain is *modular* as argued by Fodor (1983).

62. For some discussion of the role of conceptual spaces in science, see section 6.4 and Gärdenfors (1990, 1991).

63. See, for example, P. S. Churchland (1986, 281–283), and Cook (1986, chapter 2). In P. M. Churchland (1986b, 280), we find the following general idea: "[T]he brain represents various aspects of reality by a position in a suitable state space; and the brain performs computations on such representations by means of general coordinate transformations from one state space to another." The state spaces that Churchland refers to, however, are those of ANNs which in general are of a high

dimensionality at the chosen level of representation, while a conceptual space is usually represented by only a few dimensions (compare section 7.1.4).

64. On this point, Stein and Meredith (1993, 83) write in their book on the function of the superior colliculus: "At each successive level in the central nervous system the visual, somatosensory, and auditory representations occupy spatially distinct regions that are defined functionally and anatomically (i.e., cytoarchitectonically). At the cortical level and in most regions of the thalamus, the domain of an individual sensory modality consists of distinct maps. The map (or maps) of a single sensory modality in, for example, primary sensory cortex is distinguished from the map in extraprimary cortex: it abuts by mirror-image reversals in receptive field progressions, significant changes in receptive field properties, differences in afferent/efferent organization, and/or by specialization for different submodality characteristics. In cortex the interposition of "association" areas further segregates the representations of the different sensory modalities."

65. For an example from the animal kingdom, Gallistel (1990, 487–488) writes about the organization of the barn owl's tectum (that is used for vision): "Thus anatomical dimensions of the tectal area correspond to dimensions of the vector space that describes the angular deviation of the distal stimulus; the mapping carries units of angular deviation from the axis of gaze monotonically, but nonlinearly into micrometers of deviation from the orthogonal lines on the tectum that represent the horizontal and vertical meridians of the eye (the anatomical axes of the projection)." It appears that animals use several different *scales* of spatial representation in these maps. Marr (1982) shows how retinal images based on different spatial frequencies may be computationally efficient. Gallistel (1990, 214) notes that "[t]he visual systems maps the visual image onto the cortex with about ten different resolutions. . . ."

Another example from the same book is the bat's auditory cortex (Gallistel 1990, 496): "This suggests that in this area, the nervous system has opted for a polar rather than a Cartesian mapping of the descriptive space onto the cortical surface. . . . In short, there is an amplitopic representation, as well as a tonotopic representation." Spaces based on polar coordinates are discussed in section 3.5.

66. The distinction between connectionist and conceptual representations must be kept in mind. An interesting point is made by Lakoff (1988, 39), who notes in his criticism of Smolensky (1988) that "Smolensky's discussion makes what I consider a huge omission: the body. The neural networks in the brain do not exist in isolation; they are connected to the sensorimotor system. For example, the neurons in a topographic map of the retina are not just firing in isolation for the hell of it. They are firing in response to retinal input, which is in turn dependent on what is in front of one's eyes. An activation pattern in the topographic map of the retina is therefore not merely a meaningless mathematical object in some dynamical system; it is meaningful."

67. In Gärdenfors (1996b), I connect the theory of conceptual spaces to the *tensor network theory* for sensorimotor control due to Pellionisz and Llinas (1979, 1980, 1982, 1985). For detailed discussions of the philosophical relevance of this theory, see P. S. Churchland (1986, chapters 10.3–10.8), P. M. Churchland (1986a, 1986b), and Foss (1988).

68. See also Churchland and Sejnowski (1992, 163).

69. "[C]lassification theorems show that *emergent structures share properties of universality which are to a large extent independent of the specific physical properties of the underlying substrate.*" (Petitot 1995, 248)

70. There are some attempts to emulate symbol processing with the aid of ANNs (for example, Hinton 1984 and Smolensky 1991), but it is doubtful whether these models correspond to anything that goes on in the human brain.

Chapter 3

71. Sometimes the notion of a *feature* is used in this way. There appears to be a large variety of interpretations of "feature," however, some of which go beyond the dimensional structures of conceptual spaces. In particular this notion is (mis)used within connectionistic models.

72. I use the word "object," where philosophers generally use "individual." These terms can thus be treated as synonyms in the present context.

73. The extensional type of semantics is further discussed in chapter 5.

74. Again, the intensional semantics are discussed at greater length in chapter 5.

75. In Montague's semantics, the meaning of an adjective like "small" is a function from properties to properties (Montague 1974, 211–212). By this technique, the set of small emus need not be the intersection of the set of small things with the set of emus. The definition creates an abundant set (in the sense of Lewis 1986, 59–60) of adjectival meanings that will, however, in the same way as for the intensional definition of property, contain a large number of nonnatural potential meanings for adjectives (compare section 3.4).

76. These are not exactly the same as Goodman's predicates since he complicates matters by only discussing objects that are observed. For the present discussion, however, this difference will not be of any importance.

77. In connection with a discussion of inductive reasoning, a solution to the problem of separating projectible from nonprojectible properties based on conceptual spaces is presented in chapter 6.

78. It is interesting to note that already in 1928 Cassirer was aware of the problem. He wrote about the logical theory of abstraction that had been developed at that time: "And what I wanted to show was not that the theory of abstraction is 'false', i.e., formally invalid, but that it is not sufficient for the really objective foundation of concepts, for explaining their epistemological value. . . . It comprises, in a certain sense, 'valid' and 'invalid,' 'useful' and 'useless' concepts with the same love. . . . [I]n this lies, it seems to me, from a *critically epistemological* perspective, its decisive fault. Because now it becomes clear that a concept can be formally fully 'correct,' in the sense that it can be constructed thoroughly 'correctly' according to the classical logical theory, without anything that speaks for it in terms of the specific epistemological usefulness of this correctness, or even any guarantee in any sense of its usefulness." (Cassirer 1928, 132, my translation). I was led to this quotation from Mormann (1994), but he translates it in a slightly different way. Also see Quine (1969, 118).

79. X "touches" Y can be defined in topological terms as that the topological closures of X and Y share at least one point.

80. A more traditional definition is the following: *A path* from x to y in a subset C of a conceptual space S is a continuous map f: $[0, 1] \rightarrow C$ with f(0) = x and f(1) = y. A subset C of a conceptual space S is *connected*, if and only if, for all points x and y in C, there is a path between x and y such that all points on the path are in C (that is, if and only if f($[0,1]$) $\subseteq C$). The notion of a continuous map can be defined using just the betweenness relation and axiom B6 from note 23 (see Borsuk and Szmielew 1960, 66). The notion of a path, however, is definable also for other structures as, for example, graphs.

81. Foo (1994) shows that convexity of properties is closely related to classical mathematical induction. He says (1994, 39) that "if we think of classical induction in terms of some successor relation rather than a function in discrete spaces, then generalized convexity can be regarded as just a statement that the transitive closure of the relation covers the whole space starting from certain given points."

82. See Mormann (1993) for this example and some further critical remarks on the use of convexity as a criterion for natural properties.

83. Some alleged counterexamples to the conjecture are presented by Saunders and van Brakel (1997).

84. A *closure structure* on a set S is defined by an operator C defined on subsets X and Y of S which satisfies the following conditions: $X \subseteq C(X)$, $C(C(X)) = C(X)$, and if $X \subseteq Y$, then $C(X) \subseteq C(Y)$. A set X is *closed* when $C(X) = X$.

85. To verify the three conditions on closure structures, it is sufficient to note that if $C(X)$ is the smallest convex set including X, than $X \subseteq C(X)$, $C(C(X)) = C(X)$, and if $X \subseteq Y$, then $C(X) \subseteq C(Y)$. Furthermore, if X is convex, then $C(X) = X$.

86. I focus on criterion P, but also the other criteria based on connected or star-shaped regions or Mormann's closure criterion would be able to counter most of the problems.

87. As discussed in section 4.8, location functions have the same role as possible worlds in the traditional intensional semantics.

88. For example, it is not difficult to construct a conceptual space where Goodman's (1955) infamous predicate "grue" would correspond to a convex region and thus be a natural property in that space (see section 6.3).

89. Mormann (1993, 237) has the following precaution: "Of course this argument is not to be understood in the dogmatic sense that a set of traditional predicates is beyond any doubt—under certain circumstances we may be forced or, at least, be inclined to revise our conceptual system thereby changing what we regard as 'natural' and what we do not. Perhaps, contrary to the case of metrical structure of physical space, the problem of selecting natural predicates for a given conceptual space generally does not possess a clear-cut solution. Evidence for this conjecture is the fact that up to now many structurally very different colour spaces are in use and different spaces select different predicates as natural ones."

90. Quine (1969, 127–128) gives the following example: "Color is helpful at the food-gathering level. Here it behaves well under induction, and here, no doubt, has been the survival value of our color-slanted quality space." Barsalou and Prinz (1997, 298) write: "For all of the differences among individuals, there are many more similarities. Because human biology endows all people with roughly the same perceptual system, this guarantees a high degree of similarity in the perceptual symbols they construct. Although variable embodiment may tune these systems in important ways, the amount of tuning may be relatively small compared with the amount of shared structure."

91. Quine (1969, 125) states the following about learning words by ostension: "Always, induction expresses our hope that similar causes will have similar effects; but when the induction is the ostensive learning of a word, that pious hope is a foregone conclusion. The uniformity of people's quality spaces virtually assures that similar presentations will elicit similar verdicts."

92. In particular, do not always trust results about inductive inferences that have been obtained under laboratory conditions.

93. Human perception of heat is basically determined by the amount of heat *transferred* from an object to the skin rather than by the temperature of the object.

94. Different kinds of inductive inferences are compared in chapter 6.

95. A *self-approved* vowel is one that was produced by the speaker and later approved of as an example of the intended kind. An *identified* sample of a vowel is one that was correctly identified by 75 percent of the observers. The *preferred* samples of a vowel are those that are "the most representative samples from among the most readily identified samples" (Fairbanks and Grubb 1961, p. 210).

96. As discussed in section 4.9, however, there are several other concept theories than prototype theory that are compatible with the framework of conceptual spaces.

97. Hampton (1998, 159) notes that "the reason that conceptual borderline disputes are so common and so puzzling is that category borderlines themselves are *not* firmly represented in memory. Change in perspective and classification context may then affect how different attributes are weighted and how broadly or narrowly the category should be defined."

98. It can be noted that on the basis of a Voronoi tessellation one can define the following discrete function: $d(x, y) = 0$, if x and y belong to the same category; and $d(x, y) = 1$ otherwise. This function is "almost" a distance function (only the requirement that $d(x, y) = 0$ only if $x = y$ is violated). The function d can be said to be a "coarsening" of the original distance function that generated the tessellation. One possible way of interpreting categorical perception is that it is based on something like this "coarse" distance function.

99. This way of analyzing relations was proposed by Holmqvist (1988).

100. This analysis is expanded in Marr (1982, chapter 5). A related model, together with some psychological support, is presented by Biederman (1987). Also compare the "superquadrics" in the models of Pentland (1986) and Chella, Frixione, and Gaglio (1997) that are presented in chapter 7.

101. There is an alternative account of how shapes are represented cognitively (see, for example, Tarr and Pinker 1989, Ullman and Basri 1991, Ullman 1995). The key idea is that a view of an object is mentally transformed to a canonical direction, for example a face view, and objects are then categorized by the appearance of the object in that direction.

102. Some of the models are proposed with the goal of explaining human representation of shapes, while others, like Pentland (1986) and Chella, Frixione, and Gaglio (1997), are suggested as appropriate for constructing artificial systems that can recognize or generate shapes.

103. See Hemeren (1996) for a study of similarity and prototype effects among biological motions and for references to further literature in the area.

104. To be accurate, Marr and Vaina (1982) only use differential inequalities, for example, expressing that the derivative of the position of the upper part of the right leg is positive in the forward direction during a particular phase of the walking cycle.

105. See, for example, Talmy (1988) and Winter and Gärdenfors (1995) for the role of forces in a cognitive analysis of *modal* verbs.

106. For the notion of "affordance," see, for example, Gibson (1979) and Shepard (1984).

107. Goldstone (1994b, 148–149) distinguishes between four kinds of categories "in order of their grounding by similarity": natural kinds, man-made artifacts, ad hoc categories (Barsalou 1983), and abstract schemas or metaphors. It is clear that the theory of properties and concepts based on conceptual spaces, as developed in this book, applies primarily to natural kinds, and it may only be indirectly useful for an analysis of the other types. Metaphors, however, will be analyzed in section 5.6.

Chapter 4

108. For a similar idea, see Böök (1973, 1998) who traces it back to Husserl.

109. Some verbs like "support" do not involve any movements, but they can be said to be dynamic in the sense that forces (and counterforces) are involved.

110. Already Locke was aware of this phenomenon: "In some this complex idea contains a greater, and in others a smaller number of qualities. . . . The yellow shining colour makes gold to children; others add weight, malleableness, and fusibility; and others

yet other qualities, which they find joined with that yellow colour, as constantly as its weight and fusibility. And therefore different men, leaving out or putting in several simple ideas which others do not, according to their various examination, skill, or observation of that object, have different essences of gold, which must therefore be of their own and not of nature's making" (1690/1959, book III, chapter VI, 31).

111. Marr (1982, 358) says: "The perception of an event or an object must include the simultaneous computation of several different descriptions of it that capture diverse aspects of the use, purpose, or circumstances of the object."

112. Compare Nosofsky (1986). Smith and Heise (1992, 242) confirm the role of salience: "[P]erceived similarity is the result of psychological processes and it is highly variable. The central process that changes perceptual similarity is attention. The perceived similarity of two objects changes with changes in selective attention to specific perceptual properties."

113. Prototype theory normally treats concepts as context independent. In contrast, Roth and Shoben (1983) have shown that typicality judgments depend on context. Introducing context in the model of concepts makes the model more difficult to test empirically. This may not be such a severe limitation, however, as regards psychological experiments. If anything, such experiments are good at eliminating contextual factors.

114. Compare Kornblith's (1993, 96–100) discussion of our excellence in finding correlations between properties. The capacity of finding correlations between domains will be treated in section 6.6.

115. See also Sloman, Love, and Ahn's (1998) notion of "mutability."

116. As Medin (1989, 1475) formulates it: "Because a major problem with similarity is that it is so unconstrained, one might ask what constrains theories. If we cannot identify constraints on theories, that is, say something about why we have the theories we have and not others, then we have not solved the problem of coherence: It simply has been shifted to another level."

117. Quine (1969, p. 138) even claims that in advanced science, the notion of similiarity becomes superfluous: "In general we can take it as a very special mark of the maturity of a branch of science that it no longer needs an irreducible notion of similarity and kind. It is that final stage where the animal vestige is wholly absorbed into the theory. In this career of the similarity notion, starting in its innate phase, developing over the years in the light of accumulated experience, passing then from the intuitive phase into theoretical similarity, and finally disappearing altogether, we have a paradigm of the evolution of unreason into science."

118. Medin and Ortony (1989) suggest that people's beliefs in ultimate causes of category membership is sometimes so strong that it can function as an unidentified *placeholder* in the core of a concept.

119. How can one answer the Mad Hatter's question "Why is a raven like a writing-desk?" without knowing in what respect they are supposed to be similar?

120. Medin, Goldstone, and Gentner (1993, 255), distinguish among similarity as measured indirectly, direct judgments of similarity, and similarity as a theoretical construct. In this classification, they do not consider the realistic position (1). Their first two types correspond to a partitioning of the empirical conceptualist position, that is, (2), while their third is basically the same as (3).

121. Lewis Carroll's own answer to why a raven is like a writing-desk is: "Because it can produce a few notes, tho they are *very* flat; and it is never put with the wrong end in front."

122. Nosofsky (1992, 38) says: "I believe that some of the force of Tversky's demonstrations is diminished, however, when MDS representations are viewed as components

of cognitive process models. As I have argued previously, observed behavior reflects only indirectly the underlying similarity representation. Process models that incorporate symmetric-similarity representations can predict asymmetric patterns of proximity data."

123. Smith and Heise (1992, 243) say that ". . . if perceptual similarity is some weighted combination of dimensional similarities, then perceptual similarity necessarily varies with the magnitude of the difference between stimuli on the dimensions *and with the dimension weights."*

124. Different solutions to the problems raised by Tversky and Gati have been proposed by Krumhansl (1978) who views similarity as a function not only of distance but also of the *spatial density* of points in the surrounding configuration, and Nosofsky (1991) who incorporates a general notion of *bias* into spatial models. Such a bias can be generated with the aid of the prominence factors in criterion C. Also Johannesson (1997) develops a "relative prominence model" and performs some experiments that he compares to the results in Nosofsky (1991). Johannesson's model proposes that the directed similarity from *I* to *J* is proportional to some symmetric similarity measure between *I* and *J*, and the quotient between the "prominences" for *J* and *I*. His analysis of data from different areas shows that it is possible for a procedure to estimate the parameters of the model quite well.

125. A similar construction is given in intensional semantics where the intersection is taken over the extensions in all possible worlds.

126. See Rips (1995) for a discussion of this principle and other proposals for concept combinations. I will not go into the details, but I believe that most of the problems that Rips indicate for the "theory-theory" can be avoided if the minitheories of this account are interpreted as domains with certain geometrical or topological structures (see section 4.2.2).

127. A similar analysis can be provided for the combinations *giant midget* and *midget giant* (Kamp and Partee 1995, 159), provided the treatment of contrast classes to be given in the following subsection.

128. Another possibility is to consider the "mutability" of properties (or "features"). Sloman, Love, and Ahn (1998, 190) introduce this notions as follows: "We will therefore measure the degree of coherence associated with a feature by asking people how easily they can transform their mental representation of an object by eliminating the feature, or by replacing the feature with a different value, without changing other aspects of the object's representation. We call such judgments measures of "mutability" . . . , because they reflect how much a feature of a concept of an object can be mentally transformed."

129. This is essentially what happens in *metaphorical* uses of concepts. Metaphors are analyzed in section 5.4.

130. Compare the "head primacy principle" of Kamp and Partee (1995, 161). As they note (1995, 162), however, this principle must be overridden in the *stone lion* example.

131. Compare Langacker's (1991b, 176) image-schematic representation of "tall."

132. For even further combinations see Halff, Ortony, and Anderson (1976). Clark (1992, 369–372) uses this example to make a somewhat different albeit related point. Also see Broström (1994, 101–102).

133. One way to account for the phenomenon would be to say that it is only in "red book" that the word is used in its proper meaning, while in the other cases it is used as a *metaphor*. This proposal is discussed and rejected in section 5.4.3.

134. Broström (1994) speculates that when we assign properties to nonnormal objects— for example, the skin color of Martians—we choose a property that is as exceptional as possible. This is why Martians are green.

135. Balkenius (1996) presents a connectionist model of stimulus generalization, however, based on *multiscale representations* that avoids many of the problems that other connectionist models have. He notes that the multiscale architecture makes it "... possible to describe a stimulus dimension, not as an objective dimension outside the animal, but instead as a collection of subjective similarities and differences. Any such collection of similarities and differences that is sufficiently dense would act as a subjective stimulus dimension, although no explicit representation of that dimension is necessary in the network. Such dimensions need not necessarily correspond in a simple way to a single observable stimulus dimension" (Balkenius 1996, section 5).

136. Nosofsky (1988b, 707) compares the prototype model, defined by equation (4.1) and a summed similarity model, which gives slightly different results, in particular when the values along different dimensions are strongly correlated.

137. It is possible that an exemplar will lie *outside* the Voronoi region assigned to the corresponding prototype. Such an exemplar would be an anomaly for the classification.

138. See Gabbay et al. (1993) for a survey of current research areas. In Balkenius and Gärdenfors (1991), nonmonotonic reasoning is connected to representations in artificial neuron networks, and in Gärdenfors and Makinson (1994) it is connected to expectation structures.

139. The different perspectives on *observations* corresponding to the three levels of representing information is treated extensively in chapter 6.

140. The meaning of "analytic-in-a-conceptual-space" is further discussed in chapter 5.

141. I am grateful to Renata Wassermann for pointing this out to me.

142. The meaning of an atomic sentence consisting of a predicate and a name (or relational predicate and several names) can thus be represented as an assignment to an object of a location in a certain region of a conceptual space. For example, the observation that is described on the symbolic level as "x is red" is expressed on the conceptual level by assigning x a point in color space. Such a predicate is *satisfied* by an individual just in case the location function locates the individual at one of the points included in the region assigned to a predicate. This provides us with the basic notion of "satisfaction" from which most of traditional model theory can be constructed, should we want it.

143. Compare Stalnaker's arguments as presented in section 3.6.

144. This rule is the same as the "prototype model" in Reed (1972).

145. The proof, due to Kenneth Holmqvist, is quite simple: Expanding equation (2) gives

$$\Sigma_i(p_i^2 - 2p_ix_i + x_i^2) - c_p = \Sigma_i(q_i^2 - 2q_ix_i + x_i^2) - c_q, \tag{3}$$

which simplifies to

$$\Sigma_ip_i^2 - \Sigma_i 2p_ix_i - c_p = \Sigma_iq_i^2 - \Sigma_i 2q_ix_i - c_q. \tag{4}$$

Since the first term on each side is a constant (4) can, after some simplification, be written as

$$\Sigma_i(p_i - q_i)x_i + k = 0 \tag{5}$$

for some constant k, which is the equation of a straight line. Each pair of prototypes p and q thus divides the spaces into two half-spaces. Since a half-space is a convex set and the intersection of convex sets is again a convex set, it follows that the partitioning generated by equation (2) results in a convex partitioning of the space (see Okabe, Boots and Sugihara 1992, sections 3.5.3 and 3.1.4). It is easy to show that all points in the plane will belong to a region associated with one of the prototypes, which means that the partitioning is indeed a Voronoi tessellation of the plane. The proof generalizes to any number of dimensions.

146. The choice that c_p represents exactly *one* standard deviation is, however, arbitrary.

147. Smith and Sloman (1994, 380) write: "In Rips's study, subjects in the categorization condition were instructed to talk aloud as they made their choices. This instruction may have suggested to subjects that they base their categorization decisions on factors that could be articulated and that seemed principled; this could have fostered rule-based processing."

148. In the literature, there are several other examples of categorization rules that are based on dimensional representations of stimuli: however, these rules will not be discussed here.

149. Reed (1972, 385–86), calls this rule the "proximity algorithm."

150. This rule is the same as the "summed-similarity" decision rule discussed by Nosofsky (1988b).

151. It appears that this point is sometimes missed in the psychological literature. For example, Ashby and Gott (1988) work with stimuli composed of two lines—one horizontal and one vertical—joined at the upper left corner (compare their figure 2, 35). The stimuli are described by a two-dimensional vector (x, y), where x denotes the length of the horizontal component and y the length of the vertical component. Throughout the article, Ashby and Gott discuss the space generated by these axes and define their decision rules using this metric. From a number of observations in their article, however, which are problematic for them, it seems that these coordinates do not produce an appropriate metric for the phenomenal space producing the categorizations. It appears that if one makes a (nonlinear) coordinate shift by defining $x' = x/y$ and $y' = x \cdot y$, one obtains a metric that is much better suited to explain the observed phenomena. The dimension x' measures the *proportions* of the lengths of the two line segments, while y' is a measure of the *relative size* of the stimulus.

152. An alternative method would have been to use multidimensional scaling (Shepard 1962a, 1962b, 1987) as was described in section 1.7. This would have involved, however, asking the subjects to make comparisons of the relative similarity of two *pairs* of shell figures, instead of the question concerning triples of shells that was used in our pilot studies. Johannesson (1996) has continued our studies of shell shapes using multidimensional scaling methods.

153. As noted in section 4.9, this distance is not real-valued if x is located inside the circle.

154. See Gärdenfors and Holmqvist (1994) for details.

155. Our methodology is similar to that of Nosofsky (1988a) except that he did not show any new stimuli in the test phase (which he calls the transfer phase).

Chapter 5

156. Here "conceptualist" refers to the old philosophical debate in ontology between realists, conceptualists, and nominalists (see Woozley 1967 for an overview).

157. See, for example, the analysis of modal expressions in Winter and Gärdenfors (1995) and Gärdenfors (1998).

158. This is not to say that the robot's behavior should not depend on the state of the world, nor that the meanings of words cannot change as a result of the robot's interaction with the world.

159. Jackendoff (1987a, 122) calls this the "mentalist postulate."

160. A more traditional account of the relation between the conceptual structure and the world would be some kind of *correspondence theory*. In agreement with Thompson

(1995) (see below), I do not believe that there is always such a correspondence. Yet another account would be that of *radical constructivism* (see von Glasersfeld 1995) which, in its most orthodox form, denies that the external world has any role to play in determining the semantic relation. This view of semantics is discussed and criticized in Gärdenfors (1997) (see also Wallin 1997). In my opinion, any defensible account of constructivist semantics will come close to a pragmatic account.

161. This is basically a neo-Kantian position (compare Stegmüller 1976, 217–218).

162. A heavy source for this purpose is Lakoff's book (1987), which is an intense criticism of realist semantics which he calls "objectivist semantics."

163. I am grateful to Hans Rott for pointing this out to me (see Rott 1997, 88–89).

164. Compare Rott (1997, 88–91).

165. I am grateful to Annette Herskovits for making this clear to me. See also Zlatev (1997).

166. Putnam's own diagnosis of the problem emanating from his theorem is close to my own. He thinks that it springs from viewing a language as separate from its interpretation (Putnam 1980, 481–482):

> The predicament only *is* a predicament because we did two things: first, we gave an account of understanding the language in terms of programs and procedures for *using* the language (what else?); then, secondly, we asked what the possible "models" for the language were, thinking of the models as existing "out there" *independent of any description*. At this point, something really weird had already happened, had we stopped to notice. On any view, the understanding of the language must determine the reference of the terms, or, rather, must determine the reference given the context of use. If the use, even in a fixed context, does not determine reference, then use is not understanding. The language, on the perspective we talked ourselves into, has a full program of use; but it still lacks an *interpretation*.
>
> This is the fatal step. To adopt a theory of meaning according to which a language whose whole use is specified still lacks something—viz. its "interpretation"—is to accept a problem which *can* only have crazy solutions. To speak as if *this* were my problem, "I know how to use my language, but, now, how shall I single out an interpretation?" is to speak nonsense. Either the use *already* fixes the "interpretation" or nothing can.
>
> Nor do "causal theories of reference", etc., help. Basically, trying to get out of this predicament by *these* means is hoping that the *world* will pick one definite extension for each of our terms even if *we* cannot. But the world does not pick models or interpret languages. *We* interpret our languages or nothing does.

For further discussion of Putnam's theorem and its relevance for semantics, see Lakoff (1987, chapter 15).

167. Regier (1996, 27) says: "The idea is that since the acquisition and use of language rest on an experiential basis, and since experience of the world is filtered through extralinguistic faculties such as perception and memory, language will of necessity be influenced by such faculties. We can therefore expect the nature of human perceptual and cognitive systems to be of significant relevance to the study of language itself. One of the primary tasks of cognitive linguistics is the ferreting out of links between language and the rest of human cognition."

168. For accounts of the cognitive evolution of language that are relevant in the present context, see, for example, Bickerton (1990), Gärdenfors (1996f) and Deacon (1997).

169. That is, if x is earlier than y and y is earlier than z, then x is earlier than z.

170. An equivalent way of defining the notion is to say that an analytic statement is one that is satisfied for all location functions (see section 4.8).

171. Thus, the epistemology underlying the theory of conceptual spaces could be described as a version of neo-Kantianism (compare Stegmüller 1976, 217–218).

172. This process can be described as a spatial or topological analogue to *unification* in Prolog.

173. Of course, not all of syntax can be predicted or explained from semantics or pragmatics. The syntax of a language can be seen as a way of fulfilling a number of communicative functions. For example, syntax has a role in disambiguating ambiguous word combinations.

174. It is interesting to note that using semantic, syntactic, and morphological criteria, Dixon (1982, 16) distinguishes seven semantic types of adjectives in English: dimension ("big," "long," etc.), physical property ("hard," "heavy," etc.), color, human property ("happy," "generous," etc.), age, value ("good," "pure," etc.) and speed ("fast," "quick" and "slow").

175. The spatial relations are often *dynamic* as is emphasized by Zlatev (1997). Consider, for example, "into" which denotes a trajector moving from the outside of some region to the inside of it.

176. Zlatev (1997) points out, however, that the general proposal by Landau and Jackendoff is falsified in Japanese where nouns and postpositions express "where" information.

177. Again, the division between the theses LA, LV, and LN is not universally valid, since there are, for instance, languages like Mandarin and Quechua that do not have a separate syntactic category of adjective. In these languages, property words function more like verbs (Smith, Gasser, and Sandhofer 1997, 223).

178. It should be noted that what counts as "distant" is context-dependent—compare "leaving the chair" and "leaving the country." The same context-dependence appears, however, with "in"—compare "in the chair" and "in the country." The landmark (the chair or the country) constitutes the relevant region both for "leave" and for "in."

179. See also Zwarts and Winter (1998) and Helmantel (1998) for some extensions and modifications of the vector theory of prepositions.

180. One important reason why Zwarts uses vectors rather than just regions comes from the fact that prepositions can be *modified* in different ways. For example, "behind the castle" can be modified as "far behind the castle," "just behind the castle," "ten meters behind the castle," and so forth. If, for example the region corresponding to "behind the castle" is represented by a set of points, then the modifiers will be interpreted as functions mapping the set onto the subset of points that are "far" from the house (compare Zwarts (1995), 3–4). To handle this, the modifiers must refer to the distances $d(o, c)$ between the points and the castle. Zwarts argues that such a definition faces a serious problem since it is *noncompositional*: to get the relevant distances, the modifiers have to use the denotation of the reference *object*, "which is not their sister in syntactic structure." If vectors are used to represent the denotation of prepositions, however, we can immediately determine the denotation of "far behind the castle" as the set of all vectors v in the denotation of "behind the castle" which satisfies the condition that $|v| > r$, where r is some pragmatically determined distance and $|v|$ is the length of v (among other things, r depends on which object is the landmark). This definition is clearly compositional and similar conditions are easy to formulate for the other modifiers.

181. For many prepositions, two different uses exist: one object centered where the relation is determined in relation to the object (like in "Oscar is in front of the castle") and one speaker centered where the relation is defined in relation to the speaker (as in "the lion is in front of the acacia tree" when the lion is between me and the tree). Vandeloise (1991) gives this phenomenon a thorough discussion. This additional

complexity does not change Zwarts' basic vectorial analysis, however, since it will apply to both types of uses.

182. Zwarts (1995) calls the properties radially and linearly "continuous" but I think "convex" is more appropriate.

183. This is not completely true since Broschart proposes that the transfer dimension is not primitive but composed from a (+source, –source) and a (+control, –control) distinction. For details, see Broschart (1996, 17–22).

184. Lakoff's earlier "spatialization of form hypothesis" appears to be a variation of the invariance principle. He writes (1987, 283): "Strictly speaking the spatialization of form hypothesis requires a metaphorical mapping from physical space into a "conceptual space." Under this mapping, spatial structure is mapped into conceptual structure. More specifically, image schemas (which structure space) are mapped into the corresponding abstract configurations (which structure concepts)." He also draws the more radical conclusion that "[a]bstract reasoning is a special case of image-based reasoning. Image-based reasoning is fundamental and abstract reasoning is image-based reasoning under metaphorical projections to abstract domains." (1994, 229)

185. Lakoff formulates the general mechanism as follows (1994, 206): "[T]he metaphor can be understood as a mapping (in the mathematical sense) from a source domain . . . to a target domain. . . ." For a penetrative criticism of the use of "mappings" in the analysis of metaphor, however, see Broström (1994, chapter 6).

186. This thesis is challenged by Engberg Pedersen (1999). She claims that it is not possible to distinguish space and time as perceptual domains and that space is not a basic domain. Instead, she argues that the perception of *events* is basic and views the static-dynamic distinction as more central than that between space and time. She says that ". . . we can perceive time as little as we can perceive space. What we perceive are events and locomotions occurring in an environment that is rigid and permanent" (1999, 17).

187. Annette Herskovits has pointed out to me that it is not shape alone that determines the metaphorical use, but their place within the whole and their function. For example, the hands of a clock also "point" to certain positions and the legs of a table "support" it.

188. Black (1979, 31) makes essentially the same point: "Every metaphor is the tip of a submerged model."

189. Compare Verbrugge (1980) ". . . the medium of metaphoric comprehension is closely related to direct experience" (104) and ". . . semantic descriptions should be cast in terms of the invariants that structure perception and action, rather than forcing all of them into a single mathematical mould, such as a calculus of propositions. . . . Since metaphor traffics in similar and transformed identities, the assumptions one makes in defining 'identity' are crucial to a theory of metaphoric structure and process. Realism suggests that a linguistic semantics rooted in perception and action is the most appropriate basis for explaining the comprehension process and the experienced identities of topic and vehicle" (105).

190. See Osgood (1980, 204): ". . . the cognitive processes in both color-music synesthesia and in metaphorical use of language can be described as the parallel alignment of two or more dimensions of experience, definable verbally by pairs of polar adjectives and with 'translations' occurring between equivalent regions of the continua." Also compare Cytowic (1989).

191. There are cases, however, when the influence appears to go in both directions. Brinck (1992, 206–207) introduces a distinction between "transfer" metaphors, where structures from one domain is transferred to another, and "adjustment" metaphors where

the influence is bidirectional. As an example of the latter kind, she argues that in "time is a bridge," "time" obtains the characteristic of connecting events and situations, and "bridge" the characteristic of connecting periods of time.

192. It is possible that force dynamics in the sense of Talmy (1988) is even more fundamental than spatial notions. A similar thesis about the relation between spatial and temporal expressions is defended by Engberg Pedersen (1999).

193. I am grateful to Enric Vallduvi for this useful piece of information.

194. The meaning of "same form," naturally, depends on the level of description. I understand the thesis to be interpreted on the conceptual level.

195. Compare Gärdenfors (1996d).

196. This conceptual framework is, of course, dynamic in the sense that a child adds new dimensions and accommodates the structure of the domains as a result of normal (Piagetian) learning development.

197. For some recent accounts of communication and language learning, see, for example, Gallistel (1990), Hauser (1996), and Deacon (1997).

198. Some further aspects of referential communication, in particular the relevance of *contrast classes*, are treated in Winter and Gärdenfors (1998). Barsalou and Prinz (1997, 297) emphasize the role of embodiment: "Variable embodiment ensures that different individuals can match their perceptual symbols optimally to their perceptions. . . . Thus, if one individual represents color categories in a somewhat idosyncratic manner, his or her perceptual symbols will reflect this structure, such that they will be optimally tuned to match subsequent perceptions of color."

199. This is a so-called *discrimination game* that has been simulated in an autonomous agent setting by Steels (1996) and others.

200. See also Smith and Sera (1992, 132).

201. This partitioning is supported by a couple of theorems in Gärdenfors (1993a).

202. See Lakoff (1987, 122–125), for an analysis of "hedges."

203. The only remark in this direction is the following: "It would be of interest, in particular, to discover if extremely primitive peoples were sometimes exceptions to this hypothesis (which would indicate that the division of linguistic labor is a product of social evolution), or if even they exhibit it" (1975, 229).

204. This term has been proposed to me by Jordan Zlatev.

205. I believe it is is also compatible with Putnam's "internal realism."

206. A caveat: the cognitive structures should be flexible enough to account for context-dependence and other pragmatic factors.

207. For examples in the social sciences, see Foucault's "archaeological" investigations of the terminologies in various areas ("madness" for instance).

208. For a cognitively oriented analysis of quantifiers, however, see Moxey and Sanford (1993), and on negation see Holmqvist and Pluciennik (1996) and Lewandowska-Tomaszczyk (1996).

Chapter 6

209. One notable exception is Shapere (1982), who is discussed in section 6.5.1.

210. I cannot talk about three ways of *describing* observations because the very notion of "describing" presumes the symbolic level.

211. As shown in section 6.3.2, Carnap later changed his mind.

212. Compare the quotation from Cassirer in footnote 8 in section 3.3.

213. For a criticism of this interpretation, see Persson (1997).

214. Note that this criterion can only be seen as supplying necessary but not sufficient conditions. For example, for any sentence α such that Γ logically entails α, the

sentence $\neg\alpha \vee \&\Delta$ (where $\&\Delta$ is the conjunction of all elements in Δ) would fulfil this condition: it is consistent with $\Gamma \cup \Delta$ and $\Gamma \cup \{\neg\alpha \vee \&\Delta\}$ logically entails Δ.

215. For a similar approach, see Michalski and Stepp (1983).

216. One exception are theories with so-called sortal predicates.

217. In concordance with this, learning such a nonnatural disjunctive property can only be achieved by learning each of the disjuncts.

218. In contrast to convex or star-shaped regions, the *union* of two connected and overlapping regions is again connected.

219. Meinong (1906/1973) makes a distinction between *a priori* and *empirical* propositions (see Mulligan 1991, 78). The *a priori* propositions correspond to Carnap's phenomenological assumptions.

220. As a matter of fact, the characterization of mass occurs on the very first pages of his *Principia*.

221. See Stegmüller (1976) for an extensive discussion of Sneed's proposal and for a presentation of the so-called "structuralist view" of scientific theories. As a side remark, I believe that many of the notions from the structuralist position can be given a more fertile interpretation if they are reformulated in terms of conceptual spaces rather than in naked set theory as Stegmüller and his followers do.

222. For example, as mentioned in section 1.8, time and space are *separable* in Newtonian mechanics, while the four-dimensional space-time is *integral* in relativity theory and it has a different metric.

223. It should be clear from the discussion in the previous section, however, that a reduction of the number of dimensions is not the only process that creates representations on the conceptual level. The addition of new theoretical or explanatory dimensions is also extremely significant. Alas, this process is very difficult to mechanize.

224. See Shepard (1962b), (1987) and Kruskal and Wish (1978) for several examples of the results of the procedure.

225. Furthermore, new learning by instances that do not follow the previous pattern can always change the mapping function. This means that it is impossible to talk about a "final" mapping function.

226. For a more precise statement of this result and a proof, see Kohonen (1988, 145–148).

227. Garcia and Koelling (1966) showed that rats can quickly learn correlations between domains (as for example a particular kind of food and sickness) if the connection between the domains has some *ecological validity*. Without such a correlation the rats perform very poorly. Presumably, similar mechanisms operate in humans.

228. See Holland et al. (1986, 200–204) and Kornblith (1993, 101–103) for a discussion of Billman's results.

229. $F(P) \cdot F(C)$ is the *inner product* of the two vectors, defined as $\Sigma_i F(P)_i \cdot F(C)_i$ and $|F(C)|^2$ is the inner product of $F(C)$ with itself, defined as $\Sigma_i F(C)_i^2$.

230. These examples were briefly reported in Gärdenfors (1994) where the results of an experiment concerning classification of wasps were also presented.

231. The linguistic form of the names must, of course, be provided by the user.

232. The mathematical form of the connections are closely related to Hintikka's (1968, 328) measures of "evidential support," in particular the measure $(p(e/h) - p(e/-h))/(p(e/h) + p(e/-h))$ defined in his equation (27)*, where e is the evidence and h the hypothesis.

233. The sense in which neural networks perform implicit statistic inferences can be made precise. For example, see Lippman (1987) for a presentation of some of the results connecting least mean square and maximal likelihood solutions to the computations of neural networks.

234. Some similar structures can be found in the brain as is seen from the following quotation from Gallistel (1990, 520): "It appears that the nervous system is committed to representing diverse aspects of the experienced world by means of the positions of the activated neurons within modules in which neuronal units are arranged anatomically in accord with the best values of their tuning curves. It is this commitment to a positional code that makes vectorial positions a general feature of the nervous system's approach to representation." See also P. M. Churchland (1986b).

Chapter 7

235. Fodor and Pylyshyn (1988, 29–30) clearly make inferences the engine of cognition: "It would not be unreasonable to describe classical cognitive science as an extended attempt to apply the methods of proof theory to the modeling of thought (and similarly, of whatever mental processes are plausibly viewed as involving inferences; preeminently learning and perception)."

236. See Lakatos (1976), however, for a fascinating example of changes of concepts within mathematics.

237. For example, Gallistel (1990, 484–485) argues that a transformation to distal representation in mammals takes place in the superior colliculus. See also Stein and Meredith (1993).

238. The question of how the mapping is *learned*, however, is a different story which is badly understood.

239. Matters are complicated a bit by the fact that in most *simulations* of ANNs, the network is implemented in a traditional symbolic computer program (which does not involve parallel computing at all). There are other truly parallel implementations of the ANNs, however, which do not involve rule following.

240. Gallistel sometimes also writes, however, as if the brain is a rule following symbolic system. In my opinion, this is a cardinal mistake, if not just a confusion.

241. Compare the analysis of communication given in section 5.6.

242. Kohonen (1996) shows how to create an "adaptive subspace self-organizing map" that can filter away translations, rotations, and random displacements of patterns. Such mechanisms are obviously important in the process of creating object-centered spatial models.

243. Churchland and Sejnowski (1992, 32) say: "The network processes information by nonlinear dynamics, not by manipulating symbols and accessing rules. It learns by gradient descent in a complex interactive system, not by generating new rules. . . ."

244. Per se, this does not entail that the information on the conceptual level is more "correctly" represented than on the subconceptual level, only that the representation is more economical.

245. For example, Gallistel (1990, 519) writes: "At the retina, the infinitely dimensional spectral vector is collapsed into a three-dimensional representation by the cones. The cone representation of spectra, while it grossly reduces the dimensionality of the stimulus, at least preserves the unipolarity of light. This unipolarity is lost, however, in the coordinate transformation that occurs between the cones and V1. By the time color signals appear in V1, they are bipolar variables." A bipolar variable is one that varies between two extreme points. Such a variable can be seen as a special type of dimension.

246. He gives the following example of how the conceptual "scaling representations" can be used in modeling learning processes: "[S]uppose that one wanted to test the quantitative predictions of a given connectionist model of category learning. As a first step, one could fit the model to a set of identification learning data. This step

would involve searching for the input representation of the stimuli that maximized the likelihood of the data with respect to the model—the portion of the modeling in which a scaling representation is derived. Then using the same basic connectionist architecture and scaling representation, one could use the model to predict category learning in situations involving the same set of objects. With an invariant scaling representation, we gain greater confidence that a successful connectionist model captures psychological processes in a meaningful way" (Nosofsky 1992, 49–50).

247. In Petitot (1995), he uses the same strategy to derive the topology of syntax.

248. It should be emphasized that there is a different, even slower, process in an ANN, namely the *learning* that occurs from new instances being presented to the system and which causes the connections between the neurons to change. The Kohonen networks presented above illustrate this kind of slow learning. This kind of change within a network corresponds to another kind of process, namely, a sort of *inductive inference*.

249. For a general analysis of the role of resonant states in connectionist systems, see Balkenius and Gärdenfors (1991) and Gärdenfors (1994b). Barsalou (to appear) argues that everything that is required of a symbolic system can be handled by what he calls perceptual symbols systems. He claims that "a perceptual symbol is an attractor in a connectionist network" (to appear, section 2.2.1). It is unclear whether all attractors in such a system would count as perceptual symbols.

250. See Gärdenfors (1994b) for further discussion on inferences on different levels of representation.

251. A group of researchers work on implementing the features of symbolic systems with the aid of ANNs, for example Smolensky (1990), Sharkey and Sharkey (1993), and Niklasson and van Gelder (1994). In particular, the *systematicity* of symbol systems, that Fodor and Pylyshyn (1988) claim cannot be implemented in ANNs, has been investigated (for example, Bernsen and Ulbæk 1992, Hadley 1994, and Niklasson and van Gelder 1994).

252. Compare the quotation from Fodor (1981, 230) in section 2.2.1.

253. Similar complexity arguments apply to vectorial computations.

254. The symbolic level they call the "linguistic" level, and the subconceptual level the "subsymbolic" level.

255. As pointed out by the authors, the distinction between the associative and the symbolic [linguistic] expectations is a soft one.

Chapter 8

256. See Amit (1989) for an extended analysis of several such emerging structures. Petitot (1992, 37) argues that such an "emergentist" view on the relations between different levels of representation is incompatible with a purely symbolic paradigm.

257. A similar thesis is proposed by Petitot (1992, 49), although he stresses the physical origin of his intermediate "morphological" level.

258. Havel (1995) discusses scale dimensions in nature, although from a realist perspective.

259. There is some neuropsychological evidence that completely amodal representations occur only in humans (see, for example, Wilkins and Wakefield 1995).

References

Aisbett, J., and Gibbon, G. 1994. "A tunable distance measure for coloured solid models." *Artificial Intelligence 65*: 143–164.

Allwood, J., and Gärdenfors, P., eds. 1999. *Cognitive Semantics: Meaning and Cognition.* Amsterdam: John Benjamins.

Amit, D. A. 1989. *Modeling Brain Function.* Cambridge: Cambridge University Press.

Anderson, J. R. 1983. *The Architecture of Cognition.* Cambridge, MA: Harvard University Press.

Armstrong, D. M. 1978. *A Theory of Universals.* Cambridge: Cambridge University Press.

Ashby, F. G., and Gott, R. E. 1988. "Decision rules in the perception and categorization of multidimensional stimuli." *Journal of Experimental Psychology: Learning, Memory, and Cognition 14*: 33–53.

Ashby, F. G., and Lee, W. W. 1991. "Predicting similarity and categorization from identification." *Journal of Experimental Psychology: General 120*: 150–172.

Attneave, F. 1950. "Dimensions of similarity." *American Journal of Psychology 63*: 516–556.

Bailey, D., Chang, N., Feldman, J., and Narayanan, S. 1998. "Extending embodied lexical development." To appear in the *Proceedings of CogSci98.*

Balkenius, C. 1995. *Natural Intelligence in Artificial Creatures.* Lund: Lund University Cognitive Studies 37.

Balkenius, C. 1996. "Generalization in instrumental learning." In Maes, P., Mataric, M., Meyer, J.-A., Pollack, J., and Wilson, S. W., eds. *From Animals to Animats 4: Proceedings of the Fourth International Conference on Simulation of Adaptive Behavior,* 305–314. Cambridge, MA: MIT Press.

Balkenius, C., and Gärdenfors, P. 1991. "Nonmonotonic inferences in neural networks." In Allen, J. A., Fikes, R., and Sandewall, E., eds. *Principles of Knowledge Representation and Reasoning: Proceedings of the Second International Conference,* 32–39. San Mateo, CA: Morgan Kaufmann.

Balkenius, C., and Morén, J. 1998. "Computational models of classical conditioning: A comparative study. Lund: *Lund University Cognitive Studies 62.* A shorter version of the paper will appear in *From Animals to Animats 5.* Cambridge, MA: MIT Press.

Barcan Marcus, R. 1987. "Believing and claiming to believe." Manuscript, Department of Philosophy, Yale University.

Barclay, J. R., Bransford, J. D., Franks, J. J., MacCarrell, N. S., and Nitsch, K. 1974. "Comprehension and semantic flexibility." *Journal of Verbal Learning and Verbal Behavior 13*: 471–481.

Barsalou, L. W. 1983. "Ad hoc categories." *Memory and Cognition 10*: 82–93.

Barsalou, L. W. 1987. "The instability of graded structure: implications for the nature of concepts." In Neisser, U., ed. *Concepts and Conceptual Development: The Ecological and Intellectual Factors in Categorization,* 101–140. Cambridge: Cambridge University Press.

Barsalou, L. W. 1992. "Flexibility, structure, and linguistic vagary in concepts: manifestations of a compositional system of perceptual symbols." In Collins, A. F., Gathercole, S. E., Conway, M. A., and Morris, P. E., eds. *Theories of Memory*, 29–89. Hillsdale: Lawrence Erlbaum Associates.

Barsalou, L. W. (to appear). "Perceptual symbol systems." To appear in *Behavioral and Brain Sciences*.

Barsalou, L. W., and Prinz, J. J. 1997. "Mundane creativity in perceptual symbol systems." In Ward, T. B., Smith, S. M., and Vaid, J., eds. *Creative Thought: An Investigation of Conceptual Structure and Processes*, 267–307. Washington, DC: American Psychological Association.

Bartsch, R. 1996. "The relationship between connectionist models and a dynamic data-oriented theory of concept formation." *Synthese 108*: 421–454.

Barwise, J. 1981. "Scenes and other situations." *Journal of Philosophy 78*: 369–397.

Barwise, J., and Perry, J. 1983. *Situations and Attitudes*. Cambridge, MA: MIT Press.

Beale, R., and Jackson, T. 1990. *Neural Computing: An Introduction*. Bristol: Adam Hilger.

Bealer, G. 1989. "On the identification of properties and propositional functions." *Linguistics and Philosophy 12*: 1–14.

Berlin, B., and Kay, P. 1969. *Basic Color Terms: Their Universality and Evolution*. Berkeley, CA: University of California Press.

Bernsen, N. O., and Ulbæk, I. 1992. "Two games in town: systematicity in distributed connectionist systems," *AISBQ Special Issue on Hybrid Models of Cognition*, part 2, no. 79: 25–30.

Bickerton, D. 1990. *Language and Species*. Chicago, IL: The University of Chicago Press.

Biederman, I. 1987. "Recognition-by-components: a theory of human image understanding." *Psychological Review 94*: 115–147.

Billman, D. O. 1983. *Procedures for Learning Syntactic Structure: A Model and Test with Artificial Grammars*. Doctoral dissertation, University of Michigan.

Billman, D. O., and Heit, E. 1988. "Observational learning from internal feedback: a simulation of an adaptive learning method." *Cognitive Science 12*: 587–625.

Billman, D. O., and Knutson, J. 1996. "Unsupervised concept learning and value systematicity: a complex whole aids learning the parts." *Journal of Experimental Psychology: Learning, Memory and Cognition 22*: 458–475.

Birkhoff, G. 1967. *Lattice Theory*. Providence: American Mathematical Society.

Black, M. 1979. "More about metaphor." In Ortony, A., ed. *Metaphor and Thought*, 19–45. Cambridge: Cambridge University Press.

Böök, L. 1973. "Zum Problem der Konstitution der wissenschaftlichen Objektivität zur der Intersubjektivität der Lebenswelt." Manuscript, Universität Konstanz.

Böök, L. 1998. "Against representationalism." Manuscript, Lund University Cognitive Science (to appear in *Synthese*).

Borsuk, K., and Szmielew, W. 1960. *Foundations of Geometry*. Amsterdam: North-Holland.

Bowermann, M. 1991. "The origins of children's spatial semantic categories: cognitive vs. linguistic determinants." In Gumperz, J. J., and Levinson, S. C., eds. *Rethinking Linguistic Relativity*. Cambridge: Cambridge University Press.

Bowerman, A., and Choi, S. (to appear). "Shaping meanings for language: Universal and language specific in the acquisition of spatial semantic categories." To appear in Bowerman, M., and Levinson, S. C., eds. *Language Acquisition and Conceptual Development*. Cambridge: Cambridge University Press.

Bowerman, A., and Pedersen, E. 1992. "Cross-linguistic perspectives on topological spatial relationships." Paper presented at the annual meeting of the American Anthropological Association, San Francisco, CA.

Brachman, R. J., and Schmoltze, J. C. 1985. "An overview of the KL-ONE knowledge representation system." *Cognitive Science 9*: 171–216.

Braitenberg, V. 1984. *Vehicles*. Cambridge, MA: MIT Press.

Brinck, I. 1992. "Metaphor, similarity and semantic fields." In Emt, J., and Hermerén, G., eds. *Understanding the Arts: Contemporary Scandinavian Aesthetics*, 195–214. Lund: Lund University Press.

Brooks, R. 1991. "Intelligence without representation." *Artificial Intelligence 47*: 139–159.

Broschart, J. 1996. "A geometrical model of the emergence of case relations." Manuscript. Universität Köln: Institut für Sprachwissenschaft.

Broström, S. 1994. *The Role of Metaphor in Cognitive Semantics*. Lund: Lund University Cognitive Studies 31.

Brugman, C. 1981. *Story of Over*. Bloomington, IN: Indiana Linguistics Club.

Bryant, D. J. 1997. "Representing space in langauge and perception." *Mind and Language 12*: 239–264.

Burge, T. 1979. "Individualism and the mental." In *Midwest Studies in Philosophy, vol. 4: Studies in Metaphysics*, 73–121. Minneapolis: University of Minnesota Press.

Buss, A. H. 1973. *Psychology: Man in Perspective*. New York, NY: Wiley.

Carey, S. 1978. "The child as a word learner." In Halle, M., Bresnan, J., and Miller, G., eds. *Linguistic Theory and Psychological Reality*, 347–380 Cambridge, MA: MIT Press.

Carey, S. 1985. *Conceptual Change in Childhood*. Cambridge, MA: MIT Press.

Carnap, R. 1950. *Logical Foundations of Probability*. Chicago, IL: Chicago University Press.

Carnap, R. 1971. "A basic system of inductive logic, part 1." In Carnap, R., and Jeffrey, R. C., eds. *Studies in Inductive Logics and Probability, vol. 1*, 35–165. Berkeley, CA: University of California Press.

Cassirer, E. 1928. "Zur Theorie des Begriffs." *Kantstudien 33*: 129–136.

Chella, A., Frixione, M., and Gaglio, S. 1997. "A cognitive architecture for artificial vision." *Artificial Intelligence 89*: 73–111.

Chella, A., Frixione, M., and Gaglio, S. (to appear). "An architecture for autonomous agents exploiting conceptual representations." To appear in *Robotics and Autonomous Systems*.

Churchland, P. M. 1986a. "Cognitive neurobiology: a computational hypothesis for laminar cortex." *Biology & Philosophy 1*: 25–51.

Churchland, P. M. 1986b. "Some reductive strategies in cognitive neurobiology." *Mind 95*, no. *379*: 279–309.

Churchland, P. M. 1989. *A Neurocomputational Perspective: The Nature of Mind and the Structure of Science*. Cambridge, MA: MIT Press.

Churchland, P. M. 1998. "Conceptual similarity across sensory and neural diversity: the Fodor/Lepore challenge answered." *Journal of Philosophy XCV*: 5–32.

Churchland, P. S. 1986. *Neurophilosophy: Toward a Unified Science of the Mind/Brain*. Cambridge, MA: MIT Press.

Churchland, P. S., and Sejnowski, T. J. 1992. *The Computational Brain*. Cambridge, MA: MIT Press.

Clark, Austen 1993. *Sensory Qualities*. Oxford: Clarendon Press.

Clark, Andy 1993. *Associative Engines: Connectionism, Concepts, and Representational Change*. Cambridge, MA: MIT Press.

Clark, Andy 1997. *Being there*. Cambridge, MA: MIT Press.

Clark, H. H. 1992. *Arenas of Language Use*. Chicago, IL: The University of Chicago Press.

Cohn, A. G., Bennett, B., Gooday, J., and Gotts, N. M. 1997. "Representing and reasoning with qualitative spatial relations about regions." In Stock, O., ed. *Temporal and Spatial Reasoning*. Dordrecht: Kluwer.

Cook, N. D. 1986. *The Brain Code*. London: Methuen.

Cytowic, R. E. 1989. *Synesthesia: A Union of the Senses*. New York: Springer Verlag.

Deacon, T. W. 1997. *The Symbolic Species: The Co-evolution of Language and the Brain*. New York, NY: Norton.

Dellarosa, D. 1988. "The psychological appeal of connectionism." *Behavioral and Brain Sciences 11:1*: 28–29.

Dennett, D. 1978. *Brainstorms: Philosophical Essays on Mind and Psychology*. Cambridge, MA: MIT Press.

Dennett, D. 1987. "Cognitive wheels: the frame problem in AI." In Pylyshyn, Z., ed. *The Robot's Dilemma: The Frame Problem in Artificial Intelligence*, 41–64. Norwood, NJ: Ablex.

De Saussure, F. 1966. *Cours de Linguistique Générale*. de Mauro, T., ed. Paris: Payot.

Descartes, R. 1664. *Traité de l'Homme*, Angot, Paris. Published in French in vol. 11 of *Oeuvres de Descartes* 1909. C. Adam and P. Tannery. Paris: Léopold Cerf.

Desclés, J.-P. 1985. *Représentation des Connaissances*, Actes Semiotiques—Documents, VII, 69–70. Paris: Institut National de la Langue Française.

Dixon, R. M. W. 1982. *Where Have All the Adjectives Gone?* Berlin: Mouton Publishers.

Donald, M. 1991. *Origins of the Modern Mind*. Cambridge, MA: Harvard University Press.

Edelman, S. 1996. "Representation is represention of similarities." Weizmann Institute CS-TR 96–08 (to appear in *Behavioral and Brain Sciences*).

Engberg Pedersen, E. 1995. "The concept of domain in the cognitive theory of metaphor." *Nordic Journal of Linguistics 18*: 111–119.

Engberg Pedersen, E. 1999. "Space and time: A metaphorical relation?" In Allwood, J., and Gärdenfors, P., eds. *Cognitive Semantics: Meaning and Cognition*, 131–152. Amsterdam: John Benjamins.

Fairbanks, G., and Grubb, P. 1961. "A psychophysical investigation of vowel formants." *Journal of Speech and Hearing Research 4*: 203–219.

Fauconnier, G. 1985. *Mental Spaces*. Cambridge, MA: MIT Press.

Fenstad, J. E. 1978. "Models for natural language." In Hintikka, J., Niiniluoto, I., and Saarinen, E., eds. *Essays on Mathematical and Philosophical Logic*, 315–340. Dordrecht: Reidel.

Fenstad, J. E. 1998. "Formal semantics, geometry, and mind." In Arrazola, X. et al., eds. *Discourse, Interaction and Communication*, 85–103. Dordrecht: Kluwer.

Fischer Nilsson, J. 1999. "A conceptual space logic." In Kawaguchi, E., Kangassalo, H., Jaakkola, H., Hamid, I. A., eds. *Information Modelling and Knowledge Bases XI*. Amsterdam: IOS Press.

Fodor, J. A. 1975. *The Language of Thought*. Cambridge, MA: Harvard University Press.

Fodor, J. A. 1981. *Representations*. Cambridge, MA: MIT Press.

Fodor, J. A. 1983. *The Modularity of Mind*. Cambridge, MA: MIT Press.

Fodor, J. A. 1986. "Why paramecia don't have mental representations." *Midwest Studies in Philosophy 10*: 3–23.

Fodor, J. A., and Pylyshyn, Z. 1988. "Connectionism and cognitive architecture: a critical analysis." *Cognition 28*: 3–71.

Foo, N. Y. 1994. "Convex predicates and induction." *Australian Journal of Intelligent Information Processing Systems 1*: 34–40.

Foss, J. 1988. "The percept and vector function theories of the brain." *Philosophy of Science 55*: 511–537.

Freeman, W. J., and Skarda, C. A. 1990. "Representations: who needs them?" In McGaugh, J., Weinberger, N. M., and Lynch, G. eds. *Brain Organization and Memory: Cells, Systems, and Circuits*, 375–380. Oxford: Oxford University Press.

Freyd, J. 1983. "Shareability: the social psychology of epistemology." *Cognitive Science 7*: 191–210.

Fried, L. S., and Holyoak, K. J. 1984. "Induction of category distributions: a framework for classification learning." *Journal of Experimental Psychology: Learning, Memory, and Cognition 10*: 234–257.

Gabbay, D. M., Hogger, C. J., and Robinson J. A., eds. 1993. *Handbook of Logic in Artificial Intelligence and Logic Programming, volume III: Non-Monotonic and Uncertain Reasoning.* Oxford: Oxford University Press.

Gabrielsson, A. 1981. "Music psychology—a survey of problems and current research activities." In *Basic Musical Functions and Musical Ability.* Publications issued by the Royal Swedish Academy of Music, no. 32: 7–80.

Gallistel, C. R. 1990. *The Organization of Learning.* Cambridge, MA: MIT Press.

Garcia, J., and Koelling, R. A. 1966. "Relation of cue to consequences in avoidance learning." *Psychonomic Science 4*: 123–124.

Gärdenfors, P. 1988a. *Knowledge in Flux: Modeling the Dynamics of Epistemic States.* Cambridge, MA: MIT Press.

Gärdenfors, P. 1988b. "Semantics, conceptual spaces and music." In Rantala, V. Rowell, L., and Tarasti, eds. *Essays on the Philosophy of Music (Acta Philosophica Fennica, vol. 43),* 9–27. Helsinki.

Gärdenfors, P. 1990. "Induction, conceptual spaces and AI." *Philosophy of Science 57*: 78–95.

Gärdenfors, P. 1991. "Frameworks for properties: possible worlds vs. conceptual spaces." In Haaparanta, L., Kusch, M., and Niiniluoto, I., eds. *Language, Knowledge and Intentionality (Acta Philosophica Fennica, vol. 49),* 383–407. Helsinki.

Gärdenfors, P. 1992. "A geometric model of concept formation." In Ohsuga, S. et al., eds. *Information Modelling and Knowledge Bases III,* 1–16. Amsterdam: IOS Press.

Gärdenfors, P. 1993a. "The emergence of meaning," *Linguistics and Philosophy 16*: 285–309.

Gärdenfors, P. 1993b. "Induction and the evolution of conceptual spaces." In Moore, E. C., ed. *Charles S. Peirce and the Philosophy of Science,* 72–88. Tuscaloosa: The University of Alabama Press.

Gärdenfors, P. 1994a. "Three levels of inductive inference." In Prawitz, D., Skyrms, B., and Westerståhl, D., eds. *Logic, Methodology, and Philosophy of Science IX,* 427–449. Amsterdam: Elsevier Science.

Gärdenfors, P. 1994b. "How logic emerges from the dynamics of information." In van Eijck, J., and Visser. A., eds. *Logic and Information Flow,* 49–77. Cambridge, MA: MIT Press.

Gärdenfors, P. 1994c. "The role of expectations in reasoning." In Masuch, M., and Polos, L., eds. *Knowledge Representation and Reasoning Under Uncertainty,* 1–16. Berlin: Springer-Verlag.

Gärdenfors, P. 1995. "Speaking about the inner environment." In Allén, S., ed. *Of Thoughts and Words.* London: Imperial College Press.

Gärdenfors, P. 1996a. "Cued and detached representations in animal cognition." *Behavioural Processes 36*: 263–273.

Gärdenfors, P. 1996b. "Mental representation, conceptual spaces and metaphors." *Synthese 106*: 21–47.

Gärdenfors, P. 1996c. "Conceptual spaces as a framework for cognitive semantics." In Clark. A., ed. *Philosophy and Cognitive Science,* 159–180. Dordrecht: Kluwer.

Gärdenfors, P. 1996d. "Human communication: what happens?" In Reichert, B., ed. *The Contribution of Science and Technology to the Development of Human Society.* Brussels: ECSC-EC-EAEC. Abstract on p. 96. (The article is published on the accompanying CD-ROM as document C2–1A.pdf).

Gärdenfors, P. 1996e. "Ambiguity, harmony and probability." In Lindström, S., Sliwinski, R., and Österberg, J., eds. *Odds and Ends: Philosophical Essays Dedicated to*

Wlodek Rabinowicz on the Occasion of His Fiftieth Birthday, 137–149. Uppsala: Uppsala Philosophical Studies 45.

Gärdenfors, P. 1996f. "Language and the evolution of cognition." In Rialle, V., and Fisette, D., eds. *Penser l'Esprit: Des Sciences de la Cognition à une Philosophie Cognitive*, 151–172. Grenoble: Presses Universitaires de Grenoble.

Gärdenfors, P. 1997. "Does semantics need reality?" In Riegler, A., and Peschl, M., eds. *New Trends in Cognitive Science–97 "Does Representation Need Reality?"* 113–120. Vienna: Austrian Society of Cognitive Science Technical Report 97–01.

Gärdenfors, P. 1998. "The pragmatic role of modality in natural language." In Weingartner, P., Schurz, G., and Dorn, G., eds. *The Role of Pragmatics in Contemporary Philosophy*, 78–91. Vienna: Hölder-Pichler-Tempsky.

Gärdenfors, P. (to appear). "Harmony as shape in musical space." Extended abstract.

Gärdenfors, P., and Holmqvist, K. 1994. "Concept formation in dimensional spaces." Lund: *Lund University Cognitive Studies 26*.

Gärdenfors, P., and Makinson, D. 1994. "Nonmonotonic inferences based on expectations." *Artificial Intelligence* 65: 197–245.

Garner, W. R. 1974. *The Processing of Information and Structure*. Potomac, MD: Erlbaum.

Genesereth, M., and Nilsson, N. J. 1987. *Logical Foundations of Artificial Intelligence*. Los Altos, CA: Morgan Kaufmann.

Gibbs, R. W., and Colston, H. L. 1995. "The cognitive psychological reality of image schemas and their transformations." *Cognitive Linguistics* 6: 347–378.

Gibson, J. J. 1979. *The Ecological Approach to Visual Perception*. Hillsdale, NJ: Lawrence Erlbaum Associates.

Givón, T. 1984. *Syntax—a Functional-Typological Introduction, vol. 1*. Amsterdam: John Benjamins.

Goldberg, A. E. 1995. *Constructions: A Construction Grammar Approach to Argument Structure*. Chicago, IL: University of Chicago Press.

Goldstone, R. L. 1994a. "Influences of categorization on perceptual discrimination." *Journal of Experimental Psychology: General 123*: 178–200.

Goldstone, R. L. 1994b. "The role of similarity in categorization: providing a groundwork." *Cognition* 52: 125–157.

Goldstone, R. L., and Barsalou, L. W. 1998. "Reuniting perception and conception." *Cognition* 65: 231–262.

Goodman, N. 1955. *Fact, Fiction, and Forecast*. Cambridge, MA: Harvard University Press.

Goodman, N. 1961. "Safety, strength, simplicity." *Philosophy of Science 28*: 150–151.

Goodman, N. 1966. *The Structure of Appearance*, 2nd ed. New York: Bobbs-Merrill.

Goodman, N. 1972. *Problems and Projects*. Indianapolis, IN: Hackett.

Gopnik, A., and Meltzoff, A. N. 1997. *Words, Thoughts, and Theories*. Cambridge, MA: MIT Press.

Hadley, R. F. 1994. "Systematicity in connectionist language learning." *Mind and Language* 9: 247–272.

Hahn, U., and Chater, N. 1997. "Concepts and similarity." In Lambert, K., and Shanks, D., eds. *Knowledge, Concepts, and Categories*, 43–92. East Sussex: Psychology Press.

Hahn, U., and Chater, N. 1998. "Similarity and rules: distinct? exhaustive? empirically distinguishable?" *Cognition* 65: 197–230.

Halff, H. M., Ortony, A., and Anderson, R. C. 1976. "A context-sensitive representation of word meanings." *Memory and Cognition 4*: 378–383.

Hampton, J. A. 1988. "Overextension of conjunctive concepts: evidence for a unitary model of concept typicality and class inclusion." *Journal of Experimental Psychology: Learning, Memory, and Cognition 14*: 12–32.

Hampton, J. A. 1993. "Prototype models of concept representation." In van Mechelen, I. et al., eds. *Categories and Concepts: Theoretical Views and Data Analysis*, 67–95. London: Academic Press.

Hampton, J. A. 1997. "Similarity and categorization." In Ramscar, M., Hahn, U., Cambouropolos, E., and Pain, H., eds. *Proceedings of SimCat 1997: An Interdisciplinary Workshop on Similarity and Categorization*. Edinburgh University, Edinburgh: Department of Artificial Intelligence.

Hampton, J. A. 1998. "Similarity-based categorization and fuzziness of natural categories." *Cognition 65*: 137–165.

Hanson, N. R. 1958. *Patterns of Discovery*. Cambridge: Cambridge University Press.

Hård, A., and Sivik, L. 1981. "NCS-natural color system: a Swedish standard for color notation." *Color Research and Application 6*: 129–138.

Harder, P. 1996. *Functional Semantics: A Theory of Meaning, Structure and Tense in English*. Berlin: Mouton de Gruyter.

Hardin, C. L. 1988. *Color for Philosophers: Unweaving the Rainbow*. Indianapolis: Hackett.

Harnad, S. 1987. "Category induction and representation." In Harnad, S., ed. *Categorical Perception*, 535–565. Cambridge: Cambridge University Press.

Harnad, S. 1990. "The symbol grounding problem." *Physica D 42*: 335–346.

Hauser, M. D. 1996. *The Evolution of Communication*. Cambridge, MA: MIT Press.

Havel, I. M. 1995. "Scale dimensions in nature." *International Journal of General Systems 23*: 303–332.

Helmantel, M. 1998. "Simplex adpositions and vector theory." *The Linguistic Review 15*: 361–388.

Hemeren, P. 1996. "Frequency, ordinal position and semantic distance as measures of cross-cultural stability and hierarchies for action verbs." *Acta Psychologica 91*: 39–66.

Hempel, C. G. 1965. *Aspects of Scientific Explanation, and Other Essays in the Philosophy of Science*. New York, NY: Free Press.

Henning, H. 1916. "Die Qualitätenriehe des Geschmacks." *Zeitschrift für Psychologie und Physiologie der Sinnesorgane 74*: 203–219.

Herskovits, A. 1986. *Language and Spatial Cognition: An Interdisciplinary Study of the Prepositions in English*. Cambridge: Cambridge University Press.

Hintikka, J. 1961. "Modality and quantification." *Theoria 27*: 110–128.

Hintikka, J. 1968. "The varieties of information and scientific explanation." In van Rootselaar, B., and Staal, J. F., eds. *Logic, Methodology and Philosophy of Science III*, 311–331. Amsterdam: North-Holland.

Hinton, G. E. 1984. "Parallel computations for controlling an arm." *Journal of Motor Behavior 16*: 171–194.

Hintzman, D. L. 1986. "'Schema abstraction' in a multiple-trace memory model." *Psychological Review 93*: 411–428.

Holland, J. H., Holyoak, K. J., Nisbett, R. E., and Thagard, P. R. 1995. *Induction: Processes of Inference, Learning, and Discovery*. Cambridge, MA: MIT Press.

Holmqvist, K. 1988. "Aspects of parameterizing concept representations." Manuscript. Lund University: Department of Philosophy.

Holmqvist, K. 1993. *Implementing Cognitive Semantics*. Lund: Lund University Cognitive Studies 17.

Holmqvist, K. 1994. "Conceptual engineering I: from morphemes to valence relations." Lund: *Lund University Cognitive Studies 28*.

Holmqvist, K. 1999. "Conceptual engineering: implementing cognitive semantics." In Allwood, J., and Gärdenfors, P., eds. *Cognitive Semantics: Meaning and Cognition*, 153–171. Amsterdam: John Benjamins.

Holmqvist, K., and Pluciennik, J. 1996. "Conceptualised deviations from expected nor-malities: a semantic comparison between lexical items ending in -ful and -less." *Nordic Journal of Linguistics 19*: 3–33.

Honkela, T. 1997. *Self-Organizing Maps in Natural Language Processing*. Helsinki: Helsinki University of Technology.

Hopfield, J. J. 1982. "Neural networks and physical systems with emergent collective computational abilities." *Proceedings of the National Academy of Sciences of USA 79*: 2554–2558.

Hulth, N., and Grenholm, P. 1998. "A distributed clustering algorithm." Lund: *Lund University Cognitive Studies 74*.

Hutchins, E. 1995. *Cognition in the Wild*. Cambridge, MA: MIT Press.

Indurkhya, B. 1986. "Constrained semantic transference: a formal theory of metaphors." *Synthese 68*: 515–551.

Jackendoff, R. 1983. *Semantics and Cognition*. Cambridge, MA: MIT Press.

Jackendoff, R. 1987a. *Consciousness and the Computational Mind*. Cambridge, MA: MIT Press.

Jackendoff, R. 1987b. "On Beyond Zebra: the relation of linguistic and visual informa-tion." *Cognition 26*: 89–114.

Jackendoff, R. 1990. *Semantic Structures*. Cambridge, MA: MIT Press.

Jackendoff, R. 1997. *The Architecture of the Language Faculty*. Cambridge, MA: MIT Press.

James, W. 1890. *The Principles of Psychology*. New York, NY: Holt.

Janlert, L.-E. 1987. "Modeling change—the frame problem." In Pylyshyn, Z., ed. *The Robot's Dilemma: The Frame Problem in Artificial Intelligence*, 1–40. Norwood, NJ: Ablex.

Johannesson, M. 1996. "Obtaining psychologically motivated spaces with MDS." Lund: *Lund University Cognitive Studies 45*.

Johannesson, M. 1997. "Modelling asymmetric similarity with prominence." Lund: (Revised version to appear in *British Journal of Mathematical and Statistical Psy-chology*.) *Lund University Cognitive Studies 55*.

Johnson, M. 1987. *The Body in the Mind: The Bodily Basis of Cognition*. Chicago, IL: Uni-versity of Chicago Press.

Johnson, M. G., and Malgady, R. G. 1980. "Toward a perceptual theory of metaphoric comprehension." In Honeck, R. P., and Hoffman, R. R., eds. *Cognition and Figura-tive Language*, 259–282. Hillsdale, NJ: Lawrence Erlbaum Associates.

Johnson, W. E. 1921. *Logic, Part I*. Cambridge: Cambridge University Press.

Johnson-Laird, P. N. 1983. *Mental Models*. Cambridge: Cambridge University Press.

Jones, S. S., and Smith, L. B. 1993. "The place of perception in children's concepts." *Cog-nitive Development 8*: 113–139.

Jones, L. E., and Koehly, L. M. 1993. "Multidimensional scaling." In Keren, G., and Lewis, C., eds. *A Handbook for Data Analysis in the Behavioral Sciences*, 95–163. Hillsdale, NJ: Lawrence Erlbaum Associates.

Jordan, M. J. 1986. "An introduction to linear algebra in parallel distributed processing." In Rumelhart, D. E., and McClelland, J. L., eds. *Parallel Distributed Processing, vol. 2*, 365–422. Cambridge, MA: MIT Press.

Kamp, H., and Partee, B. 1995. "Prototype theory and compositionality." *Cognition 57*: 129–191.

Kanger, S. 1957. *Provability in Logic*. Stockholm: Almqvist & Wiksell.

Karmiloff-Smith, A. 1992. *Beyond Modularity: A Developmental Perspective on Cognitive Science*. Cambridge, MA: MIT Press.

Katz, J. J., and Fodor, J. A. 1964. "The structure of a semantic theory." *Language 39*: 170–210.

Keil, F. 1979. *Semantic and Conceptual Development*. Cambridge, MA: Harvard University Press.

Kirsch, D. 1991. "Today the earwig, tomorrow man?" *Artificial Intelligence 47*: 161–184.

Kohonen, T. 1988. *Self-Organization and Associative Memory*, 2nd ed. Berlin: Springer-Verlag.

Kohonen, T. 1995. *Self-Organizing Maps*. Berlin: Springer-Verlag.

Kohonen, T. 1996. "Emergence of invariant-feature detectors in the adaptive-subspace self-organizing map." *Biological Cybernetics 75*: 281–291.

Kornblith, H. 1993. *Inductive Inference and Its Natural Ground: An Essay in Naturalistic Epistemology*. Cambridge, MA: MIT Press.

Kövesces, Z. 1993. "Minimal and full definitions of meaning." In Geiger, R. A., and Rudzka-Ostyn, B., eds. *Conceptualizations and Mental Processing in Language*, 247–266. Berlin: Mouton de Gruyter.

Kripke, S. 1959. "A completeness theorem in modal logic." *Journal of Symbolic Logic 24*: 1–24.

Krumhansl, C. L. 1978. "Concerning the applicability of geometric models to similarity data: the interrelationship between similarity and spatial density." *Psychological Review 85*: 445–463.

Krumhansl, C. L., and Kessler, E. J. 1982. "Tracing the dynamic changes in perceived tonal organization in a spatial representation of musical keys." *Psychological Review 89*: 334–368.

Kruskal, J. B. 1964. "Multidimensional scaling by optimizing goodness of fit to a nonmetric hypothesis." *Psychometrika 29*: 1–27.

Kruskal, J. B., and Wish, M. 1978. *Multidimensional Scaling*. Beverly Hills, CA: Sage Publications.

Kuhl, P. K., Andruski, J. E., Chistovich, I. A., Chistovich, L. A., Kozhevnikova, E. V., Ryskina, V. L., Stolyarova, E. I., Sundberg, U., and Lacerda, F. 1997. "Cross-language analysis of phonetic units in language addressed to infants." *Science 277*: 684–686.

Kuhn, T. 1970. *The Structure of Scientific Revolutions*, 2nd ed. Chicago, IL: University of Chicago Press.

Labov, W. 1973. "The boundaries of words and their meanings." In Bailey, C.-J. N. and Shuy, R., eds. *New Ways of Analyzing Variation in English*, 340–373. Washington, DC: Georgetown University Press.

Lakatos, I. 1976. *Proofs and Refutations: The Logic of Mathematical Discovery*. Cambridge: Cambridge University Press.

Lakoff, G. 1987. *Women, Fire, and Dangerous Things*. Chicago, IL: The University of Chicago Press.

Lakoff, G. 1988. "Smolensky, semantics, and the sensorimotor system." *Behavioral and Brain Sciences 11*: 39–40.

Lakoff, G. 1994. "The contemporary theory of metaphor." In Ortony, A., ed. *Metaphor and Thought*, 2nd ed. 202–251. Cambridge: Cambridge University Press.

Lakoff, G., and Johnson, M. 1980. *Metaphors We Live By*. Chicago, IL: University of Chicago Press.

Land, E. 1977. "The retinex theory of color vision." *Scientific American 237*: 108–128.

Landau, B., and Jackendoff, R. 1993. "'What' and 'where' in spatial language and spatial cognition." *Behavioral and Brain Sciences 16*: 217–238.

Landau, B., Smith, L., and Jones, S. 1998. "Object perception and object naming in early development." *Trends in Cognitive Science 2*: 19–24.

Lang, E., Carstensen, K.-U., and Simmons, G. 1991. *Modeling Spatial Knowledge on a Linguistic Basis*. Berlin: Springer-Verlag.

Langacker, R. W. 1986. "An introduction to cognitive grammar." *Cognitive Science 10*: 1–40.

Langacker, R. W. 1987. *Foundations of Cognitive Grammar, vol. I.* Stanford, CA: Stanford University Press.

Langacker, R. W. 1988. "The nature of grammatical valence." In Rudzka-Ostyn, B., ed. *Topics in Cognitive Linguistics*, 91–125. Amsterdam: John Benjamins.

Langacker, R. W. 1991a. *Foundations of Cognitive Grammar, vol. II.* Stanford, CA: Stanford University Press.

Langacker, R. W. 1991b. *Concept, Image, and Symbol: The Cognitive Basis of Grammar.* Berlin: Mouton de Gruyter.

Langer, S. 1948. *Philosophy in a New Key.* New York: Penguin Books.

Langley, P. 1996. *Elements of Machine Learning.* San Francisco, CA: Morgan Kaufmann.

Lewandowska-Tomaszczyk, B. 1996. *Depth of Negation: A Cognitive Semantic Study.* Lodz: Lodz University Press.

Lewis, D. K. 1970. "General semantics." *Synthese 22*: 18–67.

Lewis, D. K. 1973. *Counterfactuals.* Oxford: Blackwell.

Lewis, D. K. 1986. *On the Plurality of Worlds.* Oxford: Blackwell.

Lippman, R. P. 1987. "An introduction to computing with neural nets." *IEEE ASSP Magazine*, April 1987: 4–22.

Locke, J. 1690/1959. *An Essay Concerning Human Understanding.* New York, NY: Dover Publications.

Maddox, W. T. 1992. "Perceptual and decisional separability." In Ashby, G. F., ed. *Multidimensional Models of Perception and Cognition*, 147–180. Hillsdale, NJ: Lawrence Erlbaum.

Makinson, D., and Schlechta, K. 1991. "Floating conclusions and zombie paths: two deep difficulties in the 'directly skeptical' approach to defeasible inheritance nets." *Artificial Intelligence 48*: 199–209.

Mandler, J. 1992. "How to build a baby: II. Conceptual Primitives." *Psychological Review 99*: 587–604.

Marr, D. 1982. *Vision.* San Francisco, CA: Freeman.

Marr, D., and Nishihara, H. K. 1978. "Representation and recognition of the spatial organization of three-dimensional shapes." *Proceedings of the Royal Society in London, B200*: 269–294.

Marr, D., and Vaina, L. 1982. "Representation and recognition of the movements of shapes." *Proceedings of the Royal Society in London, B214*: 501–524.

McCarthy, J., and Hayes, P. 1969. "Some philosophical problems from the standpoint of artificial intelligence." In Meltzer, B., and Michie, D., eds. *Machine Intelligence, vol. 4.* Edinburgh: Edinburgh University Press.

Medin, D. L. 1989. "Concepts and conceptual structure." *American Psychologist 44*: 1469–1481.

Medin, D. L., Goldstone, R. L., and Gentner, D. 1993. "Respects for similarity." *Psychological Review 100*: 254–278.

Medin, D. L., and Ortony, A. 1989. "Psychological essentialism." In Vosniadou, S., and Ortony, A., eds. *Similarity and Analogical Reasoning*, 179–195. Cambridge: Cambridge University Press.

Medin, D. L., and Shoben, E. J. 1988. "Context and structure in conceptual combination." *Cognitive Psychology 20*: 158–190.

Meinong, A. 1906/1973. "Über die Erfahrungsgrundlagen unseres Wissens." *Gesamtausgabe vol. V*, Graz.

Melara, R. D. 1992. "The concept of perceptual similarity: from psychophysics to cognitive psychology." In Algom, D., ed. *Psychophysical Approaches to Cognition*, 303–388. Amsterdam: Elsevier.

Mervis, C., and Rosch, E. 1981. "Categorization of natural objects." *Annual Review of Psychology* 32: 89–115.

Michalski, R. S., and Stepp, R. E. 1983. "Learning from observation: conceptual clustering." In Michalski, R. S., Carbonell, J. G., and Mitchell, T. M., eds. *Machine Learning, An Artificial Intelligence Approach*, 331–363. Los Altos, CA: Morgan Kaufmann.

Minsky, M. 1975. "A framework for representing knowledge." In Winston, P. H., ed. *The Psychology of Computer Vision*. New York, NY: McGraw-Hill.

Montague, R. 1974. *Formal Philosophy*. Thomason, R. H., ed. New Haven, CT: Yale University Press.

Morasso, P., and Sanguineti, V. 1996. "How the brain can discover the existence of external egocentric space." *Neurocomputing 12*: 289–310.

Mormann, T. 1993. "Natural predicates and the topological structure of conceptual spaces." *Synthese 95*: 219–240.

Mormann, T. 1994. "Cassirer's problem and geometrical aspects of epistemology." In Meggle, G., and Wessels, U., eds. *Proceedings of the First Conference "Perspectives in Analytical Philosophy."* 241–250. Berlin: de Gruyter.

Moxey, L. M., and Sanford, A. J. 1993. *Communicating Quantities: A Psychological Perspective*. Hove: Lawrence Erlbaum Associates.

Mulligan, K. 1991. "Colours, corners and complexity: Meinong and Wittgenstein on some internal relations." In Spohn, W. et al., eds. *Existence and Explanation*, 77–101. Dordrecht: Kluwer.

Murphy, G. L. 1988. "Comprehending complex concepts." *Cognitive Science 12*: 529–562.

Murphy, G. L. 1990. "Noun phrase interpretation and conceptual combination." *Journal of Memory and Language 29*: 259–288.

Murphy, G. L., and Medin, D. L. 1985. "The role of theories in conceptual coherence." *Psychological Review 92*: 289–316.

Murtagh, F. D. 1993. "Cluster analysis using proximities." In van Mechelen, I. et al., eds. *Categories and Concepts: Theoretical Views and Data Analysis*, 225–245. London: Academic Press.

Nelson, K. 1974. "Concept, word, and sentence: interrelations in acquisition and development." *Psychological Review 81*: 267–285.

Newell, A. 1990. *Unified Theories of Cognition*. Cambridge, MA: Harvard University Press.

Newell, A., and Simon. H. 1976. "Computer science as empirical inquiry: symbols and search." *CACM 19*: 113–116.

Niklasson, L. F., and van Gelder, T. 1994. "On being systematically connectionist." *Mind and Language 9*: 288–302.

Nisbett, R. E., Krantz, D. H., Jepson, D., and Kunda, Z. 1983. "The use of statistical heuristics in everyday inductive reasoning." *Psychological Review 90*: 339–363.

Nisbett, R. E., and Ross, L. 1980. *Human Inference: Strategies and Shortcomings of Social Judgement*. Englewood Cliffs, NJ: Prentice-Hall.

Nolan, R. 1994. *Cognitive Practices: Human Language and Human Knowledge*. Oxford: Blackwell.

Nosofsky, R. M. 1986. "Attention, similarity, and the identification–categorization relationship." *Journal of Experimental Psychology: General, 115*: 39–57.

Nosofsky, R. M. 1988a. "Similarity, frequency, and category representations." *Journal of Experimental Psychology: Learning, Memory, and Cognition 14*: 54–65.

Nosofsky, R. M. 1988b. "Exemplar-based accounts of relations between classification, recognition, and typicality." *Journal of Experimental Psychology: Learning, Memory, and Cognition 14*: 700–708.

Nosofsky, R. M. 1991. "Stimulus bias, asymmetric similarity, and classification." *Cognitive Psychology 23*: 91–140.

Nosofsky, R. M. 1992. "Similarity scaling and cognitive process models." *Annual Review of Psychology 43*: 25–53.

Okabe, A., Boots, B., and Sugihara, K. 1992. *Spatial Tessellations: Concepts and Applications of Voronoi Diagrams*. New York, NY: John Wiley & Sons.

Osgood, C. E. 1980. "The cognitive dynamics of synesthesia and metaphor." In Honeck, R. P., and Hoffman, R. R., eds. *Cognition and Figurative Language*, 203–238. Hillsdale, NJ: Lawrence Erlbaum Associates.

Osherson, D. N., and Smith, E. E. 1981. "On the adequacy of prototype theory as a theory of concepts." *Cognition 12*: 299–318.

Osherson, D. N., Smith, E. E., Wilkie, O., López, A., and Shafir, E. 1990. "Category-based induction." *Psychological Review 97*: 185–200.

Palmer, S. E. 1978. "Fundamental aspects of cognitive representation." In Rosch, E., and Lloyd, B. B., eds. *Cognition and Categorization*, 259–303. Hillsdale, NJ: Lawrence Erlbaum Associates.

Pearl, J. 1988. *Probabilistic Reasoning in Intelligent Systems*. San Mateo, CA: Morgan Kaufmann.

Peirce, C. S. 1932. *Collected Papers of Charles Sanders Peirce, volume II, Elements of Logic.* Hartshorne, C., and Weiss, P., eds. Cambridge, MA: Harvard University Press.

Pellionisz, A., and Llinas, R. 1979. "Brain modeling by tensor network theory and computer simulation. The cerebellum: distributed processor for predictive coordination." *Neuroscience 4*: 323–348.

Pellionisz, A., and Llinas, R. 1980. "Tensorial approach to the geometry of brain function: cerebellar coordination via a metric tensor." *Neuroscience 5*: 1125–1136.

Pellionisz, A., and Llinas, R. 1982. "Space-time representation in the brain. The cerebellum as a predictive space-time metric tensor." *Neuroscience 7*: 2949–2970.

Pellionisz, A., and Llinas, R. 1985. "Tensor network theory of the metaorganization of functional geometries in the central nervous system." *Neuroscience 16*: 245–273.

Pentland, A. P. 1986. "Perceptual organization and the representation of natural form." *Artificial Intelligence 28*: 293–331.

Persson, J. 1997. *Causal Facts*. Thales, Stockholm: Library of Theoria 22.

Petitot-Cocorda, J. 1985. *Morphogenèse du Sens I*. Paris: Presses Universitaires de France.

Petitot, J. 1989. "Morphodynamics and the categorical perception of phonological units." *Theoretical Linguistics 15*: 25–71.

Petitot, J. 1992. "Cognition, perception et morphodynamique." In Gervet, J., Livet, P., and Tête, A., eds. *La Représentation Animale*, 35–58. Presses Universitaires de Nancy.

Petitot, J. 1995. "Morphodynamics and attractor syntax: constituency in visual perception and cognitive grammar." In Port, R. F., and van Gelder, T., eds. *Mind as Motion*, 227–281. Cambridge, MA: MIT Press.

Pittenger, J. B., and Shaw, R. E. 1975. "Aging faces as viscal–elastic events: implications for a theory of nonrigid shape perception." *Journal of Experimental Psychology: Human Perception and Performance 1*: 374–382.

Popper, K. R. 1959. *The Logic of Scientific Discovery*. London: Hutchinson.

Port, R. F., and van Gelder, T., eds. 1995. *Mind as Motion*, Cambridge. MA: MIT Press.

Posner, M. I., and Keele, S. W. 1968. "On the genesis of abstract ideas." *Journal of Experimental Psychology 77*: 353–363.

Putnam, H. 1975. "The meaning of 'meaning'." In Gunderson, K., ed. *Language, Mind, and Knowledge*, 131–193. Minneapolis: University of Minnesota Press.

Putnam, H. 1980. "Models and reality." *Journal of Symbolic Logic 45*: 464–482.

Putnam, H. 1981. *Reason, Truth, and History*. Cambridge: Cambridge University Press.

Putnam, H. 1988. *Representation and Reality*. Cambridge, MA: MIT Press.

Pylyshyn, Z. 1984. *Computation and Cognition*. Cambridge, MA: MIT Press.

Quine, W. V. O. 1969. "Natural kinds." In *Ontological Relativity and Other Essays*, 114–138. New York, NY: Columbia University Press.

Quine, W. V. O. 1979. "Facts of the matter." In Shahan, R. W., and Swoyer, C., eds. *Essays on the Philosophy of W. V. Quine*, 155–169. Hassocks: Harvester Press.

Quinlan, P. 1991. *Connectionism and Psychology: A Psychological Perspective on New Connectionist Research*. New York, NY: Harvester Wheatsheaf.

Radermacher, F. J. 1996. "Cognition in systems." *Cybernetics and Systems 27*: 1–41.

Raup, D. M. 1966. "Geometric analysis of shell coiling: general problems." *Journal of Paleontology 40*: 1178–1190.

Reed, S. K. 1972. "Pattern recognition and categorization." *Cognitive Psychology 3*: 382–407.

Regier, T. 1996. *The Human Semantic Potential: Spatial Language and Constrained Connectionism*. Cambridge, MA: MIT Press.

Reiter, R. 1980. "A logic for default reasoning." *Artificial Intelligence 13*: 81–132.

Rips, L. J. 1989. "Similarity, typicality and categorization." In Vosniadou, S., and Ortony, A., eds. *Similarity and Analogical Reasoning*, 21–59. Cambridge: Cambridge University Press.

Rips, L. J. 1995. "The current status of research on concept combination." *Mind and Language 10*: 72–104.

Rosch, E. 1975. "Cognitive representations of semantic categories." *Journal of Experimental Psychology: General 104*: 192–233.

Rosch, E. 1978. "Prototype classification and logical classification: the two systems." In Scholnik, E., ed. *New Trends in Cognitive Representation: Challenges to Piaget's Theory*, 73–86. Hillsdale, NJ: Lawrence Erlbaum Associates.

Roth, E. M., and Shoben, E. J. 1983. "The effect of context on the structure of categories." *Cognitive Psychology 15*: 573–605.

Rott, H. 1997. "Comments on Gärdenfors' 'Meanings as conceptual structures'." In Carrier, M., and Machamer, P. K., eds. *Mindscapes: Philosophy of Science and the Mind*, 87–97. Pittsburgh, PA: University of Pittsburgh Press.

Rudzka-Ostyn, B., ed. 1988. *Topics in Cognitive Linguistics*. Amsterdam: John Benjamins.

Rumelhart, D. E., and McClelland, J. L. 1986. *Parallel Distributed Processing*, vols. 1 and 2, Cambridge, MA: MIT Press.

Rumelhart, D. E., Smolensky, P., McClelland, J. L., and Hinton, G. E. 1986. "Schemata and sequential thought processes in PDP models." In Rumelhart, D. E., and McClelland, J. L., eds. *Parallel Distributed Processing, vol. 2*, 7–57. Cambridge, MA: MIT Press.

Saunders, B. A. C., and van Brakel, J. 1997. "Are there nontrivial constraints on colour categorization?" *Behavioral and Brain Sciences 20*: 167–179.

Schiffman, H. R. 1982. *Sensation and Perception, 2nd ed*. New York, NY: John Wiley & Sons.

Schyns, P. G. 1991. "A modular neural network model of concept acquisition." *Cognitive Science 15*: 461–508.

Schyns, P. G., Goldstone, R. L., and Thibaut, J.-P. 1998. "The development of features in object concepts." *Behavioral and Brain Sciences 21*: 1–17.

Scott Kelso, J. A. 1995. *Dynamic Patterns: The Self-Organization of Brain and Behavior*. Cambridge, MA: MIT Press.

Shapere, D. 1982. "The concept of observation in science and philosophy." *Philosophy of Science 49*: 485–525.

Sharkey, N. E., and Sharkey, A. J. C. 1993. "Adaptive generalization." *Artificial Intelligence Review 7*: 313–328.

Shepard, R. N. 1962a. "The analysis of proximities: multidimensional scaling with an unknown distance function. I." *Psychometrika 27*: 125–140.

Shepard, R. N. 1962b. "The analysis of proximities: multidimensional scaling with an unknown distance function. II." *Psychometrika* 27: 219–246.

Shepard, R. N. 1964. "Attention and the metric structure of the stimulus space." *Journal of Mathematical Psychology* 1: 54–87.

Shepard, R. N. 1982. "Geometrical approximations to the structure of musical pitch." *Psychological Review 89*: 305–333.

Shepard, R. N. 1984. "Ecological constraints on internal representation: resonant kinematics of perceiving, imagining, thinking, and dreaming." *Psychological Review 91*: 417–447.

Shepard, R. N. 1987. "Toward a universal law of generalization for psychological science." *Science 237*: 1317–1323.

Shepard, R. N., and Chipman, S. 1970. "Second-order isomorphism of internal representations: shapes of states." *Cognitive Psychology 1*: 1–17.

Shepp, B. E. 1983. "The analyzability of multidimensional objects: some constraints on perceived structure, the development of perceived structure, and attention." In Thighe, T. J., and Shepp, B. E., eds. *Perception, Cognition, and Development*, 39–75. Hillsdale, NJ: Lawrence Erlbaum.

Shin, H. J., and Nosofsky, R. M. 1992. "Similarity-scaling studies of dot-pattern classification and recognition." *Journal of Experimental Psychology: General 121*: 278–304.

Sivik, L., and Taft, C. 1994. "Color naming: a mapping in the NCS of common color terms." *Scandinavian Journal of Psychology 35*: 144–164.

Sloman, A. 1971. "Interactions between philosophy and AI—the role of intuition and non-logical reasoning in intelligence." *Proceedings 2nd IJCAI*. London.

Sloman, S. A. 1993. "Feature-based induction." *Cognitive Psychology 25*: 231–280.

Sloman, S. A., Love, B. C., and Ahn, W.-K. 1998. "Feature centrality and conceptual coherence." *Cognitive Science 22*: 189–228.

Smith, E. E., and Medin, D. L. 1981. *Categories and Concepts*. Cambridge, MA: Harvard University Press.

Smith, E. E., Osherson, D. N., Rips, L. J., and Keane, M. 1988. "Combining prototypes: a selective modification model." *Cognitive Science 12*: 485–527.

Smith, E. E., and Sloman, S. A. 1994. "Similarity- versus rule-based categorization." *Memory and Cognition 22*: 377–386.

Smith, L. B. 1989. "From global similarities to kinds of similarities—the construction of dimensions in development." In Vosniadou, S., and Ortony, A., eds. *Similarity and Analogical Reasoning*. Cambridge: Cambridge University Press.

Smith, L. B., Gasser, M., and Sandhofer, C. 1997. "Learning to talk about the properties of objects: a network model of the development of dimensions." In Goldstone, R. L., Schyns, P. G., and Medin, D. L., eds. *Psychology of Learning and Motivation, vol. 36*, 219–256. San Diego, CA: Academic Press.

Smith, L. B., and Heise, D. 1992. "Perceptual similarity and conceptual structure." In Burns, B., ed. *Percepts, Concepts, and Categories*. Amsterdam: Elsevier.

Smith, L. B., and Samuelson, L. K. 1997. "Perceiving and remembering: category stability, variability and development." In Lambert, K., and Shanks, D., eds. *Knowledge, Concepts, and Categories*, 161–195. East Sussex: Psychology Press.

Smith, L. B., and Sera, M. D. 1992. "A developmental analysis of the polar structure of dimensions." *Cognitive Psychology 24*: 99–142.

Smolensky, P. 1986. "Information processing in dynamical systems: foundations of harmony theory." In Rumelhart, D. E., and McClelland, J. L. 1986. *Parallel Distributed Processing, vol. 1*, 194–281. Cambridge, MA: MIT Press.

Smolensky, P. 1988. "On the proper treatment of connectionism." *Behavioral and Brain Sciences 11*: 1–23.

Smolensky, P. 1990. "Tensor product variable binding and the representation of symbolic structures in connectionist systems." *Artificial Intelligence 46*: 159–216.

Smolensky, P. 1991. "Connectionism, constituency and the language of thought." In Loewer, B., and Rey, G., eds. *Meaning in Mind: Fodor and His Critics*, 210–227. Oxford: Blackwell.

Sneed, J. 1971. *The Logical Structure of Mathematical Physics*. Dordrecht: Reidel.

Stalnaker, R. 1981. "Antiessentialism." *Midwest Studies of Philosophy 4*: 343–355.

Steels, L. 1996. "Perceptually grounded meaning creation." Artificial Intelligence Laboratory. Brussels: Vrije Universiteit Brussel.

Stegmüller, W. 1973. *Personelle und Statistische Wahrscheinlichkeit, Erster Halbband: Personelle Wahrscheinlichkeit und Rationale Entscheidung*. Berlin: Springer-Verlag.

Stegmüller, W. 1976. *The Structure and Dynamics of Theories*. Berlin: Springer-Verlag.

Stein, B. A., and Meredith, M. A. 1993. *The Merging of the Senses*. Cambridge, MA: MIT Press.

Stewart, J. 1996. "Cognition = life: implications for higher-level cognition." *Behavioural Processes 35*: 311–326.

Suppes, P., Krantz, D. M., Luce, R. D., and Tversky, A. 1989. *Foundations of Measurement, volume II: Geometrical, Threshold, and Probabilistic Representations*. San Diego, CA: Academic Press.

Sweetser, E. 1990. *From Etymology to Pragmatics*. Cambridge: Cambridge University Press.

Taft, C. 1997. *Generality Aspects of Color Naming and Color Meaning*. Gothenburg University, Gothenburg: Department of Psychology.

Taft, C., and Sivik, L. 1997. "Salient color terms in four languages." *Scandinavian Journal of Psychology 38*: 26–31.

Talmy, L. 1988. "Force dynamics in language and cognition." *Cognitive Science 12*: 49–100.

Tarr, M. J., and Pinker, S. 1989. "Mental rotation and orientation-dependence in shape recognition." *Cognitive Psychology 21*: 233–282.

Thom, R. 1970. "Topologie et linguistique." In *Essays on Topology*, 226–248. Berlin: Springer-Verlag.

Thom, R. 1972. *Stabilité Structurelle et Morphogenèse*. New York, NY: Benjamin.

Thompson, E. 1995. "Color vision, evolution, and perceptual content." *Synthese 104*: 1–32.

Tirri, H. 1991. "Implementing expert system rule conditions by neural networks." *New Generation Computing 10*: 55–71.

Tolman, E. C. 1948. "Cognitive maps in rats and men." *Psychological Review 55*: 189–208.

Toulmin, S., and Goodfield, J. 1965. *The Discovery of Time*. Harmondsworth: Penguin.

Tourangeau, R., and Sternberg, R. J. 1982. "Understanding and appreciating metaphors." *Cognition 11*: 203–244.

Touretsky, D. S. 1986. *The Mathematics of Inheritance Systems*. Los Altos, CA: Morgan Kaufmann.

Tversky, A. 1977. "Features of similarity." *Psychological Review 84*: 327–352.

Tversky, A., and Gati, I. 1982. "Similarity, separability, and the triangle inequality." *Psychological Review 89*: 123–154.

Tversky, A., and Hutchinson, J. W. 1986. "Nearest neighbor analysis of psychological spaces." *Psychological Review 93*: 3–22.

Tversky, B., and Hemenway, K. 1984. "Objects, parts, and categories." *Journal of Experimental Psychology: General 113*: 169–191.

Uexküll, J. von 1985. "Environment and inner world of animals." In Burghardt, G. M., ed. *Foundations of Comparative Ethology*. New York, NY: Van Nostrand Reinhold Company.

Ullman, S. 1995. "The visual analysis of shape anf form." In Gazzaniga, M. S., ed. *The Cognitive Neurosciences*, 339–350. Cambridge, MA: MIT Press.

Ullman, S., and Basri, R. 1991. "Recognition by linear combination of models." *IEEE Transactions PAMI 13*: 992–1006.

Vaina, L. 1983. "From shapes and movements to objects and actions." *Synthese 54*: 3–36.

Vandeloise, C. 1991. *Spatial Prepositions: A Case Study from French*. Chicago, IL: University of Chicago Press.

Van Fraassen, B. 1969. "Presuppositions, supervaluations and free logic." In Lambert, K., ed. *The Logical Way of Doing Things*. New Haven, CT: Yale University Press.

Van Gelder, T. 1995. "What might cognition be, if not computation?" *Journal of Philosophy 92*: 345–381.

Van Gelder, T. 1998. "The dynamical hypothesis in cognitive science." *Behavioral and Brain Sciences 21*: 615–628.

Verbrugge, R. R. 1980. "Transformations in knowing: a realist view of metaphor." In Honeck, R. P., and Hoffman, R. R., eds. *Cognition and Figurative Language*, 87–125. Hillsdale, NJ: Lawrence Erlbaum Associates.

Von Glasersfeld, E. 1995. *Radical Constructivism*. London: The Falmer Press.

Waddington, C. H. 1957. *The Strategy of the Genes: A Discussion of Some Aspects of Theoretical Biology*. London: Allen.

Wallin, A. 1997. "Is there a way for constructivism to distinguish what we experience from what we represent?" In Riegler, A., and Peschl, M., eds. *New Trends in Cognitive Science—97 "Does Representation Need Reality?"* 13–18. Vienna: Austrian Society of Cognitive Science Technical Report 97–01.

Whiten, A., and Byrne, R. W. 1988. "Tactical deception in primates." *Behavioral and Brain Sciences 11*: 233–273.

Wiener, N. 1961. *Cybernetics*. Cambridge, MA: MIT Press.

Wilkins, W. K., and Wakefield, J. 1995. "Brain evolution and neurolinguistic preconditions." *Behavioral and Brain Sciences 18*: 161–182.

Winter, S. 1998. *Expectations and Linguistic Meaning*. Lund: Lund University Cognitive Studies 71.

Winter, S., and Gärdenfors, P. 1995. "Linguistic modality as expressions of social power." *Nordic Journal of Linguistics 18*: 137–166.

Winter, S., and Gärdenfors, P. 1998. "Evolving social constraints on individual conceptual representations." Lund: *Lund University Cognitive Studies 69*.

Wisniewski, E. J. 1996. "Construal and similarity in conceptual combination." *Journal of Memory and Language 35*: 434–453.

Wittgenstein, L. 1953. *Philosophical Investigations*. New York, NY: Macmillan.

Woozley 1967. "Universals." *Encyclopedia of Philosophy, vol. 8*, 194–206. New York: Macmillan and The Free Press.

Zeeman, C. 1977. *Catastrophe Theory: Selected Papers 1972–1977*. Redwood City, CA: Addison-Wesley.

Zlatev, J. 1997. *Situated Embodiment: Studies in the Emergence of Spatial Meaning*. Stockholm: Gotab.

Zornetzer, S. F., Davis, J. L., and Lau, C. 1990. *An Introduction to Neural and Electronic Networks*. San Diego, CA: Academic Press.

Zwarts, J. 1995. "The semantics of relative position." Manuscript, OTS: Utrecht University.

Zwarts, J., and Winter, Y. 1998. "The formal semantics of locative prepositions." Manuscript. Utrecht: Utrecht Institute of Linguistics.

Illustration Credits

Figure 1.5   Reprinted by permission of Cambridge University Press and the authors.
Figure 1.6   Reprinted by permission of Cambridge University Press and the authors.
Figure 1.7   Reprinted by permission of the author.
Figure 1.13 Reprinted by permission of *Psychometrika* and the author.
Figure 2.2   Reprinted by permission of MIT Press and the author.
Figure 3.7   Reprinted by permission of Cambridge University Press and the authors.
Figure 3.8   Reprinted by permission of Cambridge University Press and the authors.
Figure 3.9   Reprinted by permission of Cambridge University Press and the authors.
Figure 3.10 Reprinted by permission of Cambridge University Press and the authors.
Figure 3.12 Reprinted by permission of American Speech-Language-Hearing Association.
Figure 3.14 Reprinted by permission of the author.
Figure 3.15 Reprinted by permission of the author.
Figure 3.20 Reprinted by permission of the Royal Society of London and the authors.
Figure 3.21 Reprinted by permission of the Royal Society of London and the authors.
Figure 4.5   Reprinted by permission of Georgetown University Press.
Figure 4.6   Reprinted by permission of Georgetown University Press.
Figure 4.7   Reprinted by permission of Elsevier Science Publishers.
Figure 5.5   Reprinted by permission of Mouton de Gruyter and the author.
Figure 5.6   Reprinted by permission of John Benjamins Publishers and the author.
Figure 6.2   Reprinted by permission of Springer Verlag and the author.
Figure 6.3   Reprinted by permission of Springer Verlag and the author.
Figure 6.4   Reprinted by permission of Springer Verlag and the author.

Index